Mike Meyers' Com

Secu ty+

CERTIFICATION PASSPORT

SIXTH EDITION

(Exam SY0-601)

About the Author

Dawn Dunkerley received a PhD in Information Systems from Nova Southeastern University in 2011 with a doctoral focus on measuring information security success within organizations. Her research interests include cyberwarfare, cybersecurity, and the success and measurement of organizational cybersecurity initiatives. Dr. Dunkerley holds numerous professional certifications, including the Certified Information Systems Security Professional (CISSP), Information Systems Security Architecture Professional (ISSAP), Information Systems Security Engineering Professional (ISSEP), Information Systems Security Management Professional (ISSMP), Certified Secure Software Lifecycle Professional (CSSLP), Certified in Risk and Information System Control (CRISC), and CompTIA Security+. She is an Area Editor for the *Cyber Defense Review* published by the United States Army Cyber Institute at West Point and a Fellow of the Americas Institute of Cybersecurity Leadership.

About the Technical Editor

Bobby E. Rogers is an information security engineer working as a contractor for U.S. Department of Defense agencies, helping to secure, certify, and accredit their information systems. His duties include information system security engineering, risk management, and certification and accreditation efforts. He retired after 21 years in the U.S. Air Force, serving as a network security engineer and instructor, and has secured networks all over the world. Bobby has a master's degree in information assurance (IA) and is pursuing a doctoral degree in cybersecurity from Capitol Technology University in Maryland. His many certifications include CISSP-ISSEP, CEH, and MCSE: Security, as well as the CompTIA A+, Network+, Security+, and Mobility+ certifications.

Mike Meyers' CompTIA

Security+™

CERTIFICATION PASSPORT

(Exam SY0-601)

SIXTH EDITION

Dr. Dawn Dunkerley

New York Chicago San Francisco Athens
London Madrid Mexico City Milan
New Delhi Singapore Sydney Toronto

McGraw Hill books are available at special quantity discounts to use as premiums and sales promotions, or for use in corporate training programs. To contact a representative, please visit the Contact Us pages at www.mhprofessional.com.

Mike Meyers' CompTIA Security+™ Certification Passport, Sixth Edition (Exam SY0-601)

1 2 3 4 5 6 7 8 9 LCR 24 23 22 21 20

Library of Congress Control Number: 2020941514

ISBN 978-1-260-46795-6
MHID 1-260-46795-3

Sponsoring Editor
Tim Green

Editorial Supervisor
Janet Walden

Project Manager
Sarika Gupta,
KnowledgeWorks Global Ltd.

Acquisitions Coordinator
Emily Walters

Technical Editor
Bobby Rogers

Copy Editor
William McManus

Proofreader
Lisa McCoy

Indexer
Ted Laux

Production Supervisor
Thomas Somers

Composition
KnowledgeWorks Global Ltd.

Illustration
KnowledgeWorks Global Ltd.

Art Director, Cover
Jeff Weeks

I dedicate this book to my amazing family. Thomas, Lauren, and Max, you are the lights of my life. I couldn't be happier or prouder to be your wife and mom. I love you.

—Dawn Dunkerley

Contents at a Glance

Contents

Acknowledgments

So many thanks go to McGraw Hill Professional, especially Tim Green, Emily Walters, and Janet Walden. You've been exceptionally helpful and patient through this process.

Finally, I couldn't have completed this project without my technical editor, Bobby Rogers. He continues to be the best partner and, more importantly, the best friend I could hope to work alongside. Thank you.

—Dawn Dunkerley

Introduction

This book is your guide to CompTIA's Security+ certification, the vendor-neutral, industry-standard certification developed for foundation-level cybersecurity professionals. Based on a worldwide job task analysis, the exam structure focuses on cybersecurity core competencies, understanding governance, risk, and compliance; attacks, threats, and vulnerabilities; architecture and design; operations and incident response; and implementation.

Whether the CompTIA Security+ certification is your first step toward a career focus in security or an additional skill credential, this book is your guide to success on the CompTIA Security+ certification exam.

This book is organized similarly to the official CompTIA Security+ exam objectives, consisting of five domains, each of which is divided into objectives that align with the CompTIA Security+ exam objectives. I stick closely to the exam content that's officially stated by CompTIA, and when I don't, I provide you my expert take on the best way to approach the topics. For example, I've chosen to present Domain 5, with its coverage of risk, after Domain 1 and its discussion of threat and vulnerability.

Each domain contains some useful items to call out points of interest:

EXAM TIP Indicates critical topics you're likely to see on the actual exam.

NOTE Points out ancillary but pertinent information, as well as areas for further study.

KEY TERM Describes special terms, in detail, and in a way you can easily understand.

CAUTION Warns you of common pitfalls, misconceptions, and potentially harmful or risky situations in working with the technology in the real world.

Cross-Reference

Directs you to other places in the book where concepts are covered, for your reference.

ADDITIONAL RESOURCES Where you can find books, websites, and other media for further assistance.

The end of each objective gives you two handy tools. The *Review* covers each objective with a synopsis—a great way to quickly review the critical information. Then the *Questions* and *Answers* enable you to test your newly acquired skills. For further study, this book includes access to online practice exams that will help to prepare you for taking the exam itself. All the information you need for accessing the exam questions is provided in the appendix. I recommend that you take the practice exams to identify where you have knowledge gaps and then go back and review as needed.

The IT industry changes and grows continuously, *and so should you.* Finishing one certification is just a step in an ongoing process of gaining more knowledge to match your constantly changing and developing skills. Remember, in the cybersecurity business, if you're not moving forward, you're way behind!

Threats, Attacks, and Vulnerabilities

Domain Objectives

- **1.1** Compare and contrast different types of social engineering techniques
- **1.2** Given a scenario, analyze potential indicators to determine the type of attack
- **1.3** Given a scenario, analyze potential indicators associated with application attacks
- **1.4** Given a scenario, analyze potential indicators associated with network attacks
- **1.5** Explain different threat actors, vectors, and intelligence sources
- **1.6** Explain the security concerns associated with various types of vulnerabilities
- **1.7** Summarize the techniques used in security assessments
- **1.8** Explain the techniques used in penetration testing

Compare and contrast different types of social engineering techniques

Security is not just about technological controls. Although security solutions such as firewalls, antivirus software, and intrusion detection systems can help protect against many types of threats, they cannot completely protect your users from social engineering attacks. This objective discusses different social engineering tricks that attackers use to bypass security controls and obtain elevated access or confidential information.

Understanding Social Engineering

The easiest way to discover someone's password often is simply to ask for it. *Social engineering* is defined as using and manipulating human behavior to obtain a required result. It typically involves nontechnical methods of attempting to gain unauthorized access to a system or network. This typically means the attacker tricks a person into bypassing normal security measures to reveal information that can help the attacker access the network. The attacker, in effect, acts much like a con artist, attempting to uncover sensitive information by manipulating someone's basic human nature.

Social Engineering Techniques

Social engineering is effective when it takes advantage of trust in the message being delivered—in any form—to the victim; for example, when an attacker takes the time to gather information, otherwise known as conducting *reconnaissance*, regarding the organization or a specific user, the attacker can then use that information to build a sense of familiarity between himself and the recipient. Consider the wealth of information that most people now share on social networks and how an attacker can use that information to tailor e-mails or telephone calls to target specific victims. Because social networking is here to stay, user education is key to preventing security issues arising from social engineering attacks. Awareness training helps users to understand the dangers of various social engineering techniques and to be wary of intrusions when working through their day-to-day activities. Users communicate with other external users every day via e-mail, phones, social media, instant messaging, and file-sharing applications, and each medium has its share of security issues, including the risk of malware and phishing. Although technological security controls help, user education and awareness are the most effective security measures against the risks of social engineering attacks.

Through social engineering, an attacker might easily lead a user to reveal her account password or to provide personal information that might reveal her password, a technique known as *eliciting information*. For example, a social engineer might call a user on the phone, pretending to be from another department and asking for the user's password to retrieve a file. The user, thinking she knows who she is talking to, might give the unauthorized person the password without officially authenticating who the caller is or why he needs the information. Alternatively, if the caller believes a less direct approach is necessary to elicit the user's password, instead of asking for the user's password outright, the caller might make small talk with the user and trick her into revealing names of family members, her birth date, or other personal information so that he can try out this information as potential passwords to the user's account.

Another typical example of this type of security breach is *impersonation*. A common example of impersonation is that a social engineer calls a helpdesk operator, claims to be a high-level user, and demands that the operator reset the user's password immediately so that the user can complete an important task. Having performed his reconnaissance to determine the company's line of business and the high-level user's scope of responsibility, the social engineer can provide very believable details supporting the urgency of the password reset. The helpdesk operator, if not trained properly, could instantly give this user a new password without properly identifying the user. The social engineer can then log in using the account of the high-level user and access any sensitive information that the user is authorized to access.

Protecting against social engineering security abuses requires user education and emphasis on the need to always follow security procedures, even when dealing with someone an employee knows within the company. In short, users should be taught to recognize that social engineering attacks prey on misplaced trust and to have strategies to deal with those attacks.

Users should be taught the following *principles (reasons for effectiveness)* that social engineers rely on to design successful attacks, and also be aware that *pretexting* is a technique in which a social engineer creates a story, or *pretext*, that employs one or more of these principles to motivate victims to act contrary to their better instincts or training. Social engineers often claim positions of authority to intimidate the victim into giving them access rights (the *authority* principle), or they act belligerently if denied (the *intimidation* principle). Conversely, they may be very personable or seek common interests to create a bond between the social engineer and the victim (the *familiarity* principle). They may cite professional credentials, known organizational information, or organizational status to create a feeling of confidence (the *trust* principle). They might also try to make a social connection, claiming that another trusted individual can vouch for their authenticity (the *social proof* principle, otherwise known as the *consensus* principle). Finally, a social engineer might claim that a situation is urgent (the *urgency* principle) or that she has very little time to verify her identity (the *scarcity* principle).

EXAM TIP Be able to differentiate between the different types of social engineering attacks and the reasons why they are effective.

Phishing

A *phishing* scam is a social engineering technique that targets a large group of recipients with a generic message that attempts to trick at least the most gullible among them into responding or acting, generally into either visiting a website and entering confidential personal information, responding to a text or SMS message (known as *smishing*), or replying to an e-mail with private information, often a username and password, or banking or credit card details.

Like other forms of social engineering, phishing relies on creating a false sense of trust, and therefore phishing e-mails often contain familiar logos, official-looking messages, and links to well-known trusted sites, such as a real bank or credit card company. However, the links (often using *URL redirection* techniques in the background, as described in Objective 1.4, later in this domain) send users to the website of the phishing scam operator rather than to the trusted site. These websites are often made to look just like a real bank or credit card site. The user then enters his login and password information and personal details into the website, not realizing that the data is actually being added to the database of the phishing website operator. This activity is most commonly related to *identity fraud*, where the unauthorized user collects enough personal information about his target victim to perform forged credit card and banking transactions using the victim's financial and personal details.

A variant attack called *spear phishing* is a targeted type of phishing attack that includes information familiar to the user and could appear to be from a trusted source such as a company from which the user has purchased a product in the past, a financial service that the user has used previously, a social media site such as LinkedIn, or even a specific trusted user. A spear phishing attack is much more sophisticated than regular phishing; in this kind of attack, because the information is targeted at the victim, it offers a greater inducement to click the links in the message and serves to gain the user's trust to enter confidential information. For example, a spear phishing e-mail could include the user's personal information, such as full name and postal address (easily stolen from a mailing list), or could include as the sender the name of the user's bank manager.

Another variant to note is the *invoice scam*; this is similar to a phishing attack in that it often comes in the form of an e-mail with an attached invoice or link requesting payment for a good or service that has been rendered. The problem? There was never a good or service rendered, or the amount has been manipulated, and the attacker is betting on the invoice being paid without too much attention.

To help protect end users, many web browsers, e-mail clients, and antivirus software can detect behavior that may indicate the presence of a phishing e-mail or website. This is typically accomplished by parsing the uniform resource locator (URL) links in messages and comparing them to lists of known phishing websites.

User education and awareness are important tools to protect against phishing attacks. Users must be aware that financial institutions will never ask for personal details, especially bank account numbers and credit card details, in an e-mail to a user. When a suspicious e-mail is received, it is also helpful to check the destination of any clickable link—simply hovering over the link often does the trick—within the message to determine the location to which it is redirecting. If the destination site is not recognized, it is likely a phishing attempt. User education and awareness are the *most* important tools to prevent successful phishing events.

Whaling

Whaling is a type of phishing attack that is targeted at a specific high-level user. As previously discussed, most phishing attempts are sent to thousands of users, hoping that some of those users will fall prey to the attack. In a whaling attack, the victim is usually a high-profile member of the organization, such as an executive who has much more critical information to lose than the average user.

Many executives have their profile information posted on the organization's public website. Hackers can use this information to craft a unique message so specific to that user that it may seem legitimate enough for the victim to click an embedded link that either automatically downloads malware, which is then installed on the victim's computer, or redirects to a website under the hacker's control that entices the executive to enter sensitive credentials or banking information.

Whaling requires the same sort of protections as other phishing attacks, such as proper anti-malware and antivirus protection on the computer, as well as user education on social engineering techniques.

Shoulder Surfing

End users must always be aware of their environment and the people in their surroundings when entering login names and passwords or accessing sensitive data. Otherwise, they may fall victim to the social engineering technique known as *shoulder surfing*. For example, an unauthorized person could casually glance over the shoulder of an employee as she returns to her desk and enters her username and password into the computer. The shoulder surfer may be able to easily see which keyboard keys the employee is pressing and steal her username and password to access that account later.

The issue of viewing sensitive and confidential data, such as human resource records, while other employees are present is also important. As another example, a shoulder surfer could lurk behind an unobservant human resources employee and view sensitive and confidential data about personnel, a technique made even easier by today's widescreen monitors.

Users must examine their surroundings before entering or viewing confidential data. If a user has her own office, she should ensure that her monitor is not easily read from a distance in the hallway and that it is situated in such a way that a casual passerby cannot see the monitor screen. In many environments, the desk can be oriented to face away from the doorway to ensure that the monitor screen is always facing the back of the office. Blinds can be installed on windows to prevent outsiders from looking into the office. Screen filters can also be placed on monitors to prevent passersby, both innocent and malicious, from being able to view the content displayed on screens. In open-concept office spaces, these measures are more difficult to implement, and it is up to the user to ensure that no one is standing behind her as she is entering and working with sensitive data.

Tailgating

Tailgating is one of the simpler forms of social engineering and describes gaining physical access to an access-controlled facility or room by closely following an authorized person through the security checkpoint. For example, when an authorized person swipes her access card to open a door to enter the facility, the unauthorized person will follow the authorized person while the door is still open. To gain trust, the tailgater might make casual conversation with the authorized person as they are walking toward the checkpoint, and then gain entry by telling her that he has lost or forgotten his access card.

Organizations must have strict access control rules that prevent tailgating incidents so that unauthorized persons aren't allowed into any secure facility or room without proper authentication or identification. All employees should be educated to never let an unknown person enter the premises without proper authentication, including photo ID if possible (photos are commonly included in security access cards), and should be instructed to report unknown individuals they encounter within the facility. Visitors must always be accompanied by an employee and be properly signed in and given a temporary access card. Every visitor must sign out and return the access card when leaving the facility.

Cross-Reference

Physical security controls that help prevent tailgating are covered in depth in Domain 2, Objective 2.7.

Tailgating can also refer to using another user's access rights on a computer. For example, a user might leave on her lunch break and forget to lock her office or log out of her session on her computer. An unauthorized user could get access to her computer and be able to read her e-mail messages, access her files, and gain access to other company network resources. Users must be taught to always log out of sessions or lock their workstations before they leave the work area.

Pharming

Pharming is a social engineering technique that misdirects a user to an attacker's website without the user's knowledge, generally through manipulation of the Domain Name Service (DNS) on an affected server or the host file on a user's system. While much like phishing, where a user may click a link in a seemingly legitimate e-mail message that takes him to an attacker's website, pharming differs in that it installs code on the user's computer that sends them to the malicious site, even if the URL is entered correctly or chosen from a web browser bookmark. Through these methods, the user is tricked into browsing to the attacker's website even though he thinks he has gone to a legitimate destination. Just as in phishing, pharming can result in loss of confidential data such as login credentials and credit card and banking details; it can lead to identity theft as well.

Spam

Spam is a deliberate attempt to e-mail unsolicited advertisements to a large number of recipients. Any time you enter your e-mail address on a public website or a newsgroup, you open yourself up to the possibility of having your e-mail address added to spam mailing lists. These mailing lists are shared among Internet spam advertisers, and if you don't have an effective spam blocker, you may receive loads of junk e-mails every day. Spam annoys not only users but also networking administrators, because of the amount of space and bandwidth these mass mailings can consume. Many Internet service providers (ISPs) and corporate networks use anti-spam mail filters that block incoming spam e-mail from reaching users' inboxes.

E-mail spam continues to be one of the prime nuisances and security issues affecting organizations. Spam has evolved from the early years of simple text adverts to full Hypertext Markup Language (HTML) messages with clickable links, images, and even spam messages hidden in attached images and document files. The links in spam messages often direct users to malicious sites containing spyware, malware, and phishing activities.

SPIM

SPIM (spam over instant messaging) is instant messaging spam, and much like the more common e-mail spam, it occurs when a user receives an unsolicited instant message from another user, including users who are known and in the user's contact list. Instant messaging services provide a lot of information about users, including demographic, gender, and age information, that can be used for targeted spam advertising. These messages can contain ads or links to viruses, malware, and phishing sites.

Users can protect themselves from SPIM and other IM-related security issues by making sure that only people on their contact list can send them messages. In many cases, organizations have completely blocked access to external IM chat services.

Vishing

Vishing is a type of phishing attack that takes place over phone systems, most commonly over VoIP (Voice over IP) lines. Using tools specific to VoIP systems, hackers can program their autodialers to send a recorded message from spoofed VoIP addresses. For example, the recorded message may claim to be from a bank's call center, asking the customer to call back and verify her financial information. Because the VoIP source is difficult to trace, unsuspecting users might trust the call as legitimate and provide their private financial details to the hacker by inputting that information via the phone keypad.

Like other social engineering attacks, preventing successful vishing requires user education to recognize the warning signs of scams, including any attempt to get financial information such as credit cards and bank account numbers over the phone.

Hoaxes

One of the most annoying problems you may run across, a *hoax* is typically some kind of urban legend or sensational false news that users pass on to others via e-mail because they feel it is of interest. The most common type tells the user to forward the e-mail to ten friends to bring him good luck. Another type of hoax claims to be collecting e-mails for a sick person. Of course, this activity merely consumes network and computer resources because the number of e-mails grows exponentially as users send them to all their friends, and so on.

While annoying, hoaxes are generally harmless; however, some hoax e-mail messages are phishing attempts that try to get the user to visit a link in the e-mail message that redirects to a malicious website. The only cure for the spreading of hoax e-mails is user education to make sure that users know the typical characteristics of a hoax message and know not to forward it to other users. Organizational policies might also call for a notification to the security team.

EXAM TIP Know how to spot an e-mail hoax and how to handle it properly. The best solution is to delete it immediately and follow the organizational policy for notification, if appropriate.

Dumpster Diving

This social engineering technique requires almost no social skills at all! When data is to be disposed of, the job must be done completely. When destroying paper documentation, most companies use a shredder to cut the document into pieces small enough that they can't easily be put back together.

Simply putting documents in the trash or recycle bin isn't acceptable, as anyone can sift through the garbage or recycle containers for these documents, a practice called *dumpster diving*. As part of corporate espionage, some companies hire private investigators to examine garbage dumpsters of a target company, and these investigators try to discover any proprietary and confidential information.

EXAM TIP To combat the problems of dumpster diving for confidential company documents, the physical security of your facility should include your garbage disposal and recycling operations.

Influence Campaigns

Turn on the television news and you'll likely hear about influence campaigns being used, positively or negatively, to inform global change. Whether an "influencer" is using their social media platform to coax their followers to donate money to a cause, or a nation-state is hiding behind proxies to influence a foreign election, influence campaigns are here to stay.

There are many types of threat actors who conduct a variety of attacks for different reasons: activists looking to disrupt operations of an organization (e.g., mining, oil exploration) they disagree with; nation-states wishing to implant themselves within the systems of a foreign government, either friend or foe; a corporation looking to gain access to the information of a competitor; and so forth. All of these situations are as old as time, but the addition of cyberattacks has created a new type of *hybrid warfare*, where traditional methods like espionage and telecommunications tapping often are supplemented through cyberattacks to reach the desired end.

Social Media

With the massive increase in social media/social networking use, such as Facebook, Twitter, and LinkedIn, security administrators are beset with many new avenues of risk within their organization. The same security risks that affect other communications media, such as e-mail, web, IM, and peer to peer (P2P), are also inherent in social media applications; however, phishing and the spread of malware can be more prevalent via social media because most malicious links are spread by trusted users on the social network. When one person's social media application is infected with malware, it can quickly spread to other users as automatic messages are sent from the victim's computer to all her social media contacts. These types of social engineering attacks are very effective.

To provide a strong layer of security, many organizations have included social media with other restricted applications such as instant messaging and P2P apps and block their use on the network. If users do have access to social media sites, they require social engineering awareness training to educate them on the types of behavior to look out for when using social media, and specific training to not participate in influence campaigns on network-connected devices.

REVIEW

Objective 1.1: Compare and contrast different types of social engineering techniques Social engineering uses behavioral manipulation to trick users into bypassing security controls and providing elevated access or confidential data to the attacker. Hackers using social engineering techniques can cause victims to unknowingly provide their login credentials or confidential information such as personal credit card numbers or bank account information. Social engineering techniques cover a variety of mediums, including networking, SMS/text, websites, e-mail, instant messaging, telephone calls, and even personal contact.

The best defense against social engineering is to perform employee awareness training to educate users on the principles of social engineering. Employees should be instructed to always make sure no one is looking over their shoulder when entering sensitive data or login credentials; to be wary of tailgaters attempting to pass through an access door behind them; to recognize the characteristics of phishing e-mails and websites; and to ignore hoax e-mails and not forward them.

1.1 QUESTIONS

1. You have been contacted by your company's CEO after she received a personalized but suspicious e-mail message from the company's bank asking for detailed personal and financial information. After reviewing the message, you determine that it did not originate from the legitimate bank. Which of the following security issues does this scenario describe?
   A. Dumpster diving
   B. Phishing
   C. Whaling
   D. Vishing
2. During your user awareness training, which of the following actions would you advise users to take as the best security practice to help prevent malware installation from phishing messages?
   A. Forward suspicious messages to other users
   B. Do not click links in suspicious messages
   C. Check e-mail headers
   D. Reply to a message to check its legitimacy
3. Negative company financial information was carelessly thrown in the trash bin without being shredded, and a malicious insider retrieved it and posted it on the Internet, driving the stock price down. The CEO wants to know what happened—what was the attack?
   A. Smishing
   B. Dumpster diving
   C. Prepending
   D. Identity fraud
4. Max, a security administrator, just received a phone call to change the password for a user in the HR department. The user did not provide verification of their identity and insisted that they needed the password changed immediately to complete a critical task. What principle of effective social engineering is being used?
   A. Trust
   B. Consensus
   C. Intimidation
   D. Urgency

1.1 ANSWERS

1. **C** Whaling is a type of phishing attack that is targeted at a specific high-level user. The victim is usually a high-profile member of the organization who has much more critical information to lose than the average user. The messages used in the attack are usually crafted and personalized toward the specific victim user.
2. **B** To help prevent malware from being installed, make your users aware that a best security practice is to never click links in a suspicious message. The link can take the user to a malicious website that could automatically install malware on their computer through their web browser.
3. **B** Dumpster diving occurs when discarded documents (not necessarily *confidential*) that were improperly destroyed (or not destroyed at all) are reconstructed and read (or simply read as is).
4. **D** Max is being subjected to a social engineering attack that relies on the principle of urgency—he is being rushed, with the attacker hoping that the "criticality" of the task forces Max to bypass best security practices.

Objective 1.2 Given a scenario, analyze potential indicators to determine the type of attack

Systems security means not only securing sensitive data against unauthorized access but also protecting the integrity and existence of that data from malicious users and software. Most organizations use security resources, such as security guards and cameras, to prevent unauthorized physical access to their equipment and facilities; however, organizations must also protect themselves from threats originating from the numerous technological pathways that can potentially provide unauthorized system access, whether in the cloud or on-premises. This objective discusses different types of indicators that can help determine that an organization has been attacked and what method was used.

Analyze and Differentiate Among Types of Malware

Damage from a malware attack or unauthorized access gained via a backdoor or Trojan horse program can be catastrophic. A simple worm attached to an e-mail message can cause mail and network systems to grind to a halt. Other malware contains payloads that destroy or damage information that might never be recovered if a backup plan is not in place. System administrators must be aware of the numerous types of software attacks and understand how these attacks enter the system and what can be done to rectify the issue if they infect a system. First and foremost, proactive protection in the form of knowledge and user education is critical in dealing with these types of threats.

Viruses

Viruses are probably the most common and prevalent type of system attack. A *virus* is a malicious computer program that requires user intervention (such as clicking it or copying it to media or a host) within the affected system, even if the virus program does not harm the system. Most computer viruses self-replicate without the knowledge of the computer user.

Similar to human viruses, computer viruses can be passed along from one system to another—via e-mail messages, instant messaging, website downloads, removable media, and network connections. Cleaning up and restoring operations after a virus attack may be very expensive and require enormous amounts of time and effort. Some companies have taken many days, or even weeks, to get back to full operations after their systems have been infected with a virus. For certain time-sensitive businesses, a virus infection can be fatal to the entire computer system and company operations.

Types of Viruses

Viruses come in a variety of forms, with different locations and methods of infection and payloads of varying severity. The following sections outline some common virus types.

Boot Sector Viruses *Boot sector viruses* infect the boot sector or partition table of a disk. The *boot sector* is used by the computer to determine which operating systems (OSs) are present on the system to boot. The most common way a boot sector virus finds its way into a system is through an infected disk or removable media device that is inserted into the computer. After infecting the boot sector, the virus may not allow the system to boot into the operating system, rendering the computer useless until the boot sector is repaired. A boot sector virus may also be used to install additional malicious code, such as a rootkit, that would compromise the system.

The best way to remove a boot sector virus from a system is to boot the system using an antivirus or similar emergency recovery media. This lets you start up the computer with basic start-up files, bypassing the boot sector, and then run the antivirus program on the recovery media.

Companion Viruses A *companion virus* disguises itself as a legitimate program, using the name of a legitimate program but with a different extension. For example, a virus might be named *program.com* to emulate a file called *program.exe*. Typically, the virus runs the legitimate program immediately after installing the virus code, so the system appears to be performing normally. Some viruses replace the original legitimate file with their version that performs the same tasks but includes new malicious code to run with it.

File Infector Viruses *File infector viruses* generally infect files that have the extension .com or .exe. These viruses can be extremely destructive because they try to replicate and spread further by infecting other executable programs on the system with the same extension. Sometimes, a file infector virus destroys the program it infects by overwriting the original code.

CAUTION If your computer is afflicted with a file infector virus, do not attach it to a network because it could start infecting files on other workstations and file servers.

Macro Viruses A *macro* is an instruction that carries out program commands automatically within an application. Macros are typically used in popular office applications such as Microsoft Word and Excel. A *macro virus* uses the internal workings of the application to perform malicious operations when a file containing the macro is opened, such as deleting files or opening other virus-executable programs. Sometimes, these viruses also infect program templates that are loaded automatically by the applications. Each time the user creates a file using the default template, the macro virus is copied to the new file. Macro viruses are often written with Visual Basic for Applications (VBA). The Melissa virus was a prime example of this.

Cross-Reference

"Macros" is listed under Objective 1.4 within the CompTIA exam objectives.

Memory-Resident Viruses When a system is infected by a virus that stays resident in the system memory, the *memory-resident virus* continues to stay in memory and infect other files that are run at the same time. For a memory-resident virus to spread, the user must run an infected program that, once activated, inserts the virus into system memory, where the virus examines each new program as it is run and, if the program is not already infected, infects it.

Stealth Viruses A *stealth virus* hides from antivirus software by encrypting its code. Stealth viruses attempt to cover their trail as they infect their way through a computer. When a stealth virus infects, it takes over the system function that reads files or system sectors. When something or someone attempts to access the corrupted file, the stealth virus reports that the original file is there. However, the original information is gone, and the stealth virus has taken its place.

Armored Viruses *Armored viruses* are designed to make detection and reverse engineering difficult and time consuming, either through obfuscation (hiding in one place and attempting to trick antivirus programs or researchers into believing they reside elsewhere) or through techniques that add substantial amounts of confusing code to hide the actual virus code itself.

While armored viruses are often quite good at what they are designed to do, they are significantly larger than necessary, which makes their presence easier to detect.

File Types That Commonly Carry Viruses

Some types of files are susceptible to virus infections because they are common to certain types of computer systems and applications. The following are a few of the most common types of program files targeted by viruses:

- **.com** MS-DOS command files usually execute within a command shell interface, or they can be executed from a user interface such as Windows. Most early computer viruses were created as .com files because the main DOS program files were in this form.
- **.doc/.docx** These file extensions are associated with Microsoft Word. Along with Microsoft Access and Excel files, files with the .doc or .docx extension are susceptible to macro virus infection.
- **.dll** A dynamic link library (DLL) is a library of executable functions or data that can be used by a Windows application. Typically, a DLL provides one or more functions, and a program accesses these functions.
- **.exe** An executable file is most commonly found on MS-DOS and Windows OSs.
- **.html** The .html or .htm extension is used for a document written in Hypertext Markup Language (HTML) coding that can be opened by web browsers.
- **.mdb/.accdb** This file extension is associated with a Microsoft Access database. As with Word and Excel files, the .mdb file is susceptible to macro virus infection.
- **.scr** This is the default file extension for Microsoft Windows screensavers. Because screensavers are popular items to copy to other users, .scr files are typically easy targets for viruses.
- **.vbs** Files with the .vbs extension are for Microsoft Visual Basic Scripting, a subset of the Visual Basic programming language. This powerful language can create scripts that perform a wide variety of functions, such as control applications and manipulate the file system. VBScript is powerful and can be used to create malicious code.
- **.xls/.xlsx** These file extensions are associated with a Microsoft Excel spreadsheet. As with Word and Access files, .xls and .xlsx files are susceptible to macro virus infection.
- **.zip** This extension is used for a compressed file that contains one or more other files. ZIP files are compressed to save space and to make grouping files for transport and copying faster and easier. ZIP files must also be checked by antivirus software to ensure that the files in the archive are not infected.

NOTE Be able to recognize which types of files are most likely to carry a virus.

Polymorphic Malware

Polymorphic malware changes with each infection. These types of viruses were created to confuse virus-scanning programs. These viruses are difficult to detect by scanning because each copy of the virus looks different from previous copies.

Metamorphic Malware

Metamorphic malware can recompile itself into a new form, and the code keeps changing from generation to generation. Metamorphic malware is like polymorphic malware because both types can modify their forms. However, a metamorphic virus does not decrypt itself to a single constant virus body in memory, as a polymorphic virus does. A metamorphic virus can also change its virus body code.

Keyloggers

Keyloggers do just that: log a user's keystrokes for various purposes. This can be accomplished using a hardware device that is often discreet enough to blend in with the various cords running to and from peripherals—picture a small pass-through between the keyboard and its USB port, for example—or software that runs in the background. Keyloggers can be used by suspicious spouses, stalkers, or hackers looking to gain sensitive information, such as login credentials or credit card information (otherwise known as *credential harvesting*) and are often installed by Trojans. While antivirus can often spot a software keylogger, small, strategically placed hardware keyloggers can be almost undetectable.

Trojans

Trojan horse programs (otherwise referred to as *Trojans*) are named from the ancient myth in which Greek warriors gained entrance into the gated city of Troy by hiding inside a giant wooden horse that the Trojans presumed was abandoned. Once inside the city gates, the warriors snuck out from inside the horse and opened the gates to let in more Greek forces, which attacked the surprised inhabitants, winning a decisive battle. A Trojan horse program hides on your computer system until called upon to perform a certain task. Trojans are usually downloaded through e-mail attachments, websites, and instant messages. They are usually disguised as popular programs such as games, pictures, or music. When the program is run, it usually appears to the victim user as a functional program, but the Trojan has secretly installed itself on the user's computer.

Remote Access Trojan

A *remote access Trojan (RAT)* installs a backdoor (described in the next section) that bypasses all authentication controls and allows the attacker continuous access to the client computer. The RAT runs a service on the victim's computer and opens a port (such as TCP/IP port 12345 in the case of the NetBus Trojan software) on the system to which the attacker can connect when he runs the control application from a remote location. When connected, the attacker has full access to the infected system. Antivirus programs can detect the presence of some RAT programs. Both network and host-based firewalls can also detect suspicious incoming and outgoing network traffic from a computer. Port-scanning software can also be used to identify any open ports on the system, including those you do not recognize. These open ports can be cross-referenced with lists of ports used by known backdoor programs.

EXAM TIP A firewall can detect suspicious incoming and outgoing network traffic to and from your computer. If you do not recognize a program communicating, it could be malware communicating out to the network.

Backdoor

A *backdoor* is traditionally defined as a way for a software programmer to access a program while bypassing its authentication schemes. The backdoor is coded in by the programmer during development so that later she can "break into" her own program without having to authenticate to the system through normal access methods. This is helpful to programmers because they need not access the program as they normally would in a typical user mode, where they would be forced to enter authentication information, such as a username and password.

In hacking terms, a *backdoor* is a program secretly installed on an unsuspecting user's computer that enables the hacker to later access the user's computer, bypassing any security authentication systems. (A backdoor could also be an unauthorized account that is created on the system that the unauthorized user can access later.) The backdoor program runs as a service on the user's computer and listens on specific network ports not typically used by traditional network services. The hacker runs the client portion of the program on his computer, which then connects to the service on the target computer. Once the connection is established, the hacker can gain full access, including remotely controlling the system. Hackers usually do not know which specific systems are running the backdoor, but their programs can scan a network's IP addresses to see which ones are listening to the specific port for that backdoor.

Backdoor software is typically installed as a Trojan as part of some other software package. A user might download from the Internet a program that contains the hidden backdoor software. Antivirus programs can detect the presence of backdoor programs. Personal firewalls can also detect suspicious incoming and outgoing network traffic from a computer. Port-scanning software can also be used to identify any open ports on the system, including those you do not recognize. These open ports can be cross-referenced with lists of ports used by known backdoor programs.

Logic Bombs

Although it can be running on a system for a long time, a *logic bomb* program does not activate until a specific event, such as reaching a specific date or starting a program a specific number of times, is triggered. Logic bombs can be highly destructive, depending on their payload.

The damage done by a logic bomb can range from changing bytes of data on the victim's hard disk to rendering the user's entire hard drive unreadable. Logic bombs are distributed primarily via worms and viruses; however, there have been documented cases of malicious programmers inserting into trusted applications logic-bomb code that was subsequently triggered. Antivirus software often is unable to detect a logic bomb because most logic bombs are simple scripts that are inert (not executed and not memory resident) until executed by the event, and there may be no indication that the logic bomb is present for hours, days, months, or even years before it releases its malicious payload. Detecting a logic bomb is especially difficult if it is hidden within a trusted application. Software development companies must ensure that all application code is peer-reviewed before the application is released to ensure that a single malicious programmer cannot insert hidden logic-bomb code.

Worms

A computer *worm* is a self-contained program (or set of programs) that can self-replicate and spread full copies or smaller segments of itself to other computer systems via network connections, e-mail attachments, and instant messages. Compare this to viruses, which cannot self-replicate, but instead depend on the sharing of their host file to spread. Worms are most common in various types of networking application servers such as e-mail servers, web servers, and database servers. A user receives an attachment to an e-mail or an instant message that contains a malicious worm. When the attachment is opened, the worm infects the user's computer and then replicates itself by sending copies of the same e-mail or instant message to everyone in the user's address book. Each user, in turn, sees a message arrive from someone familiar and automatically opens the attachment, thinking it is safe. These types of worm infections can spread quickly and can bring down an e-mail server in a matter of minutes. The explosive increase in worms within e-mail attachments and instant messages has caused antivirus companies and messaging software companies to reevaluate the functionality of their applications to prevent the spread of messaging-based worms, and application server vendors have taken steps to prevent these types of worms from spreading by patching their applications to prevent malicious attachment code from executing.

EXAM TIP Watch out for a question that appears to describe a virus but alludes to its capability to self-replicate, a tip-off that it is a worm.

Adware and Spyware

Adware (advertising software) and *spyware* are a subset of software known as *potentially unwanted programs (PUPs)*, potential threats that are not always considered security risks but are still generally considered unwelcome. Software developers often eke out financial support for their free or low-cost software applications by embedding advertising content within the applications themselves. Although this provides a modest revenue stream for the software developers, it also opens the door to potential security threats, such as compromised private and personal data. Even software as simple as a downloadable screensaver may contain adware or spyware that installs code to deliver advertising to the user and/or collect personal information for use in targeted advertising. In addition to the nuisance of the advertising (which is not easily disabled) is the threat that the program itself is sending the user's personal information back to the advertiser. This information can include web surfing habits, keylogging, online purchases, and personal contact information such as e-mail address, home address, and credit card details. This personal information can be used directly by the advertiser or sold to other companies that will also use or distribute personal information.

Spyware does not necessarily involve advertising, and it might be installed by any type of software application, even trusted, popular application and entertainment software. Spyware typically tracks the user's habits while using an application, such as a music player that relays the user's musical preferences back to the application vendor. This information can then be compiled by the vendor and sold to third parties such as record companies. Many types of antivirus and personal firewall software can detect and clean software designated as adware and spyware.

It is critical that end users run some type of security software on their computers and regularly scan their hard drives for evidence of adware and spyware programs that are secretly sending personal data from their computers to advertisers. User education is also important to advise users not to download non-work-oriented software that may contain adware or spyware, such as games, screensavers, entertainment apps, or social media software, to a networked company computer.

Ransomware

Ransomware is designed to lock users out of their system until a ransom is paid. Ransomware generally enters the system much like a conventional piece of malware in a downloaded file or e-mail attachment. Once present, ransomware either encrypts the system files or simply blocks access to the user interface and plays on user fear or embarrassment to extort the desired funds via a web page or text file listing their instructions, often for hundreds of U.S. dollars per machine.

Early ransomware often displayed a page or message claiming to be from law enforcement or the operating system vendor, purporting that the software on the machine is illegal and demanding a fine be paid. Based on the geographical location of the user, the ransomware would shift its language settings, showing an initial amount of finesse.

More recent types of ransomware, such as CryptoLocker and WannaCry, also referred to as *cryptomalware*, encrypt user files and require payment within a timeframe and often through a digital currency such as bitcoin. The malware typically claims that if the ransom is not paid, the decryption key will be destroyed so that the files can never be unencrypted. The spread of this type of ransomware within an organization could potentially cause quite a dilemma for IT staff, who don't want to bow to the demands of malware authors but also stand to lose a substantial amount of data. Implementing antivirus solutions and securely backing up data regularly are almost the only ways to combat this type of malware. As with all malware, user education is a good way to combat ransomware. It can't succeed unless it's downloaded.

Rootkits

A *rootkit* is a type of backdoor program that is inserted into application software and allows a remote user *root* access (administrator access) to the system on which the software is installed, without the permission or knowledge of the user. This access potentially results in full control over the target system. Although rootkits are usually related to the malware and Trojan horse types of malicious software, they are also becoming more common in trusted applications that are potentially used by millions of users. For example, a well-known entertainment company was found to be distributing rootkits on its music CDs. This software was installed on a user's computer while the music CD was played on the system. This software installation was not disclosed to the user, and the software (primarily used for digital rights management of music copyright) allowed root access and control of the computer system for anyone aware that the software was installed.

Rootkits are not always installed by application software. They can be distributed via firmware updates for a hardware device, embedded into the primary operating system kernel (kernel rootkits), and included on application software libraries such as DLL files. Rootkits do not spread like a worm or virus; they typically infect one system only. However, rootkits themselves are typically spread as the payload of replicating worms and viruses. Several types of rootkits exist, including the following:

- **Firmware rootkit** The rootkit is embedded within the firmware of a device, such as a computer peripheral or network device. The rootkit is always available because it is embedded within the firmware of the system, thus the rootkit is available whenever the device is running.
- **Kernel rootkit** The rootkit is embedded within the operating system core itself. This effectively hides the rootkit because it runs as a hidden process and can rarely be spotted by checking active processes on the system.
- **Persistent rootkit** The rootkit is enabled when the system starts and will not turn off unless the system is shut down. This type of rootkit is often installed and activated within the Windows Registry and is run each time the system boots.
- **Application rootkit** The rootkit is activated and run in current system memory only when a specific application is launched and does not persist when the system is shut down and restarted.
- **Library rootkit** In software applications that use code library files, such as Windows DLLs, the rootkit can intercept specific system and application programming interface (API) calls and replace them with its code.

Some antivirus software applications can detect the presence of rootkits; however, rootkits may be difficult to clean from a system, especially if they are embedded in the kernel or boot sectors of an OS. In such cases, often the safest and most secure practice is to reinstall the system to ensure that any rootkit code is deleted.

Botnets

Botnet is short for *roBOT NETwork.* A *bot* is typically any type of computer system that is attached to a network whose security has been compromised and that runs malicious software completely unknown to the system users. Botnets and their bots (often called "zombie" computers) are typically used for *distributed denial-of-service (DDoS)* attacks, in which hundreds or even tens of thousands of computers are overtaken and programmed to send network attacks to a single *command and control* server. Command and control servers serve as the source to disseminate commands that spread further malware, exfiltrate data, conduct DDoS attacks, and more. An infected bot (which is typically infected by a worm, virus, or Trojan horse) that is made part of the botnet might not show any initial effects. It is only after the computer is remotely "turned on" to start its attack on another computer that the compromise becomes apparent. Typical symptoms include slow responsiveness and large amounts of network packets being sent from the infected system.

Because compromised servers are controlled by the botnets and are typically not under local control, and because of servers' distributed nature (which means the affected servers could be located anywhere in the world), it can be difficult to mitigate the effects of these types of coordinated attacks. It is also very difficult to plan and prepare for future attacks. Although the originating addresses of the systems in the botnet can be blocked, other compromised systems can be easily added to the botnet to continue the attack from different addresses. Nevertheless, regular investigations of system activity and frequent antivirus scans can help prevent a system from becoming infected with a virus or worm and becoming a bot within a larger botnet.

Malicious Code or Script Execution

Attackers are increasingly turning to shells and scripting languages, such as Bash, PowerShell, and Python, for malicious activity. Shells are ideal for an attacker, as they are native to the operating system, can execute code at an elevated level, and are less likely to be detected by antimalware software. Several famous attacks were developed to exploit these embedded tools, such as Petya/NotPetya, EternalBlue, and Shellshock. PowerShell version 5 now includes the ability to scan for malicious scripts, record sessions, and constrain the commands that can be run. Please note that an emerging type of virus called a fileless virus often piggybacks on legitimate scripts that are running and will execute their malicious commands under the cover of legitimacy. PowerShell is often used for this type of virus, which is particularly difficult for antivirus to detect due to the fact that it is resident in memory and not on the disk.

Cross-Reference

"Malicious code or script execution" is listed under Objective 1.4 within the CompTIA exam objectives.

Analyze and Differentiate Among Types of Password Attacks

Although the most common form of system authentication is a login and password procedure, this is also considered one of the weakest security mechanisms available. Users' passwords tend to be weak because users use common dictionary words or personal information that can be easily guessed by an unauthorized user. Often, a user's password is the name of a spouse or pet or a birth date. Or the user may reveal passwords to others or write them down in conspicuous locations, such as a note taped to the computer monitor.

Most operating systems come with a default administrative account called *admin*, *administrator*, or another similarly obvious name that points to this account as being necessary to manage and administer the system. For example, the *root* account is still the primary account that's been used for decades for full access to a Unix system. Most malicious users and attackers look for the admin or root account of a system or device as the first account to be compromised. It is a best practice for network administrators either to disable or rename default or administrator accounts or, if that is not possible, to create an alternative administrative account with equal access rights and name it something inconspicuous. This ensures that a malicious user cannot automatically try to log in using the well-known account names for the admin user. A recommended best practice is to use separate logins for each administrator to ensure that any admin account actions can be properly logged and audited. Generally, network administrators should never name accounts after their job functions, such as *admin*, *backup*, *databaseadmin*, and so on. Enforcing the use of strong passwords, which are not based on dictionary words or personal information but include the use of alphanumeric characters and uppercase and lowercase letters, greatly diminishes an unauthorized user's ability to guess a password.

Passwords are usually attacked in two ways: online or offline. In an *online attack*, the attacker attempts to log in as a user by guessing the user's password. If the attacker has the password already or can effectively guess the password based on knowledge of the person, this might work. However, this is usually the most ineffective and inefficient type of attack, because most systems are configured to automatically lock the user account after a certain number of unsuccessful login attempts.

In an *offline attack*, the (generally hashed) database of user credentials is usually stolen to be attacked offline by being loaded on to a system where the attacker has a variety of tools. If the attacker has the hashed passwords, he can wage different attacks against them, such as brute-force or dictionary attacks. Remember that hashing is a one-way cryptographic function that is not intended to be decrypted and that it is mathematically difficult to find two different pieces of plaintext that, when subjected to the same hashing algorithm, produce the same hash. When this does occur (and, although extremely rare, is theoretically possible), it is called a *collision* and can be used in a so-called *birthday attack*, which attempts to just find a piece of plaintext that supplies the same hashed value, no matter what the original plaintext might have been. Birthday attacks are named as such as a loose analogy to the birthday paradox, stating that if you have 23 people in a room, the probability that two or more of them share the same birthdate (without the year) is 50 percent. If you increase this number to 70 people, there is a 99 percent probability that at least two of them share the same birthdate, and that with 367 people, there is a 100 percent probability (since there are only 366 days in a year, if you include leap years). While this analogy may not seem to have too much to do with cryptography and password cracking, the same mathematical principles apply to attacks on passwords and collisions, although on a much larger and complex scale. Also, although backward compatibility with older OSs and software sounds like a safe bet, it exposes you to *downgrade attacks*, which force a system to revert to an older or less-secure mode of operation.

Cross-Reference

More information on hashing is included in Domain 2, Objective 2.8.

A *brute-force attack* is the most basic type of password attack. In this attack's simplest form, an attacker might repeatedly attempt to guess the user's password. A more effective way would be to simply start at the beginning of the character set and try all possible combinations, in order, until the attacker eventually finds the correct combination of characters and password length. This obviously would take a very long time for a person to accomplish on his own; however, improved hardware and software has reduced the time of performing brute-force attacks. Even with the best hardware and software, though, brute-force attacks could theoretically take several hundred or more years to go through every permutation. Brute force attacks can be conducted both offline and online.

More effective and efficient, a *dictionary attack* uses dictionaries, or lists of common words across various types of organizations, languages, and other words that might be used for passwords, as well as common substitutions, such as using the @ symbol in lieu of the letter *a*. *Rainbow attacks* are a variation on a dictionary attack that, instead of trying to guess the password, use precomputed hashes (called *rainbow tables*) developed by software that can process huge lists of words and spit out their hash, which is then added to the rainbow table's file. The attacker then compares the rainbow table to the password hashes he obtained illicitly, looking for matches.

Pass the hash allows an attacker to authenticate as a user without having access to the user's clear text password, bypassing standard authentication procedures that require a user to enter their credentials, and moving directly to the point where a hash is passed. This requires the valid password hash for the user to be captured for future use.

Cross-Reference

"Pass the hash" is listed under Objective 1.3 within the CompTIA exam objectives.

Finally, *password spraying* can be considered almost the converse of a brute-force attack. Instead of trying many permutations to gain access to a single account, spraying tries the most common passwords against many accounts. Known as a "low-and-slow" attack, it attempts to bypass the password lockout by trying one common password against many targets and then circling back to try the next common password after a period of time.

To ensure the usefulness and efficiency of a login and password procedure, you must create and strictly enforce account and password policies, such as enforced password expiry and rotation after a specific period, and educate users to follow those policies. Also, note that if an attacker can gain access to a piece of known plaintext, as well as its resulting ciphertext (after encrypted), they can conduct a known plaintext attack, where analysis of the plaintext and ciphertext provides clues to how other pieces of data, to include passwords, might be decrypted.

Analyze and Differentiate Among Nonstandard and Emerging Attacks

While most attacks that you'll encounter as a cybersecurity professional are those described in the previous sections involving malware, ransomware, and password attacks, you also need to understand and protect against the nonstandard and emerging attacks described in this section. From close-access attacks that require comprehensive physical security to the ever-important adversarial artificial intelligence taking the place of human hackers, these attacks are less common but still require that you guard against them.

Supply-Chain Attacks

You could securely configure all your software and make sure that all the hardware that you buy is capable of performing well and providing the necessary level of security, but that might not be sufficient to protect against embedded code and backdoors if a vendor in your supply chain has lax security. The National Institute of Standards and Technology (NIST) Special Publication (SP) 800-161 states that *supply-chain attacks* "may include insertion of counterfeits, unauthorized production, tampering, theft, [and] insertion of malicious software and hardware..." The SP also lists the following as known supply-chain threat agents:

- Counterfeiters
- Insiders
- Foreign intelligence
- Terrorists
- Industrial espionage/cyber criminals

Foreign intelligence at the nation-state level, with a higher level of sophistication, resources at hand, and the desire to insert themselves, can conduct such attacks, as well as manufacturers simply wanting to gather information and covertly send it back to themselves, even for benign reasons such as crash analysis.

The way to combat supply-chain attacks is to know which of your hardware and software contains information or communications technologies and then work to reduce the risks they pose. This is known as *supply chain risk management*. However, this management becomes exponentially difficult when you realize that the average computing system, for example, combines hardware, software, and firmware from potentially dozens of different vendors.

The motherboard, optical drive, hard drive, and memory are all likely from different suppliers, not to mention the software from the OS onward. These each, in turn, likely have components sourced from other suppliers. One method of combating supply-chain attacks is to purchase only from vendors that are certified as "trusted" through an official certifying body but be aware that this can become much pricier in the end as well.

Physical Attacks

Just when you think your systems are safe because you've blocked all the host-based, network-based, and application-based attacks, you need to consider the burgeoning world of attacks that are executed through relatively simply physical devices: a *malicious Universal Serial Bus (USB) cable* that has an embedded Wi-Fi controller that allows a remote user to send it commands; a *skimming attack* that compromises your credit card information by recording it when the card is inserted into an ATM; an individual cloning access cards, known as *card cloning* (think about badges allowing access into buildings, for example). Perhaps the most important vector to consider is the introduction of *malicious flash drives* (or "thumb" drives) within organizations. With some flash drives barely larger than a fingernail, when inserted into a system and not detected, commands can be sent and received, data exfiltrated, and malware delivered. Also, threat actors have been known to use the technique of placing a malicious flash drive near or inside an office building, tempting someone to pick it up and plug it in out of curiosity.

Adversarial Artificial Intelligence

Artificial intelligence (AI) is the future of computing. The sky is the limit; machines blocking attacks from other machines in real time based on machine learning, understanding patterns and using intellectual processes that rival the human brain, only without (or with minimal) human interaction after proper tuning. However, consider if a hacker gained access to that intellectual process and degraded it to their own ends, either through tainted training data or by tampering with the underlying algorithms. An adversary gaining access to an AI algorithm could allow them to develop inputs to purposefully cause the machine learning model to become unstable and erroneous. Unfortunately, as AI has been developed by humans, humans often find weaknesses where the developers didn't consider them.

Cloud-Based vs. On-Premises Attacks

As we will discuss several more times within this text, cloud computing has become much more prevalent as organizations look to harness the flexibility, efficiency, and increased security that having a dedicated cloud host can offer (if managed properly.) Cloud computing allows applications to be run from the web-based cloud, with no need for additional software to be run on the client. For example, word processing and spreadsheet software can now be run as a web-based application instead of a client-based application. The web-based cloud service hosts both the application and the data without the need to store anything local to the client.

This allows the user to use any client she wants to access her cloud-based services. However, while this is all true, don't assume that cloud-based solutions are impervious to the attacks that their on-premises brethren continue to suffer. Attackers, knowing that many organizations are hosted at a single provider, will attack the cloud instance itself looking to gain access to multiple organizations' data (remember the note earlier about it being more secure if managed properly), or just conduct a denial-of-service attack that slows or stops operations completely. If your organization makes a choice to move applications to the cloud, you haven't transferred complete oversight—you're still responsible in the end.

REVIEW

Objective 1.2: Given a scenario, analyze potential indicators to determine the type of attack There are a number of attack types to consider, from the ever-present malware, to password attacks, to close-access physical attacks, to the emerging AI-based attacks. Each one of these attack types has its own indicators to consider, and a defender must know how to spot the signs—from traffic flowing in and out of the network, to accounts being locked out that might indicate a brute-force attack. Thinking like an attacker helps get ahead of an attacker. Slow responsiveness and high network activity can indicate malware activity on a system. Keep antivirus software up to date to detect new types of viruses and spyware. Don't connect malware-infected host systems to a network until they are cleaned.

1.2 QUESTIONS

1. Which of the following best describes a birthday attack? (Choose two.)
   - **A.** A password attack that uses precomputed hashes in its word list
   - **B.** Two unique pieces of plaintext can have the same hash value under certain circumstances
   - **C.** In a room with 23 people, the odds of any two having the same birthdate is 50 percent
   - **D.** A password attack that attempts every single possible combination of characters and password lengths to discover a password
2. You suspect that your server has been compromised because it has been running slowly and is unresponsive. Using a network analyzer, you also notice that large amounts of network data are being sent out from the server. Which of the following is the most likely cause?
   - **A.** The server has a rootkit installed.
   - **B.** The server requires an operating system update.
   - **C.** The server is infected with spyware.
   - **D.** The server is part of a botnet.

3. Antivirus software may not be able to identify which of the following?
   A. Trojans
   B. Logic bombs
   C. Polymorphic viruses
   D. Adware

1.2 ANSWERS

1. **B C** The birthday attack looks for an input that provides the same hashed value, regardless of what the original input was. Remembering a birthday attack is easy if you understand the underlying principle that in a room with 23 people, the odds of any two having the same birthdate is 50 percent, and the odds increase commensurate with the number of people in a room.
2. **D** If your system has been infected with a worm or virus and has become part of a botnet, at certain times, it may take part in distributed denial-of-service attacks on another system on the Internet and may exhibit slow responsiveness and a large amount of network data being sent out of the system.
3. **B** Logic bombs are simply scripts that are designed to automatically execute at a particular time or under particular circumstances. While logic bombs typically perform malicious actions, they are not malicious code outright, and often are not detected by antivirus programs, especially if they reside within a trusted application.

Objective 1.3 Given a scenario, analyze potential indicators associated with application attacks

Application security is another layer of defense that provides protection for the applications that run on an organization's hosts, which include Internet servers such as web, e-mail, File Transfer Protocol (FTP), and database servers. This objective covers different types of application attacks and their impacts.

Application Attacks

Hosting and providing application services involves a wide variety of operating systems, programming languages, and application platforms. The interaction among these different levels of software greatly increases the chances of introducing security vulnerabilities. For example, a hacker may be able to insert operating system commands into a web application query input form that are run as if the hacker were the administrative user. Attacks on database servers and data queries can result in a hacker obtaining unauthorized access to confidential data stored by the database if the application is not secure and the stored data is not encrypted.

Application attacks aim to impact hosts through the applications that they host. Most applications today are web based, but in some cases, the traditional client–server model is used, where an application is hosted on a server. Generally, the threat actor seeks to deny service, steal data, implant malicious code, or gain access to the underlying systems by exploiting vulnerabilities within the applications.

Buffer Overflows

Buffer overflow is a programming term used to describe when input data exceeds the limits recognized by a program. For example, a program might be expecting only a certain number of characters in an input dialog box. If the number of characters exceeds this limit, the added information might also be processed.

In a *buffer overflow attack*, the extra characters are malicious code that causes the program or even the entire system to crash. Buffer overflow attacks typically result in command shell access that gives the attacker administrative privileges.

The buffer overflow vulnerability is a common security concern for web servers and web browsers. A malicious web server set up by a hacker can crash the systems of the users connecting to that web server by sending various HTTP buffer overflow data streams to the client. Similarly, a malicious hacker using a simple web browser can send certain HTTP data to a web server that overflows its software buffers and crashes the web server.

Buffer overflows are caused primarily by *improper input handling* that allows so much data to be entered into the application that the processing limits are exceeded. Buffer overflows have long been a thorn in the side of companies that create web server and web browser software. These vulnerabilities are easy to exploit and can significantly affect the performance of a system or cause it to crash.

An *integer overflow* is like a buffer overflow in that it simply cannot be handled within its allotted space; however, it is the result of a mathematical operation that creates a numeric value that is too large (or sometimes too small). The outcome of a successful integer overflow attack is like that of a buffer overflow attack. This type of attack can be prevented through input validation, of course, but also by implementing error-handling conditions in the web application programming that deal with such overflow conditions. *Error handling* could ensure that out-of-range numerical values are handled in safer ways, such as by converting the value to text, truncating or converting it, or ignoring unexpected values.

Resource Exhaustion

Resource exhaustion attacks take advantage of the limited resources that most modern computer systems have available for software applications. Resource exhaustion essentially creates a denial-of-service condition, because the resources that are needed to execute actions associated with an application are entirely exhausted (hence the name), leading to either an error, performance slowdown, or a denial of service. Resource exhaustion can occur through a *memory leak*, where a software application incorrectly manages its memory resources and does not sufficiently release the memory used when it is no longer needed, or it can occur due to malicious network traffic that purposefully causes resource exhaustion.

Privilege Escalation

Many software applications contain bugs that create security vulnerabilities. In a *privilege escalation* scenario, an attacker exploits a bug within an application to bypass the application and gain elevated privileges that enable the attacker to execute system commands.

Vulnerabilities that typically lead to privilege escalation scenarios are most often found in website code, where scripting and other types of running programs can potentially reveal exploits for malicious users to take control of a system. These are often buffer overflow attacks, in which conditions and boundaries are not properly set on user-entered fields in an application or website and allow malicious users to crash the program or allow highly privileged command execution.

Protection against privilege escalation requires that programmers use input validation and test their code for bugs and exploits before releasing the software. If a documented exploit is found after the software is released, it is critical that a patch be quickly made available to fix the bug to prevent proof-of-concept exploits from turning into real security threats. Systems administrators must be diligent in ensuring that any software they run is using the latest patch level to guarantee that all known bug fixes are currently deployed.

Hijacking

Cookies are a necessary part of most website application interactions, but they also represent a wide variety of security issues. Cookies contain session data for each website you visit that uses cookies. The data is usually composed of innocuous items, such as site preferences, that are reloaded when you revisit a site, but often the cookies also contain session data, including some authentication and web form information, along with referral information on websites you have already visited. *Locally shared objects (LSOs)*, often referred to as *Flash cookies*, operate in much the same manner, storing data collected from various websites.

Cookies are easily abused by malicious actors. Cookies are sent in clear text and can be easily captured by an unauthorized user using a network packet sniffer. An unsuspecting user might also click a web link that downloads a malicious script that collects data on the user's web browser cookies and transmits it back to the hacker's website.

Session hijacking can occur when a user's cookie for a website, which can contain session authentication credentials for a remote server, is hijacked by another user, who then uses that cookie to gain unauthorized access. The cookie might be transferred from the user's computer to that of the attacker, or it can be captured via a packet sniffer and an on-path network attack.

To protect against session hijacking, web applications should regenerate session keys and IDs after a successful login so that a secondary attempt to use the same session credentials from a hijacked cookie will not work. Web applications can also check other aspects of a session, such as the IP address; if the address is different from the original cookie, a new session must be created and authenticated. High-security applications such as web banking can use Transport Layer Security (TLS) or the now-deprecated Secure Sockets Layer (SSL) to encrypt sessions, including the transfer of information in user cookies. Be aware of *SSL stripping* attacks that downgrade your security from the encrypted HTTPS to plaintext HTTP in order to gain access to the information that otherwise would have been sent securely. Similar to an on-path attack, the user may not even realize they've been conned.

Clickjacking occurs with multiple layers on a page, often transparent, that trick the user into clicking a link or an image—often invisible—that is embedded within the page redirecting to a malicious site rather than to the link that the user intended to click. This is also often referred to as a *user interface (UI) redress attack*. Clickjacking is similar to another attack, *URL redirection*, in that both often redirect to a malicious site that attempts to gain credentials, but URL redirection often comes in the form of a phishing email that redirects from a legitimate site to a malicious site, while clickjacking incorporates hidden, invisible, or false elements. A small but important distinction.

Cross-Reference

"URL redirection" is listed under Objective 1.4 within the CompTIA exam objectives.

HTML Attachments

Attachments received from e-mail messages, instant messaging (IM) messages, and download sites can often contain .htm and .html documents. These document types are the default files for web browsers. These HTML attachments, if opened, can automatically open your web browser and immediately connect to a malicious website. When you are connected to the malicious website, it may transfer files such as malware and Trojan horse software to your computer. Many e-mail readers automatically open HTML attachments, which can contain malicious dynamic content and automatically load other web data, images, or even hidden code that executes on the client.

If you receive an HTML attachment, make sure it is from a trusted source. Before opening it in a web browser, you should open the HTML file in a text editor to view its contents and check for any abnormal code. Most e-mail clients have security settings that prevent the loading of images in HTML messages unless you explicitly allow them. You can add known sites to a trusted sites list, which configures the e-mail client to automatically display images that you know come from a trusted source.

Malicious Add-Ons

Most web browsers enable all the functionality of *add-ons*, which are installable modules that provide useful functionality to a user's web-browsing experience. These add-ons can be anything from decorative themes, to real-time alerts for weather and stocks, to web utilities. There is the possibility that these add-ons, if not from a trusted source, may contain malicious code that can do anything from installing a Trojan horse program that allows remote access to a user's computer, to stealing confidential personal information.

Make sure before you install add-ons to your web browser that they originate from a trusted source, such as the web browser's official site or app store. Official stores that accept add-ons uploaded by developers for public use typically thoroughly analyze and scan those add-ons for evidence of malicious code. If you download an add-on from an untrusted source, you have no verification that the code has been tested. Personal firewalls can also alert you to abnormal network connection behavior after you have installed an add-on.

Cross-Site Scripting

Cross-site scripting (XSS) is a type of website application vulnerability that allows malicious users to inject malicious code into dynamic websites that rely on user input. An example of this would be a search engine website or user message forum that utilizes user input. The malicious user can input a script or series of commands, such as JavaScript, within a legitimate input request that can provide the attacker with additional administrative access to hack user accounts and embed malicious code within cookies and other website code that can be downloaded by end users. An unsuspecting user might click a link that downloads a malicious script that collects data on the user's web browser cookies and transmits it back to the website.

Request Forgeries

Cross-site request forgery (XSRF or *CSRF)* is a type of attack that relies on the ability to use a user's current web browsing state, including session cookie data and login identity credentials, and trick that user into navigating to a website that contains malicious code. At that point, the hacker's code can use the session information to make unauthorized requests as the target user, change the user's account information, or steal the user's credentials. XSRF vulnerabilities have been found on servers hosting high-profile websites, including high-security banking sites.

While it is more common for XSRF to be conducted via a compromised server, *client-side request forgery* allows a malicious user to submit arbitrary requests to an XSRF-protected endpoint, via web browser or mobile device, by modifying the endpoint to which the client-side code makes an HTTP request with a valid XSRF token, often by form submission.

In a *server-side request forgery* (SSRF) attack, an attacker exploits the underlying functionality on a server to read or update internal resources that the attacker shouldn't have access to, using URLs which the code running on the server will read or submit data to. If conducted successfully, the attacker may be able to acquire details regarding the server configuration, connect to internal services, or send commands.

Application Programming Interface Attacks

One of the most exciting (and dangerous) innovations in recent years is the ability to integrate different applications and data sets, both internal (private) and external (partners or public) to an organization, to perform more complex analysis, data mining, and seamless functionality. This generally is done through an application programming interface (API) that serves almost as a translator between systems and software, defining what and how elements can be called. By their very nature, APIs expose some logic and data, carefully defined (hopefully) to expose only the least amount required to successfully interface. *API attacks* seek to use the API to achieve an impact such as denial of service (through forcing the API into a nonfunctional state, often by overloading it), data exfiltration (taking advantage of a lack of encryption), or code injection (through a lack of input validation).

Driver Manipulation

The constant stream of updated operating system software means that many applications must continue to perform their required functionality in an ever-changing environment. Two types of attacks that take advantage of the mechanisms put into place for continuous compatibility are shimming and refactoring. Shims intercept calls to an API, transparent to the user, and are often used to provide compatibility between an older API and newer applications, or to allow an application to be used within an incompatible operating environment. In a *shimming attack*, an attacker wraps malicious code around legitimate code, such as a driver, in an attempt to elevate their privilege or install backdoors.

Similarly, refactoring restructures older, existing code to improve it (e.g., for optimization, to remove bugs, to add functionality) without changing the output behaviors or functionality. A *refactoring attack* takes advantage of this—again, often with a driver—to add malicious code unbeknownst to the end user.

Header Manipulation

Header manipulation is a type of web application attack that inserts invalid or malicious data into HTTP headers. HTTP request and response messages have headers that include various HTTP commands, directives, site referral information, and address data. This data is simple text that can be modified by a malicious user. By manipulating this header information, a hacker can then perform a variety of attacks such as cross-site scripting, session and web page hijacking, and cookie modification.

In general, most web applications process server-side headers, which are generally safe and cannot be manipulated, while ignoring client-side headers in HTTP requests because of the security concern that they are easily manipulated.

Injections

Extensible Markup Language (XML) is like HTML in that it is a markup language that uses tags to define data. XML differs from HTML in that whereas HTML is designed to process and display data, XML is used to structure, store, and transport data. In fact, XML carries no data at all, but is designed to structure it. XML is used in a wide variety of web applications.

XML injection attacks can modify how an XML application processes data. By injecting XML content into the XML application, the attacker causes the application to process data according to the malicious injected XML code. Web applications that process XML documents require input and document schema validation to prevent XML injection attacks from occurring.

Injections insert code into a running process, forcing a program to behave in a manner that it was not intended to do. *Dynamic link library (DLL) injections* exploit DLLs by inserting code into a DLL and then having the original process load and execute the code within the DLL. DLLs were designed to be loaded when required at runtime, making them uniquely qualified for this attack.

Sometimes, web applications without proper input validation can allow operating system–level commands to be inserted into uniform resource locators (URLs) or input forms that are executed on the server. This can allow an unauthorized user to perform commands on the server with escalated privileges or to gain access to sensitive data without authentication or authorization. Each type of *command injection* attack is specific to an operating system, such as Unix or Windows, the programming language of the web application, or the back-end database, as with *Structured Query Language (SQL) injection*, in which the attacker sends SQL input (normally in the form of SQL database manipulation commands) to the database via an input form. The results returned to the attacker are responses to those commands, giving the attacker access to information stored within the database that shouldn't be available to the attacker.

For example, a malicious user might be able to specify a URL with an escape character (such as ?) and type additional commands that are executed after the main URL. Unix systems can also make use of the pipe (|) command to allow additional commands to be run as part of the primary command execution.

Applications that perform lookups to Lightweight Directory Access Protocol (LDAP) directories are also susceptible to injection attacks. *LDAP injection*, which is like a SQL injection attack, inserts code into user-based input that is utilized in a query to an LDAP server. If the application does not properly validate user input, an attacker can insert commands into the LDAP queries to perform malicious actions against the LDAP directory, including unauthorized queries and data modification.

You can prevent command injection by implementing input validation techniques that allow the user to input only limited data in web application fields and that filter out escape characters like the pipe character that a user might input to try to enter additional commands. Additional hardening techniques can be used to disable advanced functions in web applications that provide deep-level system access.

Directory Traversal

Directory traversal is a type of access vulnerability that enables a hacker to get unauthorized access to files on a web server other than the public files that are served on the website.

For example, a hacker might be able to learn the directory URL structure of a site by studying the naming conventions of the links. The hacker can input a manual URL to try to guess the link of a specific file or can actually navigate the website directory tree through the URL, via ../ on a Unix system or ..\ on a Windows system, to go to the parent directory. If permissions are not properly set on the directory tree, the hacker might be able to read and copy important system files, including user login and password databases, such as /etc/passwd on Unix systems.

You can prevent directory traversal attacks by ensuring that input validation on all website input forms prevents changing directories; by setting permissions on directories to prevent viewing their contents; by preventing debugging information (such as error messages with full URL paths) from being displayed; and by using back-end databases to store any information that needs to be viewed on a website so that any important data files are not stored on the web server.

Arbitrary Code Execution

Arbitrary code execution (sometimes referred to as *remote code execution*) describes the situation where an intruder can execute a command at will, whenever and wherever, by exploiting a vulnerability on a system, usually in an application. This type of attack has been possible within any number of applications, from operating systems to programming frameworks, and even video games.

Arbitrary code execution is considered one of the most serious types of attacks, because once an attacker has gained control of a process, he can potentially use that control to gain access to (and potentially full control of) the entire system.

Zero-Day Attacks

A *zero-day attack* is a type of threat that has rarely or never been encountered, such as an attack technique that takes advantage of previously unknown weaknesses and vulnerabilities (in turn referred to as *zero-day vulnerabilities*) in an application or operating system software. Because the attack is brand new, no existing defense has been created to detect it.

Zero-day attacks are very difficult to defend against, but in most cases, OS and software application vendors are very responsive in patching their software in the event a new vulnerability is discovered. You must always make sure your software is running the latest version with all security patches available installed.

You can also use specialized security software such as an intrusion detection system to detect anomalous events that could indicate a zero-day exploit.

Cross-Reference

"Zero-day" is listed under Objective 1.6 within the CompTIA exam objectives.

Race Conditions

Some software is designed to be executed as a series of steps: Step A is required to be performed before Step B, which in turn is required to occur before Step C, and so on. A *race condition* happens when an application is dependent on the steps to be performed in an appropriate order, and the steps are subsequently then executed out of order, creating a crash or other negative situation that can be exploited by an attacker. Race conditions can be used to cause a *null-pointer dereference*, where a pointer inside the code with a value of NULL is used rather than the valid, expected pointer. A similar term you should know is a *pointer/object dereference*, where a pointer is trusted to read valid data from a specific area, and through manipulation or just incorrect programming practices, is not loaded properly. Both of these conditions generally result in a crash and can be exploited in a variety of ways, sometimes to gain elevated access to the application or underlying system.

A specific race condition to be aware of is the *time of check/time of use*. This condition occurs when Step A (often involving successful authentication into a system) occurs and then the state changes before the use of that authentication occurs. This can be used to elevate privileges or gain access to resources using those credentials.

Replay

A *replay* attack occurs when an unauthorized user captures network traffic and then sends the communication to its original destination, acting as the original sender, as shown in Figure 1.3-1.

To prevent replay attacks from succeeding, you can implement timestamps, sequence numbers, or randomized session IDs. This allows the authentication system to accept only network packets that contain the appropriate timestamp or sequence number. If the timestamp is beyond a certain threshold, the packet is discarded. To prevent *session replay* attacks, session IDs or tokens should be randomly generated; otherwise, an attacker could guess the session ID and use it later to authenticate as a valid user.

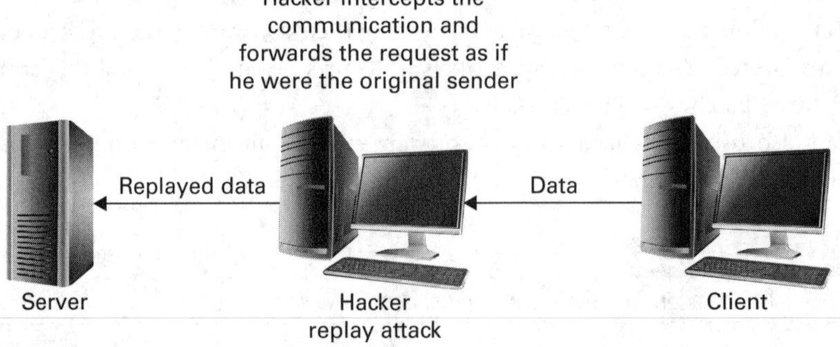

FIGURE 1.3-1 A replay attack

REVIEW

Objective 1.3: Given a scenario, analyze potential indicators associated with application attacks Application attacks aim to impact hosts through the applications that they host. Most applications today are web based, but in some cases, the traditional client–server model is used, where an application is hosted on a server. Generally, the threat actor seeks to deny service, steal data, implant malicious code, or gain access to the underlying systems by exploiting vulnerabilities within the applications.

1.3 QUESTIONS

1. While testing exception handling with a web application, you encounter an error that displays a full URL path to critical data files for the application. Which one of the following types of vulnerabilities would this application be susceptible to?
   A. Buffer overflow
   B. Session hijacking
   C. Cross-site scripting
   D. Directory traversal
2. Your web application currently checks authentication credentials from a user's web browser cookies before allowing a transaction to take place. However, you have had several complaints of identity theft and unauthorized purchases from users of your site. Which of the following is the mostly likely cause?
   A. Cross-site scripting
   B. Session hijacking
   C. Header manipulation
   D. Lack of encryption
3. During testing of a web application, you discover that due to poor input validation, you can easily crash the server by entering values in the input forms much greater than the system can handle. What type of vulnerability is this?
   A. Session hijacking
   B. Buffer overflow
   C. Privilege escalation
   D. XML injection

1.3 ANSWERS

1. **D** Directory traversal is a vulnerability that allows an attacker who knows the details of an application server's directory tree to manually traverse the directory using input commands in the URL location bar or input forms in the application. Error messages should never display the full paths of files to prevent hackers from discovering the directory structure.

2. **B** Session hijacking occurs when a malicious hacker is able to access a user's session cookie and then use the session information to make unauthorized requests as the user.
3. **B** Buffer overflows are caused primarily by poor input validation that allows illegal data to be entered into the application, causing processing limits to be exceeded.

Objective 1.4 Given a scenario, analyze potential indicators associated with network attacks

Securing a network and its systems requires protection against a variety of attacks. These attacks might affect only certain areas of operations, such as an application attack on a specific File Transfer Protocol (FTP) server, or they might disrupt your entire network, such as a denial-of-service (DoS) attack. Some attacks are attempts to gain unauthorized access to a system or to damage one user account or one server. Other attacks try to disrupt the entire network infrastructure itself or prevent customers from accessing an organization's public website.

The purpose of the attack is not the main concern, however: the main concern is how the attack occurred and how to prevent it from succeeding. By understanding the various types of protocols, attacks, tools, and resources used by malicious users, you can protect yourself and your network. By knowing where to expect attacks and how to recognize the potential indicators associated with network attacks, you can enact preventive measures.

Wireless Attacks

Numerous types of attacks can be launched against a wireless network. Some involve sophisticated methods of intercepting and cracking the secret encryption keys that wireless networks use both to authenticate clients that join it and to encrypt wireless traffic that it passes. Other attacks are more simplistic and involve low-tech methods such as using a rogue access point to fool people into joining it instead of the legitimate access point. There are also attacks against Bluetooth networks that can be effective in intercepting any data passed between Bluetooth devices. The following sections describe several of these wireless attack types and discuss how they are perpetrated.

Data Emanation

In its most basic form, *data emanation* occurs when any sort of data is transmitted over an electromagnetic medium. For example, when electricity passes through a cable, it creates an electromagnetic field that can be detected and measured. In communications, you could capture data emanation from a message and use it to rearrange the electronic signal to reveal the original communication.

This is a serious issue in wireless networking, as unprotected and unsecured wireless communications can be easily intercepted, and an unauthorized user can steal usernames, passwords, and sensitive private data. All information on an unencrypted wireless local area network (WLAN) is transmitted in clear text, and any wireless user can use a protocol analyzer or sniffer application to view the data traversing the WLAN. As will be covered in Domain 3.0, all WLANs should communicate using secure encrypted channels to prevent eavesdropping from unauthorized users. The actual equipment for the WLAN, such as access points and other wireless devices, must also be physically secure.

Jamming

Occasionally, a wireless network will experience interference from another wireless device, such as a baby monitor or cordless telephone, that is operating on the same frequency (such as 2.4 GHz). This interference can interrupt wireless network transmission and reception. For the most part, this interference is unintentional; however, *jamming* is a form of intentional interference on wireless networks, designed as a DoS attack. This type of attack is conducted by overpowering the signals of a legitimate wireless access point, typically using a *rogue access point* with its transmit power set to very high levels. However, other electronic devices can be used to intentionally create interference or jamming in wireless networks as well, including some very specialized devices that can be acquired via the Internet.

The only way to prevent jamming and interference is to proactively monitor for sources of wireless signals that are not coming from the corporate wireless network. The sources are usually in the same frequency range and may come from malicious wireless clients or rogue wireless access points.

Bluetooth Vulnerabilities

Several vulnerabilities in vendor implementations of the Bluetooth standard have allowed unauthorized access to personal data on cell phones and computer devices. Bluetooth can also be susceptible to unauthorized messages, a practice called *bluejacking*. An unauthorized user can send unwanted messages to another Bluetooth device in range of the originating device. This has most often been used for Bluetooth spam advertising, in which a Bluetooth device such as a smartphone suddenly receives a text message containing the spam message. Bluejacking is relatively harmless and a nuisance, much like spam e-mails, but there is the potential for harmful media to be transferred from one device to another.

A more serious Bluetooth vulnerability is called *bluesnarfing*. Many older Bluetooth-capable phones and devices use a discovery mode that allows a hacker to detect and connect automatically to other Bluetooth devices, much like a WLAN. Without proper authentication, an unauthorized user can connect to an unprotected Bluetooth device and access any data stored on it. If an unsuspecting user leaves his device in discovery mode, it is not protected from access by other Bluetooth devices in the vicinity.

Bluetooth defines three security modes:

- **Nonsecure mode** No security features are enabled.
- **Service-level security mode** Application security policies are used, in which the actual applications on the wireless device are responsible for security.
- **Link-level security mode** The most secure of the three modes, it authenticates the actual communications link before data transmission can begin. Data encryption can also be performed in this mode once the link is authenticated. Authentication allows the devices to decide whether to form a connection based on available identification at the hardware level. Once the link is established, additional security might be applied to the data transmission using encryption. Stronger encryption can also be enabled at the software level, if needed.

EXAM TIP Bluesnarfing is a serious Bluetooth security threat, and link-level security is recommended to protect the communications link and transfer of data. Disable Bluetooth if you are not using it.

Near-Field Communication

Near-Field Communication (NFC) is a standard used primarily in mobile devices to facilitate easy communications between two or more devices simply by bringing them into proximity (likely touching them together). NFC technology is often used within applications to send pictures, contact cards, and other media between compatible devices. However, while the range of NFC is quite limited to the immediate proximity of the devices, the standard itself is essentially an emanation, making it quite vulnerable to several types of attacks by anyone within that same vicinity. Because NFC uses *radio-frequency identification (RFID)* technologies, it is vulnerable to eavesdropping by another NFC device, on-path attacks, and relay attacks (relaying modified information back and forth from the victim's device, pretending to be the victim). Many devices that are enabled for Wi-Fi Protected Setup (WPS) also use NFC, making wireless hacking of WPS-enabled networks trivial, as discussed later in this section.

War Driving

Many corporate WLANs and home-based wireless networks are set up and configured with no encryption or access control. Hackers have been known to roam neighborhoods with a large corporate presence and use simple laptops with wireless connectivity to connect to unprotected WLANs and access their resources. This is called *war driving*. Several programs are available that allow unauthorized users to scan an area for open and unprotected wireless networks. After accessing the network, the user can attempt several types of attacks, such as eavesdropping and sniffing the wireless data, or accessing and capturing the data on other wireless devices on the network.

Administrators can lower the susceptibility of their wireless networks to war driving attacks by encrypting their networks and disabling the broadcast of their SSIDs.

Access Points (Evil Twin)

With wireless networks, much of the typical physical security that prevents someone from plugging into a network is unavailable. Anyone within the vicinity of a WLAN can connect to it easily using a laptop or other wireless-equipped device. Unauthorized users can also set up their own *rogue access points*, some of which are intended for unsuspecting users to connect and transmit sensitive and private data, including username and password credentials, directly on the hacker's network. *Evil twins* are rogue access points set up with legitimate names (for example, as a Wi-Fi hot spot for a popular network carrier). The wireless access is typically set up as password-free and unencrypted, and an unsuspecting user could connect and make an online purchase using her banking or credit card details, which are then stolen by the hacker for the purposes of identity theft and fraud.

You can prevent rogue devices and access points from connecting to your wireless network by setting a unique SSID name and encrypting the network, since any rogue access points and devices will require the SSID name and encryption passphrase to connect to the network. In certain cases, MAC address filtering can also be used to allow only certain hardware addresses access to the network; however, this is not practical for networks with hundreds of wireless clients. Your networks should be routinely scanned for evidence of rogue access points or devices; just walking the area with a laptop scanning for access points can help you determine which legit (and not-so-legit) points you have. User education is the best protection against evil twins, so make sure your users know the official access points to use and to be on guard.

EXAM TIP Never connect to a WAP that doesn't require authentication or whose SSID name is similar to that of a legitimate WAP's SSID name. It very likely is a rogue access point.

KEY TERM A **MAC address** is a unique hardware address assigned to network interface cards. (MAC stands for Media Access Control.) This address is expressed in hexadecimal format.

As an end user accessing a free access point, your best protection is to always use secure, encrypted websites via TLS or use a VPN connection when you are connected to the access point. This way, if you happen to be connected to a rogue access point, your information remains encrypted and undecipherable to the hacker. Be careful when connecting to wireless access points advertised as a popular wireless provider, and make sure that the page is legitimate before entering any type of authentication or payment card details.

Disassociation

Disassociating (also known as *deauthenticating*) a wireless host from the access point forces the client to reconnect and exchange the wireless key. There are different methods and desired ends for conducting this type of attack; if it is successful, an attacker can either join the wireless network, intercept traffic from the wireless network on-path, or prevent an authorized client from associating back to the legitimate network, essentially performing a denial-of-service.

Packet Sniffing and Eavesdropping

On an unencrypted open wireless network, any hacker can use a packet sniffer or network eavesdropping tool to analyze wireless network data as it passes through the network. The hacker can use this information to obtain authentication credentials of users, including usernames and passwords, and sensitive financial information such as credit card and bank account numbers. The hacker could also initiate an on-path attack, modifying data en route to its destination. For example, the hacker could spoof the sender or destination address, or even a network MAC address to emulate another host.

To prevent packet sniffing and eavesdropping, the wireless network must be encrypted with a strong encryption technique. While security measures such as disabling the broadcast of SSID names, authentication, and MAC address access control can help prohibit unauthorized access, only by encrypting the data can you make it indecipherable to those who are monitoring network traffic.

WPS Attacks

Wi-Fi Protected Setup was implemented for ease of use, not security. WPS attacks exploit an active WPS implementation to compromise more computing assets. For example, the Reaver tool conducts a brute-force attack against a WPS registrar personal identification number (PIN), usually residing on an access point. If the attack is successful, the tool then recovers the WPA or WPA2 passphrase for the access point.

Brute-force attacks against WPS can be mitigated by using a time-out period for the WPS-enabled device that disables the PIN. Mitigating WPS attacks is further complicated by the fact that in many WPS-enabled devices, disabling the WPS feature does not result in the feature being disabled—it only "appears" disabled to the user. The device would still be vulnerable to attack.

WEP/WPA Attacks

Several types of attacks target wireless networks utilizing Wired Equivalent Privacy (WEP), such as dictionary-based attacks that passively analyze traffic and build a dictionary file, or that utilize an open-source dictionary file that attempts to break the key. Other attacks attempt to decrypt traffic at the access point. The most serious type of attack against WEP is the IV attack.

IV Attack

On wireless networks encrypted with WEP, the WEP encryption technique uses a special 24-bit *initialization vector (IV)* that is combined with its 40-bit WEP key to encrypt each network packet. This extends the life of the WEP key, as the IV changes with each transmission. WEP has proved to be an insecure protocol, in part due to short 24-bit IV factor that is sent in clear text, which could enable a hacker to discover the IV through repetition. In very large and busy wireless networks, the IV itself can be repeated in a space of hours. The hacker can then use various utilities to decrypt subsequent packets that were encrypted with the same IV key stream. This makes it possible to decrypt packets without even needing to decrypt the WEP key.

This type of attack has become less common because WEP has been replaced by stronger encryption methods such as Wi-Fi Protected Access 2 (WPA2). IEEE deprecated WEP in 2004.

TKIP Attack

WPA networks are not impervious to attack. WPA networks utilizing the Temporal Key Integrity Protocol (TKIP) are vulnerable to attacks that decrypt and recover portions of the data, such as the Beck–Tews and Ohigashi–Morii attacks. While the size of the data decrypted can be somewhat negligible (between 12 and 596 bytes), an attacker can use the retrieved information to conduct further attacks on the network. These attacks can be mitigated through use of WPA2 combined with the Advanced Encryption Standard (AES).

WPA2 Attacks

WPA2 attacks are also possible if the WAP uses a weak passphrase ("password," for example). Cracking WPA2 is done by disassociating the client and WAP, forcing them to reestablish connections by performing a four-way handshake. If you can capture a full handshake (which is very easy to do with the command airdump-ng after disassociating them), then it's only an issue of cracking an easy-to-guess password, because you capture the key as well during the handshake. Password length and complexity are the keys to securing WPA2.

Network Attacks

Many of the types of attacks that can assault a network and computer system are geared toward specific system accounts, system services, or applications. The most damaging and, obviously, the most popular attacks by hackers involve disrupting the network itself. Because the network is the infrastructure that allows all systems and devices to communicate, disrupting those communication lines can be the most damaging attack a network can suffer.

The following sections outline some popular types of network-based attacks that have been used to intercept or disrupt communications and describe how to prevent them.

Denial-of-Service

Denial-of-service (DoS) attacks are well known for their ability to deny access to a website or other Internet site, but DoS attacks can be launched against any type of network or system and at specific layers (such as an *application-layer DoS attack*). In a DoS attack, a hacker overloads a specific server with so much data that the server is too busy to service valid requests coming from real clients on the network. System performance slows to a crawl. This affects the ability to service legitimate requests because the client does not receive responses to queries. This type of attack can also be performed on entire networks, as the DoS is targeted at the central router or firewall through which all data passes. The network traffic becomes so high that nothing can get in or out of the network. The DoS attack is more serious than a single-server attack because it compromises network bandwidth, which effectively denies access to all systems on that network rather than just one. Another type of DoS attack can occur when a wireless network is purposefully jammed, using a jammer that creates noise that interferes with the wireless signal. We will discuss that further with other wireless attacks.

While DoS attacks are often conducted against web servers, they are particularly harmful when conducted against *operational technology (OT)*, such as power generation and utility systems, which are often older and less likely to be secured against sophisticated attacks. In this situation, the systems can slow or stop, potentially leading to service outages.

Distributed Denial-of-Service

In a more organized and devastating attack, a *distributed denial-of-service (DDoS)*, the flood of data originates from multiple hosts simultaneously. The combined effects quickly overload any server or network device. As opposed to a DoS attack, which has a single origin, with a DDoS attack, a network administrator cannot pinpoint and deny access to one host because the attack comes from multiple hosts distributed throughout the Internet. Usually, these originating hosts are not willfully engaged in the attack. Malicious hackers can secretly install software on an insecure server somewhere else on the Internet and use that remotely to flood another host with data. This effectively hides the true origin of the attack, especially when the IP addresses are spoofed to show different originating addresses than those used in the attack. Botnets are often used to conduct DDoS attacks, with the computers of hundreds or even thousands of unsuspecting users conducting the attack on behalf of their remote master.

Cross-Reference

Read more about botnets in Objective 1.2, earlier in this domain.

Ping Attack

The most common form of attack uses simple TCP/IP utilities, such as ping, the command used to determine whether a certain host (classified as the destination host) is functioning and communicating with the network. A user sends an Internet Control Message Protocol (IMCP) packet to the destination host, and the destination host sends back a reply that it is indeed working and on the network. In a DoS attack, a malicious user can send a continuous stream of rapid ping attempts, called a "ping of death." The host is then overloaded by having to reply to every ping, rendering it unable to process legitimate requests.

SYN Flood

Another type of DoS attack is the *synchronous (SYN) flood*. Exchanging SYN packets is an aspect of TCP/IP that allows systems to synchronize with each other while communicating. One system sends a SYN packet that is acknowledged by another system. The target system then waits for another acknowledgment from the sender.

This process can be abused by a malicious hacker by sending forged SYN packets to a host that is unable to reply to the request because the return address is incorrect. This causes the host to halt communications while waiting for the other system to reply. If the host is flooded with a high number of forged SYN packets, it becomes overloaded and unable to respond to legitimate requests.

Other types of network flooding include ICMP floods, UDP floods, MAC floods, and other types of protocol-based flooding, and are caused by vulnerabilities in the network protocols themselves. Make sure your OS is updated to the latest version by installing any recent service packs and security patches. This ensures that your underlying network protocols do not have any unresolved security issues.

DNS Amplification

A *DNS amplification attack* uses publicly accessible Domain Name System servers to conduct a DDoS on a victim server by flooding the system with the DNS response traffic. An attacker sends a DNS lookup request to an open, recursive DNS server or DNS resolver with a spoofed source address that is the victim system and not the actual requestor (the attacker). All responses are then sent to the victim server; the amplification part comes in through the attacker querying the DNS server for *any* information regarding the zone, which creates a significant amount of information to be "returned" to the victim server. When this is amplified across a botnet, with all machines conducting the same activities, the victim server often can't handle the attack and a DDoS occurs.

Flood Protection

Some firewalls and other security products can also actively detect a network flood attack, actively block it, reclaim TCP resources used by the attack, and even try to trace it back to a source. Flood guard defenses can also prevent attacks based on multiple attempts to log in to a network device that can use up valuable networking resources.

Layer 2 Attacks

One of the more popular methods for hacking a system is *spoofing* MAC or network addresses, which involves modifying the header of a network packet to use a cloned source address of an external or internal host that differs from the original address. By spoofing the IP address, the hacker can fool the destination host into thinking the message is from a trusted source. The cause of this problem is that the architecture of TCP/IP has no built-in mechanism to verify the source and destination IP addresses of its network packets. A hacker can spoof the IP address to make it look as though a packet is coming from a different location—in fact, it can even be made to look like the IP address of an internal system. While spoofing is an attack by itself, it's more often used as a first step to carry out other attacks.

There are different ways to execute this attack, depending on what your end goal is and how you must fool other hosts. For example, to spoof a MAC address, you could use ARP poisoning (discussed a bit later) to make false updates to a host's ARP cache, causing it to communicate by MAC address to an attacker instead of the actual host.

IP spoofing is mainly used by malicious hackers to hide their identity when attacking a network system, especially in a DoS-type attack. By spoofing the IP address of the incoming packets, hackers may make it difficult for network administrators to determine the real source of the attacks before they can set up a filter to block out that IP address.

Another use for spoofing is to emulate a trusted internal system on the network. For example, if a local server has an IP address of 192.168.17.5 and accepts connections only from that network, a malicious hacker can modify the source address of the packet to mimic an internal address, such as 192.168.17.12. This way, the server thinks the packets are coming from an internal trusted host, not a system external to the network, as shown in Figure 1.4-1.

Spoofing can also occur in e-mail–based attacks, where a legitimate domain (and, by extension, its reputation) is forged to send malicious e-mails. The attacker spoofs a legitimate domain to send the e-mail, exploiting the trust that a user would have in that domain. Very often the end user does not look further into the header to determine if the e-mail was actually sent from that organization (say, a bank).

To help prevent spoofing attacks, your router or firewall might be able to filter incoming traffic to restrict network traffic coming into the external interface. By configuring the filter to prevent external packets originating from internal addresses, you prevent spoofed addresses from entering the network.

Address Resolution Protocol (ARP) poisoning is a type of network attack in which the ARP cache of systems on the network is modified to associate an IP address with the MAC address of the attacker's system. ARP is used by systems on a network to associate an IP address of a system with its hardware MAC address. The attacker sends spoofed ARP messages to the network and masquerades as another system so that returned network packets go to the attacker's system and not to their original destination. The malicious user can then modify the data in transit or modify the routing information to use the data as a DoS attack against a router.

ARP poisoning and spoofing can be mitigated by using DHCP or other network services that help network clients keep track of the MAC address of connecting systems to detect receipt of an ARP message that does not resolve properly. Physical access to the network should also be controlled by disabling unused ports on network equipment and using port security to limit who can connect to the enabled ports.

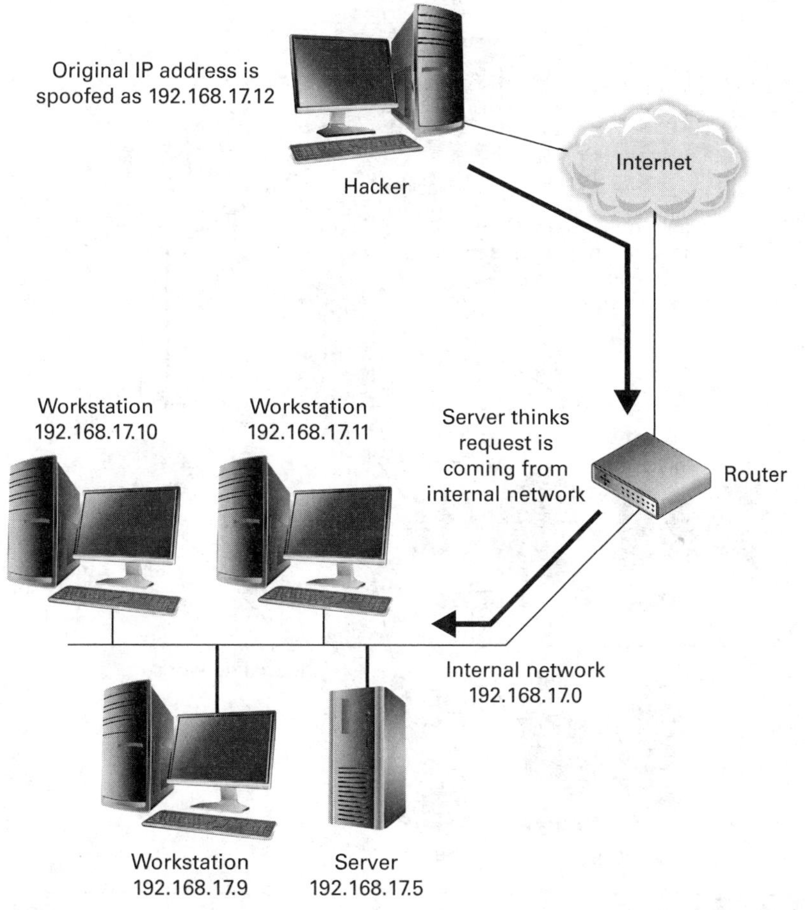

FIGURE 1.4-1 A spoofing attack

Smurf Attack

A *smurf* attack uses a spoof attack combined with a DDoS attack to exploit the use of IP broadcast addressing and ICMP. ICMP is used by networks and through administrative utilities to exchange information about the state of the network. It is used by the ping utility to contact other systems to determine whether they are operational. The destination system returns an echo message in response to a ping message.

A hacker uses a utility such as hping3 to build a network packet with a spoofed IP address that contains an ICMP ping message addressed to an IP broadcast address. A *broadcast address* includes all nodes of a certain network, and messages to that address are seen by all the nodes. The ping echo responses are sent back to the target address. The number of pings and echo responses can flood the network with traffic, causing systems on the network to be

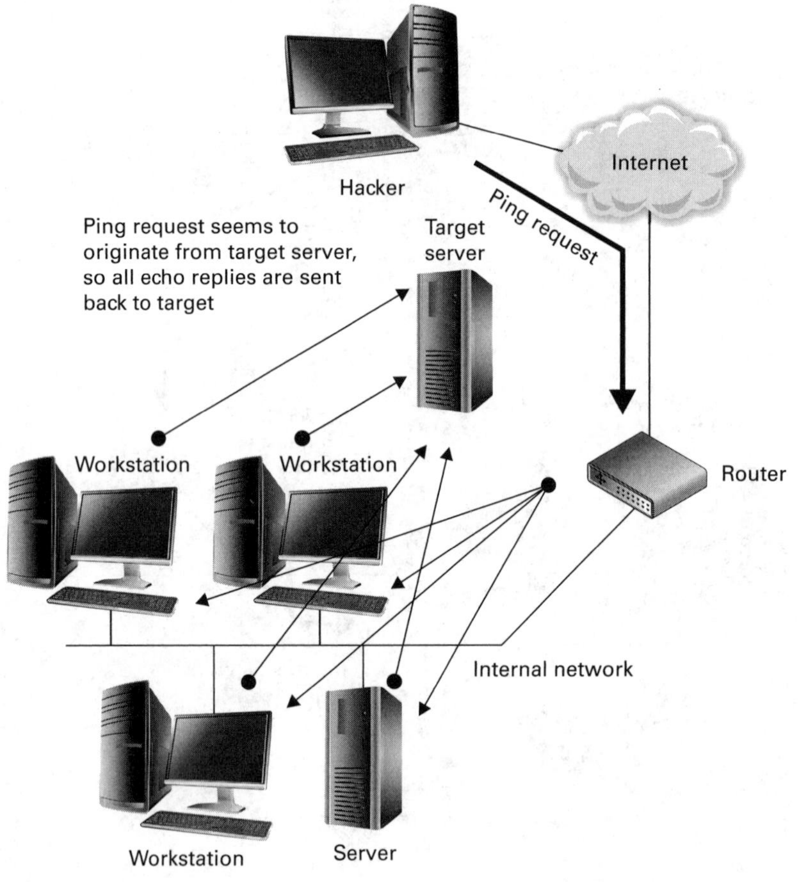

FIGURE 1.4-2 A smurf attack

unresponsive, as shown in Figure 1.4-2. To prevent smurf attacks, IP broadcast addressing should be disabled on the network router, because this broadcast addressing is used only rarely.

These attacks can be difficult to stop and prevent, but some simple configuration changes on the local routers and firewalls can help prevent them. The simplest way of protecting against ping flood types of attacks is to disable ICMP at the firewall or router level so the host will not acknowledge any ping attempts from outside the network.

NOTE Turning off ICMP can deprive you of important feedback from network troubleshooting tools because commands such as ping and traceroute use ICMP to function and can provide important network diagnostics information.

TCP/IP Hijacking

An unauthorized user can effectively *hijack* a network connection of another user. For example, by monitoring a network transmission, an attacker can analyze the source and destination IP addresses of the two computers. When the attacker discovers the IP address of one of the participants, she can interrupt the connection using a DoS or other type of attack and then resume communications by spoofing the IP address of the disconnected user. The other user is tricked into thinking he is still communicating with the original sender. The only real way to prevent this sort of attack from occurring is by installing some sort of encryption mechanism, such as IPSec.

Cross-Reference

IPSec is covered in depth in Domain 3, Objective 3.1.

On-Path

An *on-path* attack occurs when a person uses a packet sniffer between the sender and the receiver of a communication on the network and listens in on or intercepts the information being transferred, modifying its contents before resending the data to its destination. These types of attacks usually occur when a network communications line is compromised through the installation of a network packet sniffer, which can analyze network communications packet by packet. Many types of communications use clear text, which can be easily read by someone using a packet sniffer. During an encrypted communication, a hacker can intercept the authentication phase of a transmission and obtain the public encryption keys of the participants, as shown in Figure 1.4-3.

To prevent on-path attacks, a unique server host key can be used to prove its identity to a client as a known host. This has been implemented in newer versions of the Secure Shell (SSH) protocol, which was vulnerable to on-path attacks in the past.

A related type of on-path attack, known as *man-in-the-browser*, uses a Trojan horse to exploit vulnerabilities within a web browser to intercept calls to the browser and manipulate them. This type of attack is most commonly waged in an attempt to conduct financial fraud online.

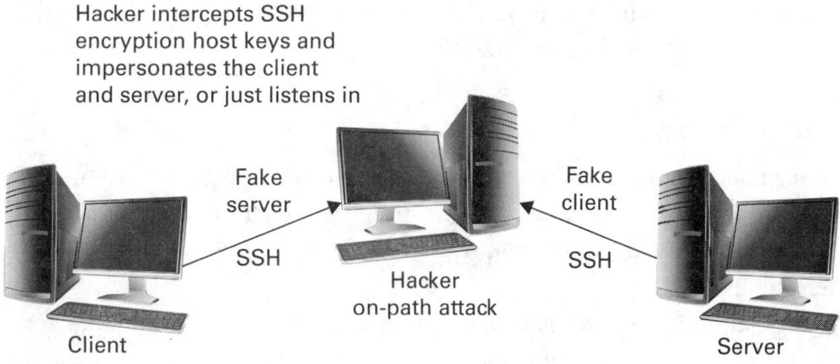

FIGURE 1.4-3 An on-path attack

EXAM TIP An on-path attack has been referred to previously as *man-in-the-middle* or *man-in-the-browser*. Be aware of this update.

Xmas Attack

An Xmas network port scan sends a network request to a system with many nonstandard TCP flag bits enabled to look for active and listening TCP ports. An Xmas scan is one of the "noisiest" scans performed simply because it uses so many nonstandard flags in combination set to "on." It can also identify operating systems based on their response to these nonstandard options. It is referred to as a *Christmas (Xmas) attack* because all the enabled flags in the TCP segment are like the lights of a Christmas tree to the scanned device, which responds to these requests (or does not reply, which can also indicate certain characteristics of the device).

DNS Poisoning

The *DNS poisoning* technique takes advantage of a DNS server's tables of IP addresses and hostnames by replacing the IP address of a host with another IP address that resolves to an attacker's system. For example, a malicious user can masquerade her own web server by poisoning the DNS server into thinking that the hostname of the legitimate web server resolves to the IP address of the rogue web server. The attacker can then spread spyware, worms, and other types of malware to clients connecting to her web server. This type of attack has a great potential for damage, as several thousand clients could be using the DNS server or its cache of IP addresses and hostnames, and all of them would be redirected to the poisoned address in the DNS cache tables.

The malicious attacker performs this attack by exploiting vulnerabilities in a DNS server that does not perform authentication or any type of checks to ensure the DNS information is coming from an authentic source. This information can be passed from one DNS server to another, almost like a worm, and the rogue address can be quickly spread.

DNS poisoning attacks can be mitigated by ensuring that your DNS server updates its information only from authoritative sources by proper authentication or the use of secure communications. Most DNS software has been updated to prevent these types of attacks, and typically, only out-of-date DNS software is vulnerable to DNS poisoning.

Domain Kiting

Domain kiting refers to the practice of registering a domain name, then deleting the registration as the five-day grace period ends, and then re-registering it to start another five-day grace period. This results in the domain being registered to the user without him having to pay for the registered domain.

The central authority for domain registrations, the Internet Corporation for Assigned Names and Numbers (ICANN), allows a five-day grace period before the registrar must pay for a new domain registration. This helps prevent mistaken domain registrations, typos, copyright infringements, and other issues related to domain name registration.

Some unscrupulous domain *registrars*, the organizations that register domains on behalf of users, take advantage of the five-day grace period by deleting the registration before the end of the grace period. The domain is then immediately re-registered, and this is repeated, allowing the registrar to register a domain name indefinitely without having to pay for it.

Malicious users or registrars have also been known to do this with recently released domains that have not been renewed (either purposely or accidentally) and effectively own the domain with no chance for the previous owner or a potential new owner interested in the domain name to officially register it.

A similar practice, called *domain tasting*, utilizes this five-day grace period to test certain domains to track the amount of traffic they receive. These domains' names often use common misspellings of popular website domain names. The domains that receive the most traffic are re-registered every five days to take advantage of the grace period and continue to generate advertising revenue for a domain that has never been paid for. These practices are often performed using fraudulent usernames and addresses of domain registrars, and a single registrar can perform this with hundreds of thousands of domain names.

Domain tasting and kiting are related to *domain hijacking*, which is very simply the theft of a domain, often through the fraudulent transfer of the domain to an unauthorized party. Often, the hijacker gains access to the control panel at the domain registrar or hosting provider and directs the domain name to a specific web server. Once control of this is gained, the domain name is then pointed to a different web server.

Network administrators with several domains under their control must keep careful track of their domains and their expiry dates to ensure that they are properly registered and renewed each time they are close to expiry to prevent the domains from being stolen by another individual or registrar. Many legitimate registrars offer several security features to prevent domain names from being transferred or renewed by a third party.

Domain Reputation

A company's reputation, while hard to put a price tag on, can be considered almost priceless when trying to recruit new customers. Similarly, domains have reputations as well; luckily for us, risk-scoring algorithms have been developed to assess *domain reputation*, often embedded within anti-malware solutions, not for brand purposes, but for the likelihood that a domain is serving malware or spam or is involved with botnet operations. These algorithms can then be used to proactively block access to risky domains.

Typosquatting

Typosquatters register domain names that are very similar to the names of legitimate domains, hoping for an unsuspecting Internet user to make a typographical error, or "typo," that directs the user to the squatter's site. Once the user is there, the squatter attempts to redirect the traffic to a competitor, install malware, or capture passwords that the user enters into the fake site.

Typosquatters also often attempt to sell their domains to the owners of the closely named legitimate websites at a substantially marked-up price or attempt to earn revenue through advertisements displayed on the illegitimate sites.

Cross-Reference

"Typo squatting" is listed under Objective 1.1 within the CompTIA exam objectives, but we feel it's more appropriate to cover the topic here.

Client-side Attacks

Often, we think of attacks as those an attacker wages against a remote server and any vulnerabilities resident on that system. However, *client-side attacks* exploit vulnerabilities in client applications, such as web browsers, using a malicious server or malicious data. A malicious website, for example, can exploit vulnerabilities within the client's web browser and facilitate the remote server's attempt to gain access to the client machine. Cross-site scripting (XSS), previously covered in Objective 1.3, is an example of an attack that uses client-side scripts to target web applications on the victim's machine. If successful, the attacker can gain elevated privileges and access to the system.

Web browsers are not the only vector of attack, however; think of all the client–server pairings that take place (for example, e-mail, FTP, instant messaging applications) and all the code operating behind the scenes to support those operations, and you will begin to realize how many opportunities there are for a determined adversary to take advantage of client vulnerabilities.

Watering Hole Attack

Watering hole attacks are designed to infiltrate a system or network through the exploitation of a secondary system or network. Think of a lion or other predator lying in wait at a watering hole, waiting for a gazelle or other prey, and you'll get the basic idea of this attack. Often, the attacker inserts malware into a website that he believes the target will visit (if the target is an organization, then one of the employees) and waits for the target to be exploited via the secondary site. The "watering hole" website is often chosen based on the organization's mission. For example, if an attacker wants to target an Internet business that ships t-shirts to customers, he might determine which shipping company the business uses and insert malware into its site, expecting the Internet business to be exploited, in turn, after an employee visits the site.

Cross-Reference

"Watering hole attack" is listed under Objective 1.1 within the CompTIA exam objectives, but we feel it's more appropriate to cover the topic here.

REVIEW

Objective 1.4: Given a scenario, analyze potential indicators associated with network attacks Understanding network attacks involves studying attacks on both wired and wireless networks and distinguishing among the types of attacks that seek to deny service, gain unauthorized access, or steal data. Many of the types of attacks that can assault a network and computer system are geared toward specific system accounts, system services, or applications. Because the network is the infrastructure that allows all systems and devices to communicate, disrupting those communication lines may be the most damaging attack a network can suffer.

Data emanation leaves a network vulnerable to unauthorized access to authentication credentials and unencrypted sensitive data. Jamming is a form of intentional interference on wireless networks, designed as a DoS attack. Hackers use war driving and war chalking techniques to drive around looking for open, unencrypted Wi-Fi networks. A rogue "evil twin" access point masquerades as a legitimate wireless access point to trick users into communicating sensitive information over a network completely under the control of a hacker. Hackers can use packet sniffers to eavesdrop on unencrypted wireless networks to discover authentication credentials and sensitive data being passed in clear text. WPS attacks can utilize tools to compromise the access point passphrase through a number of issues with WPS. IV attacks focus on the weak, 24-bit initialization vector that is used to help strengthen WEP keys, and which can then be used to break the WEP key. TKIP attacks focus on decrypting small portions of data that can be used to create more damaging attacks.

Understand how to prevent the different types of network attacks, such as denial-of-service attacks, ping and SYN floods, DNS amplification, backdoors, spoofing, smurf attacks, hijacking, on-path/man-in-the-browser attacks, replay attacks, Xmas attacks, DNS and ARP poisoning, domain kiting and hijacking, typosquatting, client-side attacks, watering hole attacks, and attacks by malicious insiders.

1.4 QUESTIONS

1. Your web server is being flooded by a denial-of-service attack. Using a network analyzer, you see that IP broadcast replies are being sent back to the address of your server from multiple addresses. Which type of network attack is this?
   A. On-path
   B. Back door
   C. Smurf
   D. DNS poisoning

2. During a denial-of-service attack, a network administrator blocks the source IP address with the firewall, but the attack continues. What is the most likely cause of the problem?
   - **A.** The denial-of-service worm has already infected the firewall locally.
   - **B.** The attack is coming from multiple distributed hosts.
   - **C.** A firewall can't block denial-of-service attacks.
   - **D.** Antivirus software needs to be installed.
3. A few systems have been infected with malware; log analysis indicates the users all visited the same legitimate website to order office supplies. What is the most likely attack the users have fallen victim to?
   - **A.** Replay
   - **B.** Watering hole
   - **C.** ARP poisoning
   - **D.** Domain kiting
4. Which of the following types of wireless attacks utilizes a weakness in WEP key generation and encryption to decrypt WEP encrypted data?
   - **A.** IV attack
   - **B.** War driving
   - **C.** PSK attack
   - **D.** Eavesdropping

1.4 ANSWERS

1. **C** A smurf attack uses a spoof attack combined with a DDoS attack to exploit the use of IP broadcast addressing and ICMP. By spoofing the address of the web server in an IP broadcast, the attacker causes all the replies from other systems on the network to the broadcast to be sent back to the web server, causing a denial of service.
2. **B** A distributed denial-of-service (DDoS) attack comes from multiple geographically distributed hosts, making it difficult for the network administrator to block it.
3. **B** The users most likely fell victim to a watering hole attack. The third-party supplier could be hosting malware with your organization as the target.
4. **A** The IV (initialization vector) attack uses the weakness in the 24-bit generated IV that is paired with the WEP encryption key. The IV can be discovered over time on busy networks that use repeated IV values, which can then be used by the hacker to decrypt the cipher stream without knowing the WEP key.

Explain different threat actors, vectors, and intelligence sources

It's easy to assume that all threats to the confidentiality, availability, and integrity of your systems and data come from malicious hackers, but that group represents only one piece of the threat puzzle. Understanding how to best defend against a variety of threats means taking a more holistic view and considering a range of threat actors and their respective attributes. This objective discusses threat actors, how they behave, and how you can learn more about them and stay informed about their latest tricks.

Understanding and Analyzing Threats

A *threat* is a negative event that creates the possibility of a vulnerability being compromised. A variety of threats can pose security risks, including the following:

- **Natural disasters** A natural disaster is a fire, flood, or other phenomenon that could cause physical damage to company assets—usually the facilities and the equipment within them.
- **Equipment malfunction** Electronic equipment is vulnerable to normal wear and tear that can result in failed components—from a failed power supply fan to a failed hard drive.
- **Employees** Assets face both malicious and unintentional threats from employees. The source of the threat could be human error, such as someone deleting a directory of files by mistake, or theft, vandalism, sabotage by a disgruntled employee, or corporate espionage.
- **Intruders** An unauthorized person can compromise the access controls of a facility to gain access and perform theft, vandalism, or sabotage.
- **Malicious hackers** Malicious hackers present a nonphysical threat that involves their ability to compromise a network.

Actors, Attributes, and Vectors

Threat actors are often seen as the "Jason Bourne" of cyberspace—individuals representing nation-states (or not) who are the stealthiest, most capable, and most damaging. Although that might certainly prove to be the case, a threat actor could also be a kid down the street or any person using "cyber" as a means to an end—generally a negative end. You should be familiar with the various different types of threat actors in order to fully protect against such threats. (Note that it is beyond the scope of this book to provide comprehensive coverage of the most sophisticated adversary tactics, techniques, and procedures [TTPs].)

Threat actors are generally assessed and categorized according to the following attributes:

- **Level of sophistication/capability** On a spectrum from the most unskilled individual to a highly technical team able to exploit niche systems and applications, often through zero-day attacks.
- **Resources/funding** On a spectrum of no funding to a full nation-state–level budget similar to other weapons program development.
- **Intent/motivation** Varies widely across poor behaviors, curiosity, fame, organizational disgruntlement, political causes, to national-level intelligence gathering, just to name a few.
- **Internal/external** Very simply, actors can be internal, such as a disgruntled employee, or external, such as a competing company.

The following are the six major threat actor types:

- **Script kiddies** Script kiddies are the lowest-common-denominator threat actor; these are delinquent teenagers sitting in their parents' basement, as the ugly stereotype goes. However, don't underestimate a so-called script kiddie! These adversaries (of all ages) excel in creating chaos based on sheer intent and numbers. Further, they can be used by more sophisticated organizations to provide larger numbers to operations. Often their tools are "point and click" or simple scripts and have little sophistication.
- **Hacktivists** Hacktivists utilize cyber means to effect an end (typically of a social or political nature). Consider, for example, Anonymous, which may be the most famous hacktivist group around. Whether you agree with its motives and approaches, Anonymous has been effective at utilizing cyberspace to draw attention to various causes, such as its campaigns against the Church of Scientology, the Westboro Baptist Church, and others. Hacktivists can utilize script kiddies or other, more sophisticated personnel, but they have a more nuanced reason behind their attacks. It is not improbable that some nation-state actors use hacktivist groups to spread their messaging, so don't discount hacktivists.
- **Criminal syndicates** Otherwise known as organized crime, criminal syndicates are exactly what they sound like: the extension of classic crime techniques into cyberspace to extort, harass, or otherwise pursue illegal ends. As with hacktivists, do not discount organized crime, and don't assume that nation-state actors don't utilize organized crime's personnel and infrastructure. Money tends to be their predominant end priority.
- **Advanced persistent threats (APTs)** As defined in the NIST SP 800-39, an APT is "An adversary that possesses sophisticated levels of expertise and significant resources which allow it to create opportunities to achieve its objectives by using multiple attack vectors (e.g., cyber, physical, and deception). These objectives typically include establishing and extending footholds within the information technology infrastructure of the targeted organizations for purposes of exfiltrating information, undermining or impeding critical aspects of a mission, program, or organization; or positioning itself to

carry out these objectives in the future. The advanced persistent threat: (i) pursues its objectives repeatedly over an extended period of time; (ii) adapts to defenders' efforts to resist it; and (iii) is determined to maintain the level of interaction needed to execute its objectives.

- **State actors** State actors are generally the top-tier cyber threat actors, and they bring a level of sophistication that, when executed well, allows them to be an APT, as discussed previously. Nation-state actors are highly skilled (some much more than others), well-funded, and motivated to use cyber tools, techniques, and procedures to gain a certain end state—whether it be the exfiltration of another country's sensitive data, the disruption of an adversary's electrical grid, intellectual property theft, election interference, or even a denial-of-service (DoS) attack targeting a multinational banking system. Stuxnet, the malicious computer worm that in 2010 targeted and caused significant damage to Iran's nuclear program, is a good example of what can occur when nations that have invested heavily in cyber capabilities flex their muscles.
- **Insider threats** Insiders may be the most dangerous type of threat actor of them all due to being employees, contractors, or other privileged parties having the access inherent to their position. Think, for example, about an administrator who becomes disgruntled and decides to turn over sensitive or classified information to a competitor or even another nation-state. The access and trust given to that insider mean that he or she has a much easier time gaining access to the information—and given that many security controls focus on monitoring and stopping external threats, it is harder to spot a malicious insider. However, you not only have to be vigilant against malicious insiders but also mindful of the friendly insider who does not follow policy or user best practices. A user who can't seem to stop clicking links in suspicious e-mails is a phisher's dream.
- **Competitors** Although competitors are generally not linked to nation-states, for a nongovernment entity, they are of tremendous concern. Organizations need to protect their intellectual property (IP), and their competitive advantage is at risk if their competitors gain access to it. Be aware that competitors could use hacking and social engineering techniques to reduce your company's competitive advantage. Competitors, especially those that are well funded, can be as capable as state actors.

KEY TERMS The terms **capability** and **sophistication** are often used interchangeably to discuss a threat actor's level of skill.

- **Hackers** Hackers often are depicted as wearing different colors of "hats" depending on their intent and motivations: a *black hat hacker* (also known as an *unauthorized hacker*), for example, is an evil hacker who uses her knowledge and skills to compromise systems. A *gray hat hacker* (also known as a *semi-authorized hacker*) is known to use her skills for both good and evil at times, and a *white hat hacker* (also known as an *authorized hacker*) is usually a penetration testing professional or ethical hacker.

EXAM TIP The terms for the various types of hackers may have changed on the most recent version of the exam. Be on the lookout for either version.

A *threat vector* describes the actual means by which a threat is realized. For example, a malicious hacker could use malware disguised as a legitimate e-mail attachment to implant a backdoor tool onto a system. In this case, the e-mail attachment is the threat vector that the attacker used to enter the system. There are a variety of threat vectors, listed here, that you'll notice probably look awfully familiar after reviewing different attacks earlier in this domain, as well as content we'll cover across different objectives to come.

Vector	Example Attack
Direct (physical) access	Dumpster diving
Wireless	Wardriving
E-mail	Phishing
Supply chain	Compromised supplier or contractor
Social media	Eliciting information
Removable media	Malicious USB drive
Cloud	Denial-of-service against cloud provider

Threat Intelligence Sources

As cyberattacks have become more prevalent, various entities have developed dedicated centers, databases, and technical specifications to catalog information about attacks (and attackers) to help understand past events and promote more predictive analysis. These *threat intelligence sources*, described in the following list, include both public sources and private sources. Combined, they provide powerful but sometimes overwhelming amounts of data. In order to avoid information overload, the future is more automated, with the end user getting a more rich, contextual perspective after the data has already been crunched through a software analytics platform.

- **Open source intelligence (OSINT)** An amazing amount of information can be gained through the use of OSINT. In fact, your organization should have someone regularly combing with search engines to look for any sensitive information about the organization that is hanging out, easily accessible on the Internet. Also be mindful that information can be aggregated from press releases, newspapers, radio, and television. This information can be used to facilitate social engineering attempts, gain insight into policy decisions before they are announced, and even reproduce emerging product designs. OSINT is a low-cost, high-reward approach.
- **Closed/proprietary** Closed or proprietary databases are managed by companies who curate and sell the information or analysis as a service to subscribers. Good examples of companies providing these services are Recorded Future and TRITON.

- **Vulnerability databases** As new vulnerabilities are discovered, they are cataloged into publicly available databases, such as the National Vulnerability Database (NVD) operated by the NIST. Each vulnerability is assigned a unique identifier and its defining characteristics are described. The NVD has standardized vulnerability identification across scanning and reporting platforms. We will discuss these databases further within Objective 1.7, later in this domain.
- **Public/private information sharing centers** As an example, Information Sharing and Analysis Centers or Organizations (ISACs/ISAOs) were created to share threat intelligence and best practices across geographical or industry segments for the common good. These organizations act as a clearinghouse for information, often ensuring that indicators of compromise are shared anonymously within their group and cannot be exploited for gain (i.e., in the case of a competitor taking advantage of another's compromise).
- **Dark web** The dark web, sometimes referred to as darknet, is often thought of as a shady place where illicit materials (e.g., drugs, stolen credit cards, child pornography) are traded. While there are certainly pockets of this activity, the dark web is also a safer haven for activists, whistleblowers, and free speech advocates who value its more private nature. That being said, the dark web can also be a great place to gather information such as hacker "how-to" guides, corporate data being sold, and even upcoming events or attacks being planned.
- **Automated indicator sharing (AIS)** While humans certainly need to be "in the loop" to provide context for and analysis of information being disseminated, they are known to slow processes down. With artificial intelligence and other "machine speed" technologies taking a larger role in cyber defense, automated indicator sharing was created to speed the process of sharing indicators of compromise to support more real-time defense. There are three major technical specifications: Trusted Automated eXchange of Intelligence Information (TAXII); Structured Threat Information eXpression (STIX); and Cyber Observable eXpression (CybOX). As defined in the NIST SP 800-150, "Indicators are technical artifacts or observables that suggest an attack is imminent or is currently underway or that a compromise may have already occurred. Indicators can be used to detect and defend against potential threats. Examples of indicators include the Internet Protocol (IP) address of a suspected command and control server, a suspicious Domain Name System (DNS) domain name, a uniform resource locator (URL) that references malicious content, a file hash for a malicious executable, or the subject line text of a malicious email message."
- **Threat maps** Threat maps are "live" graphical displays of a subset of cyberattacks that are occurring; generally, they are provided by security vendors (e.g., Kaspersky, Fortinet, and FireEye) and are meant to depict the tremendous number of malicious activities that they are continuously protecting their subscribers from. While threat maps are by no means accurate and representative of the entirety of ongoing attacks, they do serve as good marketing "eye candy" for vendors.

- **File/code repositories** Code repositories, such as GitHub, are a lifesaver for a developer who is looking to quickly churn out a product under a tight deadline, facilitating project development across geographically dispersed teams using public/private repositories. Developers write their code in their private repository and then commit it to the public repository when complete. The ability to download and study the open-source code is helpful to an intelligence analyst looking to find vulnerabilities specific to the code, as well as potential information about the developers and their respective organizations that might have been accidentally included within the published code.
- **Predictive analysis** The use of all of these data sources, and any more that can provide content and context (often alongside artificial intelligence/machine learning platforms), to deal with events more swiftly and even proactively predict events before they can occur. This is the "gold standard" of threat intelligence that organizations should strive for.

Research Sources

Security is always changing in context and content, and the security expert who doesn't constantly research won't be an expert for long. The good news is that there are quality research sources available for even the smallest of budgets. The following are some examples of research sources—some proprietary, some open—that can be used to stay on top of current activities.

Research Source	Example
Vendor websites	Microsoft Security Intelligence blog https://www.microsoft.com/security/blog/microsoft-security-intelligence/
Vulnerability feeds	U.S. National Vulnerability Database
Conferences	DefCon BlackHat BSides
Academic journals	Oxford Academic *Journal of Cybersecurity*
Request for comments (RFC)	Internet Engineering Task Force (IETF)
Local industry groups	InfraGard Information Sharing and Analysis Organization (ISAO)
Social media	Top 25 #infosec leaders to follow on Twitter (source: techbeacon.com)
Threat feeds	Secureworks AT&T Cybersecurity (formerly AlienVault) FireEye
Adversary tactics, techniques, and procedures (TTP)	SANS Internet Storm Center

One exciting new use of threat intelligence is *threat hunting*, where threat hunters combine threat intelligence with other data points about adversaries' TTPs and maneuvering capabilities to proactively hunt for the threat actors, rather than reactively waiting for an indicator of compromise. When a threat hunter finds signs pointing to a threat actor being present, the traditional incident response process begins. Threat hunting is an advanced skill for sophisticated organizations, but when done well, it can carve months or even years off a persistent threat actor's time within a system or network. Threat hunting, among many other operations, can be automated through use of a *security orchestration, automation, and response (SOAR)* platform. A SOAR platform executes many of the activities that a human would alternatively undertake, such as responding to attacks and assigning a criticality level to them.

Cross-Reference

More discussion on incident response is included within Domain 4, Objective 4.2.

REVIEW

Objective 1.5: Explain different threat actors, vectors, and intelligence sources Many types of threat actors exist and they have different attributes along a spectrum of level of sophistication/capability, resources/funding, intent/motivation, and whether they are internal or external. Doing research across a variety of threat intelligence sources can help provide content and context on threat actors and their associated activities, allowing for better, more customized protection.

1.5 QUESTIONS

1. Threat actors are generally categorized by which of the following? (Choose all that apply.)
   - **A.** Intent
   - **B.** Resources
   - **C.** Internal/external
   - **D.** Nationality
2. A company insider decides to steal data and sell it to a competitor that is offering a large amount of cash. Which of the following terms describes the insider?
   - **A.** Threat
   - **B.** Threat actor
   - **C.** Vulnerability
   - **D.** Risk actor

3. Threat hunting can be partially automated through the use of which tool?
   - A. Security information and event manager (SIEM)
   - B. Anti-malware scanner
   - C. Vulnerability scanner
   - D. Security orchestration, automation, and response (SOAR)

1.5 ANSWERS

1. **A B C** Threat actors are generally categorized using the following attributes: level of sophistication, resources/funding, intent/motivation, and whether they are internal or external in nature.
2. **B** In this scenario, the employee is a threat actor, because she is initiating a threat against an asset.
3. **D** A security orchestration, automation, and response (SOAR) platform executes many of the activities that a human would alternatively undertake, such as threat hunting, responding to attacks, and assigning a criticality level to them.

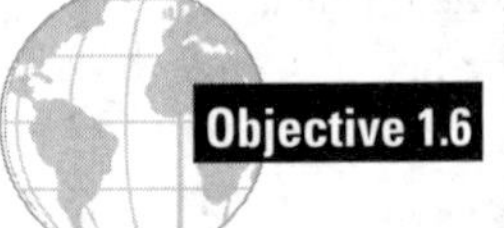

Objective 1.6 Explain the security concerns associated with various types of vulnerabilities

The networks and systems in your organization are always under constant threat of attack from hackers, physical intruders, and malware. No matter how secure your network is, there will always be risks from known and unknown vulnerabilities that can be exploited. This objective defines and describes common vulnerabilities and their associated security concerns.

Vulnerabilities

A *vulnerability* is a security weakness, such as the lack of a security control, that could be exploited or exposed by a threat. For example, an operating system (OS) that hasn't been updated with security patches might be vulnerable to network attacks. A file server that doesn't have antivirus software installed could be vulnerable to viruses. Web servers and database servers might have vulnerabilities that allow cross-site scripting and SQL injection attacks.

Physical vulnerabilities affect the physical protection of the asset. Physical assets, such as network servers, should be stored in special rooms with safeguards to protect them from natural disasters and security controls to prevent their physical theft. Nonphysical vulnerabilities usually involve software or data. Software security vulnerabilities can exist because of improper software configuration, unpatched or buggy software, lack of antivirus protection, weak access and authentication controls, unused network ports left open, and misconfigured or nonexistent network security devices.

Note that there is no situation impervious to vulnerabilities; cloud-based infrastructures have their own set of vulnerabilities that differ from on-premises infrastructures but cannot be discounted. The more control over cloud assets you give to the organization, the more vulnerabilities that are traditionally seen in on-premises infrastructures appear; in fact, without proper configuration and rigorous oversight, organizations incur most of the same vulnerabilities they would have if they maintained their on-premises infrastructure. Additionally, other vulnerabilities can affect bare-metal hypervisors that could compromise the cloud provider's customers. For the most part, however, vulnerabilities that result in attacks on cloud infrastructures are more often the result of customer configuration and patching issues.

Cross-Reference

More information on cloud models is contained in Domain 2, Objective 2.2.

Vulnerability Types

As you assess the security of your organization, you need to examine your network and systems for existing and potential vulnerabilities. The following sections discuss different types of common and emerging vulnerabilities.

Zero-day Vulnerabilities

A *zero-day vulnerability* is a software security flaw for which there is no publicly available patch or fix because the software vendor either is unaware of its existence or has just learned that it exists. The vulnerability may be in an operating system, application, or other software and typically is discovered by a threat actor or (ideally) a computer security researcher. If the vulnerability is discovered by a threat actor, the software vendor has zero days to make available a patch or fix before the threat actor potentially launches a *zero-day attack*. In the best cases, zero-day vulnerabilities are patched within days or weeks, but sometimes it takes much longer. The vendor may not even know that there is a vulnerability within their software, so they often do not have a patch or fix for it available. In the best cases, zero-day vulnerabilities are patched in days or weeks, but sometimes it takes much longer; that's plenty of time for a threat actor to take advantage of any associated vulnerabilities.

Cross-Reference

More information on zero-day attacks is contained in Objective 1.3, earlier in this domain.

Weak Configurations

After you've installed an OS, you can increase your system security by configuring the many administrative- and security-related options. However, other options might make your system more vulnerable to attack—that's why installing or enabling only the necessary options for a system is critical. By enabling unnecessary options (or failing to disable unnecessary default options), you create potential vulnerabilities for unauthorized users to exploit.

Some examples of common misconfigurations include *open permissions* (those that have not been set to restrict or deny access) or access controls, use of *unsecure protocols*, *unsecure root or administrator accounts*, weak or missing encryption, and indiscriminate acceptance of default settings. In the latter case, you should investigate the system for ports and services enabled by default that are not required, which is especially important when you are enabling services to be run on your system. Examples of services that might not be needed but that could be running are file- and print-sharing services and Internet services such as the Hypertext Transfer Protocol (HTTP), the File Transfer Protocol (FTP), the Simple Mail Transfer Protocol (SMTP), the Domain Name System (DNS), and the Dynamic Host Configuration Protocol (DHCP).

If the system you are configuring does not need to share files, disable the server service so that no one on the network can connect to a network share on that system. Enabled Internet services can cause a variety of security vulnerabilities by opening network ports on your system to which unauthorized users can connect. For example, enabling web server services on your system enables hackers to connect to your system by issuing HTTP requests to the server, where they can attempt a variety of attacks to gain access or to disrupt communications. Remember that it's always better to configure a system to have the least amount of ports and services enabled, or *least functionality*, to minimize the attack surface available to a malicious actor. Also, although backward compatibility with older OSs and software sounds like a safe bet, it exposes you to *downgrade attacks*, which force a system to revert to an older or less-secure mode of operation. Removing backward compatibility helps prevent these attacks.

EXAM TIP Services that are not required by the system should be disabled or removed, while existing services should be configured to provide maximum security.

Third-Party Risks

Every organization has third-party risks, not just organizations that rely on cloud or managed service providers. Any externally developed hardware or software introduces some level of risk that must be managed through proper integration and maintenance. When combined with other poor practices, improper integration or maintenance increases the *attack surface* within your organization. For example, your web application may listen for requests on HTTP port 80, use basic clear-text authentication credentials, and store data in an unencrypted third-party database on the same server. That expands the organization's attack surface to include three unnecessary vulnerabilities that attackers may attempt to exploit.

Reducing third-party risks requires *vendor management*, which includes regularly cataloging the vendors that your organization relies on, their *system integration*, or an understanding of what systems they are integrated with and its supporting data assets, and understanding their support agreements and their products' associated end-of-life schedules. Software that a vendor no longer supports typically is unpatched.

Any software that your organization acquires through *outsourced code development* should be reviewed internally for vulnerabilities before it is deployed on a production system. Also, any data that your organization stores at a third-party site should be regularly audited based on the data sensitivity and any service level agreements (SLAs).

Cross-Reference

Objective 1.2 earlier in this domain describes the third-party risk of supply chain attacks.

Improper or Weak Patch Management

In organizations with hundreds or thousands of workstations, it can be a logistical nightmare to keep all the operating systems and application software up to date. In most cases, operating system updates on workstations can be automatically applied via the network. However, administrators must have a clear security policy and baseline plan to ensure that all workstations are running a certain minimum level of software versions.

All software and firmware on the workstation should be kept current with the most recent patches and upgrades to remove security vulnerabilities from previous versions. The administrator should ensure that users have only the access privileges they need to perform their job functions; this is the principle of *least privilege*. For example, any system functions that enable changes to be made to the network address of a computer—or any other type of system change—should be off limits to a regular user and accessible only to the administrator. Regular users should not be able to access any application or configuration programs other than those required for their jobs. The most efficient way of preventing certain system functions from user abuse is to enact network-wide security policies that are automatically set for each workstation on the network. This can save considerable time because an administrator does not have to visit each workstation and block out items one by one.

Before you install any update or patch onto networked systems, install and test it on a test host in a lab environment. In some cases, software updates have been known to fix one problem but cause another. If no lab system is available, you can back up and then patch a server after business hours, constantly monitoring that server and having a back-out plan in place to remove the update if something should go wrong.

Legacy Platforms

In a perfect world, we would all have brand-new, freshly updated hardware and software across our architecture, all humming away with the best new algorithms and innovations. Unfortunately, the reality is that many, if not most, organizations rely on some mixture of new technologies and older, legacy systems that are integral to a critical process, such as timekeeping or payroll. Also, there is often an "if it ain't broke, don't fix it" mentality that leads to unsupported legacy platforms being used years after their prime. In these situations, the platforms introduce numerous vulnerabilities, including a lack of patch support, weak or no encryption, and obscure programming languages that are difficult to maintain. Every so often, you'll see a job posting on a recruiting website on behalf of a software vendor who built their system on COBOL or Fortran scrambling to find a programmer willing to come to their aid. It's more common than you'd think!

Shadow IT

Security professionals have a lot to do on a daily basis: keeping an accurate inventory, patching systems, writing policies, reading reports, and so on. However, they may have an additional, more dangerous issue lurking outside the confines of their traditional architecture. *Shadow IT* refers to networks and systems that are managed outside of the IT organization, often without the IT organization's permission or even awareness. Shadow IT often does not meet security requirements, which is often why it is stood up "in the shadows" to begin with and can pose a serious vulnerability to the larger architecture, especially if it's connected to the managed environment. It is important to conduct regular, thorough scans of the environment to root out any potential shadow IT assets that may have popped up.

Cross-Reference

"Shadow IT" is listed under Objective 1.5 within the CompTIA exam objectives.

Impacts

Understanding organizational risk means determining the possible impacts of a security (or even natural) failure and quantifying both direct and indirect losses. *Impact* can be defined as the level of harm that occurs when a threat exploits a vulnerability. These types of impacts include:

- Loss of organizationally sensitive or proprietary data through a breach or exfiltration
- Loss of employee or customer data leading to identity theft
- Damage to reputation and financial stability that would occur if a threat actor were to launch a successful DoS attack on the company's web servers, causing a loss of availability
- Loss of service—even for a few hours—can severely damage a company; consider, for example, the case of a company that offers stock-trading services.
- Loss of prolonged downtime must be factored into the equation; hundreds of thousands of dollars of revenue can be lost while the site is unavailable to customers, on top of the reputation hit.

Cross-Reference

Understanding and assessing risk is covered in more depth within Domain 5, Objective 5.4.

REVIEW

Objective 1.6: Explain the security concerns associated with various types of vulnerabilities Threat actors exploit vulnerabilities, so it's important to understand the different types of vulnerabilities and how they introduce security concerns. Third parties, including application developers and cloud or managed service providers, provide value but cannot operate without proper oversight and governance. Internally, weak configurations, poor patch management, and legacy platforms require mitigation strategies, as well as identifying shadow IT systems and networks.

1.6 QUESTIONS

1. A(n) __________ is a security weakness that could be exploited by a threat.
   A. vulnerability
   B. attack vector
   C. risk
   D. likelihood
2. Which of the following terms describes the level of harm that results from a threat exploiting a vulnerability?
   A. Attack
   B. Likelihood
   C. Impact
   D. Risk
3. Kevin, a college professor researching viruses, sets up a server within his campus lab without notifying the college's IT department. He doesn't want to lock the system down with security controls that could possibly slow his analysis. What is the *best* term to describe Kevin's new computer?
   A. Attack surface
   B. Shadow IT
   C. Noncompliance
   D. Impact

1.6 ANSWERS

1. **A** A vulnerability is a security weakness that could be exploited by a threat.
2. **C** Impact can be defined as the level of harm that results from a threat exploiting a vulnerability.
3. **B** Kevin has created shadow IT, meaning that he has set up IT systems that are not under the purview of the IT department and are not compliant with security requirements.

Summarize the techniques used in security assessments

A variety of tools are available to the network administrator and security professional to test networks and systems for vulnerabilities and weaknesses; unfortunately, these tools are also available to unethical hackers who use them to exploit specific vulnerabilities. By proactively monitoring your network for vulnerabilities and taking immediate steps to rectify them, you ensure that hackers using the same tools will not find vulnerabilities to exploit. You must routinely scan your network for vulnerabilities, whether they be unpatched operating systems and application software (such as web servers and database servers) or unused open ports and services that are actively listening for requests.

This objective describes how to conduct security assessments, including an overview of security testing tools, such as port scanners, network mappers, and protocol analyzers, which can aid in identifying vulnerabilities in your network.

Cross-Reference

We will cover many of the specific tools that are used within security assessments within Domain 4, Objective 4.1.

Implement Assessment Techniques to Discover Security Threats and Vulnerabilities

As part of your overall security assessment procedures, you must perform an assessment for each critical asset in your organization to ascertain the threats, vulnerabilities, and potential impact if the asset were lost or exploited. You should assess all possibilities, both physical and nonphysical. For example, confidential personal data can be stolen from a file server by someone physically stealing the system or by a hacker accessing the data through network security vulnerabilities.

Vulnerability Assessment Tools and Techniques

As part of your vulnerability and threat assessment, you need to be able to examine your network and systems for existing vulnerabilities. *Vulnerability assessment* and network-scanning programs are important tools for a network administrator who routinely runs preventive security scans on the network. These programs provide detailed information about which hosts on a network are running which services. They can also help identify servers that are running unnecessary network services that create security risks, such as a file server running FTP or HTTP services that could provide unauthorized access to data.

Common tools and techniques such as network mappers, port scanners, vulnerability scanners, protocol analyzers, honeypots, and password crackers are used by network administrators to identify and prevent such attacks. Unfortunately, these same tools are major weapons in the malicious hacker's arsenal. Assessors can use them to determine what systems are running on your network, what services and open ports those services are running, what operating system and application software they are running, and what vulnerabilities can be exploited. Due to their simplicity, these tools are commonly used to probe and scan networks, even by amateur hackers who have no knowledge of networking protocols.

Banner Grabbing

Banner grabbing is an assessment technique that allows an assessor to learn more about a system by sending data, in many cases malformed, and then waiting for the system's response. If the system replies with a standard error message, that can be used to determine the operating system and potential applications running on the system, such as web server software. This information allows a potential assessor to better craft his attacks to the specific system. The assessor wouldn't need to attempt Unix-specific attacks if he knew the system was running Microsoft Windows, or attempt Apache attacks if he knew the system used Internet Information Services (IIS). Banner grabbing can be performed with several tools, such as Telnet.

Network Mappers

A *network mapper* program scans a network to determine which hosts are available, which operating systems are running, and other types of information about a network host. For example, some network scans use the ping utility to perform Internet Control Message Protocol (ICMP) sweeps of entire ranges of IP addresses, looking for hosts that respond or are "alive" on the network. Some scans also use TCP segments with different configuration "flags" set to elicit a specific response from the host. Still other scans use UDP datagrams. But you may hear reference to scans using the generic term "packet."

Whichever type of protocol is used, the response contains a lot of information about the host and its place on the network, such as whether it's behind a router or firewall on a subnetwork. Hackers who already know the address of a specific target can also use a network mapper to analyze the host for open ports, protocols, services, and OS specifics. This information offers a virtual map of the entire network for a malicious hacker, who can narrow his scope of attack to specific systems, or for the network administrator, who needs to find and correct weaknesses on a network.

One of the most popular tools used for network mapping is an open-source and publicly available utility called *Nmap*. It is used by hackers to scan and map networks and is used by administrators to audit their networks for security weaknesses. The Nmap command-line utility uses simple text commands with switch options to perform tasks. For example, to perform a ping sweep on a system with Nmap, you'd enter the following:

```
nmap -sP 192.168.1.128

Host 192.168.1.128 appears to be up.
MAC Address: 00:B1:63:3F:74:41 (Apple)
Nmap done: 1 IP address (1 host up) scanned in 0.600 seconds
```

To perform a scan to identify the OS of a system, you'd enter this:

```
nmap -O 192.168.1.128

MAC Address: 00:B1:63:3F:74:41 (Apple)
Device type: general purpose
Running: NetBSD 4.X
OS details: NetBSD 4.99.4 (x86)
Network Distance: 1 hop
```

ADDITIONAL RESOURCES The Nmap tool can be downloaded from https://nmap.org.

Port Scanners

After an assessor has determined which systems are on a network and identified IP addresses that respond with acknowledgments of a live system at those addresses, the next step is to discover what network services and open ports are running on the system. By using a *port scanner*, an assessor can determine which ports on the system are listening for requests (such as TCP port 80) and then can decide which service or vulnerability in the service can be exploited.

For example, if an assessor sees that Simple Mail Transfer Protocol (SMTP) port 25 is open and listening for requests, he knows that an e-mail server is operating and that he can launch more probes and tests to determine which mail server software is running and whether vulnerabilities can be exploited to relay spam through the server. The following example shows a listing of a port scan from the Nmap application:

```
nmap -sT 192.168.1.128

Interesting ports on 192.168.1.128: Not shown: 1709 closed ports
PORT STATE SERVICE 21/tcp open ftp 53/tcp open domain 554/tcp
open rtsp 10000/tcp open snet-sensor-mgmt
```

A standard set of ports, including 65,535 TCP ports and User Datagram Protocol (UDP) ports, are available for running network services on a computer system. The first 1023 ports are *well-known* ports, which means they make up the most common types of network ports, such as DNS (53), SMTP (25), HTTP (80), HTTPS (443), and FTP (21). Beyond these first

1023 ports are tens of thousands of port ranges that are used by third-party applications, services, and networking devices. Two common examples of these are *ephemeral ports*, otherwise known as dynamic ports, which are allocated dynamically in the range of 49152 to 65535 for clients within a client–server communication, and *registered ports*, those used within specific applications or protocols. These generally fall in the range of 1024–49151. Table 1.7-1 lists the most common well-known protocols and services and their corresponding TCP/IP ports.

EXAM TIP Many of these services also listen on UDP ports as well as TCP. For example, the Domain Name System (DNS) uses TCP port 53 for zone transfers and UDP port 53 for DNS queries.

A port scanner sends probing network packets (sometimes called a *port sweep*) to each of the 65,535 ports (both TCP and UDP) and listens for a response. If the system port does not respond, the assessor knows it is either disabled or protected (behind a network firewall or proxy server, for example). If the port does respond, it means this service is running on the target system, and the assessor can then use more focused tools to assault that port and service. For example, a SQL server may be listening on port TCP/UDP 1433. If a port scanner receives a response from this port, the assessor knows that this system is running a SQL server, and he can then direct his attacks against specific SQL vulnerabilities.

TABLE 1.7-1 TCP/IP Services and Port Numbers

Service	TCP/IP Port Number
HTTP	80
FTP (Data)	20
FTP (Control)	21
DNS	53
DHCP	67
SMTP	25
SNMP	161
Telnet	23
POP3	110
IMAP	143
NTP	123
NNTP	119
SSH	22
LDAP	389

The following are different types of port-scanning methods that can be used to detect open ports on a system:

- **TCP scanning** A TCP scan uses the TCP protocol and its commands to connect to a port and open a full TCP connection before breaking off the communication. For example, when scanning a system for Telnet port 23, the port scanner fully connects to that port on the destination host. If no response is received, the port is deemed closed or protected by a firewall.
- **SYN scanning** A SYN scan uses TCP segments with the SYN flag set to "on" to scan a host but does not open a full TCP connection to the destination host. The SYN scan breaks off the communication before the handshake process is complete. This is often called *stealth* scanning and is less intrusive than a TCP scan, which opens a full connection to receive its information.
- **UDP scanning** The UDP scan is not as effective as other scans, because UDP is a connectionless protocol. This scan gets its open-port information by detecting which ports are not returning acknowledgments to requests, because a UDP request will receive a "host unreachable" message via ICMP in response. If no response is received, the port is open and listening for requests. However, this method is not foolproof, because if the port is blocked by a firewall, the user/assessor receives no response and might assume the port is open.

Port scanners are often built into popular network-mapping and vulnerability assessment tools such as Nmap because they provide the foundation for determining what services and open ports are on a system, which then leads to a specific vulnerability scan against those services and ports.

Vulnerability Scanners

When an assessor has ascertained which systems are available on the network, his next step is to probe these systems to see what vulnerabilities they might contain. At this point, he has an idea of which systems are alive and which network ports are open and listening for requests.

A *vulnerability scanner* is a software program specifically designed to scan a system via the network to determine which services the system is running and whether any unnecessary open network ports, unpatched operating systems and applications, or backdoors can be exploited. Network administrators can use the same vulnerability scanner software to take preventive measures to close vulnerabilities that exist on their systems.

ADDITIONAL RESOURCES Nessus (available at www.tenable.com) is a popular commercial vulnerability scanner, available in both Linux and Unix versions, that scans systems for thousands of vulnerabilities and provides an exhaustive report about the vulnerabilities that exist on your system.

Vulnerability scanners typically include a few scanning and security assessment capabilities, such as configuration scanning, port scanning, network scanning and mapping, and OS and application server scanning. A vulnerability scanner accesses a database of known OS weaknesses and application program vulnerabilities (often using the Common Vulnerabilities and Exposures [CVE] list that maps to the NIST NVD, discussed earlier in Objective 1.5), and it scans the target system to determine whether any of the vulnerabilities listed in its database exist. These are generally scored using the Common Vulnerability Scoring System (CVSS), which applies a 0–10 score to a vulnerability based on its criticality. For example, a vulnerability scanner can scan a database server and front-end web application to determine whether they are vulnerable to specific database and web server attacks. By determining the OS of a system, such as Windows or Unix, and then using the database of known vulnerabilities and weaknesses for that OS, and understanding the criticality based on its CVSS score, the assessor can target his attacks to be most effective.

The following are some vulnerability-scanning considerations:

- **Passive testing** Vulnerability scanning is a passive test of your security controls and configuration using tools such as port scans, network mappers, and protocol analyzers. *Passive scanning* means that you are not actively probing your system, as you would do in a penetration test, but you are making a step-by-step examination of your system to look for vulnerabilities that can lead to an attack.
- **Vulnerability identification** Vulnerability scanning is specifically used to identify certain vulnerabilities. A port scanner can instantly detect which ports are running on your system. Operating system scans can identify whether or not your OS is running the latest patches and software. A vulnerability scan involves simple, fact-oriented information gathering and can identify vulnerabilities but can't determine whether they have been exploited.
- **Lacking security controls** Vulnerability assessments specifically identify areas that lack technical security controls. With its all-encompassing scope of scanning, vulnerability scanning examines all aspects of your system for issues, including the configuration of your operating system or application.
- **Common misconfigurations** Using vulnerability-scanning techniques, you can also identify specific areas of your system's configuration that require tightening to prevent security issues stemming from a poor default or user-defined configuration.
- **False positives** A false positive occurs when a vulnerability scan reports a vulnerability that does not actually exist. You likely will come across false positives while conducting a vulnerability assessment. These may be caused by tools alerting on the presence of vulnerabilities within software that doesn't exist on the system, or perhaps even wrongly flagging patches as out of date. It's worth looking at each result to be sure it is legitimate, especially if you plan to use the results to make enterprise-wide changes.

- **False negatives** Even more dangerous than a false positive, a false negative occurs when a vulnerability indeed exists but it is not detected by the scanner. Using a combination of different types of vulnerability scanners or assessment methods can help eliminate false negatives.

Protocol Analyzers

A *protocol analyzer* (also sometimes referred to as a *network sniffer*) can intercept, record, and analyze network traffic. Network administrators use protocol analyzers to track specific network protocols as they send out queries and receive responses and to narrow down sources of communications issues; however, hackers also use protocol analyzers to intercept clear-text communications (such as user account and password information) that are transmitted over unsecured protocols. For example, HTTP web traffic is transmitted in clear text, and any information transmitted to a website in clear text, such as a login ID and password, is not encrypted and can be easily viewed by a hacker using a protocol analyzer. Confidential information can also be captured from sensitive e-mail messages passed over the network.

OVAL

The *Open Vulnerability and Assessment Language (OVAL)* is a security standard that provides open access to security assessments using a special language to standardize system security configuration characteristics, current system analysis, and reporting. OVAL is not a vulnerability scanner, but it provides a language and templates that help administrators check their systems to determine whether vulnerabilities, such as unpatched software, exist.

OVAL uses Extensible Markup Language (XML) schemas as its framework, with three schemas geared toward specific parts of the security standard (system characteristics, current system definition, and reporting the assessment results). These XML files can be fed through an OVAL interpreter program that examines the system, compares it to public databases of known vulnerabilities, and generates the test results that indicate any open vulnerabilities on the system.

This information relies on repositories of publicly available security content that contain a collection of security definitions provided by the security community, which continually adds to the collection and drives OVAL development and evolution. This process provides a comprehensive testing and reporting standard supported by the security community that creates a baseline and checks for known vulnerabilities on computer systems.

Security Information and Event Management

Until recently, the traditional way to assess logging and monitoring in a network was to sit down at a system and look within the operating system's log facility, such as Windows event viewer or syslog, at the files generated by the system, reviewing them for any events of interest; however, this is not the most efficient way. A newer paradigm that falls under continuous security monitoring, but is also very useful for security assessments, is *security information and event management (SIEM)*. SIEM solutions comprise an enterprise-level technology and infrastructure that aggregates all the different data points from the network, including network alerts, packet capture, user behavior and sentiment analyses, data inputs, log files, physical security logs, and so on, from every host on the network. SIEM solutions can collect all this different data into one centralized location and allow an analyst to look for correlations related to security and performance issues, as well as negative trends, all in real time, and can automate alerts to analysts based on preset triggers. SIEM solutions also can generate a variety of reports for review, handy for everything from an assessment to briefing management.

SIEM infrastructures usually require a multitier setup consisting of servers designated as centralized *log collectors*, which pass log events on to other servers designated for mass log aggregation, which are then accessed by devices focused purely on real-time correlation and analysis. When you're using a SIEM solution, it is important to make sure that the time is synchronized between the various devices providing data for aggregation and analysis; otherwise, your trend analysis will be incorrect, providing either false positives or false negatives. Also, because events can generate duplicate data (think of multiple logs across multiple devices), *deduplication*, or the reduction of duplicate events, is an important SIEM feature; otherwise, your analysts might be drowning in data.

REVIEW

Objective 1.7: Summarize the techniques used in security assessments Vulnerability assessment tools can be used by network administrators to find and mitigate vulnerabilities, but malicious hackers have access to the same tools to find vulnerabilities to attack. Perform port scanning to determine what services and open ports are running on your systems, and then disable those that are not required. Protocol analyzers can capture and analyze individual network packets, including any clear-text data sent within them. Use vulnerability scanners to determine whether your operating system and application software are up to date with the latest updates and patches.

1.7 QUESTIONS

1. Bobby is performing a vulnerability assessment for a web server. Which of the following vulnerability assessment findings should he be concerned with?
   A. Operating system not updated to latest patch level
   B. HTTPS server listening on port 443
   C. Network packets being sent in clear text
   D. HTTP server listening on port 80

2. Lauren is performing a vulnerability assessment for a web server. Which of the following tools should she use to determine what active ports, protocols, and services are running?
   A. Wireshark
   B. Nmap
   C. Honeypot
   D. Banner Grabber
3. Which of the following is the most dangerous type of finding because it can actually mean that a potential vulnerability goes undetected?
   A. False positive
   B. False negative
   C. False flag
   D. False scan
4. Tom is looking for a single tool that aggregates all the different data points from the network, including network alerts, packet capture, user behavior and sentiment analyses, data inputs, log files, and physical security logs, from every host on the network. What is the *best* option?
   A. Anti-malware scanner
   B. Vulnerability scanner
   C. Port scanner
   D. SIEM solution

1.7 ANSWERS

1. **A** A vulnerability scanner is designed to scan a system and determine what services that system is running and whether any unnecessary open network ports or unpatched operating systems and applications exist. In this case, HTTP listening on port 80 and HTTPS listening on port 443 are normal operating parameters for a web server. Unless you are using HTTPS, web network packets are always sent in clear text. The vulnerability scanner will detect that the system is not running the latest operating system patches and advise you to update the system.
2. **B** Nmap is a popular port-scanning tool used to determine what active ports, protocols, and services are running on a network host.
3. **B** A false negative can mean that an actual vulnerability goes undetected.
4. **D** A security information and event management (SIEM) solution aggregates all the different data points from the network, including network alerts, packet capture, user behavior and sentiment analyses, data inputs, log files, physical security logs, and so on, from every host on the network.

Objective 1.8 Explain the techniques used in penetration testing

The preceding objective discussed the use of vulnerability scanning to examine your network systems for unnecessary running services and open ports, unpatched operating system and application software, or any other types of network vulnerabilities that can be exploited by a hacker. *Penetration testing* evaluates the security of a network or computer system by actively simulating an attack.

Penetration Testing Techniques

Penetration tests are performed using the same types of tools and exploits that malicious hackers use to compromise system security. These tools can be used to test network and system resilience to a real attack scenario and test the effectiveness of existing security measures implemented after a vulnerability assessment. While a vulnerability scan can identify security risks and vulnerabilities, it cannot simulate the effect of real attacks. Further, penetration tests are often performed by outside vendors who are allowed access to the network by upper management, rather than being conducted by an internal team. This can often bring a fresh, unbiased perspective to the process and more realistic results.

EXAM TIP A vulnerability scan is used to identify specific weaknesses in current systems and networks, but it cannot simulate real attacks. Penetration testing is used to simulate an actual attack on a system and can be used to test your security countermeasures and resilience to an attack. In short, a vulnerability scan tells you what is theoretically possible. A penetration test proves or disproves whether it is actually possible.

Penetration testing provides the following additional benefits beyond vulnerability scanning:

- **Threat verification** Penetration testing can verify that a real threat exists if a specific identified vulnerability is exploited. The outcome of an exploit is never certain unless you take active steps to test the vulnerability and realize how deep a threat it represents.
- **Passive and active reconnaissance** *Passive reconnaissance* techniques involve gathering information about a target without their knowledge and attempting to remain unnoticed, whereas *active reconnaissance* activities use tools and techniques that may or may not be discovered by the target, but put the activities as a tester at a higher risk of discovery. While vulnerability scans generally involve only a set

of quite passive tools that look at patching adherence, configurations, and more compliance-based activities, penetration tests often involve real-world, active attack approaches, including the use of exploitation tools (such as Metasploit) and the use of drones/unmanned aerial vehicles (UAVs) to conduct "warflying" reconnaissance, and war driving, with a more traditional vehicle. Port scanning is a great example of a technique that can be both passive or active, with the more active port scans being quite noisy to a network defender. The purpose of both reconnaissance types is to gather information in the same way a threat actor would, at varying levels of "noise."

Cross-Reference

Many of the tools commonly used within both passive and active techniques will be covered in Domain 4, Objective 4.1.

- **Bypassing security controls** You can use penetration testing to find out what occurs when specific security controls are bypassed. For example, a simple vulnerability scan on weak passwords in your authentication system will not be able to detect any issues in the event a hacker can disable or bypass the authentication system. Penetration testing uses real-time attack scenarios that can't always be addressed through vulnerability scanning alone.
- **Actively testing security controls** Penetration testing actively tests security controls by simulating real attacks against the host system or application. This differs from the passive nature of vulnerability testing and can test the true depth of security controls, along with the level of weakness for specific vulnerabilities.
- **Exploiting vulnerabilities** Vulnerability scanners can detect a potential security issue, but only penetration testing can reveal whether that vulnerability could result in a specific security threat. Through active penetration testing, the vulnerability can be exploited, and the result will determine how deep the vulnerability is. After initial exploitation, a penetration team can assess the ability to move laterally within the network and pivot to other systems and networks, escalate privileges, and maintain persistence in the same way an adversary would. This provides a more realistic picture of your vulnerability.
- **Credentialed versus noncredentialled access** You can provide your testing team with credentials to gain ready access to the system, or you can take a more external approach and ask them to attempt to gain credentials, in much the same way as a threat actor would working from the outside. There are benefits to both: providing credentials may allow the team to do a more thorough job assessing your security posture, whereas not providing credentials could be a more realistic assessment.
- **Intrusive versus nonintrusive testing** If your organization hires a third-party penetration tester, you can specify (in advance and in writing, in the *rules of engagement*) how intrusive you want your testing to be. Do you want the test to really determine

how a system would handle an attack in a legitimate incident scenario? That might end up halting regular business for a time, or even causing lingering issues that need time to be resolved. This would be more intrusive, but also more realistic. Consider how realistic you want the test to be, and weigh that against the potential drawbacks posed by active testing. Penetration tests are generally much more intrusive than vulnerability assessments.

One of the drawbacks to penetration testing is that it can disrupt a live production system. To lessen the effects of the simulated attack, you could specify in the rules of engagement that the test team may perform penetration testing only after regular work hours at a time when any disruption to the network will not affect many users. Because of the disruptions tests can cause, many network administrators are able to perform only vulnerability assessments on their networks and systems; they cannot go a step further and perform actual penetration testing.

CAUTION Check with your company's security policies to determine whether you can perform penetration testing before you start such a process. Authorization is critical!

Penetration tests are often performed by outside vendors who are allowed access to the network by upper management—in some cases, without the network administrator's knowledge. This ensures the testing scenario is as close as possible to a real, unsuspected attack, and it provides a detailed analysis of any weaknesses in network and system security that remain even after vulnerability assessments have been performed.

Another increasingly common testing scenario is the *bug bounty*, where a company or even a government agency pays a reward to anyone who finds a bug and reports it to the company or agency. This is a win-win, allowing talented researchers to get recognition and compensation, and the company to have fresh eyes combing for vulnerabilities in a monitored environment.

Be sure to clean up after a completed penetration test! Otherwise, any reconfiguration, malware, or other changes made to the environment to properly exploit the network are lying in wait to be used by an actual hacker.

Known, Unknown, and Partially Known Environment Testing

When performing vulnerability and penetration testing, you can use any of several types of methods, each with its own advantages and disadvantages. What is important is that you use a variety of methods, from detailed internal testing of software code and internal processes to simulations of attacks from users who are completely unfamiliar with the inner workings of the system. By testing the software from different viewpoints and attack scopes, you can uncover vulnerabilities that might not have been apparent during other types of testing.

EXAM TIP These types of environment testings were previously referred to as white, black, and gray box testing, respectively. Be aware that you might see those terms during the transition period.

Do not confuse known, unknown, and partially known environment testing with authorized, unauthorized, and semi-authorized hacking. The latter are terms used to describe the different intentions of various types of hackers, as previously covered in Objective 1.5. For example, authorized hackers use their skills to—legally and within the confines of an agreement with the organization they're supporting—attack the security posture of a defined set of systems or a whole network infrastructure. Compare that to an unauthorized hacker, who attacks for glory, financial gain, or any number of other reasons. We generally associate these people with the "hacker" stereotype. Somewhere in the middle is the semi-authorized hacker, who might have good intentions but still conducts illegal activities within his "testing."

Known Environment Testing

A *known environment* test refers to the testing scenario where the user testing the system has prior knowledge of the system coding and design and is not testing the system from the perspective of an end user who would have no access to the internal details of an application.

Known environment testing is usually performed by quality assurance and system integration specialists who can test every aspect of the application, including deep levels of the application programming interface (API), network services, the underlying operating system, and manipulation of the input to the system for the full range of input validation.

This type of detailed testing is usually conducted with direction from development using detailed test plans and test cases for the code. The goal of known environment testing is to deeply test the internal code of the system in terms of every functional operation the application can perform. Through this vigorous testing, the most obvious and critical of internal architectural errors can be discovered and resolved.

Unknown Environment Testing

Unknown environment testing is a method of security vulnerability and penetration testing that assumes the tester does not have any prior knowledge of the system she is trying to crack. The tester has no idea how the software was developed, what languages are used, or what network services are running.

Unknown environment testing is an excellent way to test your system's security by simulating an attack. From the tester's perspective, she is seeing this system or application for the first time and therefore can be a very objective and unbiased evaluator. Without any prior knowledge of the underlying code or operating system, the tester can start off using the simplest penetration and vulnerability-seeking techniques and then proceed to more advanced methods to try and break the system.

Unknown environment testing is a complementary testing method to known environment testing and can often find bugs that the original developer could not find. However, because the tester has only limited access to the system and no access to back-end aspects of the software, an unknown environment test is not a comprehensive full-system test and cannot be solely relied on for accurate vulnerability and penetration testing.

CAUTION Before penetration testing begins, be sure to clearly define the *rules of engagement* in writing and get the proper signatures from management. Be sure the rules of engagement cover the scope, limitations, and possible repercussions of the testing. Getting a legal review isn't a bad idea either!

Partially Known Environment Testing

Partially known environment testing is a hybrid method that includes aspects of both known and unknown environment testing. Partially known environment testing uses some prior knowledge of how the software application is designed, as in a known environment test, but the testing is performed from the perspective of an attacker, as in an unknown environment test.

By combining the best of both methods, partially known environment testing can find security issues and bugs that may not have been discovered using one of the other primary testing methods.

EXAM TIP Known, partially known, and unknown environment testing require varying levels of prior tester knowledge and access to the system. Understand the differences between those terms and the terms authorized, semi-authorized, and unauthorized hackers, which describe the *intent* of the hacker.

Exercise Types

While penetration tests are often done with little to no coordination with the network defenders to maintain a true sense of vulnerability to different attacks, exercises are events that are coordinated across various teams assigned different colors. The colors are important, as they designate the roles of the respective teams within the exercise. *Blue teams* play defense and are ideally the same personnel defending against real-world attacks. *Red teams* play offense, emulating different types of threat actors to realistically portray their level of skill and known TTPs against the defense. *Purple teams* are somewhat of a hybrid, in that the red and blue teams coordinate and share information to improve the defense through active learning. Finally, *white teams* lead and adjudicate the exercise.

NOTE While some people use the terms penetration test and red team exercise interchangeably, they are not the same. Red teams emulate specific threat actors and can operate for weeks, months, or even years at a time, while penetration tests often have a predefined start date, duration, and end date.

REVIEW

Objective 1.8: Explain the techniques used in penetration testing Penetration testing evaluates the security of a network or computer system by simulating an actual attack. Vulnerability testing and assessments are helpful in identifying existing vulnerabilities and weaknesses, but only penetration testing can determine the effectiveness of the countermeasures used by the network administrator to fix these vulnerabilities. They both have their strengths and weaknesses and should be used within their appropriate contexts. Known environment testing is a detailed test by users who are familiar with the system design and code. Unknown environment testing simulates an attack from a user who is not familiar with the inner workings of a system. Partially known environment testing is a combination of known and unknown environment testing.

1.8 QUESTIONS

1. Match the following testing methods with their proper definitions:

The person testing the system has some prior knowledge of the system, but the test is performed as if he is an end user.	A. Unknown environment testing
The person testing the system has prior knowledge of the system and is not testing from the perspective of an end user.	B. Known environment testing
The person testing the system tests from the perspective of an outside user who has no knowledge of the system.	C. Partially known environment testing

2. After a security audit and vulnerability assessment, several servers required software patches and unused open network ports needed to be disabled. Which of the following should be performed after these vulnerabilities are fixed to ensure that the countermeasures are secure against a real attack?
   - **A.** Advertise the system's IP address publicly.
   - **B.** Put systems back into live production.
   - **C.** Perform additional port scanning.
   - **D.** Perform penetration testing.
3. New management has decided to test the security of the existing network infrastructure implemented by the current network administrators. Which of the following should be performed to provide the most objective and useful test of your security controls?
   - **A.** Hire a real hacker to attack the network.
   - **B.** Perform third-party penetration testing.
   - **C.** Perform penetration testing by the network administrators.
   - **D.** Initiate an external denial-of-service attack.

1.8 ANSWERS

1. The answers are as follows:

The person testing the system has some prior knowledge of the system, but the test is performed as if he is an end user.	C. Partially known environment testing
The person testing the system has prior knowledge of the system and is not testing from the perspective of an end user.	B. Known environment testing
The person testing the system tests from the perspective of an outside user who has no knowledge of the system.	A. Unknown environment testing

2. **D** Penetration testing evaluates the security of a network or computer system by simulating an actual attack. This helps test a network's and system's resilience to a real attack as well as test the effectiveness of existing security measures implemented after vulnerability assessments.

3. **B** Penetration tests are often performed by third parties who are allowed access to the network by upper management—in some cases, without the network administrator's knowledge. This ensures the testing scenario is as close to a real unsuspected attack as possible and provides a detailed analysis of existing vulnerabilities.

Governance, Risk, and Compliance

Domain Objectives

- **5.1 Compare and contrast various types of controls**
- **5.2 Explain the importance of applicable regulations, standards, or frameworks that impact organizational security posture**
- **5.3 Explain the importance of policies to organizational security**
- **5.4 Summarize risk management processes and concepts**
- **5.5 Explain privacy and sensitive data concepts in relation to security**

Objective 5.1 Compare and contrast various types of controls

The term "control" is thrown around quite a bit within cybersecurity, as professionals discuss different methods to secure an organization's people, processes, and technology. But what actually is a control? This objective explains the different categories and types of controls and how they work together to protect an organization.

Control Categories

The CompTIA Security+ exam objectives group controls into three basic categories: managerial, technical, and operational. These are the broad categories that then generally encompass six types of controls that can be applied to reduce risk: compensating, corrective, detective, deterrent, physical, and preventive. When you're choosing controls that will serve to protect a particular organization, it is critical that you choose the combination of controls that will best support the security goals of that specific organization. For example, is the organization most concerned about data confidentiality? Perhaps constant availability is central to mission success. Considerations such as these will both ensure that your choices are focused on your specific organizational needs and increase the likelihood of management support.

EXAM TIP Although most classical security theories define control categories as managerial, technical, and *physical*, the updated CompTIA Security+ objectives state that the three control categories are managerial, technical, and *operational*. You should be familiar with the definitions for all three of those control types.

Managerial Controls

Managerial risk controls are the high-level risk management, assessment, and mitigation plans that define your overall organization security. Risk management is an ongoing function within your organization. It begins with risk assessment and analysis to identify the risk of security breaches against company assets, assess the probability of a risk and estimate its impact, and define the steps to reduce the level of that risk. The solutions to these risks must be properly analyzed and budgeted to ensure that the probability and impact of the risks are properly factored into a cost-effective solution. Many risk management best practices include controls encompassing managerial, technical, and operational aspects of the organization, including implementation of an overall risk management framework and efforts to improve documentation. Common managerial controls include administrative policies, procedures, and plans and management programs.

Technical Controls

The category of technical risk controls encompasses the actual technical measures used to reduce security risks in your organization, which include deep-level network and system security (firewalls, antivirus scanning, content filters, and other network security devices) and improvements in secure coding practices. The controls in this category may perform the bulk of the risk mitigation and deterrence defined in your organizational risk analysis.

Operational Controls

Controls in the operational risk category address how the organization conducts its daily business and are designed to minimize the security risk to those business activities. This category could include, for example, company-wide policies that are created, distributed, and used to educate employees on how to conduct their day-to-day activities while being vigilant about organizational security, and improvement initiatives to make organizational processes more efficient and effective. Managing risk operationally includes controls such as fences, alarms, armed guards, gates, CCTVs, and access badges, as well as user education and vigilant monitoring and testing to make sure the organization is adhering to its plans and that its activities are constantly analyzed to protect against new threats.

EXAM TIP Managerial risk controls are the high-level risk management, assessment, and mitigation plans that define your overall organization security. Technical risk controls are technical measures deployed to mitigate security risks. Operational risk controls deal with your day-to-day physical security and the security of your organizational business activities. Understand that the controls are not applied as one group at a time only (e.g., only applying technical controls to mitigate a risk); in fact, most of the time, a combination of controls is used. For example, a managerial control might be a password policy, the technical control might be the enforcement of the use of complex passwords on the system through technical means, and the operational part might be guards walking through your building making sure written passwords are not left on desks unsupervised.

Control Types

As noted previously, controls serve different functions in an organization and are generally either compensating, corrective, detective, deterrent, directive, physical, or preventive in nature.

- *Compensating* controls compensate for weaknesses or inherent flaws within other controls or a lack of controls, such as regularly scheduled third-party review of logs based on an inability to enable proper separation of duties across system administrators.

- *Corrective* controls correct back to a trusted or "known-good" state; an example is regularly tested backups limiting the time a critical database is offline.
- *Detective* controls detect and characterize events or irregularities as or after they occur, such as internal or external audits conducted on a no-notice basis.
- *Deterrent* controls deter and discourage an event from taking place (for example, roaming security guards and cameras placed around the facilities that are continuously monitored by personnel).
- *Physical* controls include physical access controls (perimeter fencing, security passes, and surveillance) and environmental controls (fire suppression and temperature controls).
- *Preventive* controls are implemented to prevent negative events from occurring, such as locks that prevent portable systems from being removed from their desktops.

REVIEW

Objective 5.1: Compare and contrast various types of controls Choosing the correct combination of controls leads to a defense-in-depth approach where the controls are balanced and there are no gaps between them. Choose managerial, technical, and operational risk controls and understand their compensating, corrective, detective, deterrent, physical, or preventive functions.

5.1 QUESTIONS

1. Which of the following is *not* a control function?
   - **A.** Deter
   - **B.** Detect
   - **C.** Destroy
   - **D.** Compensate
2. Which of the following are control categories? (Choose all that apply.)
   - **A.** Mitigation
   - **B.** Recovery
   - **C.** Operational
   - **D.** Managerial

5.1 ANSWERS

1. **C** The functions of controls are to prevent, detect, correct, deter, compensate, or physically protect.
2. **C D** The three categories of controls are managerial, operational, and technical.

Objective 5.2 Explain the importance of applicable regulations, standards, or frameworks that impact organizational security posture

We've talked previously about the different types of controls and how they work together to cover the different functions of protecting an organization. However, how do you choose the right combination of controls? Certainly, without a guideline, wading through the thousands of combinations can set your head spinning. That's where prescriptive and guidance documents come in; these different types of documents range from mandatory to best practice, but all provide a different view and combination of what is needed to accomplish risk mitigation for their specific contexts.

Understanding Guidance Documents

One of the first things a cybersecurity professional should do when preparing to implement a new program is to identify any applicable regulations, standards, legislation, frameworks, or benchmarks and determine which documentation provides the best implementation guidance, as there is a variety to choose from. You must try to use the best framework or guidance documents (or combination of several) that is most appropriate for the organization, and you can't do that unless you have at least a basic understanding of the more defined, standardized options used in the industry. The following sections will define the differences, as well as the leading examples within each type.

Regulations, Legislation, and Standards

Very simply, regulations, legislation, and standards are mandatory documents handed down for an organization to implement across their systems, either from an executive branch, a legislature, or another governing body. Generally, these guidance documents have an associated penalty, such as a denial to connect to a network, if the guidance is not followed appropriately.

- *Regulations* have the backing of the executive branch and are enabled by a statute. U.S. regulations carry out the president's policies. An example of a regulation is GDPR (discussed later).
- *Legislation* is a law or statute passed by a legislative body, such as the U.S. Congress.
- *Standards* are published publicly and are mandatory for use within the covered organizations but are also often used (such as in the case of NIST standards) privately as a vetted source of guidance.

The following sections describe some examples of these documents that you should know for the exam.

General Data Protection Regulation

The *General Data Protection Regulation (GDPR)* is a European Union (EU) regulation with a whopping 99 articles governing data protection and privacy for individuals residing in the EU whose private information is accessed and used by organizations operating within (not necessarily located within) member countries. GDPR, which became effective in May 2018, is centrally concerned with personal data of EU citizens and how it is used, stored, transferred, or processed, even if it's in a nonmember country (such as the United States). This data can be anything from personally identifiable information (PII), such as name, location, or a username, to the IP address and cookies associated with Internet use. If you've recently noticed pop-up screens on your favorite websites asking for your permission to store cookies and giving you the ability to choose settings, GDPR is the likely catalyst. GDPR requires businesses that acquire personal data of EU citizens to provide appropriate protections for the data and also grants the subjects of that data certain rights, including the right to be forgotten, data correction in the event of errors, and erasure of information.

Payment Card Industry Data Security Standards

The *Payment Card Industry Data Security Standard (PCI DSS)* is a standard for—you guessed it—the payment card industry, namely, companies that process payment card information. A merchant of any size that uses payment cards is required to be compliant with PCI DSS, and compliance is self-mandated by the card issuers. The organization responsible for the oversight of PCI DSS is the PCI Security Standards Council, which was formed in 2006 by American Express, Discover, JCB International, MasterCard, and Visa. PCI DSS has its own set of controls that payment card processors are required to implement in terms of network and host security. Note that PCI DSS is not a law or regulation, but any merchant that wishes to process payment card transactions must comply with it. This is an example of self-governance by an industry versus laws imposed on an industry by the government.

National, Territory, or State Laws

As with most statutes, those that apply to cybersecurity vary among different nations, territories, and states. Within the United States, there is a wide range of laws either on the books or in the process of being enacted that cover everything from individual rights to reporting requirements. For example, the state of New York has a regulation for the financial services industry mandating specific cybersecurity requirements. Another example is the California Consumer Privacy Act (CCPA), enacted in June 2018, which actually has very similar requirements to GDPR. All U.S. states also have reporting timelines and requirements for instances where a government entity or business within the state has a data breach of citizens' personally identifiable information.

Key Frameworks

A *framework* is an overarching methodology for a set of activities or processes. Frameworks may not get into the specifics of the processes and procedures required to complete the tasks, but most frameworks provide the general requirements to build a program, as a guiding architecture for a larger effort. A framework generally includes defined categories or control groups, provides measurement of the cybersecurity or risk maturity, and lends itself to the development of a roadmap toward improvement. Frameworks are often used to explain complex cybersecurity concepts at a strategic level for management. The following sections introduce the key frameworks to be familiar with for purposes of the CompTIA Security+ exam.

Center for Internet Security

The *Center for Internet Security (CIS) Critical Security Controls (CSC)*, otherwise known as the "Top 20 Controls" or "CIS Controls," is a framework composed of 20 control groups covering topics that range from hardware inventory to penetration testing within an organization. The underlying thesis for the CSC framework is to pare down the controls to those that are most critical, helping prevent organizations from becoming overwhelmed or choosing the wrong controls to apply to reduce risk. The Top 20 is a maturity model as well, with an organization's maturity measured from policy development all the way through proper reporting.

NIST Risk Management Framework/Cybersecurity Framework

The National Institute of Standards and Technology (NIST) *Risk Management Framework (RMF)* is a seven-step methodology that was introduced in NIST SP 800-37, Rev. 2, *Risk Management Framework for Information Systems and Organizations: A System Life Cycle Approach for Security and Privacy*. The RMF provides for risk management through the entire information systems life cycle. The RMF phases are iterative, as follows:

- Preparing the organization
- Categorizing information systems
- Selecting the controls
- Implementing the controls
- Assessing the control compliance
- Systems authorization by a higher authority
- Continuous monitoring

Existing controls are monitored for continued compliance and effectiveness against identified threats, and the system will have to be reauthorized after a certain period of time. Note that the RMF is a cycle, and all steps will need to be undertaken potentially multiple times for each system during its life cycle.

Similar, but different, to the RMF is the NIST Cybersecurity Framework (CSF). The CSF was originally designed for organizations that are part of the U.S. critical infrastructure, but has emerged as a solid, public framework for other organizations as well. It contains a set of controls that are sorted into five categories to reduce risk and help organizations respond more rapidly when incidents do occur:

- Identify
- Protect
- Detect
- Respond
- Recover

The CSF is not one-size-fits-all and should be tailored to an organization's mission requirements and data criticality.

ISO 27001/27002/27701/31000

Where the NIST RMF is very much an American framework, the International Organization for Standardization (ISO) frameworks are used globally. The ISO family is largely focused on keeping information assets secure, ensuring privacy, and managing risk across the following major documents:

- **ISO/IEC 27000:2018** Provides the overview of information security management systems (ISMS).
- **ISO/IEC 27001:2013** Specifies the requirements for establishing, implementing, maintaining, and continually improving an ISMS within the context of the organization. It also includes requirements for the assessment and treatment of information security risks tailored to the needs of the organization.
- **ISO/IEC 27002:2013** Gives guidelines for organizational information security standards and information security management practices, including the selection, implementation, and management of controls, taking into consideration the organization's information security risk environment(s).
- **ISO/IEC 27701:2019** Specifies requirements and provides guidance for establishing, implementing, maintaining, and continually improving a Privacy Information Management System (PIMS).
- **ISO 31000:2018** Provides guidelines on managing risk faced by organizations.

SSAE Service and Organization Controls 2

The American Institute of Certified Public Accountants (AICPA) developed the Statement on Standards for Attestation Engagements (SSAE) no. 18, which is used to audit service providers. SSAE-18 provides a third-party attestation of an organization's cybersecurity controls through a *SOC 2* report. Whereas a SOC 1 report is a statement of an organization's financial posture through a test of its accounting controls, a SOC 2 report is a snapshot of an organization's security posture and comes in two "types" that test on the design of cybersecurity controls:

- **Type I assessment** Validates the presence of the controls
- **Type II assessment** Shows the effectiveness of an organization's controls over a designated period of time

A SOC 2 assessment is based on five criteria: security, availability, processing integrity, confidentiality, and privacy. Cloud service providers and managed services providers often furnish SOC 2 reports to their current or prospective customers to provide assurance that their cybersecurity controls are strong.

Cloud Security Alliance Frameworks

The Cloud Security Alliance (CSA) is an organization dedicated to developing evolving best practices to secure cloud environments. CSA operates the CSA Security Trust Assurance and Risk (STAR) program, a provider assurance program of self-assessment, third-party audit, and continuous monitoring requirements. CSA also publishes two key artifacts:

- **Cloud Control Matrix (CCM)** A set of principles for cloud vendors to follow and prospective cloud customers to use for assessing the cybersecurity posture of a provider
- **Enterprise Architecture** Formerly known as the Reference Architecture, a methodology and associated tools to both design and maintain cloud services and assess vendors across a common set of capabilities

Benchmarks and Secure Configuration Guides

Benchmarks and secure configuration guides allow an organization to compare its current security posture to industry and government best practices. A good example of secure configuration guides are the U.S. Department of Defense (DoD) Security Technical Implementation Guides (STIGs), which provide the specific configurations across platforms and vendors for web servers, application servers, operating systems, and network infrastructure. While these are mandatory configuration guides for organizations that conduct business with the DoD, they're also excellent resources for external organizations looking to understand and implement best practices. Specific software and hardware vendors also maintain their own secure configuration guides for their products.

REVIEW

Objective 5.2: Explain the importance of applicable regulations, standards, or frameworks that impact organizational security posture Guidance documents nest together, from the strategic view to daily operations, from mandatory to best practice, all providing a different view and combination of what is needed to accomplish risk mitigation for their specific contexts. Regulations, standards, and legislation are mandatory guidance from an executive, legislative, or administrative body. Key frameworks have been developed globally to cover a variety of contexts, including cloud security. Benchmarks and secure configuration guides allow an organization to compare its current security posture to industry and government best practices.

5.2 QUESTIONS

1. You are implementing an organizational-wide risk management strategy, and you are using the NIST Risk Management Framework. You have just completed the RMF phase of categorizing your organization's information systems. Which of the following steps should you complete next in the RMF sequence?
   - **A.** Authorize system
   - **B.** Assess security controls
   - **C.** Continuous monitoring
   - **D.** Select security controls
2. A client, an American department store chain, has called for support identifying and complying with their required guidance documents. Which of the following is the *most* likely guidance document the client needs to consider?
   - **A.** Payment Card Industry Data Security Standard (PCI DSS)
   - **B.** National Institute of Standards and Technology (NIST) Risk Management Framework (RMF)
   - **C.** International Organization for Standardization (ISO) 27001
   - **D.** Center for Internet Security (CIS) Top 20
3. Which of the following is widely used for cloud or managed services providers to provide a report to their current or prospective customers that provides assurance of their cybersecurity?
   - **A.** Payment Card Industry Data Security Standard (PCI DSS) certification
   - **B.** General Data Protection Regulation (GDPR) report
   - **C.** Service and Organization Controls (SOC) 2 report
   - **D.** Center for Internet Security (CIS) Top 20 Maturity report

5.2 ANSWERS

1. **D** Step 3 of the RMF is selecting the security controls and is completed after information systems have been categorized.
2. **A** Because the client is a department store, it most likely processes payment cards and therefore is required to adhere to PCI DSS.
3. **C** The Service and Organization Controls (SOC) 2 report is often used by organizations to assure current and potential customers of their cybersecurity posture.

Objective 5.3 Explain the importance of policies to organizational security

As we've discussed different types of controls that work together to protect an organization, many of which have a technical focus. However, while the more technical approaches are quite often the stars of the cybersecurity show, the importance of the good old policy cannot be understated. In fact, without a policy, quite often the security program will fall flat due to a lack of governance, management involvement, and accountability. This objective covers different types of policies and how they work together to form the underlying foundation of human and process control, ensuring a balanced and effective security program.

Policies Supporting Organizational Security

To provide effective security, security policy and procedure creation must begin at the top of an organization with senior management that understands, supports, and holds personnel accountable to the written policies. These policies and procedures must then flow throughout the organization to ensure that security is useful and functional at every level of the organization. Understanding organizational security must begin with an understanding of the basic laws, regulations, and legal jurisdiction that policies must be informed by in order to protect not only the organization and its assets but also its employees and customers.

Using Organizational Policies to Reduce Risk

Security policies and procedures are official company communications of the organization that are created to ensure that a standard level of security requirements exists across the entire organization. These policies and procedures define how the employees must interact with company computer systems to perform their job functions, how to protect the computer systems and their data, and how to service the company's clients properly. The upcoming sections outline policies and procedures important for you to understand.

Physical Access Security Policy

As part of its overall access control policy, your organization must have a strong physical access policy and ensure that all employees are educated on its use.

Depending on the security level of the company, physical security may include guarded or unguarded entrances. Even on guarded premises, the use of security access cards ensures that only identified and authenticated employees can enter a facility. Each security access card is coded with the authorization level of the user, who will be able to access only areas of the facility that are required by his job function. For example, only network and systems administrators would be able to access a server and network communications room with their access card.

Employees must be trained to always close automatically locking doors behind them and not allow unidentified people to follow them through (known as tailgating). Most security access cards include a photograph of the cardholder to further identify users in the event they are challenged for their identity. Employees must be encouraged to report suspicious individuals within the premises who are unfamiliar and do not have proper identification.

A published organizational security policy that addresses physical access allows your employees to have proper knowledge of security procedures and to be equally active in the responsibility for physical security.

Access Control Policies

The following access control policies help provide a consistent organizational structure and procedures to prevent internal fraud and corruption in your organization:

- **Least privilege** The *least privilege* principle grants users only the access rights they need to perform their job functions. This requires giving users the least amount of access possible to prevent them from abusing more powerful access rights.
- **Separation of duties** The *separation of duties* ensures that one single individual isn't tasked with high-security and high-risk responsibilities. Certain critical responsibilities are separated between several users to prevent corruption.
- **Job rotation** *Job rotation* provides improved security because no employee retains the same amount of access control for a position indefinitely. This prevents internal corruption by employees who might otherwise take advantage of their long-term position and security access.
- **Mandatory vacation** A *mandatory vacation* policy requires employees to use their vacation days at specific times of the year or to use all their vacation days allotted for a single year. This policy helps detect security issues with employees, such as fraud or other internal hacking activities, because the anomalies might surface while the user is away Increasingly, organizations are implementing a policy requiring mandatory administrative leave for situations in which an employee is under any sort of investigation, systems related or otherwise.

Cybersecurity Policies

Several policies provide standard guidelines for cybersecurity within a company and encompass areas such as the use of the Internet and internal network, data privacy, incident response, human resources (HR) issues, and document security. These polices are often enforced by technical controls such as data loss prevention (DLP) tools that monitor for breaches of policy and issue a report when one occurs. Other tools may alert an administrator to machines joining the network that don't meet security requirements (having out-of-date antivirus signatures, for example) or report to an administrator when an unauthorized machine has been added to the network or an inappropriate website has been visited.

Cross-Reference

Data loss protection and prevention is covered in more depth in Domain 2, Objective 2.1.

Acceptable Use Policy An *acceptable use policy (AUP)* is a set of established guidelines for the appropriate use of computer networks within an organization. The AUP is a written agreement, read and signed by employees, that outlines the organization's terms, conditions, and rules for Internet and internal network use.

An AUP helps educate employees about the kinds of tools they will use on the network and what they can expect from those tools. The policy also helps to define boundaries of behavior and, more critically, specifies the consequences of violating those boundaries. The AUP also lays out the actions that management and the system administrators may take to maintain and monitor the network for unacceptable use, and it includes the general worst-case consequences or responses to specific policy violations.

KEY TERM An **acceptable use policy (AUP)** is a set of established guidelines for the appropriate use of computer networks within an organization.

Developing an AUP for your company's computer network is extremely important for organizational security and to limit legal liability in the event of a security issue. An AUP should cover the following issues:

- **Legality** The company's legal department needs to approve the policy before it's distributed for signing. The policy will be used as a legal document to ensure that the company isn't legally liable for any type of Internet-related incident the employee willfully causes, as well as other transgressions, such as cracking, vandalism, and sabotage.
- **Uniqueness to your environment** The policy should be written to cover the organization's specific network and the data it contains. Each organization has different security concerns—for example, a medical facility needs to protect data that differs significantly from that of a product sales company.

- **Completeness** Beyond rules of behavior, your AUP should also include a statement concerning the company's position on Internet use (e.g., are employees allowed to use the Internet for personal use on breaks and before/after work hours).
- **Adaptability** Because the Internet is constantly evolving, your AUP will need to be updated as new issues arise. You can't anticipate every situation, so the AUP should address the possibility of something happening that isn't outlined.
- **Protection for employees** If your employees follow the rules of the AUP, their exposure to questionable materials should be minimized. In addition, the AUP can protect them from dangerous Internet behavior, such as giving out their names and e-mail addresses to crackers using social engineering techniques.

The focus of an acceptable use policy should be on the responsible use of computer networks. Such networks include the Internet—including web, e-mail (both personal and business), social media, and instant messaging access—and the company intranet. An AUP should, at a minimum, contain the following components:

- A description of the strategies and goals to be supported by Internet access in the company
- A statement explaining the availability of computer networks to employees
- A statement explaining the responsibilities of employees when they use the Internet
- A code of conduct governing behavior on the Internet
- A description of the consequences of violating the policy
- A description of what constitutes acceptable and unacceptable use of the Internet
- A description of the rights of individuals using the networks in your company, such as user privacy
- A disclaimer absolving the company from responsibility under specific circumstances
- A form for employees to sign indicating their agreement to abide by the AUP

NOTE Many company websites contain an acceptable use policy or terms of use statement that protects the company from any liability from users of the site.

Social Media Policy Websites such as Facebook, Twitter, and Instagram are more popular than ever—and not just with teenagers. Employees often use these sites, sometime during the workday, to keep up with friends, family, and activities. While keeping your employees' morale high is a plus, it's important to limit social media usage at work, as it can be a hit to overall productivity. Perhaps even more importantly, employees who are posting negative comments about your organization, or even posting potentially private intellectual property, can be a competitor's dream. For example, consider a disgruntled employee who begins tweeting about your company's secret spaghetti sauce recipe, which is then copied by a competitor. Not good!

However, some pleasant scenarios for an organization can be directly attributed to employee social media usage. That's why it's important to determine what level of social media use your company is comfortable with while employees are on the clock. Many organizations have a policy that social media use during work is only allowed on breaks and lunch hours, and that employees may not discuss or disclose any information regarding their workplace or intellectual property. Also, the organization should consider a policy for cybersecurity personnel regarding analysis of employee social media (e.g., monitoring employee accounts for sensitive company or intellectual property information); it is important to check and see if this is legal in your jurisdiction before enacting such a policy.

Personal E-mail Policy As with social media, many employees have personal e-mail accounts that they may want to keep an eye on throughout the day; this lets them know that bills are being paid and their kids are being dropped off at sports activities. Maybe they even use e-mail to keep up with friends. Although this can be positive for employee morale, it is important that a company understand how personal e-mail is being used throughout the workday. An important consideration is the potential threat associated with sophisticated adversaries in cyberspace who know a great deal about the company's employees and may use their personal e-mail account for spearfishing and other nefarious activities. If malware is introduced through this personal e-mail usage during the workday, it then becomes your problem—assuming they're using one of your company systems. That malware could potentially leak trade or other secrets about your company. Again, as with social media, it is important for a company to dictate the terms of how personal e-mail will be used throughout the workday and whether personal e-mail is allowed to be used on the company's more sensitive systems. For example, it is generally considered a bad practice to allow personal e-mail to be used on production servers, where malware could have a catastrophic effect if introduced into the environment.

Privacy Policy *Privacy policies* are agreements that protect individually identifiable information in an online or e-commerce environment. A company engaged in online activities or e-commerce has a responsibility to adopt and implement a policy to protect the privacy of personally identifiable information (PII). Increasingly, regulations such as the European Union's General Data Protection Regulation (GDPR) and the U.S. Health Insurance Portability and Accountability Act (HIPAA) require a privacy policy that is presented to and acknowledged by an individual before use of the information system. Organizations should also take steps to ensure online privacy when interacting with other companies, such as business partners.

The following recommendations pertain to implementing privacy policies:

- A company's privacy policy must be easy to find, read, and understand, and it must be available prior to or at the time that PII is collected or requested.
- The policy needs to state clearly what information is being collected; the purpose for which that information is being collected; possible third-party distribution of that information; the choices available to an individual regarding collection, use, and distribution of the collected information; a statement of the organization's commitment to data security; and what steps the organization takes to ensure data quality and access.

- The policy should disclose the consequences, if any, of an individual's refusal to provide information.
- The policy should include a clear statement of what accountability mechanism the organization uses, such as procedures for dealing with privacy breaches, including how to contact the organization and register complaints.
- Individuals must be given the opportunity to exercise choice regarding how PII collected from them online can be used when such use is unrelated to the purpose for which the information was collected. At a minimum, individuals should be given the opportunity to opt out of such use.
- When an individual's information collected online is to be shared with a third party, especially when such distribution is unrelated to the purpose for which the information was initially collected, the individual should be given the opportunity to opt out.
- Organizations creating, maintaining, using, or disseminating PII should take appropriate measures to ensure its reliability and should take reasonable precautions to protect the information from loss, misuse, or alteration.

Each company must evaluate its use of the Internet to determine the type of privacy policy it needs in order to protect all involved parties. The privacy policy will protect the company from legal issues, raising customers' comfort levels regarding the protection of their information. A privacy policy should include the following elements:

- **Information collection** Collect, use, and exchange only data pertinent to the exact purpose, in an open and ethical manner. The information collected for one purpose shouldn't be used for another. Notify consumers of information you have about them, its proposed use, and handling, as well as the enforcement policies.
- **Direct marketing** The company can use only non-PII for marketing purposes and must certify that the customers' personal information won't be resold to third-party marketing firms.
- **Information accuracy** Ensure the data is accurate, timely, and complete and that it has been collected in a legal and fair manner. Allow customers the right to access, verify, and change their information in a timely, straightforward manner. Inform customers of the data sources and allow them the option of removing their names from the marketing lists.
- **Information security** Apply security measures to safeguard the data on databases. Establish employee training programs and policies on the proper handling of customer data. Limit the access to a need-to-know basis on personal information and divide the information so no one employee or unit has the whole picture. Follow all government regulations concerning data handling and privacy.

EXAM TIP Privacy policies must be easy to find and provide information on how to opt out of any use of personally identifiable information.

Due Care, Due Diligence, and Due Process

Due care, *due diligence*, and *due process* are terms that apply to the implementation and enforcement of company-wide security policies. A company practices *due care* by ensuring that all activities that take place in the corporate facilities are conducted in a reasonably safe manner. A company practices *due diligence* by implementing and maintaining these security procedures consistently to protect the company's facilities, assets, and employees. Although many companies outline plans for security policies and standards, they often never officially implement them or don't properly share the information with employees. Without direction from management in the form of training, guidelines, and manuals, and without employee input and feedback, security policies will not be successful.

By practicing due care, the company shows it has taken the necessary steps to protect itself and its employees. By practicing due diligence, the company ensures that these security policies are properly maintained, communicated, and implemented. If the company doesn't follow proper due care and due diligence initiatives, it might be considered legally negligent if company security and customer data are compromised.

Due process guarantees that in the event of a security issue by an employee, the employee receives an impartial and fair inquiry into the incident to ensure the employee's rights are not being violated. If, during an investigation or inquiry, the employee's rights are violated, the company may face legal ramifications via lawsuits or governmental employment tribunals.

KEY TERMS **Due care** involves taking the necessary responsibility and steps to protect the company and the employees. **Due diligence** ensures these security policies are properly implemented. **Due process** ensures an impartial and fair inquiry into violations of company policies.

Human Resources Policies

A company's HR department is an important link regarding company and employee security. The HR department is responsible for hiring employees, ensuring employees conform to company codes and policies during their term of employment, and maintaining company security in case of an employee termination. The following sections outline the responsibility of human resources during the three phases of the employment cycle: hiring, maintenance, and termination.

Hiring Policy When hiring employees for a position within the company, the HR department is responsible for the initial employee screening. This usually takes place during the first interview: An HR representative meets with the potential employee to discuss the company and to get a first impression, gauging whether this person would fit into the company's environment. This interview generally is personality based and nontechnical. Further interviews are usually more oriented toward the applicant's skillset and are conducted by the department advertising the position. Both types of interview are important because the applicant could possess excellent technical skills for the position, but his personality and communications skills might not be conducive to integration with the work environment.

During the interview process, HR also conducts *background checks* of the applicant and examines and confirms her educational and employment history. Reference checks are also performed, where HR can obtain information on the applicant from a third party to help confirm facts about the person's past. Depending on the type of company or institution, such as the government or the military, the applicant might have to go through security clearance checks or even health and drug testing.

To protect the confidentiality of company information, the applicant is usually required to sign a *nondisclosure agreement (NDA)*, which legally prevents the applicant from disclosing sensitive company data to other companies, even after termination of employment. These agreements are particularly important with high-turnover positions, such as contract or temporary employment.

When an employee is hired, the company also inherits that person's personality quirks or traits. A solid hiring process can prevent future problems with new employees.

Codes of Conduct and Ethics Policy The HR department is also responsible for outlining a company's policy regarding codes of conduct and ethics. The codes are a general list of what the company expects from its employees in terms of everyday conduct—dealing with fellow employees, managers, and subordinates, including people from outside the company, such as customers and clients.

This code of conduct could include restrictions and policies concerning drug and alcohol use, theft and vandalism, sexual harassment, and violence in the workplace. If an employee violates any of these policies, that employee could be disciplined, suspended, or even terminated, depending on the severity of the infraction.

Termination Policy The dismissal of employees can be a stressful and chaotic time, especially because terminations can happen quickly and without notice. An employee can be terminated for a variety of reasons, such as performance issues; personal and attitude problems; or legal issues such as sabotage, espionage, or theft. Alternatively, the employee could be leaving to work for another company. The HR department needs to have a specific set of procedures ready to follow in case an employee resigns or is terminated. Without a step-by-step method of termination, some procedures might be ignored or overlooked during the process that compromise company security.

A termination policy should exist for different situations. For example, you might follow slightly different procedures for terminating an employee who's leaving to take a job in an unrelated industry than an employee who's going to work for a direct competitor. In the latter case, the employee might be considered a security risk if he remains on the premises for his two-week notice period, where he could transmit company secrets to the competition.

A termination policy should include the following procedures for the immediate termination of an employee:

- **Securing work area** When the termination time has been set, the employee in question should be escorted from his workstation area to the HR department. This prevents him from using his computer or other company resources once notice of termination is given. His computer should be turned off and disconnected from the network. When the employee returns to his desk to collect personal items, someone should be with him to ensure that he does not take private company information. Finally, the employee should be escorted out of the building.
- **Return of identification** As part of the termination procedure, the employee's company identification and any company equipment should be returned. This includes identity badges, pass cards, keys for doors, and any other security device used for access to company facilities. This prevents the person from accessing the building after being escorted from the premises.
- **Return of company equipment** All company-owned equipment must be returned immediately, such as desktops, laptops, cell phones, tablets, organizers, or any other type of electronic equipment that could contain confidential company information.
- **Suspension of accounts** An important part of the termination procedure is the notification to the network administrators of the situation. They should be notified shortly before the termination takes place to give them time to disable any network accounts and phone access for that employee. The network password of the account should be changed, and any other network access the employee might have, such as remote access, should be disabled. The employee's file server data and e-mail should be preserved and archived to protect any work or communications the company might need for operational or legal reasons.

EXAM TIP All user access, including physical and network access controls, needs to be disabled for an employee once she has been terminated. This prevents the employee from accessing the facility or network.

Security Training and Awareness Policies

The first step in user security awareness is creating and maintaining proper documentation of all your security policies and procedures. Policies that apply to the company should be distributed to each employee, and each employee should sign and acknowledge receipt of them. These policies might include such areas as acceptable Internet use during work hours, employee codes of ethics and conduct, and safety and emergency contact information. More department-specific policies could be distributed only to employees in that department. The HR department wouldn't publish policies for the protection of employee salary information to other departments of the company, for example, so it wouldn't reveal or undermine any security procedures. The IT department would have different security policies from those of other departments because one of its main job functions is to be responsible for the security and protection of the company's network infrastructure and data.

Because security policies tend to change over time, manual distribution isn't always the most efficient and timely way to communicate security information. Employees should have a way to access the most current versions of these documents in a conspicuous place, such as in a binder located outside the HR area. Another, more efficient method is to publish these documents on a company intranet so that employees can easily access the most current versions. Printed versions should still be available, but because this documentation frequently changes, only a few central copies should be created to prevent excessive paper waste and circulation of stale policies. The advantages of online documents are that they're instantly available through employees' computers and they're always the most recent versions.

NOTE The best place to store company documentation for easy access by employees is a central landing page, such as the corporate intranet.

Providing access to documentation is only one part of user awareness. Although printed documentation might be handed out to all employees or electronic versions made available online, no guarantee exists that they'll be read, understood, or implemented. To supplement the documentation and to ensure employee awareness, the company should provide education and training sessions. These can be as simple as in-person training sessions or can incorporate techniques such as *gamification* (making a game out of the training to keep it engaging), *capture the flag* (a competition to hone cyber "attack" skills through capturing another team's "flag" while keeping yours safe through security to prevent yours being captured), *phishing simulations*, and *computer-based training (CBT)*. Ensuring diversity of training techniques helps keep the training fresh and relevant and improves user retention.

Onboarding and Offboarding

Training sessions should be mandatory for all employees and are especially critical for new employees during their onboarding process. The training courses ensure that employees know the company's security policies and procedures and, most important, that they understand these policies and know how to enact them within their specific positions. Having formal classes also makes it more likely that any questions new employees may have will be raised and can be discussed. Classes can be based on overall security procedures, such as virus awareness and dealing with outside clients and inquiries. These should be attended by all employees to ensure they know how to handle security problems properly with communications media used company-wide, such as e-mail or the telephone.

Your organization should also start a training record for each new employee as part of the onboarding process, for both compliance and HR purposes. IT professionals and security personnel will need additional training related to their duties, so that they are fully aware of the threats and vulnerabilities they may face and thoroughly understand their roles in dealing with these threats.

Onboarding training should include a basic overview of the company's security policies and procedures (for example, general threat awareness, acceptable use policies regarding company e-mail and telephones, virus awareness). Onboarding training also can include job-/role-specific training, as well as training targeted to the particular needs of a specific department (for example, policies for salespeople in dealing with sensitive customer data such as credit card information). All new hires should leave these onboarding sessions with a robust understanding not only of the various types of security threats they are likely to encounter but also of what is expected from them and the repercussions if they don't practice due diligence.

Employees who are leaving the company should be offboarded through an exit interview that supplies them with their responsibility to safeguard sensitive data. In the event there is a security clearance or nondisclosure agreement involved, this can be a lifetime responsibility with severe penalty. It is also helpful to gather feedback from the departing employee regarding their time at the company and their thoughts on how processes could be improved.

Nondisclosure Agreements

Nondisclosure agreements (NDAs) are often utilized when an employee, or even a third-party vendor or supplier, requires access to sensitive or proprietary information, information that could provide an advantage to a competitor, or, in the case of federal agencies or contractors, harm national security. NDAs enjoin the signee from disclosing such information under threat of serious penalty.

Awareness Training

As mentioned earlier, role-based training can be particularly important for raising security awareness. Various roles throughout the organization play a significant part in the protection of systems and data, and it is important that organizations identify those specific roles that require a more detailed level of knowledge and spend the resources to facilitate their learning and engagement.

Optimally, training should be developed to consider the role the user will have within the organization, the specific organizational context (e.g., academia, government), and the threats associated with both. Some different roles that should have specific training developed include data owners, systems administrators, system owners, users, privileged users, and executive users.

- **Users** All users within your organization need training to better understand the current security threats as well as what their responsibility is to protect against them. This training can take the form of courses, briefings, online programs, or any combination of the different available solutions. What is important is to make your personnel aware of current security threats and vulnerabilities, as well as the best practices used to counter them. Users should understand what is expected of them, as well as the repercussions for not following organizational policy. If you are conducting the training, this is a great opportunity to use any powerful, real-world anecdotes you might have (sanitized, without names, of course) to make your training more effective by showing situations that employees could be confronted with. For example, if you have had a large number of phishing e-mails targeting your organization, this would be timely and relevant information to include in your training and awareness program to let users know about it and what they should do. General security items, such as facility access control, can include training on identifying and authenticating users in the facility so that they can spot employees or strangers who are somewhere they shouldn't be. Network authentication standards, such as proper login and password management, are also applicable to all employees. Specialized training can be presented to laptop and mobile device users who'll be traveling to ensure they protect company equipment and data when they're not on the premises. Other education initiatives can be more specific to an individual user or department, depending on their job function. For example, the HR department can be given training on the security practices involved with hiring and terminating employees.

- **Privileged users** Privileged users, or those users who have increased access to systems or data, should have a level of training commensurate to their level of access. These users must understand that with their privileged access comes increased responsibility for the safety and security of their area of expertise. It is important that privileged users in particular have regular access to current threat information so that they can spot anomalies that could be attributed to malicious actors, either internal or external.
- **Executive users** Although executive users' time is often very valuable, there's no denying that they are subject to targeted threats and should have appropriate training developed for their unique context. For example, since phishing attacks are often targeted at executive users (known as *whaling*), those users should be made aware of how these attacks could be used to gain the most sensitive organizational information. Although they may not be able to give you hours of their time, focused training courses of no more than 30 minutes will put you well on your way to keeping your executive users safe.
- **Systems administrators** Systems administrators play such a huge role in protecting an enterprise that they require in-depth training programs based on current events. The informed systems administrator is a responsive, savvy systems administrator who understands the threats and recognizes anomalies and trends. Keeping these people aware and engaged is your first line of defense.
- **System owners** Although they may leave much of the day-to-day care and feeding of the system to the system administrator, system owners should be properly trained and/or certified to accept the residual risks related to the system.

- **Data owners** Data owners, similar to system owners, should receive training on the data they are responsible for, the controls put into place to protect it, and their responsibilities associated with those controls and the security and safety of their data. They should understand the sensitivity requirements specific to their organization and their department. For example, a data owner within the finance department should be aware of how and to whom financial data can and cannot be released.

Remember that the security department staff should be consulted when any type of security-related training is being developed for any population of users, because they are in the best position to know where the training deficiencies are within the organization.

CAUTION If you are working within the U.S. federal government, there are now regulations detailing the continuous certification and training of employees fulfilling certain security roles. If you are working within—or are planning to support—such an organization, you should consult the most current regulatory documents to be sure you are meeting the mandates.

Users need to understand, no matter their privilege level, how policy violations are handled, as well as what adverse actions will be associated with those policy violations. For example, if pornography is found on a business system, there may be a policy to immediately terminate the guilty employee. These implications should be communicated to the employees to give them an understanding of what is *not* okay within the work environment—this is often presented to employees through the company's acceptable use policy, as discussed earlier.

Finally, users should be cognizant of the sensitive data their organization processes—for example, personally identifiable information (discussed previously), protected health information (PHI), classified data, or financial data—and how to treat that information. Certain organizations, particularly those within government or healthcare, will likely have strict policies on the handling, dissemination, and storage of this type of information. Each of these types of data may require special controls, such as data-at-rest or in-transit encryption, special networks that are not connected to the greater Internet, and data segmentation. It is important that training and awareness campaigns include these details should any of these types of data be an issue.

Continuing Education

Just as it is important for your employees to be well trained as you bring them onboard, it is also important that they have access to continuing education opportunities. This will expand their usefulness in your workplace, as well as their proficiency, and make them more valuable employees (and it may increase morale, too). In regard to continual employee education, consider the following anecdote: An HR person once asked an HR manager, "What if we train them and they leave?" The manager replied, "What if we *don't* train them and they *stay*?"

Education is often given as a "perk" or a benefit to employees, with options such as college degrees, specialized training, certifications, and certificate programs in the field, generally in exchange for a contractual commitment to the company. Investing in your employees is a smart choice toward a happier, more knowledgeable, and more productive workforce.

Recurring Training

After employees have completed their initial training, they should receive recurring training on a periodic basis—annually at a minimum, but ideally whenever the computing environment changes or new and significant threats emerge. As mentioned previously, you can utilize classes, online documentation, and briefings. Also, information can be sent to the workforce via e-mail or even as pop-up messages that appear when their computer is loading. This is vital to ensuring that your employees are aware of the most current threats and are equipped to play their part in dealing with them.

Security Metrics

Although training can prepare users to work in an environment where spam, viruses, and network breaches are common, it is key that management follow up and measure whether the training and awareness programs are having an impact on the number of security incidents occurring within the organization. It is also important that management consider exactly what should be measured and tracked for the organization. Is constant availability critical, or is the confidentiality of data the more important factor? These considerations need to be codified by the organization's leadership.

Although metrics can focus on anything from network uptime to the time it takes for the IT helpdesk to deal with customer issues, the discussion here focuses on those security metrics that validate compliance and the organization's overall security posture. For example, a department (perhaps working with the chief information security officer) that has oversight over the organization's security posture might measure the number of unauthorized information systems plugged into the network within a month. It might also monitor the number of systems that are not properly patched or the number of viruses contracted within a given time. A common metric that aligns with training is the number of users falling prey to simulated phishing campaigns. Gathering this type of data allows management to spot trends and frequent offenders and to take corrective actions.

Data and Documentation Policies

Most organizations produce a wide variety of documentation—from publications for internal use, to confidential papers for senior management, to publicly available documents. Without proper controls, such documentation could be used to compromise an organization's security. Every company should have document control standards and guidelines that ensure that all documents produced by the company are classified, organized, and stored securely to prevent their loss, damage, or theft.

As part of its governance and risk management programs, an organization should develop data sensitivity and classification programs. This process also contributes to the business continuity plan (discussed in Domain 4, Objective 4.2). The organization takes a good look at all its data, categorizes it in terms of sensitivity and type (PII, proprietary, government classified, and so on), and assigns classification values to it. To ensure control over the protection and distribution of data, it needs to be classified with a certain designation. This data classification indicates what type of document it is, whether the information it contains is confidential or can be made public, and to whom it can be distributed. The classification also defines what levels of data retention and storage are needed for that document. Finally, policies must exist concerning the legal status of data and what can be destroyed and what needs to be retained.

Standards and Guidelines

To ensure the continuity of documentation across the company, a set of documentation standards and guidelines should be introduced. These standards and guidelines can serve as templates for all documentation to guarantee that documents have the same look and feel and to ensure they'll all be distributed and stored securely, according to their scope or sensitivity.

The standards and guidelines should address the following topics:

- Data governance
- Data classification
- Document retention and storage
- Disposal

Data Classification A company's documentation can be voluminous, comprising a variety of documents of varying value and importance. Depending on the type of document, the amount of security and types of procedures used in storing and distributing that document can greatly vary. Some documents might be considered public, so they can be posted in a public forum or distributed freely to anyone. Other documents might be highly confidential and contain information that only certain individuals should be allowed to see.

To aid in the document management effort, documents need to be assigned security classifications to indicate their level of confidentiality and then labeled appropriately. Each classification requires different standards and procedures of access, distribution, and storage. The classification also sets a minimum standard of privileges required by a user to access that data. If a user doesn't have the necessary access privileges for that classification of data, the user won't be able to access it. Typically, access is delineated using subjective levels such as high, medium, and low. These should be agreed upon by management, based on the data's sensitivity and the damage to the organization if the data is subjected to unauthorized access.

Several levels of classification can be assigned, depending on the type of organization and its activities. A typical company might have only two classifications: private and public. *Private classified documents* are intended only for the internal user of the company and can't be distributed to anyone outside the company. *Public documents*, however, would be available to anyone. Government and military institutions might have several levels of confidentiality, such as Unclassified, Confidential, Secret, Top Secret, and so on. Each level of classification represents the level of severity if that information is leaked. For example, the lowest level (Unclassified) means that the document is not considered confidential or damaging to security and can be more freely distributed (though not necessarily releasable publicly). At the highest level (Top Secret), documents are highly restricted and would be severely damaging to national security if they were to fall into the wrong hands. Each document needs to be assigned a classification depending on the sensitivity of its data, its value to the company, its value to other companies in terms of business competition, the importance of its integrity, and the legal aspects of storing and distributing that data.

EXAM TIP The type of security protections, access controls, data retention, and storage and disposal policies to be used all depend on a document's security classification.

Document Handling, Retention, and Storage Depending on the classification of a document, the procedures and policies for handling and storing that document can be quite different. For example, an organization might incur certain legal liabilities if it doesn't properly store, distribute, or destroy a document containing PII. To ensure proper document management, companies have implemented data retention policies to help reduce the possibility of legal issues.

Certain documents are required by law to be archived, stored, and protected for a prescribed period of time, while others should be disposed of after a certain period. These policies must be created by senior management and the legal department, which can define what retention policies apply to different classifications of documents. The data retention policy needs to be specific to your company's data. It also needs to consider items that could be legally damaging and information that could be damaging to the business if it were lost, leaked, or stolen.

To protect documentation properly, it should be kept offsite at a special document storage facility. In case of a disaster, such as a fire at the company facility, this will ensure that all important documentation is secure and can be recovered.

Document Disposal Document disposal can often be a tricky issue. In some cases, a document needs to be destroyed to avoid future legal or confidentiality ramifications. In other cases, it's illegal to destroy certain documents that are required by law as evidence for court proceedings. Only your company's legal department can decide on retention and disposal policies for documents. Once decided on, these policies need to be communicated to the employees to ensure that sensitive documents are either destroyed or retained as per their classification. Without proper disposal techniques, the organization is susceptible to dumpster diving attacks.

Cross-Reference

More information on dumpster diving is provided in Domain 1, Objective 1.1.

Data Retention Policy

Many companies have been affected legally by archived e-mail or data that offers evidence against them during court proceedings. To prevent legal liabilities, companies have implemented *data retention* policies to help reduce the possibility of legal problems arising from past messaging communications and data.

Data retention policies should apply to electronic information, such as files, e-mails, and instant messages, and traditional paper documentation. Some clashes might occur between data retention policies and backup policies, where certain files are required by law to be archived, while others should be disposed of after a certain period. Only management and the legal department can define which data is covered under either policy. The data retention policy needs to be specific to your organization's information and consider items that could be damaging legally, as well as information that can be damaging to business if lost. In the case of e-mail, the concept of data retention becomes complicated because e-mail can contain file attachments. Part of your policy might require that e-mail be retained for a certain amount of time before deletion, while the policy for actual electronic files could be different.

Hardware Disposal and Data Destruction Policy

Any policies must also include guidance for the disposal of old hardware that might contain data. As the lifetime of computers is very low (three to five years), older equipment is constantly swapped out for newer, faster machines with more capabilities and resources. However, a critical security issue is apparent regarding the proper disposal of these systems. Servers and personal computers are typically returned with their original hard drives, which could contain sensitive and classified data. System administrators must follow a specific policy for the removal and disposal of hardware to ensure that any media containing data is completely erased or overwritten.

For electronic files, this process is more complicated. Merely deleting a file or e-mail from a hard drive doesn't necessarily delete the data. Many operating systems use a special recovery method that enables you to recover deleted files easily. When a file is deleted, only the locator for the file in the hard drive directory has been removed; the data itself usually still exists in its original location. To ensure complete destruction of data on magnetic media such as hard drives, the media should be overwritten or the drive physically destroyed. Many "shredder" utilities are available that can overwrite the contents of a hard drive with random data to ensure that any information on the drive is unrecoverable. Also, many high-security organizations, such as the military and national security agencies, opt to destroy the drives physically instead of using a shredding application.

Cross-Reference

Secure data destruction is described in greater detail in Domain 2, Objective 2.7.

IT Documentation Policies

Beyond standard company documents, such as policies, procedures, guidelines, and training manuals, some specialized document sets require unique policies regarding security and storage. Network architecture diagrams, change logs, and system logs and inventories are all documents created and managed specifically by the company's IT department. Because these documents can contain specific information on system and network devices such as logs, audit trails, network addresses, and configuration data, they are usually accessible only by authorized persons within the IT department and aren't accessible by other employees in the company.

Systems Architecture The IT department should always have current diagrams of your overall company network architecture on hand. When troubleshooting network problems or security issues, engineers who have network diagrams are ready to identify devices and overall data flow within the company's network.

A variety of diagrams is needed to show different aspects of the architecture. Overall diagrams should be general and show the company network. These diagrams should indicate offices only by name, with wide area network (WAN) links in between them for companies that have geographically distant offices. More detailed diagrams can be made of the internal network structure, showing all the routers, switches, firewalls, hubs, printers, and servers.

Each device should be clearly labeled with identifying information, such as the system name and the network address. Including end-user workstations on systems architecture diagrams is rare because in many organizations the number of workstations is so large that it would be difficult to include all of them on a single diagram. The general network used by the end users should be indicated, however.

As a security precaution, network diagrams generally shouldn't be published, because the information can be used maliciously by a hacker to give him a roadmap of the company's network, including the IP addresses of the most critical network devices and servers. Network architecture diagrams should be accessed only by authorized individuals from the IT department. Printouts of diagrams should never be posted in public places, such as on a notice board or even in the office of the network administrator. The diagram could be easily stolen, or a person could use a digital camera to quickly take a picture of it for later use.

EXAM TIP System architecture diagrams should never be displayed or stored in a public area, especially if they contain system IP addresses and other information hackers can use to compromise a network.

Logs and Inventories General application logs, audit logs, maintenance logs, and equipment inventory documentation are also important documents within an IT department. Most of this documentation is related to the maintenance and operation of the company's computer equipment, but certain logs, such as system activity logs, should be carefully archived and preserved as evidence in case of a security compromise.

System and audit logs provide snapshots of what's happening on a system at a specific point in time. These logs need to be retained for auditing in case of a security compromise. For example, the hacking of a certain server could have gone unnoticed for a long period of time. But if the logs of that system are retained and archived, they can be audited to reveal when the compromise began and how it happened. To ensure the company's backup procedures and policies are being followed, the IT department might have to retain and store copies of backup application logs, which indicate when certain data was backed up and where it's now stored. Inventories of computer equipment enable the company to keep track of its assets and know where they're located. Maintenance logs also provide important evidence for service and warranty claims.

User Behavior Policies

Beyond security awareness training, organizations must enact several policies based on best practices that users should adhere to during their day-to-day activities within the office. Security is an ongoing practice, and concepts learned in awareness training must be enacted within the office to make them effective. The following sections describe several interoffice security practices that should be followed by an organization's users.

Credential Policies

Strong credential policies should be implemented by an organization and followed by all employees in the organization. Credential policies ensure that all network administrators and users are aware of the rules and procedures in place for managing the user accounts and passwords that allow access to company resources. Credential policies should be part of the company's overall security policy.

Typically, users create passwords that are easy to remember—such as the names of family members or pets, phone numbers, and birth dates, all of which can be easily discovered by someone who knows the user, or even by a stranger who, through simple social engineering, asks the user only a few questions about her personal life or discovers the answers via social media. Other types of passwords that aren't secure are those based on any word found in the dictionary. Many password-cracking programs based on dictionary attacks are available that can find out any password in a short amount of time if it's based on a common dictionary word.

A policy establishing the minimum length of passwords should be enforced for all employees. This prevents users from using easy-to-guess passwords of only a few characters in length. The recommended minimum password length is 8 characters, with 10–12 characters being ideal (15 for an administrative or root account.) Password complexity must be part of your password policies to ensure that the password is not easy to guess (such as a dictionary word) and does not contain information specific to the user (such as a birth date). Passwords should contain a mix of uppercase and lowercase characters, numbers, and symbols, and they should not be based on any word that can be found in a dictionary.

Most login and password authentication systems can remember a user's last five to ten passwords (password history) and can prevent the user from using the same one repeatedly. If this option is available, it should be enabled so a user's password will always be different. Also, the longer a password has been in existence, the easier it is to discover eventually, simply by narrowing the options over time. Forcing users to change their passwords regularly (password aging) prevents the discovery of a password through brute-force attacks.

EXAM TIP Different types of accounts should have different credential policies. In addition to credential policies for personnel, don't forget to consider credential policies for third parties who have access to systems (such as vendors for maintenance), device accounts, service accounts, and administrative/root accounts. Not all accounts are the same!

Clean Desk Space Policy

Users should be aware of the risk of leaving confidential papers, sticky notes with sensitive information, cell phones, portable devices, and removable media on or near their desks unattended. These items can be quickly stolen or copied while a user is away from his desk. A clean desk space policy maintains that any such items should be always kept in locked drawers. Users also should never write down login credentials and leave them on their desk or stuck on the front of their monitor, where they can be easily found by other unauthorized users. Whiteboards or drawings should be wiped clean or removed after they are used to prevent leaving confidential information on the board for passersby to view.

Personally Owned Devices

Users might bring a variety of personally owned devices, such as laptops, USB keys and drives, cameras, and other peripherals, into the workplace. To protect organizational security, your company must have a defined security policy in place that spells out the types of personally owned devices that are allowed in the workplace and the conditions under which they may be used. For example, you may have a policy in place (and enforced through technological controls) that allows personal laptops but prevents them from connecting to a corporate wired or wireless network unless a full virus scan is performed. Smartphones that can access corporate messaging servers should be protected with a password so that if a user ever loses her personal phone, an unauthorized user cannot access her company e-mail account. These security controls ensure that all devices have a minimum standard of security before they can connect to company resources and access data.

In very high-security environments, personal devices, especially cameras and smartphones with cameras, are banned and must be turned in to security personnel before entrance into the facility.

Workstation Locking and Access Tailgating

Users must ensure that they lock and password-protect their workstation sessions whenever they are away from their desk. If a user leaves his current computer session still logged in to the network, any passerby can "tailgate" onto his privileges and access confidential data, e-mail messages, and shared network resources. Network-wide policies implemented by the network administrator should automatically make sure workstations lock after a specified period of inactivity, such as ten minutes, but even that is enough time for a malicious user to find what she needs on an unprotected workstation.

Data Handling

Users should be aware of the classification of the data they are working with and should be properly trained on how to handle that data. Data that is highly sensitive likely requires special procedures for dissemination and destruction, and it is the responsibility of the users to follow organizational policies. If this is not done properly, an incident could occur. Data-handling policies and procedures should cover items such as access, use, transmission, storage, and disposal of data, based on its sensitivity and classification. Examples of data handling that a policy might address include who has permissions to be able to print a sensitive document or even transport one from one company location to another.

Instant Messaging

One of the most popular Internet services is *instant messaging (IM)*, which allows users to send real-time messages to each other via their PCs. Web links, files, and other types of multimedia can also be exchanged between IM users.

Whereas e-mail messages can be protected by authentication and encryption tools, IM applications reside on a user's hard drive and are usually not protected by a firewall by default. This issue is even more critical in corporate environments, where IM programs used by employees make the corporate network vulnerable to attack because these programs are often not part of a company's traditional network security plan. To prevent users from using IM in the workplace, the administrator can configure the firewall to block specific IM ports. In certain cases, it may be necessary to allow IM within the company network but not allow it to connect to clients outside of the network.

IM can be used to send files to another user, and the same risks associated with attachments exist, such as receiving virus-infected files. When receiving a message with an option to download a file, the user must always establish the identity of the sender before replying or downloading the file. The best practice is simply to ignore the message unless the user has no doubt about its origin. Some IM programs enable the user to create a list of senders whose messages will be automatically rejected. This is helpful if the unknown sender continues to send messages to the user even after being ignored the first time. Of course, an antivirus scanner should always be running on the system to protect against any type of virus, spyware, or other malware in downloaded files.

Social Networking/Media

With the massive increase in social media use, security administrators are beset with many new avenues of risk within their organization. The same security risks that affect other communications media, such as e-mail, Web, IM, and P2P, are also inherent in social media applications such as Facebook, Twitter, and LinkedIn; however, phishing and the spread of malware can be more prevalent in social media because most malicious links are spread by trusted users on the social network. When one person's social media application is infected with malware, it can quickly spread to other users as automatic messages are sent from the victim's computer to all her social media contacts. These types of social engineering attacks are very effective.

To provide a strong layer of security, many organizations include social media applications with other restricted applications such as instant messaging and P2P apps and block their use on the network. If an organization has a policy that allows users to access social media sites, the organization should require social engineering awareness training to educate users on the risks and types of behavior to look out for when using social media.

Compliance with Laws, Regulations, Best Practices, and Standards

In the end, how an organization performs regarding compliance with applicable laws, regulations, best practices, and standards must often be tracked and reported to appropriate governing bodies. In some sectors, this is simply the security staff that is responsible for tracking and reporting compliance to company leadership. In others, detailed reports must be released to government bodies charged with oversight. Noncompliance can mean fines, legal action, censure, or, in the worst case, dissolution of the department or entire organization.

To prevent noncompliance and avoid penalties, it is important to have a very comprehensive understanding of what laws, regulations, best practices, and standards your organization is mandated to adhere to. Metrics should be developed to track the compliance with those requirements, and swift action must be taken to remediate any issues that seem probable. Consistent enforcement of those actions, from training to personnel dismissal, will facilitate a more positive security culture and improve compliance.

NOTE The previous objective, 5.2, discussed different regulations and frameworks. Be sure to know the specific guidance documents your organization is required to adhere to, if any. Remember that one size does *not* fit all!

Change Management Policies

Change management policies are official company procedures used to identify, control, and communicate current or forthcoming changes to some aspect of the company's networks and communications services. For example, the IT department might issue a change control document to all employees to notify them of a network outage that will be occurring to perform an upgrade to networking equipment or that an application will be down for several hours for a software upgrade. More detailed change control communications describe longer-term outages for specific technical changes to the company's systems or network infrastructure, such as taking down part of the network for a weekend for router and switch upgrades.

Tracking, controlling, and communicating outages and changes to your network infrastructure, assets, and applications are important to keep all departments in your organization up to date with IT maintenance activities to prevent accidental loss of data and services. For security reasons, this activity also ensures that any unplanned changes or outages are quickly detected and investigated. System and network changes without prior knowledge or approval of management and the IT department could indicate a hacker or an intruder has compromised the network.

Incident Response Policy

Incident management and response should be part of a company's overall security policy. In the event of some form of security incident—be it physical intrusion, network attack, or equipment theft and vandalism—some form of procedure should be in place to deal with the incident as it happens. Without any clear directives, the aftermath of a security breach can cause even more damage if employees don't know how to handle an incident properly. A clearly defined incident response policy can help contain a problem and provide quick recovery to normal operations.

The incident response policy should cover each type of compromised security scenario and list the procedures to follow if it happens. For example, in the case of a hacked server, procedures might be in place to deal with removing the server from the network, shutting down related network servers and services, and preserving evidence, such as audit trails and logs. The incident response policy should cover the following areas:

- Contact information for emergency services and other outside resources
- Methods of securing and preserving evidence of a security breach
- Scenario-based procedures of what to do with computer and network equipment, depending on the security problem
- How to document the problem and the evidence properly

Cross-Reference

Incident response is described in greater detail in Domain 4, Objective 4.2.

Third-Party Risk Management

Third-party risk is often managed through interoperability agreements, which differ in content and context but typically have one tie that binds: they are designed to lay out the terms of agreement between two different entities—be they two internal entities (e.g., different departments or divisions) or an internal entity and an external entity (e.g., vendors, managed service providers)—who are working toward a mutual goal. Interoperability agreements are typically legally enforceable agreements that cover responsibilities both parties have toward each other in terms of service, data protection, and use, and may even allow access to each other's confidential or proprietary information. In some cases, these agreements may even allow access to customer or privacy data, so it's important to ensure adequate security protections are included in these agreements. The following are other areas to consider:

- Onboarding and offboarding business partners at the *end of service (EOS)* or equipment *end of service life (EOSL)*; that is, how you deal with creating and removing business partner accounts from your systems when those conditions are met
- How your organizations will choose to handle official and unofficial interaction with social networks
- How success (or failure) will be measured and how those measurements will be calibrated to be sure that there are no arguments; otherwise known as *measurement systems analysis (MSA)*
- The level of assessment and metrics associated with the supporting supply chain of suppliers and vendors (which can also bring risk to your organization)

Putting these terms in writing might seem laborious and time consuming, but delineating expectations at the beginning can save serious time and money if an incident is prevented.

Service Level Agreements

A *service level agreement (SLA)* is an understanding among a supplier of services and the users of those services that the service in question will be available for a certain percentage of time. For example, a web-hosting company could have an SLA that states the web servers that host the customer's web pages will be available 99.8 percent of the time. The SLA might specify that if the service level drops below this percentage, the customer will be reimbursed for business lost during the downtime.

The SLA policy refers to a service provider's internal SLA policy for meeting its SLA obligations to customers, including the services performed to preserve the SLA uptime and the contingency plans and communications that must be performed if the availability of the organization's services exceeds the thresholds agreed to in the SLA.

Business Partnership Agreements

A *business partnership agreement (BPA)* describes how a new business will be established among partners. In general, there are three types of BPA arrangements:

- **General partnerships** *General partnerships* are devised under the assumption that all profits and liabilities will be divided equally among the business partners. To this end, all management decisions, large or small, are generally divided among those same partners equally. If this is not the case, it should be noted within the BPA.
- **Limited partnerships** A *limited partnership* is similar but more complex than a general partnership, in that it allows partners to have limited liability and corresponding input based on the investment percentage.
- **Joint ventures** *Joint ventures* begin in the same way as a general partnership but have a shorter time frame, often for a single project. If the partnership is to continue past that defined point, a general or limited partnership must be filed.

Memorandums of Agreement/Understanding

Memorandums of agreement and understanding (MOA/MOU) are common within the government sector and relate terms of cooperation between two organizations seeking a common goal, such as a joint continuity of operations site. As well, MOUs/MOAs are often used internally between different divisions or departments within an organization, especially large ones. These documents detail the distinct roles and responsibilities of both parties and are generally signed by a high-ranking staff member. These documents are often high level in nature and are often accompanied by more technical documentation, such as an interconnection security agreement.

REVIEW

Objective 5.3: Explain the importance of policies to organizational security There are a variety of policies that should be adopted within an organization to ensure governance and accountability. Personnel policies include such policies as the acceptable use policy, clean desk space policy, and nondisclosure agreements. An acceptable use policy is a set of established guidelines for the appropriate use of computer networks and equipment. A specific separation of duties ensures that a single individual isn't tasked with both high-security and high-risk responsibilities. Users should have only the access rights they need to perform their job functions. The employee termination process includes securing the work area, returning identification and company equipment, and suspending computer accounts. The company practices due care by taking responsibility for all activities that take place in corporate facilities. The company practices due diligence by implementing and maintaining these security procedures consistently and effectively to protect the company's facilities, assets, and employees.

Third-party policies such as interconnection agreements between two or more parties detail the roles and responsibilities between organizations to manage the risk that the respective organizations bring to the table. An SLA is an understanding between a supplier of services and the users of those services that the service in question will be available for a certain percentage of time. A BPA describes how a new business will be established among partners. An ISA details a technical framework in which two information systems will connect securely.

Ensuring that user training covers a variety of techniques, such as gamification and capture the flag events, will help keep the training interesting. Further, it is critical that the training be tailored both to the role and the organization's context.

5.3 QUESTIONS

1. After a few incidents where customer data was transmitted to a third party, your organization is required to create and adhere to a policy that describes the distribution, protection, and confidentiality of customer data. Which of the following policies should your organization create?
   - **A.** Privacy
   - **B.** Due care
   - **C.** Acceptable use
   - **D.** Service level agreement
2. As a managed service provider responsible for Internet-based application services across several external clients, which of the following policies does your organization provide to clients as an agreement for service uptime?
   - **A.** Code of ethics
   - **B.** Privacy
   - **C.** SLA
   - **D.** Due care
3. There is a suspicion that Tom, a systems administrator, is performing illegal activities on your company's networks. To gather evidence about his activities, which of the following principles and techniques could you employ?
   - **A.** Password rotation
   - **B.** Mandatory vacation
   - **C.** Need-to-know
   - **D.** Separation of duties

4. You need to create an overall policy for your organization that describes how your users can properly make use of company communications services, such as web browsing, e-mail, and File Transfer Protocol (FTP) services. Which of the following policies should you implement?
   A. Acceptable use policy
   B. Due care
   C. Privacy policy
   D. Service level agreement

5.3 ANSWERS

1. **A** A privacy policy concerns the protection and distribution of private customer data. Any company, especially one engaged in online activities or e-commerce, has a responsibility to adopt and implement a policy for protecting the privacy of individually identifiable information.
2. **C** A service level agreement (SLA) is an understanding between a supplier of services and the clients of those services that the service in question will be available for a specific percentage of time. In this case, your company might guarantee clients a 99.5 percent uptime of communications services.
3. **B** When Tom is forced to take a vacation, his activities can be audited, and any suspicious behavior will be more likely to be noticed and detected because he is not there to prevent its discovery. You may also discover that the illegal activities completely cease while the user is away and then resume when he returns.
4. **A** An acceptable use policy (AUP) establishes rules for the appropriate use of computer networks within your organization. The policy describes the terms, conditions, and rules of using the Internet and its various services within the company's networks.

Objective 5.4 Summarize risk management processes and concepts

Risk management is the act of identifying, assessing, and reducing the risk of issues that can impact your organization's operations and assets. These risks can be the more technical types, such as hackers and insider threats, that are often associated with cybersecurity. However, there are other risks that must be considered to have a well-rounded risk management program. This objective discusses the different types of risks, strategies to manage them, and various documents that can be used to identify, prioritize, and plan for disasters and other negative scenarios.

Understanding and Managing Risk

Risk can be classified as internal or external:

- *Internal risk* comes from elements within the organization's control, such as organizational structure, resources (personnel, time, money, equipment, and so on), the use of legacy systems, compliance, the use of third parties, and business goals and strategy.
- *External risk* is usually the type of risk that the organization has limited control over. Examples of external risk factors include the stock market, government regulation, currency valuation, national and international events, risks that third parties present when partnering, and natural disasters. Although the organization can't control these factors, it must plan for them and develop strategies to mitigate external risk.

Some risks, such as theft of intellectual property, use of third-party partners and vendors, and software compliance and licensing, have elements of both internal risk ("How are we protecting ourselves?") and external risk ("What risks do third parties present?").

To protect their assets, employees, and customers from security risks, organizations must analyze their security practices to identify the threats to their operations and protect themselves in the most cost-efficient way. Risks to your organization must be assessed based on their probability and impact (both quantitative and qualitative), and then security measures or metrics should be implemented based on this risk assessment.

Risk Assessment

Risk assessment and mitigation deal with identifying, assessing, and reducing the risk of security breaches against company assets. By assessing the probability of a risk and estimating the amount of damage that could be caused as a result, you can take steps to reduce the level of that risk.

Suppose, for example, that your company file server contains confidential company data. The file server asset is considered extremely valuable to the company, its clients, and its competitors. In this case, a considerable amount of financial damage may be incurred by the company in the event of server loss, damage, or intrusion. The risks and threats posed to the server could be physical (such as damage caused by a natural disaster or a hardware malfunction) or nonphysical (such as viruses, network hacker attacks, and data theft if the server is easily accessible through a network). The costs associated with reducing these risks are mitigated by the potential costs of losing data on the file server.

To help reduce these risks, you can take several actions:

- Use multiple hard drives and power supplies for fault tolerance.
- Implement a good backup scheme.
- Protect the server through physical security, such as door access controls.

- Install antivirus software.
- Disable unused network services and ports to prevent network attacks.

To identify the risks that pose a security threat to your company, you can perform a risk analysis on all parts of the company's resources and activities. By identifying risks and the amount of damage that could be caused by exploiting a system vulnerability, you can choose the most efficient methods for securing the system from those risks. Risk assessment can identify where too little or even too much security exists and where the cost of security is more than the cost of the loss due to compromise. Ultimately, risk assessment is a cost/benefit analysis of your security infrastructure.

Risk assessments involve four main phases:

- **Asset identification** Identify and quantify the company's assets
- **Risk analysis** Determine possible security vulnerabilities and threats
- **Determine risk likelihood and impact** Rate your various risks according to how likely they are to occur and their impact
- **Identify cost of solutions** Identify a cost-effective solution to protect assets

EXAM TIP Often you will see the terms "assessment" and "analysis" used interchangeably; however, an analysis is part of an assessment, which contains the analysis of different risk factors, their severity if realized, and proposed solutions to reduce risk.

Asset Identification

Company assets include physical items, such as computer and networking equipment, and nonphysical items, such as valuable data. *Asset identification* involves identifying both types of assets and determining *asset value*. Asset values must be established beyond the mere capital costs; a true asset valuation should consider several factors, including the following:

- **The cost to repair the asset versus replacing the asset outright** Often, repairing the asset may be less expensive in the short run, but the cost of the different components required to conduct a repair should be considered. It's important to remember that repairing the asset might only be a temporary solution—a costly one in the long run.
- **The depreciation value of the asset over time** This might reduce the amount of capital available to make a repair-or-replace decision.
- **The amount of revenue generated by the asset** If replacing the asset costs $10,000 and that asset generates $2000 worth of revenue daily based on its function, the loss of that asset ($10,000) has to be considered along with the loss of its revenue ($2000 daily), and that contributes to the total asset valuation and quite quickly begins adding up.

- **The value of the asset to a competitor** This is harder to quantify but should be considered if applicable. For example, a list of a company's clients can be easily re-created from backup if the original is lost or destroyed, but if the list finds its way into the hands of a competitor, the resulting financial damage could be devastating.
- **The exposure factor (percentage of the asset that could be lost during an event)** In many cases, negative events do not render the asset completely unusable. For example, a server could experience degradation in its ability to effectively host a web application but not be completely offline and unavailable. Calculating the exposure factor allows you to better determine how much loss your organization can bear during an event, which in turn allows for you to better understand how much money, time, or other supporting resources should be devoted to repairing or replacing an asset. Generally, exposure factors are expressed in decimal format and relate to the percentage loss associated with the exposure. For example, a 50 percent loss would be 0.5, with a total loss being expressed as 1.

As you can see, understanding the asset value is much more complicated than the list price of the asset itself, and ultimately the value and the criticality of the assets you're trying to protect drive the costs involved in securing that asset. Also keep in mind that some assets are more difficult to place value on because it may not be the cost of replacement that you're concerned about, but instead, the capability that is lost (e.g., a machine that can only perform at half speed). That can be difficult to quantify.

Risk Analysis

To identify the critical risks that pose a security threat to your company, you can perform a *risk analysis* on all parts of the company's resources and activities. By determining the probability of a risk and estimating the amount of damage that could be caused as a result, you can take steps to reduce the level of that risk. There are two generally accepted ways to perform a risk analysis: qualitative and quantitative.

Quantitative risk analysis is a numerical calculation of the exact cost of the loss of a specific company asset because of a disaster. This is a straightforward method that can be applied for simple situations. For example, if a hard drive in a RAID (redundant array of independent disks) system fails, the hard drive is simply replaced with a new hard drive. There is no loss of data because the information is rebuilt from the rest of the array.

Qualitative risk analysis considers tangible and intangible factors in determining costs. Consider a denial-of-service network attack on your company's web store server that causes four hours of downtime and corrupted data on a back-end transactional database. Your company faces not only the monetary loss from its website being down and customers not being able to order products for many hours but also the time it takes to perform countermeasures against the attack, get its web server back into operation, recover any lost data from its database, and identify data that cannot be recovered. The costs in this scenario include the personnel hours in recovering from the attack, the loss of orders from the web store during the downtime, monetary loss from corrupted data that cannot be restored, and even potential loss of future business from disgruntled customers.

EXAM TIP Quantitative risk analysis is a dollar-amount calculation of the exact cost of a loss due to disaster. Qualitative risk analysis includes intangible factors, such as loss of potential business, in determining costs. Quantitative risk analysis relies on exact data, whereas qualitative risk analysis is more subjective and relies on opinion and experience.

Risks regarding virtualization technology and cloud computing are often ignored in a risk analysis. Using virtualization technology, a computer can host multiple instances of an operating system environment, all running from the same computer on the same hardware. The consolidation of many different types of services on the same hardware creates a security risk known as a *single point of failure*, because if that system is hacked or fails, every virtualized server that runs on the system is affected also.

The risk of a single point of failure for cloud computing is very similar. Cloud computing aggregates services in a virtual environment where all aspects of the cloud—from the platform, to the software, to the entire infrastructure—are based on a distributed web service. If the cloud service fails, you may lose all access to your services and data until the cloud service is restored.

Other concepts that should be considered when analyzing risk are the following:

- **Regulations** Any regulation that might affect the risk posture.
- **Risk awareness** *Risk awareness* is the current awareness of the risks associated with an organization, both internal and external. This awareness may be quite low when conducting an initial risk analysis.
- **Risk tolerance** The *risk tolerance* is the amount of risk that's acceptable to an organization.
- **Risk appetite** *Risk appetite* is the level of risk that an organization is willing to take before actions are taken to reduce risk. Understanding an organization's risk appetite will help guide solutions and countermeasure recommendations.
- **Inherent risk** The *inherent risk* of an organization is the untreated risk, or the level of risk before any controls have been put into place to mitigate or counter risk.
- **Control risk** *Control risk* occurs when internal controls either fail to reduce risk or misstate the amount of risk that is present or being mitigated. Control risk assumes that control effectiveness weakens over time.
- **Residual risk** The *residual risk* is the level of risk that remains after controls are put into place to mitigate or reduce risk. It is important to remember that you can never entirely eliminate risk; there will always be a level of residual risk.

Overall, your risk assessment must be wide in scope to use both quantitative and qualitative risk analyses to determine your risk factors from all aspects of your company's operations. Frequently you will find that you may use a combination of these two risk analysis methods; an example would be a semiquantitative analysis, which is essentially a qualitative analysis which uses refined numerical data.

Risk Likelihood and Impact

As part of your risk assessment and mitigation strategy, you need to rate your organization's various risks according to their likelihood of occurrence and their potential impact. The risks more likely to occur and have the highest level of potential impact are ranked toward the top of the list to indicate where solution efforts should be most concentrated. For example, for a company that already practices strict physical security and access control methods, the priority of risk could be geared toward nonphysical threats, such as viruses and network hackers, because this would have a greater impact on the company's ability to operate. This is often depicted in a *risk matrix* format, as shown in Figure 5.4-1, from NIST SP 800-30, Rev. 1.

Another example of how risks are depicted visually is the *heat map*, an example of which is shown in Figure 5.4-2. Heat maps can be helpful to quickly display the most urgent risks (red) versus less urgent risks (green) when working with decision makers; however, it can be difficult to explain how risks materially differ (how an orange risk is fundamentally different than a yellow risk, for example).

The *likelihood* and *impact* of a risk occurrence have a strong measure on your cost analysis for budgeting funds for risk countermeasures and mitigation. A calculation used to determine this factor is *annualized loss expectancy (ALE)*. You must calculate the chance of a risk occurring, sometimes expressed for convenience as a yearly number and called the *annualized rate of occurrence (ARO)*, and the potential loss of revenue based on a specific period of downtime, which is called the *single loss expectancy (SLE)*. By multiplying these factors together, you arrive at the ALE. This is how much money you expect your organization to lose on an annual basis because of the impact of an occurrence of a specific risk, ideally derived using actual

Likelihood (Threat Event Occurs and Results in Adverse Impact)	**Level of Impact**				
	Very Low	**Low**	**Moderate**	**High**	**Very High**
Very High	Very Low	Low	Moderate	High	Very High
High	Very Low	Low	Moderate	High	Very High
Moderate	Very Low	Low	Moderate	Moderate	High
Low	Very Low	Low	Low	Low	Moderate
Very Low	Very Low	Very Low	Very Low	Low	Low

FIGURE 5.4-1 Example risk matrix, from NIST SP 800-30, Rev. 1

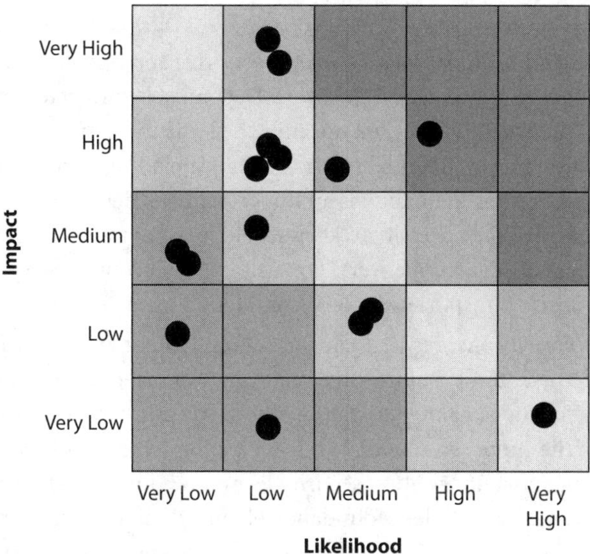

FIGURE 5.4-2 Example heat map, from RiskLens

historical or trend data. Using the ALE, you can properly budget the security measures to help protect against that risk if it occurs.

As an example of calculating ALE, if a file server has a historical precedence of being infected by a virus once every five years, its ARO is 0.20. During the time the file server is down and data is being recovered, none of your employees can work. For a downtime of two hours, you calculate $8000 of lost time and productivity. By multiplying these two factors (0.20 and $8000), you get an ALE value of $1600. You can use this amount to budget for additional antivirus software protection to help lower this risk and save money in your next annual budget.

EXAM TIP The annualized loss expectancy (ALE) is calculated by multiplying the annualized rate of occurrence (ARO) by the single loss expectancy (SLE).

Risk Control Assessment

When assessing the efficacy of current and future risk controls, the following major concepts of information security are paramount to assess. Note that these concepts run throughout most, if not all, of the objectives covered in this book. It is important that you consider how you would apply these concepts within any context; for example, some organizations, such as government agencies, value confidentiality most highly, while many commercial organizations live or die by availability.

- **Confidentiality** *Confidentiality* prevents sensitive and private data from being intercepted or read by unauthorized users. Data must be protected in its primary storage location, when it is backed up, and when it is transmitted to another user over a network. Ensuring confidentiality often entails including encryption and access control measures. Confidentiality is an important consideration when assessing risk controls because of the necessity to keep sensitive data protected in the event of a disaster and its subsequent recovery. For example, you could encrypt backup tapes for storage and offsite transport to enforce confidentiality during recovery operations.
- **Integrity** *Integrity* ensures that your data is consistent and never modified by unauthorized persons or manipulated in any intentional or accidental manner. Integrity also includes *nonrepudiation* methods to ensure information can be trusted from the supposed sender. While data integrity includes the use of proper authentication and authorization security techniques for protecting against data manipulation, it also includes redundancy planning and fault-tolerant systems that protect data from corruption. Common methods of ensuring integrity are hashing, digital signatures, and certificates. To facilitate efficient and effective recovery, you should ensure the data integrity of backup media through regular testing and validation procedures. In the event of an emergency restoration, you should be able to trust that the data is exactly what is expected.

Cross-Reference

Nonrepudiation is described in more detail in Domain 2, Objective 2.8.

- **Availability** *Availability* ensures that your systems and networks are always operational and providing service to users, minimizing downtime when patching or scanning. Your organization's networks and data must be available to authorized users as required with a minimal amount of interruption. Your disaster recovery and business continuity plans make sure, using redundancy and fault tolerance, that interruptions do not happen and that if there is downtime, it can be resolved very quickly. When considering controls to reduce risk, for example, availability might be ensured through the implementation of a cold, warm, or hot site, or a site-sharing agreement with an alternate organization.
- **Safety** *Safety* first ensures that personnel will be safe, and then that organizational priorities (as listed within disaster recovery and associated plans) will be carried out. Safety considerations often coincide with physical controls such as fencing, lighting, locks, and closed-circuit televisions (CCTV). Documentation contributing to personnel safety includes escape plans and escape routes. Finally, testing should include regular drills and controls testing. Safety in a disaster situation is paramount and can be implemented through fail-safe measures such as doors opening outward for easier personnel rescue and using safer fire suppression methods, such as water.

Solutions and Countermeasures

After you've assessed and defined risk and management procedures, you'll have collected the following information:

- **Asset identification** A list of your assets (and their criticality to the organization), including physical assets (such as server hardware and hard disks) and nonphysical assets (such as the valuable customer data stored on the hard drives).
- **Threat profiles** A list of every possible threat against your assets.
- **Risks** An evaluation of the potential risk of each threat—such as the risk of a malicious hacker being able to compromise a database server. If the database server itself is compromised and the hacker leaks the valuable and confidential data on the database server, the impact on the business is substantial, so the risk is far greater for this asset.
- **Impact** The potential loss in the event your assets are attacked or compromised by threats, including the assets' capital value (such as hardware cost), plus how much it will cost to replace those assets, especially lost customer data. A failed hard drive can be a relatively low cost to recoup, but if you have no backup of the customer data stored on that hard drive, you might have lost tens of thousands of dollars' worth of data.
- **Likelihood** How likely the event is to occur. The risks that are more likely to occur are ranked toward the top of the list to indicate where solution efforts should be most concentrated. For example, within a company that already practices strict physical security and access control methods, the priority of risk scenarios could be geared toward nonphysical threats, such as viruses and network hackers.

Once this process is complete, a list of solutions and countermeasures to protect against each threat should be reviewed and documented. Examine your solutions for what current security measures are in place and what needs to be done to make them more effective. Ensure that the functionality and effectiveness of the solutions are sufficient to reduce the risk of compromise. Purchasing a fire extinguisher for the server room could seem like a fire-prevention solution, for example, but only an automatic fire detection and suppression system can fully protect a room full of servers from a large, out-of-control fire that occurs in the middle of the night. Similarly, buying a firewall to protect your servers from outside Internet traffic is a great idea for network security, but if the network administrator hasn't been trained to configure it properly, the firewall might not be effective at all.

Any solutions must be cost-effective to ensure that the benefits are in line with the actual value of the assets. For example, there's no point in spending $100,000 on a security solution to protect data that's worth only $40,000 to the company if it's lost or damaged. Ongoing maintenance also needs to be factored into the final calculations. Although a large initial cost is incurred for a tape backup solution, the costs of purchasing new tapes as they're needed will be ongoing, and you'll have to pay for offsite storage of used tapes. Again, it is important to consider the security goals of the organization (confidentiality versus availability, for example) before expending resources.

EXAM TIP The cost of the risk management solution shouldn't exceed the value of the asset if it's lost. For example, if a file server and its data are valued at $35,000 and the proposed security solution to protect it costs $150,000, then implementing the proposed solution doesn't make sense.

Risk Register

A *risk register* is a living document used to track different types of data elements, most commonly risk factors and risk scenarios. It might also include data that describes different technical or management findings contributing to the risk. Additionally, threats, vulnerabilities, assets, likelihood, and impact data can be included in the risk register. For example, a risk register might include the following items:

- Risk factors
- Threat agents, threats, and vulnerabilities
- Risk scenarios
- Criticality, severity, or priority of risk
- Asset information
- Impact of the risk on an asset
- Likelihood of the threat exploiting the vulnerability
- Status of risk response actions
- Resources that may be committed to responding to risk
- Risk ownership information
- Planned milestones toward the risk response

Risk Management Strategies

When you have completed your risk analysis, and depending on your operations and budgets, you have several options for dealing with each risk:

- **Avoidance** Depending on the type of risk, you can opt to avoid the risk altogether. This option is typically used when the cost to mitigate a threat, especially a threat that is likely to occur and have significant impact, is higher than the value of engaging in the risky activity that is being avoided. This can also mean you take certain steps to avoid risk altogether, such as not investing in a promising company that has a great deal of risk (often this is determined during a corporate due diligence assessment, for example).
- **Transference** The organization can also transfer, or "pass on," the risk to a third party—for example, to a company offering *cybersecurity insurance* that will pay for damages incurred by the organization in the event that a certain risk is realized, or to a third-party provider that can store the organization's backup media offsite and guarantee its security and availability.

- **Acceptance** In most cases in information security, a certain level of risk must be accepted with any type of information system network. For example, your organization may want to sell its products directly from its website, and the potential revenues greatly outweigh the potential network security risks involved. On the other hand, if the risk is deemed too great in comparison to the benefit, the service might not be offered, or additional mitigation techniques might be required. Organizations also accept whatever residual risk remains after all other possible mitigation strategies have been applied.
- **Mitigation** Based on your risk analysis, specific risks must be mitigated using countermeasures—for example, implementing a network firewall for network security, installing desktop and server antivirus protection, and implementing fault-tolerant systems to mitigate the impact of failed hardware.

Types of Disasters

Many types of events can befall a company. Many are small and inconvenient, affecting only a certain part of the company or only one network server. They might affect only communications or software applications. Larger events, such as disasters, can be devastating, causing the destruction of most or all the company's physical facility. Disasters can be initiated externally to the organization (such as an environmental disaster) or internally (such as a employee who initiates a person-made disaster). This section goes into more detail on those different types of disaster scenarios that can affect an organization's operations.

Environmental

The types of environmental, otherwise known as natural, disasters that can occur depend on the location of the company facilities; natural disasters can be the most devastating emergency to affect a business. You must be aware of the types of natural disasters that can happen in your specific geographic area. A fire, flood, earthquake, tornado, or hurricane can destroy your building and its infrastructure within minutes. The only way the company can be truly protected is if its data is regularly backed up and sent to an offsite location. Your company furniture and computer equipment can be replaced relatively quickly, but sensitive company data collected over many years can't.

Person-made

Something as simple as a mistakenly deleted file can cause a company much grief if the data in that file is critical to the business operation. A spilled cup of coffee can render a server unusable within seconds. Human errors and mistakes can be expected and are much more common than natural disasters. Vandalism and sabotage, however, can be quite unexpected but cause great damage. Theft or malicious destruction of company equipment by a disgruntled employee can cause as much damage as any natural disaster. The need for access controls and physical security is emphasized with these types of disasters.

Network and Hacking Attacks

Cyber theft and vandalism are increasingly annoying, expensive, and dangerous problems for companies, especially those whose business is Internet-related. When a company is permanently connected to the Internet, the door is open for unauthorized users to attempt to gain access to company resources. Some malicious hackers simply try to gain access to a system for fun. More-malicious unauthorized users might cause widespread damage to the company's network if they gain access. Some attacks could come from within the network. A security professional needs to analyze threats coming from both outside and inside the network.

Viruses

Computer viruses are special programs able to replicate themselves, and they often perform malicious activities on networks, servers, and personal computers. Viruses can be extremely destructive, causing massive network outages, computer crashes, and corruption or loss of data. Once one computer is infected with the virus, it can quickly spread to other computers and servers on the network. E-mail–based viruses can spread quickly in a short amount of time. Protection against viruses includes the use of special antivirus software at both the personal computer level and the server level, as well as user education about computer virus prevention.

Functional Recovery Plans

Disaster recovery and continuity of operations planning are extremely important in preventing downtime for your organization in the event of equipment or communications failure. Your system's ability to recover from a disaster is greatly dependent on the facilities and equipment available if your main facility is heavily damaged or destroyed.

Although the chances of a large disaster, whatever the cause, interrupting or halting business operations are slim, all companies should be prepared for disastrous events through the development of functional recovery plans. The overall *business continuity plan (BCP)* is a detailed document that provides an initial analysis of the potential risks to the business because of a disaster, an assessment of the site and alternate sites, an analysis of the potential business impact *(BIA)*, a *disaster recovery plan (DRP)* for restoring full operations after a disaster strikes, and a *continuity of operations plan (COOP)* for best continuing operations if disrupted from normal activities by any situation, from a simple outage to an attack. The specific purpose of a disaster recovery plan is to prepare your company with a step-by-step plan to recover your networks and systems. The DRP is a technologically oriented part of the overall business continuity plan, detailing specific steps to take to return and recover systems to an operational state.

The process of creating a business continuity plan includes the following phases:

- Creating a disaster recovery team
- Performing a risk analysis
- Performing a business impact analysis

- Performing a privacy impact assessment
- Creating a disaster recovery plan
- Preparing documentation
- Testing the plan
- After-action reporting

Disaster Recovery Team

A *disaster recovery team* is responsible for creating and executing business continuity activities and a disaster recovery plan that outlines the goals for restoring company operations and functionality as quickly as possible following a disaster. The team is also available to provide for the safety and support of the rest of the company's personnel and the protection of company property.

The team should include members from all departments, including management. Including all areas of the company's operations is important because each department has its own objectives and goals, depending on its function. Disaster recovery duties should be included in the job description of each department, even though these duties go over and above regular duties. Designated backup team members should also be assigned in case an original member isn't available to perform the appropriate function.

In a disaster, each team member is responsible for certain priorities and tasks, which could include coordination of other department personnel and contact with outside emergency agencies and equipment and service vendors. The bulk of the work will be the responsibility of the IT staff, which needs to coordinate the creation of a communications and networking infrastructure, as well as restore all system functionality, including the restoration of lost data.

Site Risk Assessment

As part of your *site risk assessment*, you examine and identify any areas of your operations that stand out as a *single point of failure*. For example, you may realize that although you have several redundant web servers that process customer orders, the back-end database is located on a single server. If that single server were to fail or were damaged in a disaster, your web servers would not be able to connect to the database, causing all customer transactions to halt. Through this process, you identify areas where you can replace single points of failure with redundant and fault-tolerant systems.

Create or obtain diagrams of the facility layout, such as building blueprints, seating plans, network cabling maps, and hardware and software inventories. The effect of each disaster scenario should be more easily ascertained with the aid of these diagrams. When you finish, you'll have a detailed document outlining the possible risks for each type of disaster that might occur. Using this information, you can formulate a business impact analysis that will show how those risks can affect your business functionality.

Business Impact Analysis

A *business impact analysis (BIA)* outlines your organization's most critical functions and how they'll be affected during a disaster. The analysis examines the loss of revenue, legal obligations, and customer service interruption that can arise as the result of a disaster. Your organization's most important business functions should be prioritized so that during the disaster recovery process, they receive the attention they need to become operational before any noncritical aspects of the business. Your organization's leadership must take a hard look at what the *mission essential functions (MEFs)* are, meaning those functions that are the most important to complete. For example, if your company is in the business of logistics, the functions of distribution are more critical than, say, the function of employee morale and wellness. While that may sound harsh, getting the distribution systems up and running after a disaster is more critical than restoring the intranet portal supporting the company's holiday season party.

After you've determined, in rank order, the MEFs, you can then *identify the critical systems* that support those MEFs. This is where you'll need to take a cold, hard look at what is critical to operations and what is just "nice to have." It is extremely useful to have a session with the people doing the work; for example, to use the logistics example again, the folks watching shipments move from point A to point B are the ones who know intimately how they do their jobs and how long they could get by without their systems. Don't make the mistake of asking the IT folks how much money they've spent on different systems and using that as your prioritization schema! The on-the-ground truth from the operational personnel will give you the most reliable information for your prioritization.

EXAM TIP Critical business functions and their associated systems must be prioritized so that in case of a disaster, they'll be made operational before other less-critical functions and systems.

The business impact analysis should also include timelines estimating how long it will take to get the company operational again if a disaster occurs. The resources, equipment, and personnel required should be carefully detailed—especially the ability to recover and restore vital company information from backups.

Most important in the BIA will be examining the total financial loss incurred through certain types of disasters. This isn't only the cost of lost equipment; it's the totality of the loss of life, other property, productivity, and reputation, as well as any injury. If the company isn't prepared, it might not survive a disaster that completely halts its operations. This information can be provided to other managers, who might help fund and organize a disaster recovery plan, based on the statistics of the impact of a disaster. Many companies don't like spending significant time or money on disaster recovery preparation, but when presented with a well-prepared BIA, management typically realizes that the ability to be prepared for a disaster will quickly pay for itself when a disaster strikes.

Privacy Impact Assessment

A *privacy impact assessment (PIA)* begins with *a privacy threshold analysis (PTA)*, the purpose of which is to determine if a system is using privacy information or connecting to one that is. If that is the case, a full PIA is required. An organization's *data privacy officer (DPO)* should begin the PIA by determining what type of data is being stored, how it is being stored, where it is being stored, and what would trigger a privacy issue. Systems that require a PIA should incorporate increased controls to mitigate the risks of processing and storing privacy data. Keep in mind that different types of privacy data, such as personally identifiable information (PII) and protected health information (PHI) (and, within the PHI category, even different types of PHI), often require additional controls, which should be identified during the PIA. Normally, laws and regulatory guidance dictate how the PIA should be conducted for privacy data as well as the controls that must be in place.

Disaster Recovery and IT Contingency Plans

Organizations must devise disaster recovery and IT contingency plans to establish the procedures that can quickly recover critical systems after a service disruption. This includes defining and prioritizing specific tasks to aid in the process and defining clear objectives that must be met during the recovery phase.

Responsibilities must be clearly defined for individuals participating in the recovery as part of the disaster recovery team. Tasks should be divided and assigned to the appropriate people and departments. Everyone must be trained on the specific procedures, and those procedures must be properly documented. Team leaders must be established, and central authorities can guide the recovery process through each of its critical steps.

Each organization also needs to decide which aspect of the business is the most critical and must be up and running first if a disaster occurs. Different departments in the company have unique objectives and priorities, but certain functions can be delayed if they don't immediately impact the company's ability to function.

The most important part of the company to get operational is basic communications, such as desk phones, mobile phones, networking connectivity, and e-mail. Until these communication lines are functional, the company's ability to coordinate the disaster recovery effort will be greatly reduced, causing much confusion and chaos. Business-critical items should come next, such as file servers, database servers, and Internet servers that run the company's main applications or anything specifically needed by customers. Most of these responsibilities are defined in the IT department's contingency plan.

The company's ability to restore full operations as quickly as possible depends on the efficiency with which it meets the objectives and goals outlined in the disaster recovery plan.

Your organization's DRP must also contain information on succession planning for key employees. Depending on the type of disaster, specific employees might not be available or could be directly affected by the disaster. You must identify key positions that can be filled in by other employees who can take over and execute the same responsibilities. These positions can be very technical in nature, such as a network administrator, or at the executive level to provide direction during a disaster.

Documentation

Each phase of your organization's recovery plans should be carefully documented, and the resulting documentation should be readily available to all members of the disaster recovery team. The documentation should also be safely stored in both hard copy and software form to reduce the potential for damage or loss. In case of a real disaster, a lack of documentation will cause nothing but chaos because no one will know how to get all aspects of the company running again, especially during a stressful and frantic time.

The disaster recovery plan must be precise and detailed so that anyone can follow the instructions without requiring further clarification. Each person on the disaster recovery team will have clear responsibilities and duties that must be performed in the most efficient manner possible.

The DRP documentation should include the following items:

- **Notification lists** A list of people and businesses to notify in case of a disaster.
- **Contact information** Phone numbers and contact information for employees, vendors, data recovery agencies, and offsite facilities.
- **Networking and facilities diagrams** Blueprints and diagrams of all networking and facilities infrastructure so they can be re-created at the new site.
- **System configurations** Configuration information for all servers, applications, and networking equipment.
- **Backup restoration procedures** Step-by-step information on how to restore data from the backup media.
- **Location of backup and licensing media** To reinstall the servers, you will need the operating system software, the appropriate license keys, and the backup media. These should be stored in a safe location so that they are ready and available during the installation process.

Finally, copies of the DRP should be stored and secured both onsite and in an offsite facility—especially any designated alternative company site. If a physical disaster strikes your main facility, the plan will be useless if it's destroyed along with the building.

EXAM TIP Be aware of the types of information that should be documented in your disaster recovery plan.

Testing

To complete your disaster recovery plan, you must fully test it to ensure all parts of the plan work as they should. Re-creating a disaster without affecting the current operations of your company might be difficult, but some form of test should be performed at least once a year.

One common type of test is a *tabletop exercise*, which requires the involved parties to sit around a—you guessed it—table and step through a scenario to discern weaknesses in the plan. Conducting this type of test several times will make participants more comfortable in the event they must conduct the plan, almost like muscle memory.

Most disaster recovery tests involve the choice of a scenario, such as a fire in a certain part of the building. In the test, your disaster recovery team must consult the recovery plan documentation and execute it accordingly. Depending on the size of the company, it might be feasible to involve only certain departments, but the IT department should always be included because its main responsibilities are the network infrastructure and data recovery. During the testing, every phase should be fully documented using a checklist. Any exceptions or problems encountered during the procedure should be thoroughly documented.

After the test has been completed, the original disaster recovery plan should be reviewed for any procedures that didn't work correctly or that need to be modified because of the test. The DRP should be updated with any new information emerging from the testing. Any changes to the existing facilities or infrastructure should initiate a review of the current disaster recovery procedures. Any necessary changes to the recovery procedures should be made immediately to reflect the new environment.

After-Action Reporting

After you have completed testing, documenting your findings—good and bad—in an after-action report (AAR) allows you to give an honest assessment of the testing, detail the areas that should be improved upon, and identify the path forward for filling any gaps. Often called a *lessons learned report*, the AAR should be focused on measurement and improvement. Were organizational policies sufficient? Were they followed? What are recommendations for improvement?

High Availability and Redundancy Planning

High availability, redundancy planning, and fault tolerance are extremely important factors in ensuring business continuity, and they are implemented at the system and network levels to protect the confidentiality and integrity of data as well as to maintain data availability.

The ability to provide uninterrupted service consistently is the goal of maintaining a high-availability system. This initially requires that you identify systems that need to provide services always. Answer the following questions to help you in planning for high-availability systems:

- What is the monetary cost of an extended service downtime?
- What is the cost to a customer relationship that can occur because of an extended service downtime directly affecting that customer?
- Which services must be available always?

Based on the answers to these questions, rank the services in order of priority. If your company hosts several services required by customers, these services should be given higher priority than your own systems because the service level promised to customers must be maintained always.

Service Levels

Many companies measure their ability to provide services as a *service level*. For example, a web-server-hosting company might promise 99 percent service availability for the systems and services it hosts. The other 1 percent of the time, the systems might be unavailable because of maintenance, equipment failure, or network downtime.

KEY TERM A **service level** specifies in measurable terms the level of service to be received, such as the percentage of time services are available. Many Internet service providers (ISPs) and cloud service providers provide a service level agreement (SLA) to guarantee customers a minimum level of service. Some IT departments now provide a measured service level to the rest of the company.

The most common examples of servers and services that require high availability and high service levels include the following:

- **Internet servers** These include Internet services, such as web and FTP servers. These types of servers usually require that the information and data stored on them be always available.
- **E-mail** E-mail is the most commonly used Internet service because all users need and use it. Therefore, high levels of service availability must be maintained for mail servers and gateways.
- **Networking** As the backbone of all computer communications, the networking equipment that provides the infrastructure for private and public networks must be always available.
- **File servers** File servers house all data needed by users. Without access to this data, users can't perform their job functions.
- **Database servers** Database servers are typically required as back-end servers to web servers and other applications that use database transactions. Data stored on database servers, just like that stored on file servers, must be always available.
- **Telecom** Even in an Internet-centric organization, phone and other voice telecommunications systems are still services that require high availability. In the event of a disaster, your voice communications will be of the highest critical priority in order to coordinate disaster recovery efforts.

Reliability Factors

Several industry-standard terms are used in the IT world to refer to the reliability of services and hardware products. These terms are often used in maintenance contracts that identify how long it takes a manufacturer or a service company to repair a failed service or server. They can also refer to service levels provided by a company to customers depending on their services, such as a web hosting company that hosts and services thousands of websites for many customers.

- **Mean time to repair (MTTR)** The average length of time from the moment a component fails until it is repaired. For spare parts for a failed server hard drive, your service contract may state that the web hosting company can provide a new hard drive within 4 hours, but in other cases, this could be 24 to 48 hours. Don't forget to include all the time from failure until the full determination of cause, receipt of a new part (as required), proper testing, all the way up to the actual working order is restored.
- **Mean time to failure (MTTF)** The length of time that a component is expected to last in regular service. For example, when you're comparing component prices, one device may have a lower initial price and a lower MTTF, which could mean that your company spends more in the end replacing components if the lower-cost device is chosen for implementation. MTTF assumes the component will *not* be repaired.
- **Mean time between failures (MTBF)** The average length of time a specific component is expected to work until it fails. A mathematical formula is used to determine how long a specific product should last based on previous measurements of failure rates. For example, a mechanical or electrical device such as a hard drive or power supply may have an MTBF rating of 500,000 hours; after that, it is more likely to fail. MTBF assumes components will be replaced or repaired upon failure.
- **Recovery time objective (RTO)** The maximum amount of time that is considered tolerable for a service or certain business function to be unavailable. Organizations use this as a key factor in their ability to provide specific guaranteed service levels. Different functions and services may have different RTOs. For example, a company may determine that its website from which customers purchase the company's products is of the highest importance, and set the RTO for the website as 60 minutes. RTOs are typically defined in the business impact analysis of the business continuity and disaster recovery plans.
- **Recovery point objective (RPO)** The maximum acceptable amount of lost data due to an outage or disaster. This is defined in terms of time, such as one hour. For example, if a database server fails, up to one hour of data can be considered an acceptable loss. These policies are defined in the business impact analysis of your business continuity and disaster recovery plans. RPOs can help define other security policies, such as the backup frequency, to make sure that a data backup occurs at least every hour to preserve the RPO.

REVIEW

Objective 5.4: Summarize risk management processes and concepts Risk can be internal or external in nature and can be accepted, avoided, transferred, or mitigated. In order to determine the risks to the organization, a risk assessment should be undertaken, either qualitative or quantitative, that considers the likelihood of risk occurrence and the impact if the risk is realized. Calculations such as single loss expectancy (SLE), annualized loss expectancy (ALE), and annualized rate of occurrence (ARO) help quantify reliability and financial costs associated with different loss scenarios.

Consider the security concepts of confidentiality, integrity, availability, and safety to select appropriate access controls before disaster strikes. Create a disaster recovery plan that documents your organization's risks, an analysis of the potential business impact of a disaster, a contingency plan, succession planning, and network and facility documentation. Don't forget to identify mission essential functions and associated critical systems. Test your business continuity and disaster recovery plans regularly, and conduct any applicable privacy impact assessments if privacy data is being processed.

5.4 QUESTIONS

1. As part of a risk analysis of a very large and extensive back-end database, you need to calculate the probability and impact of data corruption. Which of the following impact factors allows you to calculate your annualized losses due to data corruption?
   - **A.** SLE
   - **B.** SLA
   - **C.** ARO
   - **D.** ALE
2. As part of business continuity planning, it is discovered that the organization is processing PII unknowingly. Which of the following should be conducted?
   - **A.** Privacy implication assessment
   - **B.** Privacy processing assessment
   - **C.** Privacy impact assessment
   - **D.** Privacy identification assessment
3. AJ's management tasks him with determining the right reliability factor to track for the company's new engines. The management wants to know how long they can expect the engine to last before failure, with the expectation that it will then be replaced. What is the best reliability factor?
   - **A.** Recovery point objective (RPO)
   - **B.** Mean time to repair (MTTR)
   - **C.** Mean time between failures (MTBT)
   - **D.** Mean time to failure (MTTF)

4. A(n) __________ tracks different types of data elements, most commonly risk factors and risk scenarios. It might also include data that describes different technical or management findings contributing to the risk, as well as threats, vulnerabilities, assets, likelihood, and impact data.
   - **A.** Acceptable use policy
   - **B.** Business continuity plan
   - **C.** Risk register
   - **D.** Risk matrix

5.4 ANSWERS

1. **D** ALE (annualized loss expectancy) describes how much money you expect to lose on an annual basis because of the impact of an occurrence of a specific risk. ALE is calculated by multiplying the annualized rate of occurrence (ARO) by the single loss expectancy (SLE).
2. **C** A privacy impact assessment (PIA) is conducted when privacy data is being stored or processed; when conducted, the PIA determines what type of data is being stored, how it is being stored, where it is being stored, and what might trigger a privacy lapse. Systems that require a PIA should incorporate increased controls to mitigate the risks of processing and storing privacy data.
3. **D** When the management assumes that the engines will not be repaired and will be replaced, the mean time to failure (MTTF) is the best reliability factor to track.
4. **C** A risk register tracks different types of data elements, most commonly risk factors and risk scenarios. It might also include data that describes different technical or management findings contributing to the risk. Additionally, threats, vulnerabilities, assets, likelihood, and impact data can be included in the risk register.

Explain privacy and sensitive data concepts in relation to security

With growing regulatory requirements associated with breaches of privacy and data, there are more reasons than ever for organizations to pay sharp attention to guarding the privacy of sensitive data. This objective discusses some concepts you should understand regarding privacy and sensitive data.

Privacy and Sensitive Data

Many people confuse the concepts of security and privacy. While these concepts certainly complement each other, privacy relates to the control an individual has over their personal information and how it is used and disseminated, while security relates to how that information is protected. In the following sections, we'll discuss the important elements regarding the classification and management of privacy and other types of sensitive data that you need to understand for the exam.

Organizational Consequences of Privacy and Data Breaches

As noted, now more than ever before, there are organizational consequences when a privacy or data breach occurs. Some consequences are easy to quantify, such as a fine from a government entity. Others are less easily quantified, such as damage to organizational reputation or theft of intellectual property (IP), but still equate to real money lost by a company, even if calculating the loss can be somewhat tenuous. Another consideration is the loss of private information leading to identity theft, which can affect both employees and customers alike, sometimes leading to lawsuits and substantial payouts (such as the Equifax breach in 2017).

There are some emerging resources that can help organizations better quantify the losses associated with potential breaches of private or sensitive data. For example, the Ponemon Institute conducts an annual study, sponsored by IBM Security, of the costs associated with data breaches in various industries and how security controls affected those losses. The results of the study are published in an annual *Cost of a Data Breach Report*. Figure 5.5-1 shows a graphic from the 2019 Cost of a Data Breach report that details the four major loss categories: detection and escalation of the breach, notification after the breach, post breach cost, and lost business cost. In addition to the aspects previously mentioned, this report also includes the personnel costs associated with remediation and cleanup, the productivity losses to the organization, and any costs associated with third-party losses. This can add up quickly!

It is prudent for every organization, ideally during their risk assessment process, to assess the impact to the organization of such a breach of private or sensitive data to better understand the ramifications and help justify the measures to protect it. Such a *privacy impact assessment (PIA)* should include all of the direct and indirect costs previously mentioned, allowing for better risk prioritization and decision-making. Figure 5.5-2 shows the NIST SP 800-60, Vol. 1, Rev. 1 impact assessment model as an example of what can be used to derive organizational impact.

Cross-Reference

Additional information on conducting a privacy impact assessment is provided in the previous objective, 5.4.

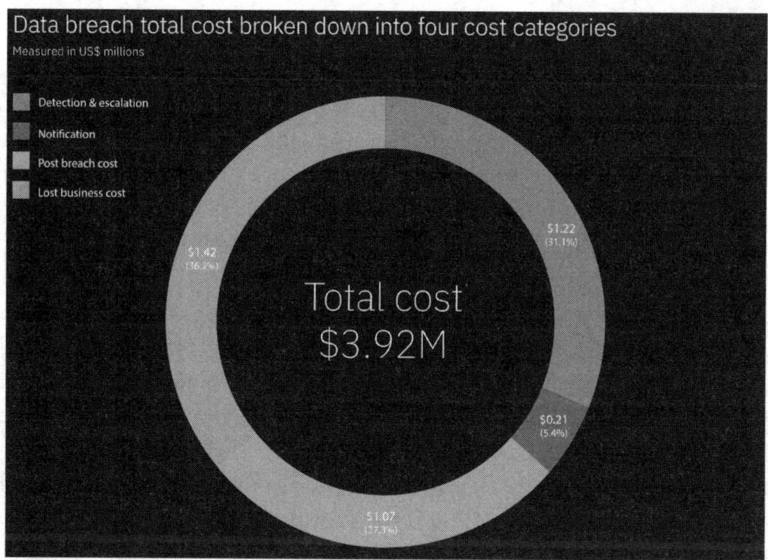

FIGURE 5.5-1 Data breach total cost broken down into four cost categories (source: IBM Security/Ponemon Institute, 2019)

Potential Impact	Definitions
Low	The potential impact is **low** if—The loss of confidentiality, integrity, or availability could be expected to have a **limited** adverse effect on organizational operations, organizational assets, or individuals.[7] A limited adverse effect means that, for example, the loss of confidentiality, integrity, or availability might: (i) cause a degradation in mission capability to an extent and duration that the organization is able to perform its primary functions, but the effectiveness of the functions is noticeably reduced; (ii) result in minor damage to organizational assets; (iii) result in minor financial loss; or (iv) result in minor harm to individuals.
Moderate	The potential impact is **moderate** if—The loss of confidentiality, integrity, or availability could be expected to have a **serious** adverse effect on organizational operations, organizational assets, or individuals. A serious adverse effect means that, for example, the loss of confidentiality, integrity, or availability might: (i) cause a significant degradation in mission capability to an extent and duration that the organization is able to perform its primary functions, but the effectiveness of the functions is significantly reduced; (ii) result in significant damage to organizational assets; (iii) result in significant financial loss; or (iv) result in significant harm to individuals that does not involve loss of life or serious life threatening injuries.
High	The potential impact is **high** if—The loss of confidentiality, integrity, or availability could be expected to have a **severe or catastrophic** adverse effect on organizational operations, organizational assets, or individuals. A severe or catastrophic adverse effect means that, for example, the loss of confidentiality, integrity, or availability might: (i) cause a severe degradation in or loss of mission capability to an extent and duration that the organization is not able to perform one or more of its primary functions; (ii) result in major damage to organizational assets; (iii) result in major financial loss; or (iv) result in severe or catastrophic harm to individuals involving loss of life or serious life threatening injuries.

FIGURE 5.5-2 Low/moderate/high impact assessment model, from NIST SP 800-60, Vol. 1, Rev. 1

Notification of Breaches

Notification as a cost is worth noting, both as an internal and an external endeavor. Once a breach has occurred, incident response procedures often dictate internal escalation to internal teams, such as legal, communications, and upper management, that have a stakeholder role within the process. Breaches can be quite technical in nature, but if decisions need to be made that involve significant financial resources, upper management may require their signature authority. An organization's legal department may be required to alert authorities to start an investigation, while the communications team should be prepared to notify employees or customers in a timely manner. External parties that organizations may be legally required to notify include the United States Computer Emergency Readiness Team, commonly known as US-CERT (for breaches of private or sensitive U.S. government data), and individual U.S. state governments (depending on the state and where the data is stored or processed; a good example of a state that has its own privacy standards is California, with its California Consumer Privacy Act).

Often these disclosures directly lead to public disclosure to affected parties within a set time period of days to weeks, depending on the entity and severity. An example of this is the Health Insurance Portability and Accountability Act (HIPAA) Breach Notification Rule, found in U.S. 45 CFR §§ 164.400-414. The rule requires HIPAA "covered entities" and their business associates to provide notification following a breach of unsecured protected health information (PHI). If a breach of PHI occurs, covered entities must notify affected individuals via individual notice in written form by first-class mail or, alternatively, by e-mail if the affected individual has agreed to receive such notices electronically. If the covered entity has insufficient or out-of-date contact information for ten or more individuals, the covered entity must provide substitute individual notice either by posting the notice on the home page of its website for at least 90 days or by providing the notice in major print or broadcast media where the affected individuals likely reside. The covered entity must include a toll-free phone number that remains active for at least 90 days that individuals can call to learn if their information was involved in the breach. If the covered entity has insufficient or out-of-date contact information for fewer than ten individuals, the covered entity may provide substitute notice by an alternative form of written notice, by telephone, or other means. Knowing the specific notification requirements is key when handling PHI is central to your business.

Cross-Reference

More information on some key regulations and frameworks, such as the European Union (EU) General Data Protection Regulation (GDPR), is offered in Objective 5.2, earlier in this domain.

Data Types

Different types of data should (and in some cases must) be handled in an appropriate manner. Failing to do so can lead to stiff fines or even the inability to conduct business. When looking for the best strategy to protect the private and sensitive data within an organization, a good first step is to catalog what data the organization collects and processes, which systems conduct these activities, and where the data is stored. Table 5.5-1 lists important types of data to understand, along with a brief description of each.

Cross-Reference

Additional information on data types is found in Objective 5.3, earlier in this domain.

TABLE 5.5-1 Important Data Types

Data Type	Description
Public	Any information, regardless of form or format, that an organization discloses, disseminates, or makes available to the public.
Private	All information that is not meant to be publicly disclosed or disseminated. Some, but not all, private information is subject to privacy laws.
Sensitive	Information that is privileged and requires special access to view or process.
Confidential	Information subject to restricted access, whether regarding an individual or a company. This term is often used interchangeably with *sensitive*.
Critical	Any information whose loss, misuse, disclosure, unauthorized access, or modification would have a debilitating impact on the organization.
Proprietary	Information that, if disclosed, could harm a business's interests, often through loss of a competitive advantage.
Personally identifiable information (PII)	Information that can be used to distinguish or trace an individual's identity, either alone or when combined with other personal or identifying information that is linked or linkable to a specific individual.
Protected health information (PHI)	Individually identifiable information relating to the past, present, or future health status of an individual that is created, collected, transmitted, or maintained by a HIPAA covered entity in relation to the provision of healthcare, payment for healthcare services, or use in healthcare operations.
Sensitive personal information (SPI)	Defined in the EU GDPR as personal data revealing racial or ethnic origin, political opinions, religious or philosophical beliefs; trade-union membership; genetic data, biometric data processed solely to identify a human being; health-related data; or data concerning a person's sex life or sexual orientation.
Financial information	Information relating to personal finances, such as a credit score, or corporate finances, such as private earnings figures that have not been released.
Government data	Information that is created, collected, or transmitted on behalf of a government.
Customer data	Information that is created, collected, or transmitted to serve a customer interest, generally to deliver a service or good, such as customer address.

Privacy Enhancing Technologies

Protecting private and sensitive data involves a number of privacy enhancing technologies that either make the data anonymous (*anonymization* and *pseudo-anonymization*), obfuscate the data (*data masking*), or substitute tokens in lieu of the data itself (*tokenization*). Organizations often use data loss prevention (DLP) tools across an enterprise to minimize the ways in which private and sensitive data can potentially be exfiltrated, even innocently, such as a person e-mailing their Social Security number without encryption.

Finally, information has a life cycle: information comes into the organization, is processed, is stored, and then is purged. Each phase of this cycle should have appropriate privacy enhancing measures associated with it, and data shouldn't linger forever, if possible, unless its retention is legally required. Not only does this take precious space, it requires more resources to continue to protect it commensurate with its value. Ideally, the best practice of *data minimization* should be considered at all times, meaning that the amount of sensitive or private data that is collected, processed, and stored is minimized. It's much easier to protect something you don't have!

Cross-Reference

Additional information on data loss prevention is provided in Domain 2, Objective 2.1.

Data Ownership Roles and Responsibilities

Within partnerships where data is "owned" by one organization and stored and processed by another, it is important to detail within any agreement the requirements for legal and regulatory authority over the data. Particularly within the U.S. government, the *data steward* (aka *data custodian*) has succeeded the concept of a *data owner*, because the true owner is the American public. Within this construct, a steward is appointed the responsibility for establishing the policies and procedures for the handling and dissemination of that data. Further, that steward will have the regulatory approval for any interconnections.

Now that we've determined who owns or stewards the data, the *data controller* (either a person or an organization) determines what data will be collected and how it will be used. Subsequently, the *data processor* processes the data in accordance with the data controller's requirements. Overseeing this entire process is the *data protection officer (DPO)*, who is responsible for ensuring that there is a data privacy strategy and that its implementation meets requirements. A good example of a regulatory mechanism that mandates all of these roles is the previously discussed EU GDPR, which enacts strict guidelines for all these roles, as well as for the proper disclosure of breaches, with big fines resulting from lack behavior.

Terms of Agreement and Privacy Notices

Since the GDPR became enforceable in May of 2018, you've probably noticed that many more websites have screens that pop up and ask you to choose your privacy settings upon your first visit. This is because the GDPR has globally changed the requirements for how websites

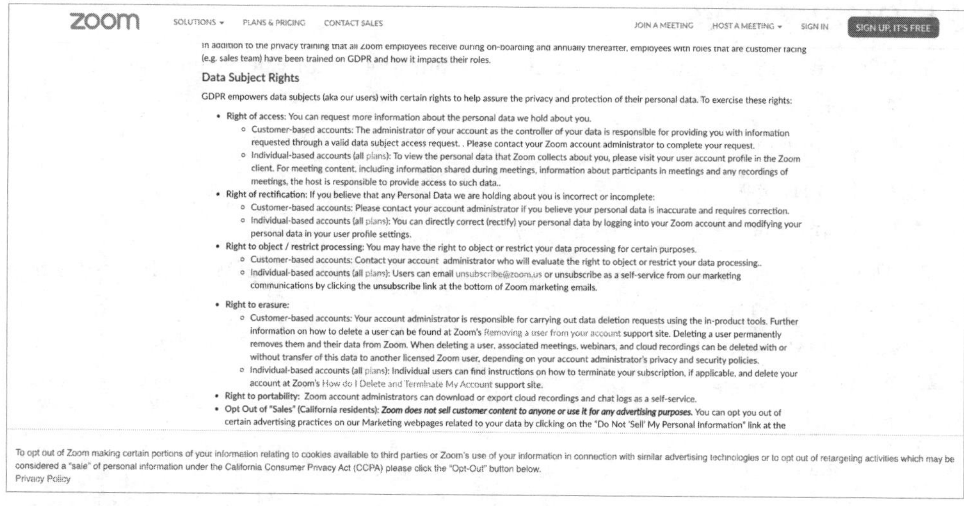

FIGURE 5.5-3 Zoom Terms of Agreement and Privacy Notice

collect, process, and store data, even cookies that are connected to your web browsing. Each website that is accessible to EU citizens is required to have a public copy of its privacy policies available, and the use of the website requires the user to accept the terms of agreement. Basically, if you don't agree to the terms, you can't use the website. However, many websites do allow you to choose how cookies are used, which does limit some customization options if disabled. Figure 5.5-3 shows an example of how Zoom informs consumers of its Terms of Agreement and links to its privacy policy.

REVIEW

Objective 5.5: Explain privacy and sensitive data concepts in relation to security It is important for an organization to understand the consequences of a privacy breach, from the easily quantified consequences such as monetary penalties to the not easily quantified consequences such as identity theft, reputation damage, and intellectual property theft. When a breach occurs, it should be escalated to the proper stakeholders, and both internal and external (as necessary) notification procedures should be executed.

The first step to preventing a breach of private or sensitive data is to catalog what data your organization has, how it is processed, and where it is stored. Understand the different types of data, and conduct a privacy impact assessment. Once you have a clear view of what data is at stake, apply appropriate privacy enhancing technologies, such as data loss prevention tools that offer data masking, tokenization, and anonymization features, but keep in mind that minimizing the data collected is the best approach. Finally, understand the varying roles and responsibilities associated with the information life cycle.

5.5 QUESTIONS

1. Which of the following is *not* a standard classification for private or sensitive data?
   - **A.** Public
   - **B.** Confidential
   - **C.** Proprietary
   - **D.** Consensual
2. The __________ determines what data will be collected and how it will be used within an organization.
   - **A.** Data steward
   - **B.** Data controller
   - **C.** Data processor
   - **D.** Data protection officer

5.5 ANSWERS

1. **D** Public, confidential, and proprietary are all examples of valid data types that should be considered when cataloging private and sensitive data within an organization.
2. **B** The data controller determines what data will be collected and how it will be used within an organization.

Architecture and Design

Domain Objectives

- **2.1 Explain the importance of security concepts in an enterprise environment**
- **2.2 Summarize virtualization and cloud computing concepts**
- **2.3 Summarize secure application development, deployment, and automation concepts**
- **2.4 Summarize authentication and authorization design concepts**
- **2.5 Given a scenario, implement cybersecurity resilience**
- **2.6 Explain the security implications of embedded and specialized systems**
- **2.7 Explain the importance of physical security controls**
- **2.8 Summarize the basics of cryptographic concepts**

Explain the importance of security concepts in an enterprise environment

The previous domain broadly covered the different types of controls and how they support the confidentiality, integrity, and availability of an organization. This objective kicks off the discussion of specific security solutions and how their implementations support a robust, defense-in-depth approach to secure an enterprise.

Enterprise Security

Pick up a trade magazine or browse LinkedIn for cybersecurity vendors, and you're bound to find dozens (or more) companies with different tools that claim to provide enterprise security. However, the judicious use of industry-standard best practices such as Transport Layer Security (TLS), hashing, and application programming interfaces (APIs) are the foundation for any smart security program. Understanding how to get the basics right is essential before spending time and money investing in more complex techniques that we'll discuss later.

Cross-References

More details on TLS and APIs are available in Domain 1, Objective 1.3.
For more on hashing, see Objective 2.8, later in this domain.

Change and Configuration Management

Change management policies are official company procedures used to identify and communicate current or forthcoming changes to some aspect of the company's networks and communications services. For example, the IT department might issue a change control document to all employees to notify them of a network outage because of an upgrade to networking equipment, or that an application will be down for several hours for a software upgrade. More detailed change control communications describe longer-term outages for specific technical changes to the company's systems or network infrastructure, such as taking down part of the network for a weekend for router and switch upgrades.

Tracking, controlling, and communicating outages and changes to your network infrastructure, systems, and applications are important to keep all departments in your organization up to date with IT maintenance activities to prevent accidental loss of data and services. For security reasons, this activity also ensures any unplanned changes or outages are quickly detected and investigated. System and network changes without prior knowledge or approval of management and the IT department could indicate a hacker or an intruder has compromised the network.

The U.S. Department of Defense (DoD) Architecture Framework (DoDAF) 2.02 provides a good definition of the *Configuration Management* (CM) function: "CM provides an orderly way to facilitate change, based on a documented requirements baseline, and utilizing best practices in the change management process. This is intended to ensure that expectations are fully understood and realized in an efficient manner, including proper consideration of all potential impacts on customers and resources." CM should include such elements as the network and architecture diagrams, the agreed-upon baseline configurations of hardware and software, standard naming conventions (such as username_workstation or firstname.lastname), and the Internet Protocol (IP) schema used across the enterprise.

EXAM TIP Note that the overall program for the entire organization is called *change* management, while changes at the actual host or network level of baseline configurations is called *configuration* management.

Data Protection

Most security concerns are centered on preventing inbound threats such as network attacks, malware, and viruses from entering your organization's network. For organizations that operate in a 24/7 digital world where there is a constant flow of data being passed in and out of their networks via e-mail, instant messaging, web, and other communications channels, the concept of data protection and loss prevention has quickly become of equal importance.

Data loss prevention (DLP) is the concept of using security and content control features to prevent confidential, private data from leaving your organization's networks. DLP has become so important that certain types of organizations, including financial and medical companies, must adhere to strict guidelines and regulations regarding the storage and communication of private data. For example, banks and other financial companies must ensure that a customer's banking and credit card info are secure and never transmitted without being encrypted. Hospitals, doctors' offices, and other health-related organizations must ensure patient confidentiality regarding personal health records.

DLP requires that organizations create compliance policies that detail which users can send certain types of documents and data outside of their networks and the types of actions that should be applied to outbound messages that violate a policy. From a technical perspective, DLP techniques use deep content scanning (such as with a content filter network device) on outbound network traffic to act on messages or requests, depending on various criteria about their content. For example, a company can create content rules that automatically encrypt any outbound e-mail messages that contain patterns of credit card numbers or Social Security numbers. A high-security organization may block document attachments to e-mails, or even HTTP or FTP uploads of documents marked as "confidential" or "secret," to prevent them from leaving the network. DLP requires the ability to scan multiple network protocols and services (e-mail, web, IM, and so on) to ensure that there is no way that sensitive data can leave the network.

DLP becomes even more difficult when dealing with cloud computing, where data can be stored and transmitted within a distributed service cloud across public networks. Once the data is transmitted in the cloud, ensuring confidentiality is much more challenging. Your DLP policies must ensure that specific confidential data is not transmitted out of your organization into the cloud.

Related data protection concepts include the following:

- **Data masking** Obfuscates sensitive data by substituting it with a different value ("dummy" value.) Note this data is not encrypted and is often taken from elsewhere in the database.
- **Tokenization** Similar to masking, replaces sensitive data, but instead of replacing it with dummy data, the data is replaced with a token that refers back to the actual, sensitive data and represents the data in lieu of the real deal.
- **Digital rights management (DRM)** Embeds a digital watermark, generally within audio or video data, to prevent that data from being copied. In the years before streaming services became prevalent, DRM was very popular as a way to prevent movies and records from being copied and shared.

Data Encryption

For data confidentiality, the ability to render data unreadable through encryption is a key component of data loss prevention. Most security resources are dedicated to protecting the confidentiality of data while *in transit/motion* over a network using secure cipher suites and implementations. Of equal importance is the protection of data while it is stored *at rest* on server hard disks, mobile devices, and USB flash drives. Emerging techniques, such as homomorphic encryption, encrypt data while *in processing*, removing the concern of unencrypted data being exploited while actively being used by an application and residing in memory. The following sections describe how data is encrypted using both hardware and software technologies to protect the confidentiality of stored data.

Cross-Reference

For details on cryptographic techniques for encryption, see Objective 2.8, later in this domain.

Trusted Platform Module

A *trusted platform module (TPM)* is a special hardware chip that is typically installed within a computer system or device, such as on the system motherboard of a computer desktop or laptop. This module provides authentication by storing security mechanisms such as passwords, certificates, and encryption keys that are specific to that system hardware. The chip itself contains a built-in RSA (Rivest, Shamir, and Adleman) key that is used for encryption and authentication. In the past, hardware-based passwords on desktops and laptops were typically stored in cleartext and, therefore, vulnerable to unauthorized access. With the advent of TPM, any system passwords are now stored and encrypted on the TPM chip. The TPM provides greater security benefits over software-based solutions because it runs in a closed hardware subsystem that mitigates external threats. TPM-based systems are compatible with most popular operating systems.

Laptops are especially prone to physical theft because of their portability, and if the hard drive contents are not encrypted, an unauthorized user can easily access these files. The TPM allows the contents of the hard drive to be encrypted; the user simply generates a key that is stored on the TPM chip. When the user needs to access the hard drive, she uses operating system software, such as Windows, to send the key to the TPM chip for authentication. This prevents an unauthorized user from accessing the hard drive contents of equipment.

Hardware Security Module

A *hardware security module (HSM)* is a specialized hardware appliance used to provide onboard cryptographic functions and processing. This physical hardware device can be a stand-alone device attached to a network or connected directly to a server as a plug-in card. HSMs are primarily used to host integrated cryptographic functions, such as a Public Key Infrastructure (PKI) server for encryption, decryption, and secure key generation and management, but they can also be used to provide onboard secure storage of encrypted data. With their processing speed and security, HSMs are often used for banking applications (such as ATMs) that require scalable, performance-based solutions for critical key management and security.

Full Disk Encryption

With *full disk encryption*, the entire contents of a computer system's hard drive are encrypted, typically by encrypting the disk volume that contains all the operating system data; this does not include the booting instructions located in a boot volume or master boot record (MBR). By encrypting all files, including temporary and swap space files, you ensure that no unauthorized user can access this data if the system is compromised or stolen.

Many operating systems come with their own proprietary whole-disk encryption mechanisms (such as Microsoft BitLocker) that encrypt data at rest and decrypt data in transit/motion as the user is operating the computer. You can encrypt a system's operating system volume on the hard drive and provide authentication for the boot process (which cannot be encrypted). It is critical that disk encryption systems use some form of authentication for the boot process, such as a locked-down mini operating system or a TPM mechanism whose only function is to authenticate the user before booting the system. Otherwise, an unauthorized user can still boot the system and access user files as if he were the original user. To authenticate the user, a combination of passwords, passphrases, personal identification numbers (PINs), or hardware tokens can be used before allowing access to the encrypted disk volumes.

Database Encryption

Company databases can consist of millions of records and terabytes of data. Data is the heart of a company, and if this data is damaged, lost, or stolen, it could mean the end of that company. Although most security resources are spent on encryption of data in transit, you must also consider the confidentiality of data at rest.

Databases can be encrypted so that even if an attacker were able to gain unauthorized access to a database, she would not be able to read the data without the encryption key. You can encrypt the entire database itself or the actual physical database files (which also protects backups of the database). For more granularity, you can even encrypt individual cells/records in the database that are decrypted as authorized by the user.

As with other encryption methods, key management and authentication can create security issues, and it is a best practice that the encrypted key never be stored with the encrypted data. Encryption keys should be stored and managed by external devices such as an HSM.

Individual File Encryption

Data encryption can also be taken to a very granular level where only individual files and folders are encrypted by the file system itself, rather than the contents of entire partitions or a whole disk. A good example of this is Microsoft's Encrypting File System (EFS) that's been native to Windows since Windows 2000. This type of encryption has the benefit that each encrypted file or folder has a different encryption key. This approach provides more strict access control; however, it requires efficient key management to properly oversee different keys with different user authorizations.

Encrypting Removable Media and Mobile Devices

The ability to transfer information easily from one computer device to another has been made easier with removable media and mobile devices. Technologies such as removable hard drives, USB keys, and flash memory in mobile devices give users flexibility in moving data from one system to another.

Removable media can contain critical and confidential data that must be protected from unauthorized access and physical damage or destruction. The portable nature of many types of computer media means more opportunities for an unauthorized user to obtain or damage the information they contain. Security must be a priority to protect the confidentially and integrity of data, especially when this information is being physically moved from one place to another. This involves the use of encryption and authentication to secure access to the data, as well as physical and environmental protection of the removable media itself.

While the data is protected by encryption, there are security concerns with the methods used to access and decrypt data. A user must authenticate using a password, passphrase, or some other identifier before he can decrypt the contents of the device. If the authentication process is weak, the strong encryption techniques can be easily subverted. More advanced USB flash drives can store the actual encryption key on a separate controller part of the USB device that is protected from the main flash drive where the data is encrypted.

Data Destruction and Media Sanitization

There are several basic types of data destruction and media sanitization techniques. According to NIST SP 800-88, Rev. 1, media that will be reused and will be leaving an organization's control should be purged, meaning the data cannot be recovered. If the media will be reused and will not be leaving an organization's control, then clearing through a simple overwrite is a sufficient method of sanitization. Finally, if the media will not be reused at all, then destruction is the method for media sanitization. The following options can be used to either destroy data and securely reuse the media, or destroy the associated media completely:

- **Wiping** The use of a program to conduct "passes" of random or nonrandom data, overwriting a file or an entire drive. This is generally done in one or more passes, with the larger number of passes taking more time, but considered more secure. Reuse is possible after wiping.
- **Burning** Tossing whatever media you wish to destroy into an incinerator that burns it beyond recovery.
- **Shredding** Commonly used with paper or optical media to shred the item beyond recovery, generally in strips or further into small, confetti-style pieces; it is important when employing the shredding technique that your chosen shredding solution creates such small pieces that they cannot be pieced back together.
- **Pulverizing** Much like shredding but reduces the media to dust.
- **Pulping** Mixing water and special chemicals with the paper to remove any ink; the paper can then be recycled.
- **Degaussing** Involves running a strong magnet over magnetic storage (such as a non–solid-state hard drive) to erase the contents and restore it to a blank and generally unusable state.

Cross-Reference

More details on the policies associated with data destruction are provided in Objective 2.7, later in this domain.

Cloud Storage

Cloud storage is such an amazing concept—the ability to seamlessly store files in a remote infrastructure where they are kept safe and secure, ready to be retrieved when you need them. Some implementations even keep files locally and sync them remotely as soon as you connect to the Internet. It's a great solution for writers, students, and people who simply want the peace of mind that a current backup of their data being stored in an offsite location brings. However, cloud servers have the same inherent security concerns that other servers have. Hackers can download sensitive data for exploitation. Fire and flood can cause availability issues. How can a user balance these concerns with the clear benefits cloud storage brings?

Understanding how a cloud solution brings potential pros and cons versus an on-premises or hosted solution is important to address this balance.

A cloud storage solution might employ a few mechanisms designed to provide defense-in-depth. For example, a provider might require multifactor authentication that includes a username/password combination along with a *time-based one-time password (TOTP)* token to access the data. The provider might also encrypt data that has been classified as particularly sensitive by the data owner. Utilizing a *cloud access security broker (CASB)*, which acts as an intermediary between the user of the cloud service and the cloud provider and enforces the enterprise security policy, can also ensure that the appropriate levels of visibility and security are met.

To address availability concerns, cloud providers can take a page out of the high-availability handbook and implement redundancy and well-established (and tested) policies and procedures in the event of a disaster or disruption. Cloud storage also often resides within large server facilities that generate immense amounts of heat; to keep the systems properly cooled, effective heat dissipation and cooling solutions should be considered.

Cross-Reference

More details on cloud computing are provided in Domain 3, Objective 3.6.

Storage Area Networks

Storage area networks (SANs) are, funny enough, networks devoted to storage, and are often useful during disaster recovery situations. They generally allow attached devices to appear as local drives within the operating system environment. This differs from network-attached storage (NAS) in that NAS is presented to a client system like a file server, whereas SAN disks are available in a manner like a local disk.

SAN storage security often implements the concept of *zones*, which allows segmentation of data by classifications and restriction of that data by device. For example, sensitive HR data can be restricted to access only by devices within the HR department.

The SAN should also provide data security while data is at rest and in transit. Data at rest often requires encryption while residing on the SAN. Communication between devices should be encrypted also to protect data while in transit.

Handling Big Data

Big data is simply that: *big*. The thought is generally to collect everything—logs, files, even data thought to be previously frivolous—and perform analysis on it to determine trends and make decisions. Generally, the purpose of collecting and storing big data—including logs, files, and even data previously thought to be frivolous—is to perform analysis on it to determine trends and make decisions.

However, consider for a moment the implications of collecting and storing this much data. Imagine, if you will, a box of black dots. If you start pulling dots out of the box, you can connect them. Now, if those dots are data, such as phone numbers, IP addresses, and physical locations, you could potentially gain a robust picture of a situation through their analysis.

This is both positive and negative. Security administrators can store much more data and use analytical tools to spot anomalies within operations. However, malicious intruders can use those same "dots" for business intelligence, identity theft, or just general threats to privacy.

Data Sovereignty

Legal implications of where data are stored is also an issue to be considered, with data sovereignty being one of the most important considerations. Because different nations have different laws governing what can be done with data processed within their borders, it is important to take those requirements into consideration when choosing where to locate an alternate site. For example, the European Union, which encompasses many of the most important data processing centers in the world, has different data processing standards than the United States, with penalties for companies that do not comply. A multinational company that chooses to have a European alternate site may find that it is not prepared to protect the data to the standards set by the European Union. This could set up a company for big problems if it does not comply with the data handling and processing requirements. It truly is a tricky time to be a multinational company that relies heavily on data, especially privacy data.

Cross-Reference

Different requirements for collecting, processing, and storing sensitive or private data are discussed in Domain 5, Objective 5.5.

Response and Recovery

When a security incident (or disaster scenario) occurs, the initial response can make all the difference—either it quickly mitigates a threat, preventing it from spreading and causing further issues, or the incident spins out of control, causing irreparable damage to your organization's ability to function. Effective recovery, in turn, includes a step-by-step plan for recovering your networks and systems after a disaster, perhaps from a redundant site. It is essential to protect employees, the company's ability to operate, its facilities and equipment, and its vital data. Bad things will inevitably happen; the best organizations are prepared for them.

Cross-Reference

More details on incident response and disaster recovery are presented in Domain 4, Objective 4.2.

Site Resiliency

Not all alternate considerations are technical; you should also consider people and processes. For example, if you have a system that processes contracting data and it goes offline, an alternate business process could be to write contracts by hand, have them legally reviewed, and then enter them into the system once it's brought back up. Most functions can be done without their information systems. It may be annoying, or even painful; however, understanding how the business can continue, even in the most degraded or disrupted conditions, can mean the difference between recovering the business and closing shop for good.

Hot Site A *hot site* is a facility that's ready to be operational immediately when the primary site becomes unavailable. All equipment and networking infrastructure the company requires are already in place and can be activated quickly. The equipment duplicates the setup installed in the original building. The hot site facility is usually provided by another company, which hosts your company's equipment. Hot sites should be tested frequently to ensure the switchover runs smoothly and quickly. This is an expensive solution, but for companies that offer critical services, the costs of losing money and customers during an extended downtime warrant the expense of a hot site.

Warm Site A *warm site* is like a hot site but without most of the duplicate servers and computers that would be needed to facilitate an immediate switch-over. The warm site is there to provide an immediate facility with some minimal networking in place. In the event of a disaster, a company will transport its own equipment to the new facility, or if the original equipment is destroyed with the facility, new equipment can be purchased and moved there. A warm site could take several days to restore and transfer data to and bring the business back to full operation, so this option makes sense for companies that don't offer time-critical services. This is the most widely used alternate site option because of its relatively lower price compared to hot sites, as well as its flexibility. The disadvantages of a warm site are that it's not immediately available after a disaster and isn't easily tested.

Cold Site A *cold site* merely offers an empty facility with some basic features, such as wiring and some environmental protection, but no equipment. This is the least expensive option, but this also means when a disaster strikes, it might be several weeks before the facility and equipment are ready for operation, as almost all the networking and server infrastructure will need to be built and configured.

EXAM TIP Be aware of the advantages and disadvantages of the different types of alternate sites, depending on your environment.

Deception and Disruption

At the beginning of this objective, the point was made that you need to get the basics right before diving into more advanced techniques. These techniques include *deception* and *disruption* tools, which can be effective additions to a sophisticated enterprise security program. However, if these tools are implemented incorrectly, they can actually do more harm than good. Therefore, it's best to be sure that you have professionals on staff who are experienced with the techniques for implementing, maintaining, and monitoring such tools. Some examples of deception and disruption tools include the following:

- **Honeypot** A device or server used to attract and lure attackers into trying to access it, thereby removing attention from actual critical systems.
- **Honeynet** A large-scale network of several honeypot servers that more accurately resembles a target network.
- **Honeyfile** "Bait" files that send an alarm when accessed.
- **Fake telemetry** Inaccurate measurement data from a remote source forwarded on to an entity that is monitoring it.
- **DNS sinkhole** A Domain Name Server (DNS) that provides false DNS results. This can be used to identify infected hosts within an enterprise.

REVIEW

Objective 2.1: Explain the importance of security concepts in an enterprise environment Use data loss prevention concepts such as outbound content filtering and encryption to prevent confidential data loss and interception. Use TPMs for secure storage of encryption keys and certificates for hardware platforms. HSMs are used for high-end security applications that require secure key generation and management on a separate hardware appliance. Whole-disk encryption encrypts an entire disk or volume while providing authenticated access for the boot partition of the disk. Database encryption can secure data at rest on a database server. You can encrypt the physical database files, or you can encrypt data cells/records within those files for granular protection that includes user authorization for accessing specific encrypted data. Understand how to securely destroy data and media. SAN data should be protected while on the SAN and in transit. Big data collects a wealth of data that can be used for security analytics and many other applications, but generates many privacy and security concerns. Once you have mastered these basics, deception and disruption tools can take your security program to the next level.

2.1 QUESTIONS

1. Bobby's management has asked him to explore an alternate site solution that can be operational somewhat quickly when needed but does not require duplication of the primary network. What is the *best* solution?
   - **A.** Hot site
   - **B.** Cold site
   - **C.** Mobile site
   - **D.** Warm site

2. __________ is a data protection approach that obfuscates sensitive data by substituting it with a different value ("dummy" value), available to unauthorized users.
   - **A.** Data masking
   - **B.** Data obfuscation
   - **C.** Data transference
   - **D.** Data rights management
3. SAN storage security often implements the concept of __________, which allows segmentation of data by classifications and restriction of that data by device.
   - **A.** masking
   - **B.** encryption
   - **C.** zones
   - **D.** tokenization
4. Barbara needs to destroy a set of sensitive printed documents. Her management tasks her to find the *most* secure solution, as shredding is not up to standard. Which of the following is the *best* option?
   - **A.** Degaussing
   - **B.** Pulverizing
   - **C.** Washing
   - **D.** Wiping

2.1 ANSWERS

1. **D** A warm site is Bobby's best choice, as it can be prewired for systems to become operational quickly but still requires systems to be moved or purchased if a disaster does occur.
2. **A** Data masking is a data protection approach that obfuscates sensitive data by substituting it with a different value ("dummy" value), available to unauthorized users.
3. **C** Storage area network (SAN) storage security often implements the concept of zones, which allows segmentation of data by classifications and restriction of that data by device.
4. **B** Of the options presented, pulverizing, which would reduce the printed documents to dust, is the best option.

Objective 2.2 Summarize virtualization and cloud computing concepts

Few concepts have revolutionized how enterprises—large and small—harness computing power more than virtualization and cloud computing. Once upon a time, it was common for a mainframe to be the back-end horsepower, but as technology evolved, the client–server architecture became the norm. It was then very common for a user to have a beefy desktop PC—and often a laptop if they traveled for business or took work home—connected to a corporate data center that required a full staff to maintain and monitor the entire architecture. However, the increasing global reach of the Internet and the demand for faster, more secure computing has given way to organizations relying on cloud and managed service providers to take care of their sensitive data in lieu of larger IT staffs. This objective discusses virtualization and cloud computing concepts and their impact on enterprises of all sizes.

Cloud Computing

Cloud computing is a technique that allows network services to be distributed from a central web-based "cloud" that can be updated from any device connected to it. Cloud computing provides a distributed service-based model where all aspects of the cloud—from the platform, to the software, to the entire infrastructure—are based on a distributed web service. This differs from the traditional client–server network model, where specific servers host network services and data and client device applications connect to the servers for the applications to work properly.

Most people now use multiple devices to access and manage their applications and data, including computer desktops, laptops, smartphones, and tablet devices. Before cloud computing, each device needed to have its own copy of the data the user wanted to work on. For example, the latest version of a spreadsheet file that the user was working on with his desktop computer had to be transferred to a laptop so that he could work on it as he commuted home. When he returned to the office, the file would have to be transferred back to the work desktop again.

Cloud computing allows the user to save the file to his cloud web service, and the file is automatically synced to all other devices that are connected to the same cloud. With this model, the user always has access to the latest version of the file no matter which device he uses to access it, and the file is stored in a safe location that is also backed up by the cloud service provider.

Cloud computing also allows applications to be run from the web-based cloud, with no need for additional software to be run on the client. For example, word processing and spreadsheet software can now be run as a web-based application instead of a client-based application.

The web-based cloud service hosts both the application and the data without the need to store anything local to the client. This allows the user to use any client she wants to access her cloud-based services.

Security and authentication services for cloud-based services are centralized, and each device must authenticate and be authorized before being allowed access to the cloud. Device security is critical for protecting access to the cloud. For example, if you lose your smartphone or laptop and you do not have adequate security for accessing the device and its applications and data, such as a password, you risk providing access to your cloud data to the person who finds the device and is able to launch the cloud application.

Edge computing evolved from the concept of content distribution networks (CDNs) that were developed to improve the response time of very bandwidth-intensive, speed-dependent activities such as streaming services by bringing the content to "edge devices" that are closer to the end users, thereby reducing the amount of time the content takes to make its way from the provider to end users. In the same way, edge computing uses edge devices to improve response times for end users who are accessing data storage and other more traditional computing needs within an enterprise. In a related concept, *fog computing* places some computing requirements at edge devices at the edge of the network to provide computational power rather than offloading all computing to the cloud. Fog computing assumes that a device that is closer to the user will provide a better quality of service in the end.

Managed service providers (MSPs) and managed security service providers (MSSPs) are becoming increasingly popular as companies look to outsource everything from their IT services to their security services to save money and reduce risk. MSPs are often viewed as less risky because they offer service level agreements (SLAs) with high uptimes guaranteed, typically have experience hardening resources to comply with NIST or other certification bodies, and may have more experienced handling incident response and other critical processes than an in-house shop. However, before choosing an MSP or MSSP, it is critical to be diligent and consider what your requirements are, research potential providers, and perhaps talk to their existing customers. Remember that while these service providers might be more experienced in providing the resources you need, they don't absolve your organization of the risk of sensitive or private data being compromised, so consider the use of an MSP to be a partnership, not a method of risk transference.

Anything as a Service

The concept of *Anything as a Service (XaaS)* means that, for a price, nearly anything that a user or company would want to use a computing system for can be delivered to them by a *cloud service provider* through the cloud infrastructure—typically through a thin client (a lightweight software program designed to establish a server interface) or web interface. In such a *serverless architecture*, a cloud provider manages the server and associated architecture and allocates resources as necessary to the end users. This requires less up-front investment in hardware and software by the customer, greater scalability, and centralized management for administration and security concerns. Here are some examples of cloud service models:

- *Infrastructure as a Service (IaaS)* provides the ability to quickly stand up virtual machines (VMs), storage devices, and other infrastructure that would otherwise require the purchase of physical devices.
- *Platform as a Service (PaaS)* provides the framework of an operating system and associated software required to perform a function (for example, the Linux operating system and components needed to run a web server).
- *Software as a Service (SaaS)* allows a customer to essentially lease software, such as applications and databases, thus enabling rapid rollout to the greater user community.
- *Security as a Service (SECaaS)* allows an organization to offload its security monitoring and administration to a third-party provider on a subscription model. Often, this third party is responsible for antivirus, anti-malware, intrusion detection, and other security-focused monitoring services.

EXAM TIP It is critical to understand the differences between the various cloud service models.

It is common for an IT service provider to offer end-to-end support of its enterprise under one branded "umbrella" for a price. Considering the variety of cloud service models previously discussed, offering everything from infrastructure to security to event response as a service, an organization might use a dozen different cloud service providers to fulfill its computing requirements. Managing the respective service providers and their associated agreements may be daunting because the providers do not present a cohesive and integrated interface to the organization. Services integration and management (SIAM) is the answer and is exactly what it sounds like—the integration and management of multiple services to provide a seamless one-stop shop to a customer. A SIAM provider closely tracks the key performance indicators (KPIs) of the cloud services that the SIAM client is receiving from various service providers to ensure that the client and its users are receiving a maximum return on value and are not exceeding the specified total cost of consumption. SIAM providers sometimes work separately from the IT provider, on behalf of the client, to corral the client's entire service chain and manage it for ease of use.

Cloud Deployment

Cloud-based technologies can be deployed in several ways—either on-premises, hosted, or cloud—to fit the unique needs of the users who will be using the cloud services. These cloud deployment models include the following:

- A *private cloud* is available only to one organization and can be managed either internally by the organization or externally by a third party.
- A *public cloud* is available to the greater public, with security segmentation between users.
- A *community cloud* is created when two or more organizations create a mutual cloud.

- A *hybrid cloud* combines two or more different cloud deployment models (such as private and community) to perform specific tasks not easily completed through one standard solution. For example, an organization could utilize a community cloud for its greater workforce but segment a portion of its most sensitive data to a private cloud managed internally.
- An example of a *virtual private cloud (VPC)* offers an organization the ability to provision a logically isolated section and launch resources in a virtual network as defined by the organization's requirements. The organization then has control over the virtual networking environment, including the selection of its IP address range, creation of subnets, and configuration of route tables and network gateways. The Amazon VPC, for example, offers a *transit gateway*, a network transit hub that connects the VPC and on-premises networks.

EXAM TIP Compare and contrast the different cloud deployment models and how they can support varying organizational needs.

Virtualization

Virtualization technology allows computer desktops or servers to host and run additional "virtual computers." Using virtualization technology, a single computer can host multiple instances of an operating system environment, all running on the same hardware. These virtualized environments run as if they were a separate system and can run applications, be networked, operate remotely, and perform almost any type of function that a single computer running a single operating system can perform. Virtualized systems are very popular for cross-OS and application testing that allows software to be run and tested on several different types of operating systems, all on the same server.

The concept of virtualization is expanding from the desktop into concepts such as the following:

- *Infrastructure as code (IaC)*, which enables data centers to be managed and provisioned as machine-readable "definition" files that can be deployed much more rapidly than standing up new physical hardware
- *Software-defined networking (SDN)*, which allows greater agility and scalability to meet demand, with less physical overhead through centralized control of the network and a simplified design, ideal when rapid failover is needed
- *Software-defined visibility (SDV)*, which pulls the feeds from SIEMs, IDSs, and other network and security data collection and analysis tools into one seamless "visibility fabric" that is less likely to promote blind spots within the monitoring of the network and allows faster event analysis and response through increased automation

High-powered servers can run several virtualized systems simultaneously, thus helping to reduce the cost of additional hardware and power resources. In addition, virtual systems provide improved security, high availability, and better disaster recovery by running as separate processes on the same hardware.

Virtualization emulates a complete computer system environment by sharing a single system's processors, memory, and hard disks for several individualized operating system environments. These virtual machines run their own separate operating systems and run their own separate applications like a real system. Several different operating system types, such as Linux, Windows, macOS, and Unix, can all run together on one computer in separate virtualized environments while sharing the same hardware resources. Any software crashes or security issues in one virtual machine typically do not affect another virtual machine running on the same computer.

The advantages of virtualization are that the number of physical systems running in your environment can be consolidated on several high-end servers, allowing several virtualized environments to be running on each server. In large-scale data centers, this can greatly reduce the amount of hardware required and thus the space taken up by the hardware; it can likewise reduce the amount of infrastructure resources required, such as power and environmental controls, thus significantly reducing overall operating costs. In terms of desktop computing environments, administrators can deploy secure desktop and network environments that can be accessed remotely without the need for separate keyboards, monitors, and input devices, thus greatly reducing the number of access points that create security risks.

Virtual machines can take snapshots that allow the administrators to "roll back" to a point in time, perhaps before data loss or the introduction of malware into the enterprise. Virtualization allows *elasticity*, where resources can be divided ad hoc upon demand, with minimum—or no—downtime. This also provides a near-automated course of action as required, with the added benefits of being highly scalable and allowing resources to be allocated in a distributed manner. Virtual machines also allow so-called *sandboxing*, where the underlying machine layer supposedly is unharmed in the event of a malware outbreak or other security breach. To ensure that the machine layer is protected, penetration tests that encompass virtualization should be conducted in any enterprise that uses virtualization.

Containers are similar to VMs but do not contain a full operating system, instead of sitting on top of the host operating system. Another emerging software development technique that takes advantage of virtualization is the use of *microservices*, a collection of small services coupled together that operate on top of a well-defined application programming interface (API), allowing more rapid software development with easier integration. Microservices often use containers or serverless architectures for their computing power.

Hypervisors

A *hypervisor* is an application that creates and runs virtual machines. There are two types of hypervisors: Type 1 and Type 2. A Type 1 hypervisor is essentially a bare-bones operating system that runs the host machine and serves to provide the single functionality of managing the VMs installed on it. These types of hypervisors are usually called *bare-metal* (or sometimes *native*) hypervisors, simply because they provide a very limited functionality and exist to load the physical machine and handle resource access from the virtual machines, generally installed directly on the hardware rather than on a conventional OS. For the most part, Type 1 hypervisors are usually installed and then run in "headless" mode, meaning that they don't require a user to be located at the console, but are generally managed remotely through client software on a workstation. For larger environments, Type 1 hypervisors are normally used and typically use powerful physical hardware.

KEY TERM A **hypervisor** is an application that creates and runs virtual machines. There are two types of hypervisors: Type 1 and Type 2. Understand the difference between the two for the exam.

A Type 2 hypervisor is an application that runs on top of a more conventional operating system. Popular Type 2 hypervisors include VMware and Oracle VirtualBox software. Type 2 hypervisors can create and manage a limited number of VMs and are often used in small environments to create and test different aspects of virtualization, including applications that would not run natively on the host OS.

Virtualization Risks

Virtualization is the solution to many problems, such as scalability, hardware production, and even security in some respects, but there are also risks that go with it. One risk of virtualization is that the host machine represents a single point of failure, simply because if the host machine becomes unavailable, loses connectivity, or encounters a serious hardware error, all the VMs that reside on it are also lost. Another risk is that because there may be multiple VMs running on a host, some of which may have several different services or even levels of security controls running on them, the attack surface of the host is expanded, especially if the number of VMs has grown out of hand (known as *VM sprawl*), making their maintenance increasingly difficult. To avoid VM sprawl and maintain a manageable attack surface, it is important to set *resource policies* that limit users' ability to dynamically allocate new resources on the fly. This also avoids the potential pitfall of the organization receiving a whopping bill after unknown or unplanned resources have been consumed. The different services that the VMs run communicate with the outside world and the network, so they represent different attack vectors as well. These represent a threat not only to each individual VM but also to the host overall. Finally, there are attacks, known as *VM escapes*, that attempt to "break out" of the VM environment and attack the hypervisor, or even the host operating system. Protection against a VM escape requires good old defense-in-depth techniques that we've already discussed, such as sandboxing, diligent patching of the hypervisor, and continuous monitoring.

REVIEW

Objective 2.2: Summarize virtualization and cloud computing concepts Use virtualization and cloud computing to simplify and centralize network security administration. A cloud infrastructure can be used to provide a variety of different services such as infrastructure (raw computing power and storage), platforms (operating systems and web server software), and software (applications and databases). Cloud services can be deployed in a few ways—as public, private, or community clouds—or they can be a hybrid of two or more other types. Virtualization is the solution to many problems, such as scalability, hardware production, and even security in some respects, but there are also risks that go with it. Without resource policies, unexpected costs can occur from unplanned resource usage. Also be on the lookout for VM sprawl and potential VM escapes when implementing virtualization within an enterprise.

2.2 QUESTIONS

1. Match the cloud type to its description.

Combines two or more different types of clouds to perform specific tasks not easily completed through one standard solution	A. Private cloud
Is available to the greater public, with security segmentation between users	B. Community cloud
Is available only to the organization and can be managed internally by the organization or externally by a third party	C. Hybrid cloud
Is created when two or more organizations create a mutual cloud	D. Public cloud

2. You have been tasked by your manager with performing an evaluation of the benefits of using virtualization in your quality assurance (QA) testing environment. Which of the following is an advantage of using virtual machines in terms of security and cost efficiency?
   - **A.** It reduces the need to install operating system software updates.
   - **B.** Multiple operating systems can be installed and run in their own separate, secure area on a single hardware device.
   - **C.** It helps secure the hardware from unauthorized access.
   - **D.** Antivirus and other security software must be installed only once.
3. Sam's manager is fed up with managing the dozens of service providers across the corporate portfolio and tasks Sam with finding the best way to provide a seamless view to the corporation's users. What is the *best* option?
   - **A.** Security information and event management (SIEM)
   - **B.** Services integration and management (SIAM)
   - **C.** Microservices
   - **D.** Managed service provider (MSP)

2.2 ANSWERS

1. The answers are as follows:

Combines two or more different types of clouds to perform specific tasks not easily completed through one standard solution	C. Hybrid cloud
Is available to the greater public, with security segmentation between users	D. Public cloud
Is available only to the organization and can be managed internally by the organization or externally by a third party	A. Private cloud
Is created when two or more organizations create a mutual cloud	B. Community cloud

2. **B** Virtual machines all run in their own separate and isolated area on the system as if they were each on a separate physical machine. This greatly increases security because any issues arising in one VM will not affect another VM. This also allows multiple operating systems to be installed on the same physical hardware, which saves money by avoiding the need to buy multiple hardware systems.

3. **B** Services integration and management (SIAM) providers can be hired to corral the corporation's entire services chain and manage it for ease of use.

Objective 2.3 Summarize secure application development, deployment, and automation concepts

Application security is a critical layer of defense that requires not only careful consideration of how applications are designed and developed but also adherence to secure coding techniques. Fortunately, tools and resources are available that can help developers follow best practices and conduct dynamic testing, monitoring, and deployment of applications. Working to integrate secure application practices into the software development life cycle helps ensure that when the application is created, deployed, and used, it is an asset to your organization, not a liability.

Secure Application Development, Deployment, and Automation

With a wide variety of attack vectors, applications are extremely vulnerable to security issues. Poor input validation, weak error and exception handling, and misconfiguration can create vulnerabilities in your applications that can lead to crashes, unauthorized access, and loss of data. Application security begins in the design and development phase to create a secure architecture, whereas application hardening, configuration baselines, and software update maintenance provide continued security when the application is deployed and in use. The following sections describe important concepts and best practices for application security.

Development Life-Cycle Models

EXAM TIP Understand the concepts of scalability and elasticity, not only for software development, but also for cloud resources. They are much the same.

Software development methodologies generally divide the software development process into a series of phases to allow the process to be managed in much the same way as traditional projects, incorporating much more *scalability* (can handle a larger workload through provisioning and deprovisioning of resources) and *elasticity* (fitting the resources to the increased scaled workload). Taken together, these phases are known as the *software development life cycle (SDLC)*. The Waterfall and Agile development methods are two of the most popular SDLC methodologies.

Waterfall Method

The Waterfall method, named after the fact that its steps flow steadily downstream (much like a waterfall, if you can visualize it), is based on a more traditional project management model in which software development proceeds through the phases of conception, initiation, analysis, design, construction, testing, production and implementation, and maintenance. The Waterfall method is not iterative, and when used, organizations do not move to the next phase until the current phase is assessed to be complete.

Agile Method

The Agile software development methodology, as introduced by the Agile Manifesto, is iterative in nature and utilizes teams to deliver earlier and continuously improve more rapidly (hence the name Agile) than the Waterfall development method. The Agile Manifesto states that the software development methodology is based around the values of individuals' interaction being more valuable than tools and processes; working software as more important than comprehensive documentation; customer collaboration being more valued than contract negotiation; and the ability to respond to change as being more important than following a specific plan. Comparing these values to the Waterfall methodology, you can see why this methodology might be valued in some organizational constructs but seen as riskier within others.

Secure Coding Concepts

Developers must build their applications from a secure base and use secure coding concepts to make sure that when an application is deployed, it does not contain security issues and is designed to be resistant to application errors and crashes that can create a condition of vulnerability within the application and potentially expose sensitive data or allow the system to be exploited. The following sections describe some basic secure development concepts that should be applied when creating software.

Open Web Application Security Project

Thankfully, application developers now have invaluable resources such as the *Open Web Application Security Project (OWASP)* to help them improve their application development techniques. OWASP describes itself as "a nonprofit foundation that works to improve the security of software. Through community-led open source software projects, hundreds of local chapters worldwide, tens of thousands of members, and leading educational and training conferences, the OWASP Foundation is the source for developers and technologists to secure the web." One of the best resources that OWASP offers the new (and experienced) developer is the "Top 10 Web Application Security Risks" list, which not only lists the most common vulnerabilities but also provides detailed explanations of how they are exploited and how to prevent them through secure coding techniques. Many automated tools now offer the capability to scan applications for these most common vulnerabilities, as well as others.

ADDITIONAL RESOURCES The OWASP website (https://owasp.org/) is a terrific resource to understand not only current attacks (regularly updated) but also techniques to improve your organization's coding practices.

Secure Development Operations

Development operations (often shortened to *DevOps*) brings together the project and product managers, software developers, and the operations group to better facilitate rapid but secure software development, testing, deployment, and change management through a combination of automation, continuous integration, and secure baselines. As more organizations utilize more rapid software development methodologies, such as the Agile method discussed previously, DevOps became more important to securely but swiftly release software into production.

Emerging tools available to DevOps personnel include immutable infrastructure, infrastructure as code, and automation/scripting tools. *Immutable infrastructure*, although not completely standardized as a definition, means the infrastructure can never be changed once instantiated. If a change needs to be made, it must be replaced fully with another instance of the infrastructure that is fully tested and secure. Think about it this way: as software changes are made, the software and its infrastructure are tested and are ready to be deployed and made immutable (or unable to change). The infrastructure is deployed as a single set, and the old iteration is removed and its resources freed for use. This provides both performance and security benefits.

The rapid development timelines made possible through DevOps are also supported by *automation/scripting tools*, particularly in testing. These tools can check the various courses of action within the code, validate inputs, and even play a role in the integration, delivery, deployment, and monitoring while providing reporting and analytics. Emerging tools can even perform these functions continuously.

Software applications cannot be considered only in a bubble; you must also consider the surrounding infrastructure that supports them, often called a *data center*. DevOps personnel are required to consider these aspects and *provision* (appropriately prepare) and *deprovision* (appropriately release or redirect resources) data center assets to support software and user requirements. Whereas this is often done through the configuration of servers, network hardware, and software residing on subsequent software, *infrastructure as code (IaC)* manages and provisions data centers through machine-readable files rather than the physical hardware. The physical equipment is generally a "bare-metal server" with virtual machines and configurations that all come together to be considered the "infrastructure." Infrastructure as code enables DevOps personnel to be much more agile by automating the process of spinning up or shutting down resources as needed.

Version Control and Change Management

Version control and *change management* are critical because they keep developers from stepping all over themselves and deploying outdated or insecure code into the production environment. They also keep multiple developers from overriding changes that might be written by other developers. Change management also ensures that all the stakeholders associated with a software change, from the developers to the security management, thoroughly understand what changes need to be made, when they will be made, and any second- or third-order effects that might be associated with these changes. Ineffective or missing version control and change management procedures will end up putting your systems at risk—either of wasted time and effort or, more seriously, of an attack associated with improperly vetted software.

Input Validation

Input validation refers to the process of coding applications to accept only certain valid input for user-entered fields. For example, many websites allow users to fill in a web form with their name, address, comments, and other information. If proper input validation code has not been included in these types of web forms, in certain cases a malicious user can enter invalid input into a field that may cause the application to crash, corrupt data, or provide the user with additional unauthorized system access. Invalid input often leads to buffer overflow types of errors that can be easily exploited. Encoding proper input validation within an application reduces the risk of a user inadvertently or intentionally entering input that can crash the system or cause some other type of security concern.

Another concept related to input validation is *escaping*. Without proper validation, hackers can input actual commands into input fields that are then run by the operating system. Escaping recognizes specific types of command characters and parses them as simple data rather than executing the text as a command.

Software Diversity

Software diversity is the practice of using either predetermined processes or synthetic processes to create diversity within the software development process. By analogy, some organizations purposefully use hardware from different manufacturers within their infrastructure to ensure that if hardware from one manufacturer has a zero-day exploit or another serious issue that is presenting vulnerability, the supporting hardware around it will help mitigate the risk and will not have similar vulnerability. The same is true with software diversity in a development environment, such as using randomness within functions and core processes. This is increasingly possible as an automated feature within the compiler itself and allows for diversified software to be distributed within its binary form prior to compilation. Further, software diversity can also be improved by varying the languages that are used within software development, as well as varying the applications that are deployed within an infrastructure to ensure one manufacturer is not overwhelmingly represented, much as in the hardware example. These are great illustrations of how defense-in-depth across an enterprise strengthens an organization—there is no silver bullet to security!

Code Testing and Validation

Dynamic code analysis is conducted by executing software on a real or virtual processor, with inputs that allow the tester to determine how the software will behave in a potentially negative environment, looking for race conditions, incorrectly handled exceptions, resource and memory release issues, and potential attack vectors. It is critical to check for errors on both the client side and the server side. *Fuzzing* is a dynamic technique that can help test input validation and error/exception handling by entering random, unexpected data into application fields to see how the software program reacts. Many application vulnerabilities originate from input validation issues, buffer overflows, and error handling, and fuzzing helps make sure that the software does not crash, lose or manipulate data, or provide unauthorized access based on input validation defects. It is also possible to perform dynamic verification of code at runtime by executing the software and extracting information to determine if it is operating in a secure state and within its modeled specifications.

Static analysis, conversely, is performed without executing the program, either through a manual code review or by using an automated tool, the latter of which is increasingly more common as many programs have become so large that having someone (or a group of people) simply look through the code is not enough.

Stress testing checks the ability of a piece of software to undergo large amounts of stress, or extremely heavy operating loads. Stress testing pushes the software beyond its normal or best-scenario operating environments and determines what the behavior would be in a real-world, heavy-load situation. Stress testing is critical for software and supporting infrastructure where resiliency, reliability, and error handling might mean the difference between life and death, such as in industrial control systems or weapons platforms—though large retail outlets also find it important to use stress testing to understand how the holiday rush might affect their systems.

Finally, *integrity measurement* is emerging to provide key performance indicators (KPIs) of software integrity, such as how many defects are present in the software before testing versus after testing, or before delivery to the customer versus after delivery. These KPIs can help measure how effectively software is developed and how efficiently it is tested prior to deployment.

Error and Exception Handling

Developers must be careful when coding applications to determine how the software program should react to error conditions and exceptions. In many cases, an unexpected error condition can reveal security vulnerabilities that can be exploited. For example, a software program may crash and drop to a command line that can be used by a hacker, or error messages may indicate full file and directory paths that the hacker can use as knowledge to further penetrate the system.

Error and exception handling is largely determined by the operating system and the programming language environment in use because they can offer varying levels of tools to deal with software exceptions. Generally, developers must make sure that a program should still be able to retain its state and continue to function in the event of an error condition. The program should be able to roll back to its previous state without interrupting the flow of the application.

Error messages must be informative to the user, but system details should never be revealed unless the software is running in a special debugging mode only available to the developers, where verbose error logging can help them trace a problem to fix a programming issue.

Memory Management

As we discussed in Domain 1, Objective 1.3, resource exhaustion attacks take advantage of the limited resources that most modern computer systems have available for software applications. Resource exhaustion essentially creates a denial-of-service condition, because the resources that are needed to execute actions associated with an application are entirely exhausted—hence the name—leading to either an error, performance slowdown, or a denial of service. This can be prevented through *memory management* techniques that prevent memory leaks that are either inadvertently written into the code (generally where the software doesn't properly release the memory resources) or through malicious techniques that purposefully cause resource exhaustion.

Transitive Access

Transitive access occurs when you have access permissions or systems of trust between different components of a software application that allow users to pass through unexpectedly and without proper authorization to access another software component.

For example, consider an application or operating system that establishes a trust relationship between two software components, A and B, that allows full access for data passing between these components. Another separate trust relationship is set up between components B and C that allows similar full access between those two components. If there is no explicit nontransitive access specified, any user who is authenticated and authorized for component A is allowed access through component B, and then by the separate trust relationship, unauthorized access to component C.

You must be careful when coding software that no software components allow pass-through transitive access by ensuring that trusts between components are nontransitive and require explicit authorization before access is granted.

Server-Side vs. Client-Side Execution and Validation

As you know by now, validation is a strong mitigation strategy to prevent many attacks. The two main ways to conduct this are client-side validation and server-side validation, and they both have pros and cons.

For example, client-side validation can respond to the user more quickly because the feedback can be generated almost instantaneously; if a user inputs numeric digits in a nonnumeric field, for instance, he can receive instant feedback rather than waiting for the server to respond. This type of validation requires fewer server resources for processing and is generally considered faster.

Server-side validation is more widely compatible; what if the user doesn't have the software installed that you require? A server-based implementation is more software agnostic. It also is generally considered more secure because the server doesn't show its code to the client.

Before implementing a validation technique (and it's incredibly important that you do), consider these benefits and drawbacks, and make the appropriate choice for your situation.

Cross-Site Scripting

Cross-site scripting (XSS) can be prevented via careful web programming and strong input validation that does not permit additional code to be included in dynamic input and is effectively ignored by the application. To prevent command insertion, any special characters that could be interpreted as a command should be "escaped" as harmless data strings.

Cross-Reference

More details about cross-site scripting are covered in Domain 1, Objective 1.3.

Cross-Site Request Forgery

To prevent cross-site request forgery attacks (CSRF), a web application must verify that a request came from an authorized user, not just the browser of an authorized user. Web applications can require a second identifying value saved in a cookie that is compared with every request to the website. This ensures that the request is coming not only from the same user and browser but also the same authenticated session. A hacker who manages to get a user to go to his malicious website and steals her session cookie still requires the temporary session request value to take any action as the target user.

Cross-Reference

Cross-site request forgery is covered in more depth in Domain 1, Objective 1.3.

Secure Coding Techniques

Code reuse is the use of existing source code for a new purpose, either for a new program or for a new environment. Although code reuse obviously can have some cost- and time-saving benefits by eliminating duplication of effort, there are negative aspects to be considered. Reuse of code that contains weak cipher suites and implementations, often incorporated to better integrate with legacy software, can introduce inherent weaknesses into your new project. Similarly, *third-party libraries and software development kits (SDKs)* may not have had adequate quality or security vetting and can also introduce unknown weaknesses. One way to mitigate this is by looking for signed code where possible; *code signing* entails using a certificate to digitally sign executables and scripts to confirm that the software was developed by the appropriate author and has not been manipulated in any way, thus providing integrity and a measure of authenticity. Also, when uploading code to be reused or shared with third parties, be careful to guard against *data exposure*, where sensitive data such as passwords is hard-coded and shared. This can create an easy avenue of approach for an attacker who is combing repositories looking for potential targets. Finally, be on the lookout for *dead code*, which can either be code that is executed but the results are never used or code that is never executed at runtime. This can create issues, not only for code optimization, but also because its removal can sometimes cause unforeseen consequences, such as exceptions or a change in the program's output.

Another important secure coding technique is *normalization*, which basically refers to simplifying the design of a database to remove redundancies and improve integrity. Very simply put, normalization is the design of a database to remove redundancies and improve integrity through simplifying the design. Data redundancies not only consume resources but also create situations where data (let's use "Employee ID" as an example) repeats in multiple database fields or tables. What happens when Employee ID isn't updated properly or consistently across these multiple fields or tables? There is a loss of data integrity, or the trust in the data, and likely the results achieved will be incorrect. Normalization sets a single, primary key that relates fields, and the fields that aren't related via the primary key are ignored or eliminated.

As previously discussed in Domain 5, Objective 5.5, data *anonymization* and *pseudo-anonymization*, *obfuscation* (*data masking*), and the use of tokens in lieu of the data itself (*tokenization*) are security functions for maintaining data privacy, but they also have a role in secure application development. Organizations often use data loss protection or prevention tools across an enterprise to minimize the ways that this data can potentially be exfiltrated, even innocently, such as a person e-mailing their Social Security number without encryption, but when working with databases, for instance, incorporating these techniques can help keep sensitive data more secure from prying eyes.

In a similar manner, *stored procedures* are saved subroutines that can be used within applications accessing databases, saving time and memory by combining the execution of several statements into one stored procedure and allowing applications to call that procedure. This also reduces code duplication, thus further allowing for consolidation and centralization of that procedure. Although using stored procedures can provide security benefits through the central management and less code sprawl, you need to be diligent in reviewing any stored procedures to ensure that you understand clearly what they are executing.

Secure Deployment

It's important to understand the different environments that are involved in securely staging and deploying software applications, most commonly in the following steps:

- **Development (DEV)** The development environment is where software is developed. This is often done in a sandbox, meaning far away from the production systems and data, to minimize any impact from spillover that harms other code and processes resident on the system.
- **Test (TEST)** The testing environment is where the software is tested, either in a static or dynamic manner (or a combination of the two), often using a subset of production data to best mirror the live environment.
- **Quality control/quality assurance (QC/QA)** The QC/QA environment is built for iterative testing to assure new code does not have negative impacts on the functionality.
- **Staging (STAGING)** The staging environment occurs prior to the production environment and allows the code to be subjected to final testing, in as close to a duplicate live environment as possible, before being moved into production.
- **Production (PROD)** Production is the final, live environment that users interact with to get work done. Because this is the most critical environment to keep resilient, it is important to baseline and monitor the integrity of the production environment after every code deployment.

Deploying through these steps properly will ensure that your code is thoroughly tested and securely integrated into the environment in a way that does not introduce risk to your missions.

REVIEW

Objective 2.3: Summarize secure application development, deployment, and automation concepts Applications must be designed and developed with security in place. The OWASP website is a great place to start reviewing secure coding practices. Use input validation to make sure hackers cannot insert malformed input or command requests in application input forms. Escape out special characters and command characters so that they are processed as data, not actual commands. Software should be developed to combat resource exhaustion and memory leaks. Use fuzzing to test input validation by entering random, unexpected characters into application input forms. Don't display filename and directory paths in error messages. Make sure your application handles exceptions without crashing or providing unauthorized access. Make sure applications have secure configuration baselines and that all software is up to date with all security patches installed. Don't forget that there's a full software development life cycle, so paying attention to not only development but also testing, deployment, and maintenance is key.

2.3 QUESTIONS

1. As part of your application-hardening process, which of the following activities helps to prevent existing vulnerabilities in applications from being exploited?
   - **A.** Exception handling
   - **B.** Fuzzing
   - **C.** Updating to the latest software version or patch
   - **D.** Escaping
2. Which of the following is *not* part of the secure deployment process?
   - **A.** Production (PROD)
   - **B.** Testing (TEST)
   - **C.** Quality control/quality assurance (QC/QA)
   - **D.** Sandbox (SAND)
3. __________ is the design of a database to remove redundancies and improve integrity through simplification of the design.
   - **A.** Normalization
   - **B.** Anonymization
   - **C.** Masking
   - **D.** Obfuscation

2.3 ANSWERS

1. **C** Application vendors will release updated software versions of their products or provide a security patch to resolve any security vulnerabilities in previous versions of the software. It is a best practice to always keep your application software up to date.
2. **D** A sandbox allows for malicious code testing as well as preventing legitimate code from conducting unexpected activities that could cause harm, but it is not part of the secure deployment process.
3. **A** Normalization is the design of a database to remove redundancies and improve integrity through simplifying the design.

Objective 2.4 Summarize authentication and authorization design concepts

To use the resources of a computer system or network or to enter a secure facility, a user must first be authenticated. Identification and authentication verify that the user is who he says he is and has the credentials to access these resources. The most common form of authentication requires a username and password, but more secure schemes can use multiple factors to strengthen the authentication process and confidence in the identity and credentials of a user. This section describes the types of authentication models, services, and protocols available that help to provide secure, authenticated access to your networks.

Authentication Concepts

Before a user is allowed access to a facility or resource, the user must pass these levels of security:

- **Identification** The user must initially identify herself as a valid user for that network, usually with a login username or account name, or other recognized credential, such as a smart card. *Identification*, also referred to as *identify proofing*, is the process of presenting valid credentials to the system for identification and further access. For example, before performing any type of online banking, a customer must identify who she is and have sufficient identification, such as a bank card, password, personal identification number (PIN), and so on, to be able to prove her identity before the process goes any further.
- **Authentication** *Authentication* is the process of validating the user's identification. This means that the user is verified as being the person whose identity she has claimed to be. After presenting identifying credentials, the user must then pass the authentication phase. If the credentials she provided match entries in the global database of login usernames and passwords stored on the network, the user is authenticated and is granted access to the network. To be authenticated properly, the user must provide proof that she should be using the login name by supplying a password, PIN, or token. If the identity and password or PIN match the central database, the user is authenticated.
- **Authorization** When a user tries to access a resource, the system must check to see if that user ID is authorized for that resource and what permissions or privileges the user has when using it. *Authorization* is the act of granting permission to an object. Just because a user has been identified and authenticated to a network doesn't mean she should be able to access all resources. If the system determines that the user may access the resource, the user is authorized and allowed access with the privileges she has been granted.
- **Accounting** In the context of network security, accounting is the process of logging users' activities and behaviors, the amount of data they use, and the resources they consume. This allows for a trending analysis that enables both planning and control of authorization, both business focused and security focused.

EXAM TIP Be aware of the differences between identifying a user, authenticating, and authorizing. In a secure, access-controlled environment, these terms specifically correspond to different steps in the process.

Accounting is often grouped with authentication and authorization as *the authentication, authorization, and accounting (AAA)* framework, with one server handling all three needs. Two popular protocols that are often used for centralized AAA are Remote Authentication Dial-In User Service (RADIUS) and the newer Diameter. These protocols are used to manage the full AAA process by authenticating users through a comparison of the user's authentication credentials against those of the server's database. If the credentials match, the user is granted access to the rest of the network.

Cross-Reference

More information on implementing authentication and authorization solutions is contained in Domain 3, Objective 3.8.

There is one other concept that you'll need to know about, *attestation*. While related to authentication, it is slightly different. Authentication verifies who a user is, while attestation is a method of confirming an identity that is based on a third party or a device. An example is attestation tied to a vendor and a specific model of mobile device that verifies that device in order to download a mobile authenticator.

Multifactor Authentication

Single-factor authentication refers to requiring only one factor (such as a password) to authenticate a user. The system compares the password for the account with the database of known usernames and passwords and then authenticates the user if they match. This is the simplest but weakest form of authentication because users' passwords tend to be weak or are easily compromised.

Single-factor authentication can also involve a magnetic swipe card or token used to open a locked door. This is also a weak form of authentication, as the card or token can be easily lost or stolen, and an unauthorized user can simply use the card or token to access the door without needing to provide any other credentials.

Two-factor authentication typically combines two single-factor authentication types, such as something the user knows and something the user possesses. For example, most automated teller machine (ATM) banking transactions require two-factor authentication: the user inserts a physical banking card into the machine and then types a PIN, which is matched with the electronic information contained on the card's magnetic strip. One authentication factor should be physical, such as a smart card or access token (something the user possesses) or a biometric factor (something physically unique about the user), and the second factor should be a password or PIN (something the user knows). Without these two items, no access can be granted.

Multifactor authentication (MFA) is the strongest form of user authentication and involves a combination of a physical item, such as a smart card, token, or biometric factor, and a nonphysical item, such as a password, passphrase, or PIN. Typically, the biometric factor is the third and deciding factor used in combination with an access card and password. For example, before he can enter a high-security facility, a user might have to insert a smart card into a door, enter a PIN on a keypad, and then insert his finger into a scanner.

MFA Factors

A user-authentication system must be able to confirm a user's identity and level of authorization. Combining three of the following common authentication factors provides the highest level of assurance in authenticating a user's identity:

- **Something you *know*** A username, password, or PIN. This is sometimes referred to as the *knowledge factor*.
- **Something you *have*** An ID badge or smart card the user possesses. This is also called the *possession factor*.
- **Something you *are*** A unique physical aspect of the user, such as a biometric characteristic. Sometimes you will see this expressed as the *inherence factor*.

MFA Attributes

Less common are the following attributes that can be used to authenticate users, often in conjunction with the more common authentication factors:

- **Some*where* you are** Location-based authentication, using GPS or another geolocation device. This is also known as the *location attribute*. This is often seen in applications that compare your location to the known-good locations of the authorized user.
- **Something you can *do*** A unique swipe or gesture pattern (often used on mobile devices). Microsoft Windows uses this attribute in its Picture Password feature.
- **Something you *exhibit*** Authentication through a unique trait, such as a neurological pattern or behavioral trait, such as personality.
- **Some*one* you know** Validation provided by another person, through a chain of trust or social network graph.

Authentication Methods

The following sections will discuss established and emerging methods for authenticating users.

Directory Services

Directory services are a repository of information regarding the users and resources of a network. Directory services software applications and protocols are often left open and unprotected because the information they contain sometimes isn't considered important, compared to file server or database server information. Depending on the level of information they provide, however, directory services can be an excellent resource for unauthorized users and attackers to gain knowledge of the workings of the network and the resources and user accounts they contain.

The standard Lightweight Directory Access Protocol (LDAP) service is the underlying protocol that is found in most modern directory service implementations. Examples of directory services include Microsoft Active Directory and OpenLDAP implementations for Linux. Directory services databases contain usernames, e-mail addresses, phone numbers, and user locations, and can be a fantastic resource of information for an unauthorized user or malicious hacker looking for an accounting user or an engineering user for purposes of corporate espionage. Specific directory services that use LDAP may contain more critical network and user information, such as network addresses, user account logins and passwords, and access information for servers.

All LDAP servers have some security controls in place for allowing read and update access to the directory database. Typically, all users can read most of the information held in the database (via specific LDAP-enabled applications or utilities), but only a few users have update privileges. Large directories usually have multiple information administrators who have access to update only information pertaining to their departments or regions.

For a client to access an LDAP server, it must first be authenticated, unless the server allows anonymous connections. This type of access control allows the LDAP server to decide exactly what that client can access and what information it can update.

At the bare minimum, users who query directory services should be authenticated via a login ID and password. This will at least prevent casual unauthorized users from accessing the data on the network's directory services through queries. This is especially important for protecting more critical network-wide directory services, such as Microsoft Active Directory. Only the administrators of the network should have access to read and change the highest levels of the directory hierarchy, whereas common users should be allowed only to look up basic information, such as the e-mail address of another user. Most LDAP servers support the use of encrypted secure channels to communicate with clients, especially when transferring information such as usernames, passwords, and other sensitive data. LDAP servers use the Secure Sockets Layer (SSL) or Transport Layer Security (TLS) protocol (also called *LDAPS*, or sometimes also *Secure LDAP*) for this purpose.

EXAM TIP Remember that LDAP (unencrypted) uses TCP port 389, LDAP over SSL uses TCP port 689, and LDAP over TLS uses TCP port 636.

Single Sign-On

In early computer systems, when networking wasn't as available as it is today, each computer contained a set of resources the user could access. To access the resources of a computer system, the user used a specific login and password. Each specific computer needed a separate login and password. This was tedious for computer users and administrators alike because of the frequency with which login accounts and passwords needed to be reset for each computer if a user forgot them.

Nowadays, modern networks provide resources that are spread throughout the computer network and that can be accessed by any user from any location. The user can be onsite on her own computer, or she can be logged in from home or on the road by using dial-up methods or via the Internet. With the vast amount of resources that can be contained on a large computer network, the concept of different logins and passwords for each resource has been eliminated in favor of a *single sign-on (SSO)* to the network; the user must be authenticated only once on the network to access the resources on it. This type of centralized administration is a much more efficient way for a network administrator to control access to the network. User account policy templates can be created and used network-wide to remove the need to configure each user's account settings individually, except for a unique login and password.

An example of single sign-on is a Microsoft Active Directory username and password required for accessing directories, files, and printers on a network, along with Microsoft Exchange mail servers and SQL database servers.

Federation

Related to single sign-on is the concept of *federation*, often implemented through an enterprise-wide identity management system where a user's identity and associated attributes are carried across enterprise boundaries. This allows a user to log in one time, with his credentials following him through the enterprise and across enterprise boundaries. Federated identities center around the foundational concept of *transitive trust*, where the trust relationship between two domains allows authentication of trusted users across both domains. Transitive trust requires the two (or more) organizations to agree on standards for sharing identity attributes and for the organizations to accept and authenticate identities based on attributes received from external organizations. A great example might be a university student logging in to his school's portal account and then having access based on his associated attributes to external library or academic publication resources that are granted based on his active student status.

Smart Card Authentication

The most common method of personnel access control used today is the smart card. Typically, each employee receives a card with a magnetic strip or computer chip that contains her access information. These cards are swiped in magnetic card readers that are stationed outside important access points, such as doors and elevators. If the card uses a chip, the card is inserted into a card reader. The information on the card is then compared with the security access of the area the person is about to enter. If she doesn't have access to that area, the door won't open.

NOTE Smart cards should include no company identification. If a card is lost or stolen, the unauthorized user would have no idea from which company or facility the card came.

Another type of access card system is the proximity reader, which doesn't require the physical insertion of a card. The reader can sense the card if it's within a certain minimum distance. The information is read through an electromagnetic field.

The card can also be used as a requirement to log in to sensitive networks and computers. Using a card reader, the computer will not allow you to log in until you have inserted your smart card to verify your identity and access level.

EXAM TIP Smart cards can be complemented with access codes or PINs. In the event the card is lost or stolen, it can't be used for access if the proper corresponding PIN is not keyed in. This makes it a multifactor authentication system, since it must use at least two factors to authenticate to the system.

Technologies

Many technologies are available to implement the authentication methods previously discussed. However, with unwieldy solutions, users are less likely to use strong authentication, to security's detriment. The following are current, common solutions that are used to provide authentication in both enterprise and personal environments:

- **HMAC-based One-Time Password (HOTP)** The HOTP algorithm can be used to generate the one-time password values often used to authenticate users via an authentication server. This standard was developed as an interoperable, two-factor algorithm to be used across a variety of platforms, both commercial and open source. You will often hear HOTP and variant algorithms referred to as *two-step authentication* within many web applications.
- **Time-based one-time password (TOTP)** TOTP extends the general HOTP concept through the adoption of a time-based factor, generally measured in seconds. Adding the element of time means that even a second's difference will result in a totally different value for the two passwords generated.
- **Short Message Service (SMS)** SMS is often used to receive a 6- to 8-digit PIN that must be then entered into an interface for authentication.
- **Token key** A token key is a physical device that is inserted into a system to validate your identity through the "something you have" factor.
- **Authentication applications** A growing number of major commercial entities, such as Google, Microsoft, and Blizzard, have adopted authenticators using TOTP as added measures to protect their users. This requires the user to input a username and password combination, and then the user is challenged for a one-time password, generally displayed from a separate device such as a smartphone.
- **Push notifications** Smartphones have the ability to receive push notifications from an app that display a code to be entered for authentication.
- **Phone call** The good old-fashioned phone call is often offered as a backup method, with an automated system providing a code for entry.
- **Static codes** Generally, static codes are generated as a set through a website or application and meant to be stored in hard copy as a backup method to other code delivery methods.

Biometrics

Biometric access control offers the most complete and technologically advanced method for securing access. The technology used to be available only to extremely high-security installations because of the high costs, but it has become less expensive over time and is now becoming more commonplace in small businesses and even consumer-grade devices. Biometrics uses a unique physical attribute—such as a fingerprint, voice scan, or retinal scan—to identify a user.

Initially, the user requesting access must have the particular attribute scanned so that a perfect copy is on file for comparison when the user tries to gain access in the future. These types of biometric systems are complex and sensitive, and they can often result in false permissions and denials for access. These events effect the *efficacy rate* of that biometric method, or how well it can perform the authentication task at hand. Efficacy is measured through the *false acceptance rate (FAR)*, which is the rate at which a biometric system allows access to an unauthorized individual based on an incorrect identification, and the *false rejection rate (FRR)*, which is when the biometric system incorrectly rejects access to an authorized user. A system that has a high FAR—allowing unauthorized access—is considered to be more dangerous than one with a high FRR, which is generally just annoying due to the unnecessary rejections. The *crossover error rate (CER)* is the rate where the system has been tuned to be precise enough that the FAR and FRR are equal. Note that the FAR is considered a "false negative" reading, and a FRR is considered a "false positive." It is also important to note that biometric systems must be constantly calibrated, so repeated measurements of users' biometric data are often required.

Table 2.4-1 lists a number of the most common types of biometric collection and analysis methods, along with their description.

Cloud vs. On-Premises Requirements

Whether in the cloud, on premises, or some hybrid of the two, identification, authentication, authorization, and accounting are central to the security of an organization. As discussed previously, authentication services for cloud-based services are centralized, sometimes through a combination of cloud and on-premises solutions, and each device that will access cloud services and data should authenticate and be authorized before being allowed access. Because of this, device security is critical for protecting access to the cloud. If a device, such as a user's mobile phone, that is used for MFA is lost or stolen, it can be used to authenticate into cloud services and associated data, either through access to authentication methods, such as on-device authenticators or push notifications, or through access to cloud-connected applications. A further concern with the cloud is misconfiguration leading to data exposure. It is important that successful user authentication only allow access to the user's specific data in the cloud and not to other users' data that is stored. Cloud service providers must practice diligence and defense-in-depth to ensure that users only receive access to their own resources.

Cross-Reference

More info on cloud computing can be found within Objective 2.2 earlier in this domain.

TABLE 2.4-1 Biometric Methods and Descriptions

Method	Description
Palm/fingerprint	No two fingerprints are alike. A user must place his hand on a biometric scanner that compares it to the palm scan and fingerprints on file for that user.
Retinal	A person's retina is a unique attribute, like a fingerprint. The user must place his eye up to a device that projects a light beam into the eye to capture the retinal pattern.
Iris	Much like the retina, a person's iris is unique and very complex. The iris also has the benefit of being very stable over the human lifetime, whereas the retina can be affected by disease, pregnancy, and chronic health conditions and change over time.
Facial	A facial scan records the unique characteristics of each user's face, such as bone structure and the shape of the eyes and nose. These characteristics can be captured in the scan and compared to the facial scan on file.
Voice	The voice is also a unique characteristic for each user. The user is recorded speaking a set of access words, and the captured voice print can be compared to the same spoken words the next time the user tries to gain access.
Vein	Alternately known as *vascular biometrics*, a scan is made of the unique vein patterns within a finger, palm, or eye.
Gait analysis	Every person has a unique gait, or walking pattern. The gait analysis is performed through scanning or sensors (either worn or embedded within the floor).

On-premises authentication becomes the organization's configuration and security concern, but also allows for the inclusion of some unique attributes, such as only allowing users who are on premises to authenticate. Users who require remote access to on-premises systems and data often must connect to a remote authentication server that exists on the premises and then, after successful authentication, treats the users as if they were onsite. Active Directory is a good example of a traditional on-premises solution that has begun to bridge between the traditional enterprise and the cloud, with its Azure AD solution, to allow users a "seamless" experience as they move between different operating environments.

REVIEW

Objective 2.4: Summarize authentication and authorization design concepts Identification ensures that a user (which could also be an application program or process) is who the user claims to be. The user must then pass the authentication phase using a unique logon username or account number and a password. If these two criteria are matched with the global database of login usernames and passwords stored on the network, the user is granted access to the network. Finally, when a user tries to access a resource, the system must check to see if that user ID is authorized for that resource and what permissions or privileges the user has when accessing it. Multifactor authentication schemes build upon single-factor authentication by combining multiple single-factor authentication types, such as something the user knows (a password or PIN) and something the user possesses (a magnetic swipe card or token). Biometric systems offer the most complete and advanced methods to identify people through a unique physical attribute, such as a fingerprint, voice scan, or retinal scan, but a balance between the FAR and FRR must be achieved in order to find the CER.

2.4 QUESTIONS

1. You are tasked with setting up a single sign-on authentication system for a large enterprise network of 5000 users. Which of the following is the best option?
   - **A.** Local login and password database
   - **B.** Login and password with a security token
   - **C.** Authenticated access to an LDAP database
   - **D.** Smart card with PIN number
2. Bobby is tasked with creating a high-security authentication system for physical access control to a military installation. Which of the following authentication systems would be most appropriate?
   - **A.** Smart card and PIN
   - **B.** Security badge and guard
   - **C.** Biometric eye scanner
   - **D.** Username and password
3. A web services provider wants to improve its security through the implementation of two-factor authentication. What would be the most likely authentication method?
   - **A.** TOTP
   - **B.** SIEM
   - **C.** TACACS
   - **D.** LDAP
4. After a user is identified and authenticated to the system, what else must be performed to enable the user to use a resource?
   - **A.** Authorization
   - **B.** Authentication by token
   - **C.** Encryption of network access
   - **D.** Biometric scan

2.4 ANSWERS

1. **C** An LDAP server provides a centralized directory that can be used to securely authenticate a user to multiple services on the same network. This is the most efficient and secure method for a large network of 5000 users. Other methods would require tedious configuration and management of each individual user.
2. **A** Of the examples, the smart card (something you have) and the PIN (something you know) combine as a multifactor authentication solution that is more robust than single-factor solutions.
3. **A** Time-based One-time Passwords (TOTPs) allow users to log in to a system with a username and password combination and then a one-time token, usually generated from a separate device.
4. **A** Although a user has been given access to log in to the network, the user still needs to be authorized to use a particular resource based on access permissions.

Objective 2.5 Given a scenario, implement cybersecurity resilience

Disaster recovery and continuity of operations planning are extremely important in preventing downtime for your organization in the event of equipment or communications failure. Your system's ability to recover from a disaster is greatly dependent on the facilities and equipment available if your main facility is heavily damaged or destroyed. Backup equipment and facilities are vital elements in planning for recovery, and each should be examined for both onsite and offsite strategies.

High availability, redundancy planning, and fault tolerance are extremely important concepts in ensuring cybersecurity resilience, and they must be implemented in an in-depth manner across an enterprise.

Resiliency Concepts

Earlier, Objective 2.1 discussed resiliency in the context of the different types of alternate sites (cold, warm, hot) that an organization can choose to have on standby in case of a disaster. This objective discusses resiliency in the context of ensuring that your organization's cybersecurity is resilient to all types of interruption. *Resiliency* means that an organization's IT systems are capable of operating continuously through adverse events (though possibly at a less-than-optimal level temporarily). The ability to provide uninterrupted service consistently is the goal of maintaining a *high-availability* system. This initially requires that you identify systems that need to provide services always. Answer the following questions to help you in planning for high-availability systems:

- What are the customer's availability requirements?
- What is the monetary cost of an extended service downtime?
- What is the cost to a customer relationship that can occur because of an extended service downtime directly affecting that customer?
- Which services must be available always? Rank them in order of priority.

If your company hosts services that are required by customers, these services should be given higher priority than your own systems because the service level promised to customers must be maintained always.

KEY TERM Often you'll hear the term *scalability* mentioned alongside *high availability*. They are related, but not the same. **Scalability** allows resources and systems to grow or shrink based on demand.

Service Levels

Many companies measure their ability to provide services as a *service level*. For example, a web server–hosting company might promise 99 percent service availability for the systems and services it hosts. The other 1 percent of the time, the systems might be unavailable because of maintenance, equipment failure, or network downtime.

NOTE A service level specifies in measurable terms the level of service to be received, such as the percentage of time that a particular service is guaranteed to be available. Many Internet service providers (ISPs) provide a service level agreement (SLA) to guarantee customers a minimum level of service. Some IT departments now provide a measured service level to the rest of the company as an internal metric. Service levels with high guaranteed uptimes help ensure resilience through high availability.

Service levels can also specify minimum bandwidth, guaranteed low latency, and other quality of service (QoS) functions. The most common examples of servers and services that require high availability and high service levels include the following:

- **Internet servers** These include Internet services, such as web and File Transfer Protocol (FTP) servers. These types of servers usually require that the information and data stored on them be always available.

- **E-mail** E-mail is the most commonly used Internet service because all users need and use it. Therefore, mail servers and gateways must maintain high levels of service availability.
- **Networking** As the backbone of all computer communications, the networking equipment that provides the infrastructure for private and public networks must be always available.
- **File servers** File servers house all data needed by the users. Without access to this data, users can't perform their job functions.
- **Database servers** Database servers are typically required as back-end servers to web servers and other applications that use database transactions. Data stored on database servers, just like that stored on file servers, must be always available.
- **Telecommunications** Even in an Internet-centric organization, phone and other voice telecommunications systems are still services that require high availability. In the event of a disaster, your voice communications will be of the highest critical priority in order to coordinate disaster recovery efforts.

Redundancy

The key components of redundancy planning are high availability and fault tolerance. Maintaining high availability is the premier goal of most businesses that guarantee access to data and provide host services and content that must be always available to the customer. To protect your systems and network equipment and to provide redundancy for maintaining high-availability service, you must implement *fault-tolerant* systems. To make a system fault tolerant, it should contain several redundant components that will allow it to continue functioning if an equipment failure occurs. For example, a server with only one hard drive and one power supply isn't fault tolerant: if the power supply fails, the entire server is rendered useless because there's no power to the system. Similarly, if your file server's hard drive crashes and is unrecoverable, all data on that hard drive is lost. Fault-tolerant systems are important for maintaining business continuity. The key point about redundancy is that it helps to eliminate single points of failure.

Equipment Redundancy

Most disasters and disruptions are localized in nature and typically involve only one room or one piece of equipment. Failed hardware, such as a blown power supply, damaged network cabling, failed hard drive, or broken tape backup drive, is the most common type of service interruption. Having spare hardware onsite to fix these small problems is vital to handling these smaller disruptions quickly. Many companies have vendor maintenance contracts that require the vendor to replace failed hardware, but in case of an emergency, the spare parts might not be delivered for many hours or even days. It's critical for hardware components that are commonly prone to failure to be switched quickly with an onsite spare.

The following spare components should always be kept onsite:

- Hard drives
- Redundant array of independent disks (RAID) controllers
- Small Computer System Interface (SCSI) controllers
- Hard-drive cabling
- Memory
- Central processing units (CPUs)
- Network cards
- Keyboards/mice
- Video cards
- Monitors
- Power supplies
- Network switches, hubs, and routers
- Phones

It is also highly recommended that you have a contact list on hand for the manufacturers/vendors of your components in the event a replacement part needs to be ordered.

Redundant Servers In high-availability environments such as e-commerce and financial websites, where servers must be up and running 24 hours a day and seven days a week, a downed server can cause a company severe financial damage. Customers will be unable to make purchases online while the server is down, and critical stock trades or financial transactions cannot take place. In these environments, redundant servers are installed that will take over in the event the primary server is unavailable. For example, an organization with a critical web server can install a secondary identical web server that can be swapped with the primary if the primary is down. If redundant servers are not running concurrently, having spare servers and workstations on hand means that if the primary server goes down, the failed file server hardware can be quickly replaced and the data restored from backup. This is often the preferred method for smaller organizations that do not have the resources or budget to run live redundant systems.

KEY TERM **High availability** ensures that a service, such as a web or database server, is always available. Redundancy via live or spare replacement servers is a recommended method of ensuring high availability.

System Configuration Backups The use of backups in a business continuity sense involves backing up not only important data but also the system files and configuration settings of your server and network equipment.

When equipment failure causes the loss of your server, you not only lose the data and services housed on that server but also lose all your system settings and configuration. Depending on the type of server, these configuration settings can be complex and can take many hours, or even days, to restore. For example, an e-mail server is usually configured with many options and settings that are unique to your location. If the server has failed or is destroyed and needs to be rebuilt, you'll need to reinstall the operating system (OS), reinstall your e-mail server applications, and configure the system properly before you can restore your mail files that were backed up. If you didn't back up your system files, you'll need to recall and enter your system settings manually, which can take up too much time when a high-availability server is down.

Most modern backup applications have disaster recovery options that save important elements of the OS and application configuration files so that they can be instantly restored in case of a disaster. If you're recovering a server, you need only install the OS and the required media device drivers for your backup media device to retrieve the rest of your server files and system configuration from the backup media.

Redundant Internet Connectivity It might be surprising to learn that many organizations rely on only one ISP to host their connections to the Internet. If any communications issues occur with the Internet line or the ISP itself, the organization's communications are instantly crippled. Users will not be able to access the Internet or e-mail and, for organizations that have deployed Voice over IP (VoIP) telephony applications, the telephones will not be operational. It is difficult to think that so much time and money can be spent on redundant servers and equipment, while no thought is put into communications redundancy.

It is a best practice to have two or even three completely different ISP services and connections to provide a backup line of communication or to run concurrently with your current ISP line. In the event one of the ISPs or lines goes down, users will still be able to communicate to the Internet via the redundant connection. The ISP lines must be from different companies, or else your supposedly redundant Internet lines will be going to the same point of failure at the same ISP, and if the central router fails at the ISP, both your connections to the Internet will be down.

Many organizations also use redundant ISPs to provide some bandwidth control. For example, critical applications and services can be routed to one ISP, while general company connectivity (such as e-mail or web browsing) can be directed to the second ISP to ensure critical applications receive the maximum bandwidth they require from their own dedicated Internet connection.

Geographical Redundancy

In the event of a physical disaster such as a fire or a flood at your main company site, or even a disruption in power or Internet service, you need to plan for alternate facilities (or, in some cases, alternate capabilities) to get your company operational again. In some cases, your original server and networking equipment could be damaged or destroyed, and then a new infrastructure must be created at a new site. For a company with no alternate site in its disaster recovery plan, this could mean many weeks before a facility is secured and new equipment is set up in the new building. The purpose of an alternate site is to have a facility already secured and, in some cases, already populated with a network and server infrastructure to minimize downtime. The choice of alternate sites comes down to how time-sensitive your company's product or services are and how fast you need to be operational again.

Is important to consider where you place your alternate site geographically. For example, for truly mission-critical systems, it is better to have the site be in an area that is not too close to an ocean (missing hurricanes) and not prone to tornadoes, flooding, or other damaging natural weather scenarios. Take, for example, the Cheyenne Mountain Complex in Colorado Springs, Colorado. It's built into the side of the mountain, and its natural attributes, along with a great deal of redundancy that was planned in, is designed to allow missions to withstand any number of natural or man-made disasters.

Geographic dispersal from your main site is also an important consideration, for several reasons. In the event of a crisis, you will want to have maximum speed for your alternate processing, and longer distances make this more difficult. Therefore, many cloud providers have multiple locations that they can fail over to across a large geographical area. Also, it is recommended that an alternate site be at least five miles from any "prime" targets of terrorist activity, such as military installations or major government buildings. Finally, not sharing the same utility grid is smart.

Legal implications are also an issue to be considered, with data sovereignty being one of the most important considerations. Because different nations have different laws governing what can be done with data processed within their borders, it is important to take those requirements into consideration when choosing where to locate an alternate site. For example, the European Union, which encompasses many of the most important data processing centers in the world, has different data processing standards than the United States, with penalties for companies that do not comply. A multinational company that chooses to have a European alternate site may find that it is not prepared to protect the data to the standards set by the European Union, such as the General Data Protection Regulation (GDPR). This could set a company up for big problems if it does not comply with the data handling and processing requirements. It truly is a tricky time to be a multinational company that relies heavily on data, especially privacy data.

Cross-Reference

More information on different types of alternate sites is provided in Objective 2.1, earlier in this domain.

Disk Redundancy

To ensure data integrity, it isn't enough to implement redundant hardware components, such as power supplies and network cards. Emerging solutions allow true *multipath* capability, allowing uninterrupted access to critical assets in a near-seamless manner. In the event that a controller fails, for example, a multipath solution can reroute to a different controller to continue operating.

Because hard drives are partly mechanical in nature, this makes them one of the most common components prone to failure on a server. The hard drives contain all the data, and if the hard drive fails, that data can be irretrievably lost.

NOTE If a hard drive fails or its data is corrupted, the information it contains can sometimes be retrieved by special hard-drive recovery specialists. However, this recovery process can be both time consuming and expensive.

The most common method of hard-drive redundancy is to use a RAID system. RAID allows data to be spread across two or more hard drives, so if one hard drive fails, the data can be retrieved from the existing hard drives.

KEY TERM **Redundant array of independent disks (RAID)** defines the concept of using several separate hard drives to create one logical drive. If one of the drives fails, the system can rebuild the information using the remaining disks.

Some fault tolerance concepts must be understood before RAID implementation:

- **Hot swap** Refers to the ability to insert and remove hardware while the entire system is still running. Most types of hardware require that the system be shut down before components are removed or inserted. Hard drives in RAID systems are the most common type of hot-swap device.
- **Warm swap** Refers to the ability to insert and remove hardware while a system is in a suspended state. Although less flexible than hot swap, warm swap means you needn't shut down the entire server to replace hardware components. When the swap is complete, the server resumes its normal operations. Although services are shut down during the suspend period, time is saved by not having to reboot the entire system.
- **Hot spare** Refers to a device already installed in the system that can take over at any time when the primary device fails. There's no need to physically insert or remove a hot-spare device.

RAID can be implemented via hardware or software. Hardware RAID is based on a disk controller that controls the redundancy process across several physical hard drives. Software RAID relies on operating system kernel processes to control the RAID redundancy process, and although less expensive, it requires much more CPU processing power to manage the RAID process, and a software problem could put your data at risk compared to a dedicated hardware solution.

Mirroring the contents of one hard drive on another is called *RAID 1*. Several RAID levels can be implemented, depending on the number of disks you have and the importance of the information being stored. Other RAID techniques include *striping*, which spreads the contents

TABLE 2.5-1 RAID Levels

RAID Level	Minimum Number of Hard Drives	Characteristics
0	2	Striping only, no fault tolerance
1	2	Disk mirroring
3	3	Disk striping with a parity disk
5	3	Disk striping, distributed parity
6	4	Disk striping, double distributed parity
0+1	4	Disk striping with mirroring

of a logical hard drive across several physical drives and includes parity information to help rebuild the data. If one of the hard drives fails, parity information is used to reconstruct the data. Most RAID systems use hot-swap drives, which can be inserted and removed while the system is still running. To increase the fault tolerance of a RAID system, redundant RAID controllers can be installed to remove the disk controller as a single point of failure. Table 2.5-1 describes the most common RAID levels and their characteristics.

Network Redundancy

Load balancing allows administrators to balance the load traversing a network across several resources in a distributed manner. Load balancing is often used with websites that receive a large amount of traffic, ensuring that the web server is not a single point of failure. Applying the concept of load balancing allows for a failover mechanism in the event one server is lost due to mishap or disaster. This can be implemented in several ways, including clustering.

For more advanced high-availability purposes, the use of clustering technology enables you to use several servers to perform the services of one. Clustering greatly enhances load balancing, as the resources of all the servers can be used to perform the same task as one server. For fault tolerance purposes, if one system goes down, one of the other servers in the cluster can take over seamlessly without any interruption to the clients.

Two primary types of clusters are used: active/active and active/passive. *Active/active* means that both servers in the cluster are up and running and actively responding to requests. In the event one server is unavailable, no loss of availability occurs because the other server is still actively responding to requests. In an *active/passive* arrangement, one server is actively responding to requests while the other server acts as a live standby. In the event the active server is unavailable, the passive server can be triggered into becoming the active server and begin responding to requests.

For major disaster recovery scenarios, failover systems and redundant servers can be kept in buildings of other company locations. For example, a company operating in Los Angeles might have another facility operating in New York City. This allows the NYC servers to take over the services offered by the LA servers if Los Angeles suffers an interruption or disaster.

One of the most overlooked fault-tolerant-capable devices in a system is the network card. Typically, little thought is given to the scenario of a failed network card. In the real world, losing connectivity to a server is the same as having the server itself crash because the server's resources can't be accessed. Many modern servers now come preinstalled with redundant network cards. Extra network cards can also be used for load balancing, as well as being available to take over if another network card fails. For example, a file server can be configured with two network cards. In case one network card fails, network communications can continue uninterrupted through the second network card, a concept known as *NIC teaming*.

Power Redundancy

Because of their electrical nature, power supplies are another important common computer component prone to failure. As the central source of power for any computer or network device, a power supply that fails can instantly render a critical computer system useless. Most modern servers come with multiple power supplies, which are running as hot spares. If one of the power supplies fails, another immediately takes over without an interruption in service. Some high-end servers have as many as three extra power supplies. Many network devices, such as switches and routers, now come with dual power supplies. Replacing a single power supply on such a small, enclosed device would be difficult.

Although redundant power supplies can provide fault tolerance in a server if one of the power supplies fails, they can't protect against the total loss of power from the building's main power circuits. When this happens, your entire server will immediately shut down, losing any data that wasn't saved and possibly corrupting existing data. In this case, a battery backup is needed. An *uninterruptible power supply (UPS)* contains a battery that can run a server for a period after a power failure, enabling you to shut down the system safely and save any data.

NOTE Most UPSs come with software that can configure your server to automatically (and gracefully) shut down when it detects the UPS has taken over because of a power failure.

For large organizations with critical high-availability requirements, a more expensive option for backup power is the use of a *generator* that runs on a battery or fuel. When using batteries, a power generator has a finite time that it can run until the battery power runs out. A fuel-based generator, on the other hand, can be kept operational if it continues to be filled with fuel, and it provides electricity even for very long blackout periods if fuel is available.

Also very commonly seen in larger organizations, especially those with a data center, are *managed power distribution units (PDUs)*, which are rack mounted and often look like beefier home power strips. These often provide a visual "meter" that displays current power consumption and allows for monitoring to prevent overloads and the ability to hot swap between power sources without powering down the equipment.

Software and Hardware Diversity

As discussed in previous objectives, software and hardware should be diversified within an enterprise to minimize vulnerability. This is a critical consideration for cybersecurity resilience, because a vendor-specific vulnerability can potentially bring an organization to its knees if its technology is not diverse. Consider the concept of "defense-in-depth" when planning your resiliency. Being sure that you're not too reliant on a specific vendor, a specific technology, or even one type of cryptographic solution keeps an attacker on their toes.

Cross-Reference

The concept of software diversity is explored in Objective 2.3, earlier in this domain.

Backups

Critical to a company's preparedness is having a proper backup and disaster recovery plan. Without any sort of data backup, a company risks having its entire data store wiped out forever. In most cases, this would cause the company to go under immediately or face a long rebuilding stage until it can become operational again. A well-defined disaster recovery plan is coupled with a backup strategy. Although the expense and planning for such a large disaster can be costly and time consuming because of the dedication of resources and equipment costs, these must be compared to the costs involved with losing the ability to do business for many days, weeks, or months.

Planning

A good backup strategy must be clearly planned, defined, executed, documented, and tested. The first step in establishing your backup strategy is to draft a plan that covers the following points: the type of data to be backed up, the frequency with which backups will occur, the amount of data that will be backed up, the retention period for the backups, and the order in which services will be restored.

Your company's data must be separated into mission-critical data and more constant data that doesn't change much over time. Obviously, the most important data is the information the company requires during its daily business activities, especially if this information is something frequently accessed by customers. For example, a database company will ensure that it fully protects its customers' data. If the company loses that data without any procedure for disaster recovery, its business is essentially lost. Also critical to planning is to determine the *restoration order*, the order in which services (and their associated backups) will be restored. This needs to be documented in writing so that, when the time comes, there is no guesswork. Critical business services must be prioritized over important but less urgent services such as e-mail.

Depending on the type of data your company stores, a wide range of backup frequency schedules can be implemented. For example, a transactional database used every day by customers would be considered critical data that must be backed up every day. Other files such as OS and application program files that don't change often can be backed up on a lighter schedule—say, once a week. Backup frequency should depend on the critical nature of the data, as well as the costs involved with losing and re-creating data from the same point in time. Some high-end transactional databases, for example, need to be backed up many times a day because of the high rate of transactions.

The amount of data to be backed up will have a large bearing on the type of backup strategy you choose. Depending on how much information you need to save daily, you might be unable to perform a completely full backup of all your data every night because of the time it takes to perform the operation. To create a backup plan that can meet your objectives, you must achieve a balance between the type of data and the frequency with which it needs to be backed up. Instead of using full backups, you can try other alternatives, such as performing incremental or differential backups on information that has only recently changed.

You must decide how long you need to keep backed-up data. Depending on the type of business and the type of data, you might need to archive your backup data for long periods of time so it will be available if you need to perform a restore. Other data might be needed only in the short term and can be deleted after a certain period. This is often tied to data retention policies and driven by specific legal governance requirements, depending upon data sensitivity.

NOTE The legal policy of some companies is to retain information for a certain period before the information must be destroyed. Check with your legal department to create a policy for backup media retention.

Backup Hardware

Several types of backup hardware and devices are available to suit the needs of the backup strategies of most companies. In the past, the most common type of backup system used was magnetic tape. These can be simple devices that contain only one tape drive, or large jukebox tape libraries with robotic autoloaders. Magnetic tape drives and media are flexible and offer relatively inexpensive storage combined with speed and ease of use.

The vast amount of data storage used by today's disk drives that are into the terabyte (TB) territory and the speed required to back up such a vast amount of data are slowly making tape backups a thing of the past. Today's backup systems use a combination of more traditional on-premises solutions such as magnetic tape, disk drives (including removable drives), storage area networks (SANs), virtual machines (VMs), and network-attached storage (NAS), as well as more recent additions such as cloud storage.

Cross-Reference

More details on SANs and NAS are provided in Objective 2.1, earlier in this domain.

Backup hardware should be routinely inspected for faults. Because of its mechanical nature, tape backup hardware is more prone to failure than typical electrical devices. Magnetic tape drives should be maintained periodically with a special tape to clean the magnetic heads, which become dirty over time. Backup solutions that rely on disk drives, such as NAS devices, need to be monitored for failing drives, which should be immediately replaced.

Backup Types

An important part of your backup strategy is deciding what type of backup you'll perform. Depending on the size of all the data you need to back up daily, a full backup of everything every night might be impossible to do. The amount of backup media required and the time needed to perform the backup can render this option unfeasible. The goal is to achieve the most efficient backup and restoration plan possible, depending on your environment and the type of data to be backed up.

Each file on a computer system contains a special bit of information, called the *archive bit*. When a file is modified or a new file is created, the archive bit is set to indicate the file needs to be backed up. When a backup is performed, the archive bit is either cleared or left as is, depending on the type of backup method chosen.

A *full backup* includes all files selected on a system. A full backup clears the archive bit of each file after every backup session to indicate the file has been backed up. The advantages of a full backup include the fact that all data you selected is saved during every session, so all your system's data is backed up in full. If you need to restore all the information back on to the server, the recovery time is much shorter because it's saved in a specific backup session and can be restored with a single restore operation. For example, if you perform a full backup on Wednesday night and the server crashes Thursday morning, your data loss will be minimal. The disadvantages of using a full backup are that, depending on the amount of data you have, the backup could take up a large amount of media and the time it takes to perform the backup could intrude on normal working hours, causing network delays and system latency. Notable here is the difference between a full backup, which clears the archive bit, and a *copy*, which does not clear the archive bit.

With an *incremental backup*, only those files that have been modified since the previous full or incremental backup are stored. The archive bit is cleared on those files that are backed up. Incremental backups are much quicker to perform than full backups, and they use up much less space on backup media because you're saving only files that have been changed. The disadvantage of incremental backups is that to restore an entire system, you need to restore the last full backup and every incremental backup since then.

A *differential backup* saves only files that have been changed since the last full backup. In this method, the archive bit isn't cleared, so with each differential backup, the list of files to save grows larger each day until the next full backup. The advantage of differential backups is that to restore an entire system, you need only the last full backup and the most recent differential backup. The disadvantage is that backups take more time and use more media with each differential backup that takes place.

A *snapshot* enables you to take a picture of your system configuration at a known-good point in time and roll back to that configuration at some point in the future if the system becomes unstable or is corrupted. For example, suppose that your organization is about to undertake a major software upgrade that could radically change the user experience and ability to conduct daily operations. Being able to take a snapshot and then roll back in the event of an unexpected snafu would be exceptionally helpful. There are many contingencies where having that ability to revert to a snapshot and not lose hours, or even days, of rebuilding a system from scratch could keep a business afloat.

Finally, you should be aware of replication and how it can support high availability requirements. We'll talk about replication in more depth in Domain 3, Objective 3.6, but simply, *replication* allows storage to be replicated, or essentially copied, from one place to another. Replication creates, as the name suggests, an exact replica of your production or primary site, again supporting high availability requirements. While this is a powerful tool for availability in the time of crisis, do bear in mind that if you have issues such as corrupted data and it's replicated, it will indeed follow you along.

Offsite Storage

In the event of a disaster at your primary site, such as fire or a flood, any backup media stored there could also be destroyed. All the data that's saved to backup will be lost, and you won't have other backups available. Therefore, you should store copies of the backup media offsite. Offsite storage is an important part of your overall disaster recovery plan. Using an offsite storage facility means that after you successfully complete your backups, they're sent to a different location, which could be another office building or a special storage company facility.

NOTE In case you want to keep your most recent backup media onsite, you can make two copies of your full backup and send only one of them to the offsite storage company.

When choosing an offsite storage facility, you must ensure it follows the same basic rules of facility security measures that you follow at your own site. You should visit the location where your backup media will be stored to examine the environment. For example, the storage area should be regulated for temperature, humidity, fire prevention, and static electricity prevention. Access control should be strictly enforced so only authorized employees of your company can retrieve backup media from the facility. You should also consider encrypting the backups. Depending on the type of data you're sending offsite, you should identify how quickly you'll need access to the media, if this is necessary. The distance from the main site to the offsite storage is a consideration. In the event of a crisis where the offsite backup needs to be restored, if personnel need to make it onsite, time could be a factor if measured in hours, not minutes. However, storing the data too close to the primary site could subject the offsite storage to the same natural disaster scenarios. The storage facility should also allow access at all hours in case you need a backup in an emergency.

Online Backup

With the vast increase in Internet bandwidth speed and capacity, online backup services that back up your data over the Internet are a popular alternative for offsite storage of physical backup media. Client software is installed on your system, and an initial upload takes place of your data. Depending on the amount of data, this can take many days before the full body of data is synchronized. After the initial synchronization, your file system is constantly scanned, and changed files are automatically synchronized over the Internet to a secure server.

Some online servers offer synchronization services that keep only a copy of your data in its current state. There is no way to retrieve a deleted file or a file that was changed two weeks ago but has been modified several times since that initial change. Other services offer version control, where you can restore a deleted file or a version of a file several weeks old.

For security, you must make sure the online backup server stores your data in encrypted form and that all network communications with the service are over encrypted channels such as a Transport Layer Security (TLS) connection.

Online backup services are geared toward individual systems or small business servers, and they cannot scale up to handle the vast amount of data produced by a large company or data center. For these larger networks, the same online backup principles can be applied and the data kept securely within the company's networks by synchronizing or backing up data between geographically different sites.

Media Rotation and Retention

Another important factor in your backup plan is determining the length of time that backup media and their data should be retained. Theoretically, you could save every backup you create forever, but this increases costs because of the large amount of backup media you'll need to purchase on a routine basis. Magnetic tape media usually deteriorate over time, and if you use the same tapes over and over, they'll quickly wear out. The integrity of your backups might be compromised if you continue to use the same tapes. Media rotation and retention policies must be defined to form the most efficient and safe use of your backup media. Several methods can be used for rotation and retention, from simple to the most complex.

EXAM TIP Be aware of the advantages and disadvantages of each type of backup method, considering the environment and availability requirements.

Son Backup Method The *son backup method* is the simplest method to use because it involves performing a full backup every day, using the same backup media each time. This method is used only for small backup requirements. The media can quickly wear out and must consistently be replaced. The son method doesn't allow for archiving, and if you need to perform a restore, you can use only the last backup as a source—so if the file you're looking for was deleted months ago, the data can't be recovered.

Father-Son Backup Method The *father-son backup method* uses a combination of full and differential or incremental backups on a weekly basis. For example, daily media are used for a differential or incremental backup from Monday to Thursday, while Friday or weekend media are used to perform a full backup that can be archived away as a weekly backup. This method enables you to retrieve files archived from the previous week using the weekly full backup. Additional backup media can be added to the strategy if further archiving is needed.

Grandfather-Father-Son Backup Method The most common backup strategy is the *grandfather-father-son method*. This method is easy to administer and offers flexible archiving. Like the father-son method, daily backup media are assigned for incremental or differential backups. At the end of the week, a full backup is made, which is kept for one month. At the end of the month, a special monthly backup can be made, which is then kept for one year. This method enables you to archive data for at least a year.

Nonpersistence

In the event of a crisis, *live boot media* can be a great way to revert to a known state to begin recovering from any damage. Live media allows an administrator or first responder to boot directly from trusted media with the last known-good configuration, commonly a CD or flash drive, in lieu of booting from the hard drive. This supplies *nonpersistence*, meaning that anything malicious or unauthorized currently residing on the main drive can likely be overcome. Creating live media also allows for a master *image* to be stored in multiple areas both onsite and offsite, allowing an almost automated course of action as needed. Generally, you go into the BIOS of the system and change the boot order to boot from the desired media that has a last known-good operating system, configuration, and required drivers. On the other hand, live media can also be used to bypass secure operating systems and configurations for nefarious purposes if users use them instead of their required, secure operating system that would have been otherwise loaded. Take note that this is more difficult on UEFI systems and may not be possible if they are sufficiently locked down.

REVIEW

Objective 2.5: Given a scenario, implement cybersecurity resilience Consider the requirements for resiliency, high availability, and fault tolerance before disaster strikes by implementing redundancy. Perform backups to save and archive critical company data. Full backups are recommended if time and space permit, but if not, use incremental or differential schemes. Test your backups by performing a restore on a regularly scheduled basis. Consider using alternate sites for disaster recovery purposes, taking into account applicable geographical and legal constraints. RAID is a key disk redundancy solution. Determine the level of RAID redundancy appropriate to the importance of the data you're protecting. Keep spare parts of common hardware on hand so it can be replaced immediately.

2.5 QUESTIONS

1. Max is installing a database server that requires several hard drives in a RAID array. In the event one of the drives fails, he needs to be able to swap out a failed hard drive with no downtime. Which of the following types of hard drives should he use?
   - **A.** Cold swap
   - **B.** Suspend swap
   - **C.** Warm swap
   - **D.** Hot swap
2. Bobby must ensure that power is always available, 24/7, for a critical web and database server that accepts customer orders and processes transactions. Which of the following devices should Bobby install?
   - **A.** Power conditioner
   - **B.** UPS
   - **C.** Power generator
   - **D.** Redundant power supply
3. AJ's company is in the middle of budgeting for disaster recovery. He has been asked to justify the cost for offsite backup media storage. Which of the following reasons should he offer as the primary security purpose for storing backup media at an offsite storage facility?
   - **A.** So that the facility can copy the data to a RAID system
   - **B.** So that if the primary site is down, the offsite storage facility can reload the systems from backup
   - **C.** For proper archive labeling and storage
   - **D.** To prevent a disaster onsite from destroying the only copies of the backup media

2.5 ANSWERS

1. **D** A hot-swap device, such as a hard drive, can be inserted or removed without the need to shut down the server. This enables you to retain the availability of the services on that server.
2. **C** A power generator is required to ensure that there is always power for your server. A UPS battery typically contains only enough power to run a system for about 10 to 20 minutes, while a power conditioner or redundant power supply will not help if there is no power to run them.
3. **D** All backup plans should require backup media to be sent to an offsite storage facility. That way, if a disaster destroys your physical location, the backup media will be safe.

Explain the security implications of embedded and specialized systems

Thus far, this book has mainly discussed traditional computing environments, including company mainframes and mobile devices. Although these environments are still the bread and butter of a security professional's knowledge base, it's important to consider emerging, alternative environments, such as the so-called Internet of Things (IoT) and wearable devices. Control redundancy is important for true defense in depth; think of how to apply the tools, techniques, and procedures you've learned about within these scenarios.

Embedded and Specialized Systems

As you assess the various systems within your organization and how to scan, patch, and otherwise manage them, it is critical to consider the growing number of nontraditional systems that may be present within your organization. Often, these embedded and specialized systems have computing capabilities that you may not even be aware of, and this creates significant vulnerability if they are not identified and managed appropriately. Also, these systems often have one or more of the following inherent constraints to consider:

The following sections discuss the implications of these emerging technologies and how to best protect your organization while reaping the value that they bring.

Embedded Systems

Embedded systems, or computing systems that are embedded within another, larger system, with a dedicated function, are growing in number daily. These include appliances, in-vehicle systems, medical devices, cameras, home automation, and HVAC (heating, ventilating, and air conditioning) controls that are network enabled, and sometimes Internet connected, for remote access. You've likely seen the now ubiquitous devices that can be placed in your home to remotely manage all your devices in the house, including the alarm system, light timers, and even data on how much milk is in your refrigerator from barcode sensors on it.

Embedded systems are enabled by emerging concepts such as *System on Chip (SoC)*, which is a single chip, or circuit, that contains all the major components of a computing system, including the microprocessor, memory, network interfaces, power management, and more. The shrinking size and increasing speed of SoCs are enabling embedded devices to be more powerful than ever before. Another breakthrough is the use of real-time operating systems (RTOSs), which provide low-latency responses upon input. An RTOS is installed on an electronic chip, instead of on hard drive, and is static, or not easily updatable, patchable, or configurable once it is embedded. The advantage an RTOS gives is its speed and the requirement for little processor or memory overhead, while its disadvantage is the difficulty to update it in the event a vulnerability is discovered. RTOSs are common within vehicle electronics, manufacturing hardware, and aircraft.

The increased performance that embedded systems offer often comes at the cost of decreased device flexibility. One approach to strike a balance between performance and flexibility is the use of a *field-programmable gate array (FPGA)*, a type of programmable chip that is widely used in many areas, including automotive electronics, medical devices, and consumer electronics. The design of FPGAs allows programmers to reconfigure the hardware itself to accommodate new software functionality in a more agile manner.

A popular embedded system is the *Raspberry Pi*, developed by a UK-based charity. The Raspberry Pi is very popular for the education community, for the maker community, and anywhere that a low-cost, reasonably powered system makes sense. The newest versions even have support for dual monitors for only $25 USD (at time of writing). A great example of how the Raspberry Pi is used is to teach kids how to program and develop robotics.

A similar concept that you need to know about is the *Arduino*, which is a simple microcontroller. An Arduino is often used in conjunction with the Raspberry Pi or other small single-board computer to provide control to a physical system of some sort. The Arduino does one program repeatedly and is meant to be very simple; the Raspberry Pi, as a full-fledged computer, is suitable for providing the control software for a physical system. This is a great combination if you're interested in "hacking" a solution to, say, open your garage door and turn on your lights automatically. The combination of the Raspberry Pi and Arduino has been used for everything from simple hobbyist projects, such as robotics, to more complex solutions for industrial systems.

Have you ever heard of an intrusion detection system (IDS) for a smart refrigerator? Not likely, but as Internet-connected smart devices become more prevalent, it is important for you to identify all network-enabled devices that you have, determine whether they allow remote access, and analyze how they are protected. Although having an IDS for a smart refrigerator may seem ridiculous, smart devices often are connected to other systems or networks and could be used as an entry point into a larger, more critical system (like your home alarm system). Strong passwords (when possible) are the key. Version control of the firmware, when possible, will allow you to monitor any changes to the programmable aspects of your embedded systems and debug in the case of a fault or error.

Increasingly, wireless embedded systems include a variety of communications technologies, even integrated *subscriber identity module (SIM) cards*. Any wireless communications between embedded systems must be secured, so it's important to be on the lookout for these technologies. Some examples of current and emerging communications technologies that you must consider include the following:

- **5G cellular** The emerging fifth-generation cellular technology that will be significantly faster than its predecessor and open up more airwave options. Different carriers have different transition plans and different levels of progression on their move to 5G.

- **Narrowband** A narrowband system transmits and receives data only on a specific radio frequency. The signal frequency is kept as narrow as possible—large enough to communicate only the required information. A United States Federal Communications Commission (FCC) license must be issued for each site where it is employed.
- **Baseband radio** A chip (or part of a chip) that manages the radio function for a device. A baseband radio can transfer frequencies at a very low level, almost zero. Often included within mobile phones, and generally use a real-time operating system (discussed later within this objective).
- **Zigbee** Uses very low-power devices to produce short-range mesh networks, usually in an ad-hoc structure; widely used within wireless industrial control systems.

Industrial Control Systems and Supervisory Control and Data Acquisition Systems

Industrial control systems (ICSs) are systems used to integrate specialized software with physical devices. This specialized software can be written in a multitude of programming languages and run various operating systems from the centralized computer on the network. However, it communicates with specific automated devices that control systems and processes.

A *supervisory control and data acquisition (SCADA)* system is a subset of an ICS that is used to control utilities, automated systems, and machinery of all sorts, usually using an IP-based network to do so. SCADA systems are often quite geographically dispersed and may have no permanent human presence, or are periodically maintained by people, and rely on wide-area communications systems for monitoring between sites. Some of the software used in the systems is dated, highly specialized to the specific use, and not often patched or updated after installation. Generally, the software is also proprietary and sometimes uses proprietary protocols. Because of their isolation and geographic dispersal, many of these systems have never had a vulnerability scan on them. Physical vulnerabilities are also more likely with SCADA systems, as they often exist in facilities which may or may not have adequate physical security controls in place.

EXAM TIP You may encounter the "supervisory" in SCADA on the exam as "systems."

Some common industries and examples that are heavily reliant on SCADA systems include

- **Industrial** Mining and metals
- **Manufacturing** Automotive, pulp, and paper
- **Energy** Oil and gas
- **Logistics** Shipping, transportation
- **Facilities** Building management, physical security

Often, these systems use older operating systems that are not patched as regularly as traditional computing systems. A key consideration of SCADA systems is that they should *never* be connected to the public Internet; in fact, a best practice is to limit even the internal connectivity of a SCADA system, through *network segmentation*, to reduce the possibility of lateral movement within the network. Consider implementing manual updates, or updates that you push to the system after thorough testing procedures have been conducted.

Internet of Things

The *Internet of Things (IoT)* continues to grow as items that range from unmanned aerial vehicles (UAVs) and facility automation systems to personal assistants (like Apple's Siri) and wearable devices (such as the Fitbit and Apple Watch) become more intertwined with our daily lives. For example, you might listen to your morning Flash Briefing on an Amazon Echo, have the refrigerator remind you that you are running low on orange juice and need to stop by the store (or you could just use one of the growing number of online services that will ship that item to your doorstep), and have the reminder sent to your Apple Watch at a certain time or when you are within proximity to the store.

Although IoT technology makes modern life more convenient in many ways, it also introduces privacy and security concerns, as many IoT devices are wearable, constantly connected sensors. Think of how dangerous it could be for a potential home intruder to know exactly where you are based on the data streaming constantly from your devices, especially if those devices are connected to social media. Be mindful of the data that is being processed and disseminated by IoT devices, any potential third-party application or social media linkages, and the privacy settings associated with those devices. Finally, many of these devices have weak default configurations, so it is highly recommended to check the settings for each individual device for ways to harden the defenses.

Specialized Systems

Specialized systems that operate using a variety of nontraditional network technologies and computing systems have become much more common, to include embedded medical systems such as pacemakers that can provide updates to a doctor remotely when a heart condition is proactively spotted; embedded vehicle systems that, for example, alert the driver that the vehicle needs an oil change; aircraft systems that help a pilot fly more efficiently; and smart meters that can alert a homeowner when they have outsized electric or water usage that needs to be addressed. These are just some current examples of how computing technology is working to improve our daily lives that we had previously taken for granted.

Many common medical systems, such as MRI machines, have a variety of computing technologies embedded within them. Some of those same technologies are increasingly being used in small medical devices that are wearable or implanted within the body. These medical devices monitor vital signs and provide an alert if a reading falls above or below normal range.

Connected vehicle technologies are another great example of technologies that have clear positive, but also concerning negative attributes that need to be addressed. The ability to have your car send you an alert or an e-mail when your trunk has been left open, when your teenager is driving too fast after borrowing your car, or when your fuel level is dangerously low definitely has benefits in today's connected world. However, consider those same alerts for, perhaps an abusive relationship or at the hands of a hacker who wants to exploit that data for blackmail or other nefarious purposes. As always, it is important to check the settings of connected devices associated with your vehicle to determine what data is tracked. Also, most current automobiles have an on-board diagnostics port that supports a small tracking device that plugs in and can be used to geolocate your vehicle, provide the vehicle status, and even provide a Wi-Fi hotspot.

Voice over IP

Voice over Internet Protocol (VoIP) systems provide the ability to replace "plain old telephone service" (POTS) with an integrated phone system that runs over the same network as all other data services. While a VoIP system often provides additional functionality, such as the ability to transcribe voicemails and send them to a user via e-mail, for example, it is important to note that voice systems must be secured at the same level as any other critical information system on the network. There are specialized voice attacks against VoIP systems, such as flooding the system to create a denial-of-service condition in order to prevent phone calls, spoofing telephone numbers to annoy or interfere with business operations, or causing phone calls to drop completely.

Heating, Ventilation, and Air Conditioning Systems

Including discussion of heating, ventilation, and air conditioning (HVAC) systems in a cybersecurity book 20 years ago would have seemed very odd, but these systems are increasingly networked—especially within a commercial context, where saving energy really does equate to saving significant amounts of money. HVAC systems are network connected to provide the ability to remotely monitor and regulate temperatures within (sometimes giant) commercial facilities, even allowing the temperatures to be shifted based on the time of day and the number of personnel and customers within the facility. Network-connected HVAC systems have been adapted to the home context as well, as consumers with wired homes look to better regulate their energy usage and save money. Because the systems historically have not necessarily been protected at the same level as other embedded systems, there have been some pretty gnarly security breaches associated with them, most notably Target Corporation in 2013, where hackers stole approximately 40 million debit and credit card accounts using the credentials of their HVAC vendor. This breach was eventually settled for $18.5 million USD.

Drones/UAVs

Drones, also known as *unmanned aerial vehicles (UAVs)*, have risen in popularity over the last few years both in hobby and professional contexts. For example, drones are used to take photographs of industrial sites that are unwieldy to reach by traditional vehicle in order to determine if maintenance needs to occur. Drones have also historically been used by nation-states to perform intelligence, surveillance, and reconnaissance activities. Quite high-powered drones can now be bought on the Internet for $200 USD, putting them within the reach of hobbyists. Unfortunately, drones can cause quite a disturbance within commercial aviation space due to their potential interference with airplanes, even temporarily grounding flights at London's Gatwick Airport in 2018.

From a security perspective, because a drone is essentially just a flying robot with embedded computing technology, it is quite a powerful tool in the wrong hands, able to collect geolocation data, jam signals, and capture video. Who is receiving the surveillance video captured from a drone is of particular concern. In fact, in 2017 the U.S. Army banned the internal use of drones manufactured by the Chinese company DJI due to concerns that the collected data was being sent back to the Chinese government.

Multifunction Printers

A *multifunction printer (MFP)* incorporates within a single device not only printing capabilities but also scanning, copying, and faxing functions. Although MFPs typically are network connected, they often are overlooked as devices that need to be managed and updated for security purposes; consequently, they have historically been a ripe target for attackers looking to gain network access through a less-protected device. From access to the print data itself, all the way to lateral movement within the network, it is critical to consider the security of multifunction printers just as you consider the security of any other computing asset. Many MFPs now often include cloud access printing, which adds a potential attack vector to the organization's cloud storage. When administering an MFP, it is best practice to use two-factor authentication when possible (many MFPs now have the ability to require the use of a smart card, for example), at a minimum requiring a unique PIN that tracks a user back to their print job.

Surveillance Systems

While networked video camera systems have been common within commercial environments for years, a plethora of new home surveillance systems, such as the Nest and Blink systems, have greatly improved the ability for the home user to install internal and external cameras to monitor entry points and other areas of concern, alerting on sound or movement, even allowing for video and audio responses when the doorbell rings. Again, this technology has wonderful benefits, but it must be implemented responsibly. If breached, access to a home surveillance system would allow an outsider to spy on the home, take sensitive photos, and maybe even know when to physically burgle it.

REVIEW

Objective 2.6: Explain the security implications of embedded and specialized systems Consider the benefits and constraints of embedded and specialized systems. Most have a combination of power, computing, network, crypto, patching, authentication, range, cost, and trust constraints.

2.6 QUESTIONS

1. A __________ system is often used to control utilities, automated systems, and machinery of all sorts.
   A. sensor
   B. wearable
   C. SCADA
   D. smart meter
2. Tom wants to replace his company's "plain old telephone service" (POTS) with an integrated, network-enabled phone system. What is this type of system called?
   A. VoIP
   B. Narrowband
   C. Smartphone
   D. BYOD

2.6 ANSWERS

1. **C** A supervisory control and data acquisition (SCADA) system is often used to control utilities, automated systems, and machinery of all sorts.
2. **A** A voice over IP (VoIP) system replaces POTS with an integrated phone system that runs over the same network as all other data services.

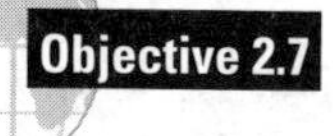

Objective 2.7 Explain the importance of physical security controls

Physical access controls differ from logical computer security controls. When securing a computer system or network, you're attempting to prevent unauthorized users from accessing the resources of your system. Physical security, however, is implemented to prevent unauthorized users from accessing an environment or a system physically—anything from the entire facility to a small network closet that contains networking equipment and wiring.

Physical Security

Much time and expense are spent on securing a computer network from unauthorized external access, but typically not enough resources are used on physical security to prevent unauthorized internal access. The possible result of lax physical security and access control includes equipment theft, physical damage and vandalism, service interruptions, and the unauthorized release of confidential data. Physical security is required to protect employees, company data, equipment, and the facility itself.

To secure access to the facility, access systems should be installed to identify employees and control what areas of the facility they can enter. Access control security also includes surveillance and monitoring of company property and the installation of physical barriers to prevent unauthorized intruders from trespassing on a company's property.

Your first line of defense is the security of the perimeter of the facility or the boundaries of its property. Unauthorized people must be prevented from accessing the property or its buildings. This could involve different security mechanisms for use during daily working hours and use when the facility is closed. Building security includes the use of physical barriers, surveillance, access control, and secure destruction of data. Objective 2.1, earlier in this domain, covered secure data destruction, but here's a recap:

- **Wiping** The use of a program to conduct "passes" of random or nonrandom data, overwriting a file or an entire drive. This is generally done in one or more passes, with the larger number of passes taking more time, but considered more secure. Reuse is possible after wiping.
- **Burning** Tossing whatever media you wish to destroy into an incinerator that burns it beyond recovery.
- **Shredding** Commonly used with paper or optical media to shred the item beyond recovery, generally in strips or further into small, confetti-style pieces; it is important when employing the shredding technique that your chosen shredding solution creates such small pieces that they cannot be pieced back together.
- **Pulverizing** Much like shredding but reduces the media to dust.
- **Pulping** Mixing water and special chemicals are mixed with the paper to remove any ink; the paper can then be recycled.
- **Degaussing** Involves running a strong magnet over magnetic storage (such as a non–solid-state hard drive) to erase the contents and restore it to a blank and generally unusable state.
- **Third-party solutions** Burn trucks, bins, and other third-party solutions allow an organization to essentially outsource document destruction using any combination of the above methods.

Physical Barriers

To deter unauthorized people from accessing a facility, physical barriers, including bollards and other barricades, can be the most effective form of security. Fencing can close off the perimeter from people who are simply passing by and could be inclined to trespass on company property. Depending on the level of protection required, the fencing can be as simple as a four-foot fence that protects against casual trespassers or animals. Higher fences of at least eight feet should be constructed to make it difficult for the average person to climb over them. For the most protection, barbed wire can be installed at the top of the fence. Electrified fences, which should be used to protect only the most sensitive facilities and data, are normally only erected around highly secure government facilities and should *not* be installed without proper safety considerations and legal approval.

Barricades are a common type of physical security device that are used to block unauthorized personnel from entering an area. You'll frequently see barricades in the perimeter area surrounding a facility, which can keep vehicles from getting too close to a building, for example. You'll also see barricades in various areas inside a facility, to control the flow of traffic through secure areas. Barricades can be temporary in nature (often using strong plastics filled with sand or water to make the barricade heavier) or permanent (using concrete or metal). Temporary barricades are commonly used to block off streets for parades or protests, for example, or when construction is taking place. For example, you'll frequently see *bollards*, vertical posts constructed from concrete or steel, at the perimeter of a facility or pedestrian area to prevent vehicles from getting too close to the building or area. Bollards are also commonly used to direct the flow of traffic, for example, in drive-through lanes and parking lots.

Badges

For personnel, more advanced access control techniques include the use of personal identification verification cards or badges. The ID card provides photo identification that can immediately identify the wearer as an authorized user. ID cards should be worn prominently so that they can always be seen by other employees. The card should identify the person and his or her job function. By listing job functions, the ID card can be used to quickly determine that person's access clearance into a certain part of the facility. Simple ID cards, however, require the presence of security guards and the training of employees to be security conscious. Access control badges can also use a wide variety of automated technologies to ensure that only authorized personnel are allowed into the facility or secure area. These technologies include RFID, proximity readers, and smart cards.

Lighting

In the interest of security and safety, all areas of the property—including all the company's buildings and the parking lot—should have proper lighting installed to discourage intruders and provide a safe environment for employees. During evening or dark hours, lighting can help ensure that trespassers, attackers, and thieves are deterred from venturing out into open areas when trying to approach a facility or harm its personnel. Floodlights are an effective way to illuminate a large area. Lighting can be placed at various points along the perimeter fence, at least at distances so that the outer edges of the areas of light each pole projects overlap with each other (usually no more than about 20 or 25 feet for tall poles, or about 8 to 10 feet for smaller ones). Lighting should also be placed at gates, door entrances, along sidewalks, and in foyers or entryways. There should also be emergency lighting throughout a facility, in the event that power to the facility goes out.

The entire lighting system should also be set on a timer, or photoelectric technology can be used to detect outside light levels. For example, some lighting, such as fence perimeter lighting, may be programmed with a timer to come on at certain hours, such as from dusk till dawn. Other types of lighting make use of motion sensors that turn on when someone approaches an area. Still other types of lighting may activate in the event an alarm or intrusion detection system is triggered.

Industrial Camouflage

Industrial camouflage, much like its name suggests, is a protective measure that hides lights, sensors, and other security measures from detection. This camouflage matches its subject device to its surroundings through paint matching, terrain matching, use of trees and bushes, and so on or by hiding the device inside another device, often to camouflage facilities from aerial surveillance (satellite, drone, etc.). A common use of industrial camouflage is to match the color of surveillance cameras to the color of the walls on which they are mounted to reduce the likelihood that they will be noticed. Note that this would decrease their effectiveness as a deterrent control.

Alarms

Physical alarm and intrusion detection systems are a critical part of the physical security program. Some alarms are purposefully loud as a deterrent measure, but alarms can also be silent and activate only at a guard station to alert security personnel without tipping off an intruder that they have been discovered, thus giving security personnel time to get to where the intruder is and subdue them. Alarm systems can be activated by any number of factors, including manually by personnel, by opening alarmed doors, and even by motion sensors in an area.

Motion detection involves using one or more different types of sensors to detect the presence of a person in a restricted area. These motion detection sensors might include:

- Invisible light beams that are emitted from photoelectric sensors in a room; breaking the light beams triggers the alarm.
- Sensors monitoring environmental factors such as temperature, humidity, and air pressure are closely monitored in an area; an individual entering that area would change those factors, causing the temperature to rise a few degrees or the air pressure or flow to change slightly. These almost imperceptible changes to the environment might indicate unauthorized personnel in the area and trigger an alarm.
- Plates in the floors that detect different weights or pressure on the plates; stepping on one of these plates triggers an alarm.

Keep in mind that motion sensors, as well as some of these other advanced types of physical intrusion detection systems, are typically installed only in highly secure areas, although there are commercial- and private-grade motion sensors that can be used in small businesses and homes.

Signage

Signage is a very important security mechanism both inside and outside a facility to help deter unauthorized activities and intruders. In addition to being a security function, signage is often used for personnel safety, such as to warn about potential safety hazards or dangerous areas and to clearly mark where exits are located in the event of an emergency. Signs can warn when entering or leaving restricted areas, as well as what the proper security and safety procedures are if they vary from the norm. In some cases, signage throughout a facility may be required by laws or safety regulations and prevent the organization from being involved in liability issues.

Signs should follow national and international standards for symbols and colors, especially those that mark hazardous conditions, show exits, or identify the location of safety equipment such as fire extinguishers. Awareness of safety signage should be included in new employee training as well as in periodic training of all employees. Signs should be placed in well-lit areas and not obstructed by large objects.

Surveillance

To maintain the physical security of an organization's premises, property, and personnel, the organization should consider employing surveillance and monitoring devices. The simplest form of surveillance is the use of common security procedures, such as stationing security guards at building or campus access points. Video cameras can be set up throughout the facility, and their feeds can be constantly monitored by security guards. Although effective, these options can be costly because of the high price of surveillance equipment and the ongoing wages that must be paid to security guards. Video camera surveillance can be coupled with recording equipment that can monitor and record all activity 24 hours a day. This is also known as *closed-circuit television (CCTV)*, as the cameras broadcast to a limited number of stations that are not publicly accessible. If a burglary or vandalism occurs, the culprits could be captured on video, which can then be analyzed to identify the unauthorized intruders. This can be both a detective control and a deterrent control; the guards monitoring the CCTV can detect, and potential intruders may be deterred if they are aware of the surveillance cameras.

Camera placement is of primary importance, both in terms of efficiency of surveillance and equipment costs, and at a minimum all entrances, doors, and access ways should be included in the coverage. All people who enter and exit the facility will be recorded on the cameras. In high-security environments, additional cameras are typically placed inside server rooms and other networking equipment areas that form the hub of the communications network.

The use of intrusion detection equipment can ensure that a surveillance and monitoring system is proactive by alerting you to suspicious behavior without the need and expense of constant monitoring by security guards. Several intrusion detection technology options are available:

- **Proximity detector** Senses changes in an electromagnetic field that surrounds a small area or object; when a change is detected, an alarm sounds.
- **Motion detector/recognition** Detects motion in a certain area; most often used in conjunction with floodlights that turn on when motion is detected. The light serves as a warning that an intruder has been detected.
- **Object detector** Uses technology that can observe and detect the presence of specific objects when seen on camera; think about how airport security can scan for firearms and explosives due to the shape of the object as an example of how this works.
- **Infrared detector** Senses changes in the heat patterns of an area that indicate the presence of an intruder.
- **Noise detector** Senses sounds and vibrations and can detect changes in the noise levels in an area.
- **Protected cable distribution** Protects sensitive cabling from taps or other malicious activity. This can also be monitored by video at critical points or through a physical intrusion detection device that monitors for potential tapping activity.

NOTE The main drawback of most intrusion detection systems is the large number of false alarms that can occur because of abnormal weather conditions, animals, and improper calibration.

Finally, drones and unmanned aerial vehicles (UAVs) are increasingly being used by organizations to monitor and surveil their premises. These systems are used to fly over different areas to take pictures, record video, or gather other data that can help an organization to physically secure its premises.

Cross-Reference

More information on drones and UAVs is provided in Objective 2.6, earlier in this domain.

Locks

The most basic and least expensive type of physical access control is the use of a lock and key. Unfortunately, in large environments, this can quickly become an administrative nightmare because the number of keys that must be distributed for each lock can grow quickly. In addition, employees lose keys, duplicate them, and let other users borrow them. When an employee is terminated, he might not return his keys or might have duplicates of the keys he returns, meaning every lock should be changed.

Depending on the environment, different types of locks can be used. For perimeter security, a simple padlock on a chained fence might suffice. For higher-security areas, electronic or mechanical locks with programmable keys can be installed. These require a combination or key code to open instead of a physical key.

Physical Locks

It's easy for an unauthorized user to walk by an unattended desk or system rack and quickly remove expensive equipment. Not only does the stolen equipment need to be replaced, but the sensitive data saved on that equipment also must be recovered. If the item was stolen for corporate espionage, the results of the theft can be devastating.

Any expensive or sensitive equipment—especially portable items such as laptops, mobile devices, and networking equipment—should be locked up when unattended. Device locks are available for both desktop computers and portable laptops. A desktop computer can be housed in a lockable cage that would require a great deal of effort to open. Also, an alarm card that sounds a loud alarm if the computer is moved can be installed in computers. Peripheral devices attached to a computer can be protected with cable traps that prevent their removal. Laptop computers should be fitted with special *cable locks* that securely attach them to a current work area. If a user will be away from a laptop for an extended period, the user should store the laptop in a locked desk or cabinet.

Physical access to special network and computer equipment rooms should be secured as carefully as access to company facilities. These rooms house the brains of company operations, concentrating a variety of critical functions, such as network communications, database servers, and backup systems. If an unauthorized user gains access to the central network room, she could cause considerable damage.

The main door to the network or server room should be secured with some type of lock, preferably with some sort of access system that incorporates picture IDs and smart cards that are only given to authorized personnel. Only those employees who need to be in the room to perform their job functions should be allowed access. Inside, servers and other sensitive equipment should be housed within a lockable cage or rack and not left running in an open area where they could be accessed or accidentally damaged. Many types of networking equipment servers come with their own locks that require keys to open them for access.

Electronic Locks

Electronic locks are more sophisticated than hardware-based locks and include one or more additional protection mechanisms. An electronic lock often uses a PIN code, and thus may be known as a *cipher lock*. The mechanisms of electronic locks generally are protected by metal containers or are embedded into walls. Electronic locks may be programmable, offering a number of configurable options, such as the ability to program separate PINs for different people, a lockout threshold for the number of incorrect PIN entries, a lockout delay, and so on. They also may be tied to other security measures, such as smart-card and biometric mechanisms.

NOTE Electronic locks should be linked with the alarm system. In case of a fire or other emergency, the locks should automatically disengage to allow people to leave the building. This mode is called *fail safe*, versus *fail secure*, which means that the locks engage in a secure manner if a facility or restricted area is subject to unauthorized entry.

Biometric Locks

Objective 2.4 already discussed biometrics extensively, but more from a technical or logical control perspective than from a physical security perspective. Biometric locks can also be used to control physical access to facilities in secure areas. In addition to smart cards and PINs, biometric locks can be used to provide for multifactor authentication that may be required for entrance into a secure area. Examples of biometric locks often used for secure entry into a facility include locks requiring thumbprints, palm scans, retinal or iris scans, and voiceprint recognition. Since each of these methods uniquely identifies an individual, combined with another factor, such as a passphrase or PIN, these methods can provide for secure access and entry into sensitive areas.

Cross-Reference

Much more information about biometric controls and methods is provided in Objective 2.4, earlier in this domain.

Access Control Vestibule

An *access control vestibule* is a two-tier, physical access control method with two physical barriers, such as doors, between the person and the resource that the person is trying to access, such as a secure building. A person is allowed access to the access control vestibule through the first door (sometimes requiring a first authentication), and then when that door closes, the person is physically caught between doors and must pass a form of authentication to gain entry through the second door. In high-security environments, the first door locks and the person is effectively trapped if he passes the first authentication but cannot be properly authenticated through the second door. Because both doors are locked, he will not be able to leave until security arrives to examine his credentials. Another purpose of an access control vestibule is to prevent tailgating by allowing only one individual to enter at a time. Access control vestibules do exist that have no authentication requirements; they only serve to stop more than one person from entering/exiting at the same time.

EXAM TIP The older term for access control vestibule is *mantrap*. Be prepared for either term to be used in the exam.

Personnel

Personnel are a valuable resource for access control, even within environments that have highly technical security controls. You may consider a security guard an "old-fashioned" method of securing access, but simply having personnel who are charged with observing and reacting to threats can be a powerful deterrent and mitigation to both internal and external threats. Security guards can monitor CCTVs and access control vestibules and check equipment being moved in and out of the perimeter. Reception personnel also serve a security role by managing a visitor log, distributing badges to visitors, and simply keeping an eye out for potential intruders and for personnel who are not following organizational security practices.

Highly secure organizations also require multiple personnel to be present for certain functions, such as opening secure vaults or safes. This is referred to as *two-person integrity* or *two-person control* and helps to ensure that a single employee doesn't become an insider threat.

A futuristic security guard that is increasingly being deployed on the campuses of high-tech companies such as Microsoft and Google is the *robot sentry*. Unlike human security guards, robot sentries are unarmed, but they use a combination of cameras, alarms, and sirens to alert their human counterparts. When their batteries begin to run low, much like a robot vacuum cleaner, they return to their "dock" to charge for next use.

Faraday Cages

Even the most secure areas behind thick walls can be reached wirelessly if proper precautions are not taken, and in extremely sensitive situations such as investigations, this can have serious impacts. For example, mobile devices especially may still communicate with other hosts and networks through wireless or cellular means. This can be problematic if you discover an unauthorized mobile device or one that has been used to take pictures or eavesdrop in a restricted area. The potential is there for the mobile device to communicate with someone on the outside of the facility, who may initiate a remote wipe of that device or get sensitive data from it before security personnel can prevent it. Since you often shouldn't turn them off in case you need to collect forensics data, you must shield them from communicating with the outside world via a special container or bag, known as a *Faraday container*, or in a larger *Faraday cage*. These special containers are made of a mesh or a continuous piece of conductive material and block RF radiation and communications to and from the device and prevent it from communicating. Be aware that emerging research has shown that systems using Faraday solutions can indeed be breached using low frequency magnetic radiation.

Visitor Logs

As part of an overall security plan, an organization should maintain visitor logs that contain the names and phone numbers of all visitors to the facility, who or why they are visiting, and their arrival and departure times. Most organizations have a policy that requires all nonemployees, including visitors and contractors, to sign in at the reception area in the front lobby of the building, and have reception personnel or security guards present to ensure that no one tries to enter the interior of the building without first completing the visitor log. If any security or emergency incident arises, the visitor log provides a record of everyone who was in the building at the time of the incident.

Visitor logs are also important for highly sensitive areas of an organization, such as the main server and telecommunications room that houses the primary system and networking equipment. All administrators should be required to record their times of entry into and departure from the server room to perform duties or maintenance. Any security issues that arise regarding activities in the server room can be tracked to whoever was in the room at the time. Most electronic card systems automatically record this information, as employees typically use their ID cards to enter and exit various parts of the building. These electronic logs can be easily obtained and scanned to determine who was at a certain location during times of a security lapse. Manual access logs can still be used for those visitors who are required to enter the controlled access area occasionally but do not have electronic cards for the area.

USB Data Blocker

USB charging ports are available in airports, airplanes, hotels, and many other public locations as a convenience for customers who need to recharge their USB devices. Because these USB ports are accessible by anyone, hackers can easily infect them with malware that siphons data from any device that is plugged into them and/or installs malware on the device. A *USB data blocker* is a device that looks similar to a USB thumb drive but has its own USB port in which you plug in your smartphone or other USB device. When you insert the USB data blocker into a USB port, it prevents any data transfer but allows your device to recharge. If your organization has employees who travel, they should be given USB data blockers to use in public places.

Secure Areas

Secure areas are a common way to segregate people from sensitive data. The following are a few key secure areas to know about:

- **Air gaps** Typically reserved for the most extreme scenarios, air gaps provide the most restrictive type of segmentation. Air-gapped systems and devices have no network connectivity with anything.
- **Vaults and safes** Vaults (larger) and safes (smaller) hold people, systems, and very sensitive materials, depending on the size of the vault or safe. They generally require at least a two-person integrity mechanism to enter.
- **Screened subnets** Screened subnets are seen throughout cybersecurity as a buffer between a public area and an internal, private area. This same concept can be both physical and logical in nature.

EXAM TIP Screened subnets were referred to as *demilitarized zones (DMZs)* on the previous version of the exam. Be aware that you might see either term.

Fire Suppression

Although fire suppression is typically already part of the facility plans, fire suppression for a computer environment can differ from techniques used to protect building structures and their contents. The most obvious difference is that suppressing a fire with water in a computer facility that's filled with many electronic servers, personal computers, laptops, printers, and network devices can be as damaging as the fire itself. Although computer-equipment-approved fire extinguishers are available, other effects of a fire, such as smoke and high temperatures, can also be damaging to computer equipment.

The key elements of fire protection are early detection and suppression. Early detection is a must in preventing fires from escalating from a small, minor flame to a raging inferno. Timing is of the essence, and you can detect a fire in several ways:

- **Smoke detectors** Smoke detectors are the most common form of warning device. Using optical or photoelectric technology, a beam of light is emitted, and the smoke detector sets off an alarm if it detects a change in the light's intensity. As smoke filters into the unit, it senses the changes in the light pattern.
- **Flame detectors** A flame detection unit can sense the movements of a flame or detect the energy that's a result of combustion. Flame detection units tend to be more expensive than other options, and they're typically used in high-security environments that require advanced fire-detection techniques.
- **Heat detectors** A heat detector can detect fires by sensing when a predetermined temperature threshold has been reached. When the temperature from the fire grows to a certain level, an alarm is triggered. Heat detector units can also detect rapid changes of temperature that indicate the presence of a fire.
- **Video monitoring** A video monitoring system allows you to look for any visible environmental concerns in a computer equipment room, such as smoke or flames that indicate a fire. Full-time video monitoring requires a dedicated security team, and this is typically reserved for protection of larger data centers.

When a fire is detected, a mechanism must be initiated to suppress the fire. A fire can be suppressed in several ways, each with its own positive and negative aspects, depending on the type of fire and the environment of the location.

Water

Water is the most common type of fire suppressant, but for computer facilities that contain a large amount of electrical equipment, water can be damaging. The use of water during an electrical fire can make the fire worse, causing even more damage. Water sprinkler systems usually consist of sprinkler heads that are distributed evenly throughout the area to provide maximum coverage. In some cases, the detection system can be configured to shut down the electrical supply before the water sprinklers turn on.

TABLE 2.7-1 Types of Fires and Their Respective Extinguishers

Class	Type	Recommended Suppression
A	Combustibles (wood, paper, etc.)	Foam, water
B	Liquids (gasoline, oil, etc.)	CO_2, foam, powder
C	Electrical (computer equipment, etc.)	FM-200, argon, CO_2
D	Combustible metals (sodium, magnesium, etc.)	Powder

Chemical-Based Fire Suppression

Older fire suppression units for computer facilities used *halon*, a special fire-suppressing gas that can neutralize the chemical combustion of a fire. Halon acts quickly and causes no damage to computers and electrical equipment. Unfortunately, because of its environmental drawbacks, including depletion of ozone and the possibility of danger to humans when used in large amounts, halon is no longer manufactured. It still currently exists in some building installations, if they were installed before restrictions on halon were put in place.

Several environmentally safe chemical-based replacements exist for halon, such as FM-200 and argon, which work the same way to neutralize a fire.

It's important to use the type of fire suppression that is appropriate for the type of fire you encounter. Table 2.7-1 lists the different classes of fires, their characteristics, and the appropriate suppression for each.

Environmental Issues

Computers and electronic equipment are sensitive to environmental factors such as temperature, humidity, and air and power quality. Imbalances in any of these factors can result in severe damage to computer equipment, and they can potentially cause even greater perils to both the people and the facilities. Environmental controls must be installed and continuously monitored for proper operation.

Temperature

Sensitive computer and electronic equipment must operate in a climate-controlled environment. To provide a proper operating environment, the temperature and humidity of a computer facility must be carefully controlled and maintained through proper heating, ventilation, and air conditioning (HVAC), and not just your run-of-the-mill home system or wall unit; computer facilities should be equipped with an industrial HVAC to keep the entire room at a steady, cool temperature. Overheating of computer equipment can cause disruption or even total equipment failure. When devices overheat, their components expand and retract, which can eventually damage them permanently. In a computer system itself, several fans circulate the air and cool the components inside.

Hot and Cold Aisles

Using hot and cold aisles is an air circulation technique often employed in large data centers with rows and rows of equipment racks. A *cold aisle* has the front of the two adjoining rows of equipment facing each other over a vented floor with cool air passing upward, which flows into the front of the equipment racks to cool them down. The backs of each row of equipment face into a *hot aisle*, where the fans from the equipment racks on each side of the row push out hot air.

Using cool air vents and hot air intakes from the HVAC units creates a constant flow of air to prevent buildup of heat emanating from the back of the equipment racks and allows cool air to flow into the front of the equipment racks.

Humidity

Humidity levels are important to the overall operating health of computer equipment because high humidity can increase the exposure of sensitive electronic components to moisture and cause corrosion of the internal parts of a system. Low humidity levels create a dry environment where the buildup of static electricity can cause great harm to electronic equipment, so humidity levels should be set between 40 and 50 percent. Static electricity can also be minimized in the environment using special antistatic mats and wristbands, which can be used by technicians who regularly touch the equipment.

Ventilation

The quality of the air circulating through the computer facility must be maintained through the proper use of ventilation techniques. Without proper ventilation, a risk of airborne contaminants occurs. These contaminants could be dust or other microscopic particles that can get inside and clog critical equipment such as the fans, which need to be running to keep the system cool. These particles can also be harmful to human beings and present a health issue, so proper ventilation is also a safety concern.

Monitoring

The temperature and humidity of your equipment rooms must be constantly monitored to make sure that a safe environment is maintained for your computer equipment. A failed air-conditioning unit can cause your computer equipment room's temperature to soar immediately, causing equipment shutdown and failure within several minutes.

The monitoring equipment must be able to actively generate alarms so that you will be alerted to a significant change in temperature. This gives you time to quickly shut down systems before they overheat. Individual devices may also have diagnostic tools that can alert you to changes in the temperature of a device.

Electrical Power

Another important environmental concern is the electrical power system that runs your equipment. Electrical power must be provided with consistent voltage levels and a minimum of interference. Even small fluctuations in power can cause irreparable damage to sensitive electronic equipment. Power protection has two aspects: ensuring the consistency and quality of your primary power source, and maintaining the availability of alternate power in a power outage.

Several types of fluctuations can occur:

- **Blackout** A prolonged period without any power
- **Brownout** A prolonged period of lower-than-normal power
- **Spike** A momentary jump to a high voltage
- **Sag** A moment of low voltage
- **Surge** A prolonged period of high voltage

To protect your equipment against these different types of perils, you can use several devices. Simple power-surge protectors generally aren't rated for expensive types of computer equipment. Usually, these types of power bars contain some type of fuse or circuit breaker that cuts off the power in a spike or a surge. By the time the breaker cuts in, the moment of high voltage has already been reached and has possibly damaged the equipment that's plugged into the power bar. The recommendation is for most computer systems, servers, and network infrastructures to use an uninterruptable power supply (UPS), which works both as a high-end surge protector and power supply during a power failure.

CAUTION Don't plug power bars or high-load peripherals, such as laser printers, into UPS power outlets because they can quickly overload them.

To provide clean and consistent power to computer equipment, a device called a *line conditioner* or *power conditioner* can be used. It plugs directly into the power supply outlet and ensures that the power that reaches the computer equipment is free of voltage fluctuations and interference.

For large organizations with critical high-availability requirements, a more expensive option for backup power is the use of a generator that runs on a battery or fuel. When using batteries, a power generator has a finite time that it can run until the battery power runs out. A fuel-based generator, on the other hand, can be kept operational if it continues to be filled with fuel, and it provides electricity even for very long blackout periods if fuel is available.

REVIEW

Objective 2.7: Explain the importance of physical security controls Physical access control security includes surveillance and monitoring, lighting, signage, ID cards, sensors, locks, access control vestibules, security guards, cameras, visitor logs, and a variety of other physical security controls. ID cards should be complemented with access codes or PINs. In case the card is lost or stolen, it can't be used for access without the corresponding PIN. Faraday cages prevent equipment from emitting or transmitting signals and are especially useful for preventing transmission in secure areas, such as vaults or safes.

2.7 QUESTIONS

1. How should lighting installed along a perimeter fence be programmed?
   - **A.** To activate when someone approaches the fence
   - **B.** To activate only when alarms detect an intruder
   - **C.** To activate between dusk and dawn
   - **D.** To be turned on 24 hours a day
2. Which of the following are advantages to employing security guards in a facility? (Choose two.)
   - **A.** CCTVs can be in places where guards cannot always be.
   - **B.** Guards can make split-second decisions during security incidents.
   - **C.** The vast majority of facility security issues can be handled by well-trained guards.
   - **D.** Guards are not susceptible to social engineering.
3. Which of the following is not a benefit of using an access control vestibule?
   - **A.** It can serve as a single controlled entry point into a facility.
   - **B.** It can assist with positive identification and authentication of individuals entering the facility.
   - **C.** It can prevent unauthorized individuals from entering a secure facility.
   - **D.** It can protect individual information systems from unauthorized access.

2.7 ANSWERS

1. **C** Lighting installed along a perimeter fence should be programmed to activate from dusk to dawn.
2. **B C** Guards can make split-second decisions during security incidents, and most facility security issues can be handled by well-trained guards.
3. **D** An access control vestibule cannot protect individual information systems from unauthorized access.

Objective 2.8 Summarize the basics of cryptographic concepts

Cryptography is the conversion of machine- and human-readable communicated information into an unreadable form that keeps the information confidential and private. The protection of sensitive communications has been the basis of cryptography throughout history. Modern cryptography performs essentially the same function but with added functionality, such as authentication, data integrity, and nonrepudiation, to accommodate personal and business communications and transactions in the digital world.

FIGURE 2.8-1 Encryption and decryption

The central function of cryptography is *encryption*, the transformation of data into an unreadable form. Encryption ensures confidentiality by keeping the information hidden from those for whom the information is not intended. *Decryption*, the opposite of encryption, transforms encrypted data back into an intelligible form. Even though someone might be able to read the encrypted data, it won't make any sense until it has been properly decrypted.

The encryption/decryption process involves taking data in *plaintext*, which is readable and understandable text, and manipulating its form to create *ciphertext*. When data has been transformed into ciphertext, the plaintext becomes inaccessible until it's decrypted. The entire process is illustrated in Figure 2.8-1.

This process enables the transmission of confidential information over an insecure communications path, greatly decreasing the possibility of the data being compromised. In a file storage system, data is protected by authentication and access controls that prevent unauthorized users from accessing some files. When this data is transmitted over a network, the data can become vulnerable to interception. If the information or the communications channel itself is encrypted, the chance of someone intercepting and deciphering the data is extremely slim.

This objective details the subjects of cryptography and encryption, including mathematical algorithms, public key cryptography, and encryption standards and protocols.

Cryptography

Today's cryptography involves more than hiding secrets with encryption systems. With the world using more technological means to perform business and legal functions, such as purchasing items from a web-based store, conducting online banking, and digitally signing documents, the need for strong and secure encryption systems to protect these transactions is vital. Security is obviously a key use, but cryptography is also used to promote other ends, such as obfuscation and high resiliency. As previously discussed in Objective 2.5, resiliency enables an organization to "operate through" attacks or other negative cyber events. Cryptographic systems that promote high resiliency are more able to operate through the resource constraints that we will discuss further.

Cryptographic algorithms and techniques are considered suitable for use based on different factors, including encryption strength, ease of implementation, high resilience to cryptographic attacks, and the requirement to use a particular cryptographic service provider or crypto-modules. Some methods are more suitable than others based on the level of protection required. Other methods, such as lightweight cryptography used within medical devices, sensors, and Internet of Things devices, may be more suitable based on practicality or required resource constraints. In any case, organizations and users must evaluate certain considerations when looking at various algorithms and methods for encryption. Some algorithms are weaker than others for various reasons, including the use of weak initialization vectors and key lengths. It's important to understand the pros and cons of various algorithms and to select algorithms that are strong and resilient against attack.

EXAM TIP Lightweight cryptography is not necessarily less secure, depending on the implementation, so it won't necessarily be an incorrect answer to a question asking for strong encryption. However, it is most often implemented in systems where low power requirements are a necessity, and trade-offs must be made in order to synchronize constraints with security.

Generally, the stronger the algorithm, the better the encryption that it provides and the more resilient it is to cryptographic attack. When you're considering your options, factors such as key length, keyspace, and mode of operation make for stronger encryption. Weak and deprecated algorithms often have common characteristics, including shorter keys and a less complex keyspace. One common flaw is poor implementation. In fact, stronger algorithms can suffer attacks if they are not implemented securely, so careful implementation is critical.

KEY TERMS The number of bits that are within an encryption algorithm's key is the **key length**, also referred to interchangeably as **key size**.

The set of all the possible permutations of a key is the **keyspace**.

Selecting strong ciphers over weak ciphers often isn't the primary consideration, however. Which cryptographic method or algorithm should be selected for a particular scenario depends on the ability of the operating system, application, or even hardware to support it, or the time that the method or algorithm requires to do its business. For example, devices that have low-power and low-latency requirements, such as embedded medical devices, require cryptographic solutions that balance strength and resource requirements in an efficient and effective manner. (Certainly, you wouldn't want your pacemaker to have resource issues!) Resource constraints must be considered alongside security constraints; understanding the context in which the cryptographic method or algorithm will be used should help you to choose the correct method that balances both considerations.

Along with the previously discussed resource and security constraints, other common considerations include

- **Speed** Different algorithms have different speed benchmarks; for example, previously conducted research benchmarked Blowfish with a variable-length key, 64-bit block at 64.386 MBps, while 256-bit key Rijndael took 48.229 MBps. While this is not a perfect comparison, it is clear that in many implementations, speed is a factor to consider.

- **Size/length** Different algorithms have different maximum key sizes; Blowfish supports up to 448-bit keys, while AES supports up to 256-bit keys. However, these have different block sizes that must also be considered, as explained later in this objective.
- **Weak keys** Different algorithms have weak keys that have been proven susceptible to attack, such as DES, RC4, and Blowfish.
- **Time** Generally, the stronger and longer the key, the more time it takes to crack the key.
- **Longevity** Otherwise known as a *cryptoperiod*, longevity is the timespan during which a specific key is authorized for use or may remain in effect. Generally, this is measured in one or more years, depending on the key type.
- **Entropy and predictability** Entropy, otherwise known as *randomness*, decreases the predictability, or ability to crack the key based on a guess or analysis. Most encryption uses pseudo-random number generation to increase the entropy within the algorithm.
- **Reuse** Improper reuse of keys leads to an increased potential for an attacker to crack the key.
- **Computational overheads** Different algorithms require different levels of computing power, and this can be a significant constraint for applications such as streaming video and low-power devices such as sensors.

Common Use Cases

Information assurance is a method of protecting information and information systems by providing confidentiality, integrity, authentication, nonrepudiation, and obfuscation. Cryptography directly supports all of these attributes in varying ways, as discussed next.

Confidentiality

Confidentiality is the concept of ensuring that data is not made available or disclosed to unauthorized people. Processes such as encryption must be used on the data, network infrastructure, and communication channels to protect against data interception and disclosure.

Integrity

Data *integrity* is the protection of information from damage or deliberate manipulation. Integrity is extremely critical for any kind of business or electronic commerce. Data integrity guarantees that when information has been stored or communicated, it hasn't been changed or manipulated in transit. The cryptologic function of hashing is often used to create signatures for files that indicate whether a file has been tampered with; if the hashed value does not match the original, the file's integrity has been compromised. Hashing is discussed in more detail later in this objective.

Authentication

Authentication is the concept of uniquely identifying individuals to provide assurance of an individual user's identity. It is the act of ensuring that a person is who he claims to be. Typical physical and logical authentication methods include the use of identification cards, door locks and keys, and network logins and passwords. For modern e-commerce and legal applications, this type of authentication needs to be tightly controlled. Encrypted digital certificates are used to identify users electronically on a network. Encrypted forms of authentication can also be used in smart cards, which are a more secure medium than a typical ID badge.

Nonrepudiation

Nonrepudiation is the term used to describe the inability of a person to deny or repudiate an action they performed, the origin of a signature or document, or the receipt of a message or document. For example, suppose a user is trying to legally prove that an electronic document or transaction did not originate with her. The user could have digitally signed a contract that was transmitted through e-mail, but if the data or transmission wasn't considered secure because of the lack of encryption, the user might legally claim it was tampered with and call its integrity into question. By implementing nonrepudiation processes, a cryptographic system can be considered secure for business and legal transactions.

Obfuscation

Obfuscation provides security through obscurity, meaning that data is modified to make it unreadable to a human or a program trying to use it. A good example is when you use your credit card on the Internet; often you will notice that, after your credit card number is entered, it morphs to the format XXXX-XXXX-XXXX-1234. This is to obfuscate the number so that someone eavesdropping cannot see it and use it; in many cases, the full card number will be sent to the credit card processor, but the last four digits are the only ones kept by the merchant. Although obfuscation cannot be the only attribute you pursue, it certainly doesn't hurt to add it into the mix. Encryption supports the concept of obfuscation quite simply through changing plaintext to ciphertext, rendering it unintelligible until decrypted. However, be aware that the bad guys often use obfuscation as a tool as well; for example, URL shorteners are tools that reduce long, complex URLs into more readily tweeted or e-mailed links. The official McGraw Hill site (mheducation.com) processed through the bit.ly URL shortener becomes https://bit.ly/387dFOi, which could then be sent to an unsuspecting user. It could be a legit site, but how would the user know? This obfuscation is helpful to a genuine user, but provides great opportunity to a phisher, for example.

EXAM TIP A specific type of encryption scheme, algorithm, or protocol may cover only certain parts of the information assurance objectives. For example, certain encryption protocols concern themselves only with authentication, whereas others cover all the objectives of confidentiality, integrity, authentication, nonrepudiation, and obfuscation.

Algorithms

A system that provides encryption and decryption services is called a *cryptosystem*. A cryptosystem uses a mathematical encryption *algorithm*, or *cipher*, to turn data into ciphertext. A cryptographic algorithm is a complex mathematical formula that dictates how the encryption/decryption process takes place. Because these mathematical algorithms are usually

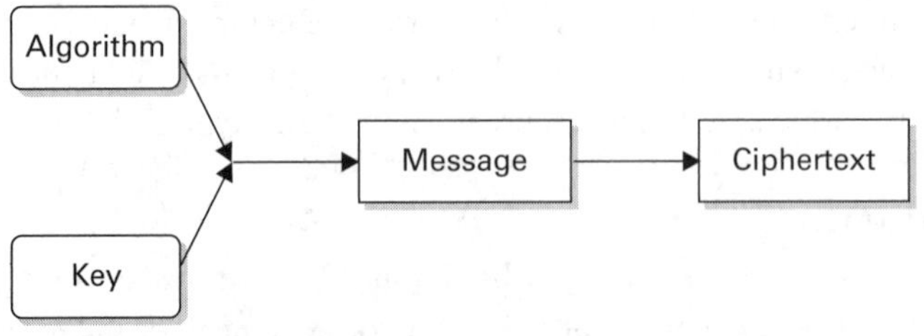

FIGURE 2.8-2 Cryptosystem using algorithms

publicly known, the cryptosystem is strengthened with the addition of a secret key, as shown in Figure 2.8-2.

A *key* is like a password that's combined with an algorithm to create the ciphertext. The encryption can't be deciphered unless the key is used to decrypt it. No one can simply unravel the algorithm to decode the message, because the key is also needed. Depending on the encryption mechanism used, the key might be used for both encryption and decryption, while different keys might be used for encryption and decryption, respectively, for other systems.

The strength of the key depends on the algorithm's *keyspace*, which is a specific range of values—usually measured in bits—that's created by the algorithm to contain keys. A key is made up of random values within the keyspace range. A larger keyspace containing more bits means more available values exist to use for different keys, effectively increasing the difficulty for someone to derive the keys and compromise the system. The smaller the keyspace, the greater the chance someone can decipher the key value.

The strength of the cryptosystem lies in the strength and effectiveness of its algorithm and the size of the keyspace. However, no matter how strong the algorithm, it will be rendered useless if someone obtains the key, so the key must be protected, and one of the methods to do this is to use encryption protocols for secure key delivery. It is also important to consider the requirements for strength versus performance when deciding which cryptosystem to implement within your organization.

CAUTION Most attacks on encryption center on the interception of keys rather than on attempts to subvert the algorithm, which requires a large amount of processing resources.

Ciphers have two major outcomes: confusion and diffusion. *Confusion* means that the ciphertext output is dependent on several parts of the key, rather than only one. This increases the change in the plaintext to ciphertext and results in a more thorough encryption process. *Diffusion* means that even a small change in the plaintext results in a significant change in ciphertext. In other words, changing a single letter of plaintext should result in a totally different ciphertext output, not merely a change of only one letter or character. To accomplish both outcomes, there are two main types of ciphers, often used in conjunction:

- **Substitution** In its most simplified form, a *substitution* cipher takes plaintext and substitutes the original characters in the data with other characters. For example, the letters *ABC* can be substituted by reversing the alphabet, so the cipher form will read *ZYX*. Modern substitution encryption ciphers are much more complex, performing many types of substitutions with more than one alphabet. A common, but weak, example of a substitution cipher is ROT13 (which means "rotate by 13 places"). In this cipher, a piece of text is encrypted by replacing it with its pair letter 13 places along in the alphabet. Using this system, the letters *ABC* would then become *MNO*. Because ROT13 is so easily decrypted, it is not recommended for use in serious contexts.
- **Transposition** In a *transposition* cipher, the characters are rearranged through mathematical permutations. When used with difficult mathematical formulas, these ciphers can be extremely complex.

Most modern ciphers use a combination of long sequences of substitution and transposition schemes. The data is filtered through an algorithm that performs these complex substitution and transposition operations to arrive at the ciphertext. The two main types of encryption—symmetric and asymmetric—use key values and complex algorithms.

Symmetric Keys

In a symmetric (sometimes referred to as *secret key*) encryption scheme, both parties use the same key for encryption and decryption purposes. Each user must possess the same key to send encrypted messages to each other, as shown in Figure 2.8-3. The sender uses the key to encrypt the message and then transmits it to the receiver. The receiver, who is in possession of the same key, uses it to decrypt the message.

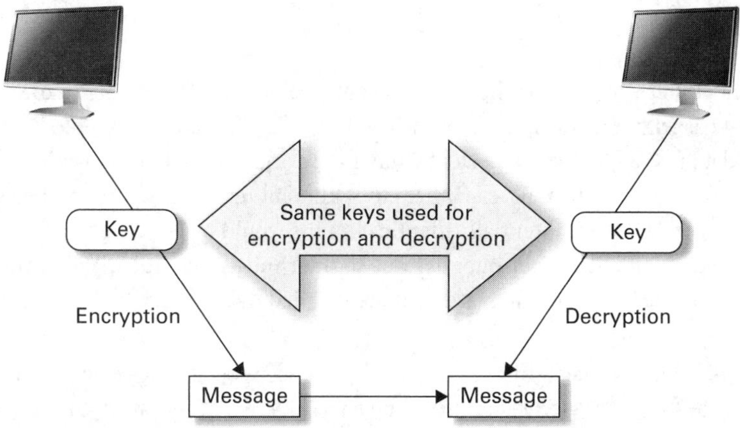

FIGURE 2.8-3 Symmetric key encryption

The security of this encryption model relies on the end users to protect the secret key properly. If an unauthorized user could intercept the key, she would be able to read any encrypted messages sent by other users by decrypting the messages with the key. It's extremely important that a user protect the key itself, as well as any communications in which he transmits the key to another user.

One of the main disadvantages of symmetric encryption schemes is that they don't scale well with large numbers of users. A user needs different keys, depending on the person with whom he is communicating. If the user communicates with a lot of people, the number of keys that need to be distributed and tracked can become enormous. Another disadvantage is that the system needs a secure mechanism to deliver keys to the end users. Symmetric systems can offer confidentiality only through encryption; they offer little in the way of authentication and nonrepudiation.

Symmetric systems, however, can be difficult to crack if a large key length is used. A symmetric system is also much faster than asymmetric encryption because the underlying algorithms are simpler and more efficient.

Two main types of symmetric encryption can be used:

- **Stream cipher** A stream cipher encrypts data one bit at a time, as opposed to a block cipher, which works on blocks of text. Stream ciphers, by design, are fast compared to block ciphers. With stream ciphers, each bit of the plaintext stream is transformed into a different ciphertext bit using a randomly generated initialization vector (IV; discussed in more detail later in this objective). A stream cipher generates a key stream that's combined with the plaintext data to provide encryption. RC4 is the most commonly found streaming cipher, and it is used in the Wired Equivalent Privacy (WEP) protocol, which was discussed in the context of IV attacks in Domain 1, Objective 1.4.

EXAM TIP RC4 is likely the only example of a stream cipher you will encounter on the exam.

- **Block cipher** A block cipher encrypts entire blocks of data, rather than smaller bits of data as with stream cipher methods. A block cipher transforms a block of plaintext data into a block of ciphertext data of the same length. For many block ciphers, the block size is 64 bits. Block ciphers use different modes of operation because large streams of data with potentially identical inputs would be less able to provide the required confidentiality or integrity due to their subsequent identical output. These modes of operation and their features are detailed in Table 2.8-1.

NOTE Authentication schemes have been developed to work with block ciphers to provide not only encryption (confidentiality) but also authentication. These are known as *authenticated modes of operation*, or *authenticated encryption*, as opposed to *unauthenticated modes of operation*.

TABLE 2.8-1 Modes of Operation (adapted from NIST SPs 800-38A and 800-38D)

Name	Acronym	Description
Electronic Codebook	ECB	A confidentiality mode that features, for a given key, the assignment of a fixed ciphertext block to each plaintext block, analogous to the assignment of code words in a codebook. ECB is vulnerable to replay attacks and has been deprecated.
Cipher Block Chaining	CBC	A confidentiality mode whose encryption process features the combining ("chaining") of the plaintext blocks with the previous ciphertext blocks. The CBC mode requires an IV to combine with the first plaintext block.
Cipher Feedback	CFB	A confidentiality mode that features the feedback of successive ciphertext segments into the input blocks of the forward cipher to generate output blocks that are XORed with the plaintext to produce the ciphertext, and vice versa. The CFB mode requires an IV as the initial input block.
Output Feedback	OFB	A confidentiality mode that features the iteration of the forward cipher on an IV to generate a sequence of output blocks that are XORed with the plaintext to produce the ciphertext, and vice versa. The OFB mode requires that the IV is a nonce—a one-time number.
Counter	CTR	A confidentiality mode that features the application of the forward cipher to a set of input blocks, called *counters*, to produce a sequence of output blocks that are XORed with the plaintext to produce the ciphertext, and vice versa. The sequence of counters must have the property that each block in the sequence is different from every other block.
Galois Counter Mode	GCM	A confidentiality mode that provides assurance of the confidentiality of data using a variation of the counter for encryption. GCM provides assurance of the authenticity of the confidential data using a universal hash function. GCM can also provide authentication assurance for additional data (of practically unlimited length per invocation) that is not encrypted.

Popular symmetric algorithms include Data Encryption Standard (DES), 3DES, Advanced Encryption Standard (AES), Blowfish, Twofish, and RC4 (Rivest Cipher), as listed in Table 2.8-2.

TABLE 2.8-2 Common Symmetric Algorithms

Symmetric Algorithm	Block or Streaming	Block Size	Rounds	Key Length	Notes
DES	Block	64 bits	16	56 bits (64 bits total, with 8 bits for parity overhead)	Uses five modes of operation: ECB, CBC, CFB, OFB, and CTR
3DES	Block	64 bits	16	168 bits (three 56-bit keys)	Repeats DES process three times
AES	Block	128 bits	10, 12, and 14 (based on key size)	128, 192, and 256 bits	Uses the Rijndael algorithm
Blowfish	Block	64 bits	16	32–448 bits	Public domain algorithm
Twofish	Block	128 bits	16	128, 192, and 256 bits	Public domain algorithm
RC4	Streaming	N/A	1	40–2048 bits	Used in WEP, SSL, and TLS; largely deprecated in current technologies

Asymmetric Keys

In an *asymmetric* encryption scheme, everyone uses different but mathematically related keys (always two keys in a *key pair*) for encryption and decryption purposes, as shown in Figure 2.8-4.

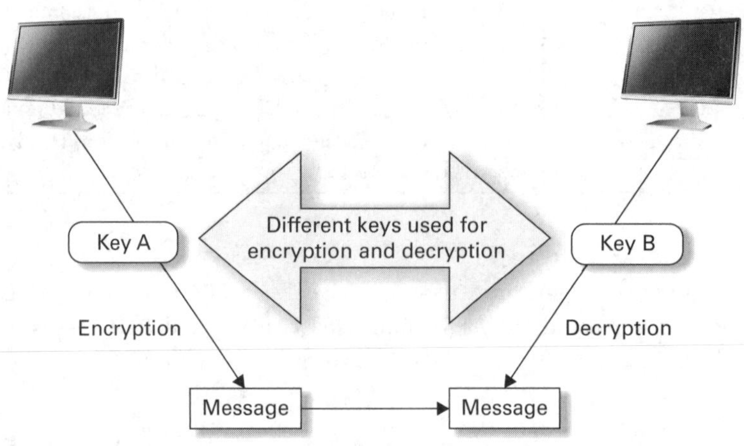

FIGURE 2.8-4 Asymmetric key encryption

Even though the keys are mathematically similar, they can't be derived from each other. An asymmetric scheme is the basis for the *public key* system. Two keys are created for encryption and decryption purposes: one key is the public key, which is known to all users, while the private key remains secret and is given to the user to keep private. To use this system, the sender encrypts a message or file with the intended receiver's public key. To decrypt this message, the receiver uses a private key that only she possesses. No one else can decrypt the message without this private key. Public keys can be passed directly among users or found in directories of public keys.

EXAM TIP For asymmetric key encryption, remember that there must always be a mathematically related key pair involved; what one key encrypts, only the other key in the pair can decrypt, and vice versa.

Another encryption concept related to asymmetric cryptography is that of key escrow. Key escrow involves a third party, such as a government agency or an authorized organization, that holds a special third key on top of your private and public key pair. The third key is used to encrypt the private key, which is then stored in a secure location. This third key can be used to unlock the encrypted copy of the private key in case of loss or the theft of the original key.

Cross-Reference

Key escrow is described in more detail in Domain 3, Objective 3.9.

The advantage of an asymmetric scheme over symmetric schemes is that it offers a level of authentication and nonrepudiation. By decrypting a message with a sender's public key, the receiver knows this message came from the sender. The sender is authenticated because, in order for the message to be decrypted with a public key, the private key had to be used to perform the initial encryption.

EXAM TIP Recognize how the different combinations of key-pair encryption methods can provide different levels of information assurance, such as authentication, nonrepudiation, confidentiality, and integrity.

The main disadvantage of asymmetric encryption is that it can be much slower than symmetric schemes. Unlike symmetric systems, however, asymmetric schemes offer confidentiality, authentication, and nonrepudiation (which prevents a user from repudiating a signed communication). Asymmetric schemes also provide more manageable and efficient ways for dealing with key distribution.

Popular asymmetric algorithms and applications include RSA (named for creators Rivest, Shamir, and Adleman), Elliptic-curve, Diffie-Hellman, and Digital Signature Algorithm (DSA).

EXAM TIP In a symmetric encryption scheme, both parties use the same key for encryption and decryption purposes. In an asymmetric encryption scheme, everyone uses a different (but mathematically related) key for encryption and decryption.

Elliptic-curve Cryptography

Elliptic-curve Cryptography (ECC) provides functionality such as encryption and digital signatures. The ECC cryptosystem uses complex mathematical structures to create secure asymmetric algorithms and keys. It is often used as the lightweight cryptographic solution for devices with smaller processing capabilities, such as smartphones, tablets, IoT devices, and other wireless devices. ECC uses smaller keys than the similar RSA; larger keys need more processing power to compute.

Key Exchange

In-band key exchanges take place within the normal communication channel. Out-of-band key exchanges utilize a separate channel outside the norm to authenticate the user; this is to verify that the original channel is not compromised. Think of e-mail, banking, or gaming services that require a time-based code from your phone or a token device, and you'll understand the out-of-band concept. Although this helps ensure that a compromise of the original channel doesn't compromise the confidentiality of the communication mechanism, it is susceptible to on-path attacks if the out-of-band channel is lost, stolen, or compromised in some way.

Ephemeral Keys

Ephemeral keys are the converse of static keys, in that they are temporary by nature, whereas static keys are semi-permanent (the typical life span of a static key is one to two years). Often, ephemeral keys are generated for each execution of the key establishment process and are unique to a message or session. However, they can be used more than once when a sender generates only one ephemeral key pair for a message and the private key is combined with each distinct recipient's public key. The benefit of using an ephemeral key is that if a particular secret key is leaked or compromised, the other messages encrypted by the system remain unreadable because each encryption session generates its own unique keys (see "Perfect Forward Secrecy," next).

Perfect Forward Secrecy

Perfect forward secrecy (PFS) is designed, through the utilization of complex cryptographic protocols, to prevent the situation where a compromise of one secret key or message leads to a compromise of previous confidential messages. For example, if my key were compromised today, use of perfect forward secrecy would mean that all my previous messages are still secret. Traditional methods assume that the underlying cipher is always secure and cannot be used to recover older plaintexts. For example, within Hypertext Transfer Protocol Secure (HTTPS), both the browser and the server exchange information toward an agreement on a secret key. In this process, if a private key is captured by an attacker, that key could be used to decrypt previous messages. PFS works because even if a private key is captured, the session key is truly ephemeral, or used only one time, as discussed in the previous section.

Random/Pseudo-Random Numbers and Inputs

Three major types of one-time use numbers are used as inputs into various algorithms: initialization vectors, nonces, and salts. A *salt* is a randomly generated input, often used within hashing schemes (discussed later in this section.) As discussed previously, both block and stream ciphers use *initialization vectors (IVs)*, which should be randomly generated to ensure that if the same message is encrypted twice, the ciphertext differs between the messages. *Nonces* are, as indicated by their name, numbers used once, and generally for a limited time; nonces are often sequential and sometimes have a salt as an input. Nonces are not required to be random, and they can be pseudo-random in nature; the sequential nature can be used to check against replay attacks. Nonces and IVs are often used interchangeably as terms, but they have one big difference: IVs must be random, whereas nonces do not need to be random.

You may have noticed a common theme in these inputs, in that they are generally dependent on randomly or pseudo-randomly generated numbers. *Random number generators* are programs that generate numbers that are statistically independent of each other. Truly random numbers are often generated by using inputs that cannot be predicted, such as radioactive decay. While random number generators are most ideal for a scenario requiring a truly random input, they are often considered very inefficient for use due to speed concerns, and they are nondeterministic, meaning that the number cannot be predetermined based on a mathematical equation or set table of inputs. In some situations, such as modeling and simulation, a *pseudo-random number generator* might be preferable due to the speed in which numbers can be created and the ability to determine how a number was generated. Pseudo-random number generators often use a mathematical formula or a set input list to generate the numbers, leading to an ability to replay; for this reason, random numbers are best for highly secure situations.

Key Stretching

Key-stretching techniques strengthen a weak key, usually a password, against brute-force attacks by increasing the time for testing each potential key. Passwords are particularly susceptible to brute-force or other password-cracking attacks because they are often quite short and are created by humans. Key stretching works to counteract this by creating an enhanced key—a result of the initial key and a hash function or a block cipher being applied in a loop. This enhanced key should be theoretically impossible (or at least cost prohibitive) to crack through various attacks. The two common functions used for key stretching are the Password-Based Key Derivation Function 2 (PBKDF2) and bcrypt.

Quantum Cryptography

Quantum cryptography is an extremely advanced technique for protecting key distribution through light-based quantum computing. The technique uses the quantum communication of light waves over fiber-optic cable to transmit code within theoretically unbreakable light pulses to distribute a shared key between two users. Theoretically, quantum states cannot be copied. Unfortunately, there are distance limitations, and the expensive hardware required to support quantum cryptography means it is limited to only the most advanced and secure of environments, such as scientific research or military applications.

Quantum computing uses quantum bits, also called *qubits*, which are units of quantum information. Whereas traditional bits are either the binary value 1 or 0, qubits can hold both values (and all values in between) at the same time and can process multiple calculations simultaneously. Quantum computers use this increased processing capability to solve huge problems—such as previously unbreakable cryptographic mathematical solutions—in a fraction of the time. This means that some current algorithms are living on borrowed time once quantum computing becomes more accessible.

Post-Quantum Cryptography

As the name suggests, post-quantum cryptography refers to algorithms, generally asymmetric, that are considered secure against attacks using quantum computing. At the time of writing, most modern asymmetric algorithms are not considered secure against attacks using quantum computing, so researchers are looking to develop post-quantum approaches to prepare for the advent of more commonplace quantum computing. Note that symmetric algorithms and hashing are not as susceptible to attacks using quantum methods; for example, simply doubling the key length is an effective solution.

Homomorphic Encryption

Most security resources are dedicated to protecting the confidentiality of data while in transit over a network using secure cipher suites and implementations. Of equal importance is the protection of data at rest, stored on server hard disks, mobile devices, USB flash drives, and so forth. Emerging techniques, such as homomorphic encryption, allow for data to be encrypted while processing, removing the concern of unencrypted data being exploited while being processed. Homomorphic encryption allows for computation to take place on ciphertext, with a result that matches what the value of the plaintext would have been if not encrypted.

Steganography

Steganography does not involve algorithms to encrypt data; it is a method of hiding data in another type of media that effectively conceals the existence of the data. This is typically performed by hiding messages in graphics images such as bitmap (BMP) files or other types of media files such as digital audio or video files. Many companies place a watermark (a hidden image) within a company image to be able to prove it is owned by the company in the event it is being used by another company or person. Unused sectors of a hard disk can also be used in steganography. These types of files contain insignificant data bits that can be replaced by the data to be hidden without affecting the original file enough to be detected.

Blockchain

Blockchain is one of the most exciting developments in cryptology in the recent years. *Blockchains* are publicly accessible ledgers that record online transactions, based on peer-to-peer technology. A party initiates a block, which is then verified by all the distributed systems and added to the chain (or rejected if not verified). Each block is bound to the other, and the distributed nature of blockchain means that the ledger is accessible to anyone, making it difficult to cheat the system. Generally, the larger the blockchain, the safer. That doesn't necessarily sound very interesting, but it is directly tied to another technology, cryptocurrency, that has become a quite successful avenue for monetary transactions (but unfortunately is often used as a ransomware demand).

Hashing

A *hashing* value is used in encryption systems to create a "fingerprint" for a message. This prevents the message from being improperly modified on its way to its destination. In the overall information assurance model, hashing is used to protect the integrity of a message and is most often used with digital signatures.

The most commonly used hashing function is the *one-way hash*, a mathematical function that takes a variable-sized message and transforms it into a fixed-length value, referred to as either a *hash value* or a *message digest*. This function is "one-way" because it's difficult to reverse the procedure, and the results are never decrypted, only compared to each other when repeating the same function on the same message. The hash value represents the longer message from which it was created. This hash value is appended to the message that's sent to another user, as shown in Figure 2.8-5. The receiver then performs the same hashing function on the message and compares the resulting hash value with the one sent with the message. If they're identical, the message was not altered.

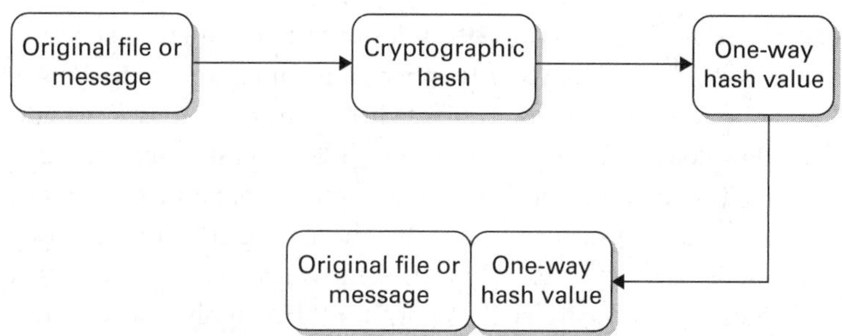

FIGURE 2.8-5 One-way hash appended to a message to protect its integrity

Attacks against one-way hash functions can be prevented by using longer hash values that are less susceptible to brute-force attacks. A good minimum starting point for the size of a hash value is 128 bits. The most common problem with weak hashing algorithms is the possibility of *hash value collisions* that occur when two different hashed messages result in the same hashing value. When these collisions are discovered, they can be used to reveal the underlying algorithm. *Birthday attacks*, a class of brute-force attacks, are often used to find collisions of hash functions. The birthday attack gets its name from this surprising result: the probability that two or more people in a group of 23 share the same birthday is greater than 50 percent. Such a result is called a *birthday paradox*. In encryption terms, if an attacker finds two hashed values that are the same, she has a greater chance of cracking the algorithm with this information.

Cross-Reference

Cryptographic attacks were covered in Domain 1, Objective 1.2.

Another attack to be mindful of is a *pass the hash* attack, which occurs when an attacker intercepts a hash and uses it to authenticate directly, rather than using the underlying plaintext password.

The following sections describe some of the common hashing algorithms in use today.

Message Digest Hashing

Message digest hashing algorithms are used for digital signature applications when a large message must be hashed in a secure manner. A digital signature is created when the digest of the message is encrypted using the sender's private key. These algorithms take a message of variable length and produce a 128-bit message digest.

EXAM TIP Remember that a digital signature is created when the digest of the message is encrypted using the sender's private key.

Message Digest 5

Message Digest 5 (MD5), developed in 1991, is a slower but more complex version of MD4. MD5 is popular and widely used for security applications and integrity checking. For example, downloaded software usually includes an MD5 checksum that the user can compare to the checksum of the downloaded file. MD5 produces a 128-bit hash value using a hexadecimal, 32-character string. Its complex algorithms make it much more difficult to crack than MD4. The algorithm consists of four distinct rounds that have a slightly different design from that of MD4. Vulnerabilities have been found in MD5 in which techniques are used to reverse-engineer the MD5 hash, and Secure Hash Algorithm (SHA) hash functions, discussed next, are often considered better alternatives to MD5 hashing.

Secure Hash Algorithm

The Secure Hash Algorithm (SHA) family was developed by the U.S. National Security Agency (NSA) for use with digital signature standards and is considered a more secure alternative to MD5. SHA is used in several popular security applications, such as Transport Layer Security (TLS), Secure Sockets Layer (SSL), and Internet Protocol Security (IPSec).

ADDITIONAL RESOURCES The NSA website (www.nsa.gov/about/cryptologic-heritage/?) provides an excellent overview of the history of cryptography for U.S. national security.

- **SHA-1** Produces a 160-bit hash value that was used as the first version of the Digital Signature Algorithm (DSA) and added the signature for the message. The sender encrypts the hash value with a private key, which is attached to the message before it's sent. The receiver decrypts the message with the sender's public key and runs the hashing function to compare the two values. If the values are identical, the message hasn't been altered. SHA-1 is no longer considered secure as of 2010, and the NSA deprecated its use in 2013.
- **SHA-2** Includes the SHA-224, SHA-256, SHA-384, and SHA-512 variants, which indicate their larger bit values. While NIST acknowledged that SHA-2 was in no imminent threat of being broken, they felt there was a need for a new, unrelated standard.
- **SHA-3** Accepted as the winner of the 2012 National Institutes of Standards and Technology (NIST) hash function competition. SHA-3 was released to the public in 2014. It includes the same hash-length variants as SHA-2, but is based on a hash function called *Keccak*, and is significantly different from the SHA-2 internal structure.

Diffie-Hellman

The *Diffie-Hellman Exchange (DHE)* isn't an actual encryption algorithm: It's a key agreement protocol that enables users to exchange encryption keys over an insecure medium. The Diffie-Hellman protocol depends on the discrete logarithmic formulas for its security. The main vulnerability with the basic protocol is that the key exchange doesn't authenticate the participants. Further enhancements to the Diffie-Hellman protocol, such as the Elliptic-curve Diffie-Hellman Exchange (ECDHE), allow the two parties to authenticate each other through the addition of more advanced technologies such as Elliptic-curve public-private key pairs, digital signatures, and public key certificates. This system is used in the Public Key Infrastructure (PKI).

ElGamal

ElGamal is an asymmetric algorithm that can be used for both digital signatures and general encryption. It was designed by Taher ElGamal in 1985 and is based partially on Diffie-Hellman key exchange algorithms. It's widely used in open standards and cryptosystems, including PGP and GPG. DSA is based upon the ElGamal signature scheme. ElGamal uses mathematical problems related to computing discrete logarithms.

Digital Signature Algorithm

The *Digital Signature Algorithm (DSA)* was published by NIST in cooperation with the NSA, as the digital authentication standard of the U.S. government. DSA is based on discrete logarithms and is used only for authentication. The algorithm is considered secure when the key size is sufficiently large; DSA was originally proposed with a 512-bit key size but was eventually revised to support key sizes up to 1024 bits. Because of DSA's lack of key-exchange capabilities, its relative slowness, and the public's distrust of the process and the government involvement that created it, many people prefer RSA for digital signatures and encryption, but both standards are used widely.

Digital Signatures

A *digital signature* is an encrypted hash value used to ensure the identity and integrity of a message. The signature can be attached to a message to uniquely identify the sender. Like a written signature, the digital signature guarantees the individual sending the message is who he claims to be. The sender runs a hash function on his message, takes the resulting hash value, encrypts it with his private key, and sends it along with the message. When the receiver gets the signed message, she first decrypts the encrypted hash with the corresponding public key (verifies the sender) and then performs her own hashing function on the message. The calculated hash is then compared against the unencrypted hash, and if they are the same, the receiver knows the message hasn't been altered in transmission.

RIPEMD

RIPEMD (RACE Integrity Primitives Evaluation Message Digest) is a hash function message digest. Originally based on MD4, RIPEMD comes in several different bit varieties, including 128-, 160-, 256-, and 320-bit versions, although the 256- and 320-bit versions don't necessarily increase security; they only reduce the chance of hash value collisions. The original weak 128-bit version has been replaced primarily by RIPEMD-160.

HMAC

Hash-based Message Authentication Code (HMAC) is used as an algorithm for message authentication purposes, where the authentication is applied using hash functions and a secret key to create an authentication code value. HMAC is used to authentic a message and provide data integrity. The Message Authentication Code (MAC) is sent along with the message itself so that the receiver can authenticate the sender of the message and verify the integrity of the message contents. The strength of HMAC depends on the size and type of hash it uses.

REVIEW

Objective 2.8: Summarize the basics of cryptographic concepts Information assurance through encryption protects information and information systems by securing their confidentiality, integrity, authentication, and nonrepudiation. An algorithm is a complex mathematical formula that dictates how the encryption and decryption processes takes place. Because these mathematical algorithms are usually publicly known, the cryptosystem is strengthened with the addition of a secret key. A key is like a password that's combined with the algorithm to create ciphertext, and encrypted data can't be deciphered unless the same key is used to decrypt it. In a symmetric encryption scheme, both parties use the same key for encryption and decryption purposes. In an asymmetric encryption scheme, everyone uses different but mathematically related keys for encryption and decryption purposes. Random numbers are often used within algorithms to prevent replay attacks. Also understand critical concepts such as quantum cryptography, homomorphic encryption, steganography, blockchain, hashing, digital signatures, RIPEMD, and HMAC.

2.8 QUESTIONS

1. You have encrypted an e-mail message because you want to ensure that it is read only by the recipient. A hacker has intercepted the message. When the hacker views the message, what does he see?
   - **A.** The plaintext of the e-mail
   - **B.** The one-way hash of the message
   - **C.** The recipient's certificate information
   - **D.** Ciphertext
2. You have been tasked with implementing information assurance principles within your organization's security and encryption functions. Which of the following isn't a function of information assurance within encryption systems?
   - **A.** Entropy
   - **B.** Confidentiality
   - **C.** Integrity
   - **D.** Nonrepudiation

3. You have sent your friend a secret, encrypted message. The key you used to encrypt the message is the same key with which your friend will decrypt the message. What type of encryption scheme is used?
   A. Asymmetric
   B. Symmetric
   C. RSA
   D. Diffie-Hellman
4. Which of the following encryption schemes would you use if your company wants to create an invisible watermark hidden within the images on its website to identify the images in case they are used by another company?
   A. One-time pad
   B. Elliptical-curve
   C. One-way hash
   D. Steganography
5. Your organization wants you to implement an encryption system that ensures that the sender and receiver of the encrypted message use different keys for encryption and decryption. Which type of encryption scheme would you use?
   A. Elliptical-curve
   B. Quantum
   C. Asymmetric
   D. Symmetric
6. Which of the following protocols would you use for message authentication and integrity in your encryption systems?
   A. Steganography
   B. Elliptical-curve
   C. HMAC
   D. One-time pad

2.8 ANSWERS

1. **D** Cleartext is transformed into ciphertext after being put through some type of cipher or encryption algorithm system. The ciphertext is unreadable unless it is decrypted back into cleartext form.
2. **A** Entropy is not a function of information assurance within encryption systems. The basic functions pertaining to information assurance are confidentiality, integrity, authentication, nonrepudiation, and obfuscation.
3. **B** In a symmetric encryption scheme, both parties use the same key for encryption and decryption purposes. Both users must possess the same key to send encrypted messages to each other.

4. **D** Steganography hides data in another type of media that effectively conceals the existence of the data.

5. **C** An asymmetric encryption scheme relies on the sender and receiver of a message to use different keys for encryption and decryption. The keys are mathematically related, but they can't be derived from each other.

6. **C** HMAC (Hash-based Message Authentication Code) is used to authenticate a message and provide data integrity. The Message Authentication Code (MAC) is sent along with the message itself so that the receiver can authenticate the sender of the message and verify the integrity of the message contents.

Implementation

Domain Objectives

- **3.1** Given a scenario, implement secure protocols
- **3.2** Given a scenario, implement host or application security solutions
- **3.3** Given a scenario, implement secure network designs
- **3.4** Given a scenario, install and configure wireless security settings
- **3.5** Given a scenario, implement secure mobile solutions
- **3.6** Given a scenario, apply cybersecurity solutions to the cloud
- **3.7** Given a scenario, implement identity and account management controls
- **3.8** Given a scenario, implement authentication and authorization solutions
- **3.9** Given a scenario, implement public key infrastructure

Given a scenario, implement secure protocols

Security must also include the network devices, protocols, and communications technologies that enable users to access the network's resources. Network devices such as routers, switches, and firewalls can be compromised, causing potentially much more damage than the simple theft of a laptop computer. Secure network administration means knowing how data flows in your network and how to properly configure your communications devices for maximum security. Not only do you need to be aware of how protocols support critical functions such as routing and switching, e-mail and web traffic, file transfers, and remote access, you also need to know about less obvious uses of protocols, such as time synchronization across the network.

Protocols and Use Cases

To understand the types of attacks that can occur against a network, it is useful to know the basic underlying protocols of Internet-based computer networks and the application protocols that use them. You should already be familiar with the Open Systems Interconnection (OSI) model, which divides communications functions among seven layers. Within the model, a layer provides services to the layer above it and receives services from the layer below it. The OSI layers and some common protocols are presented in Table 3.1-1.

TCP/IP

The *Transmission Control Protocol/Internet Protocol (TCP/IP)* is the most basic communications protocol of the Internet. TCP/IP communications are "point to point," and together the two aspects of the protocol, TCP and IP, manage and route network messages. TCP/IP is a request/connection type of protocol, where a client requests a service from a server—for example, a web browser that sends a request to a web server to retrieve a web page for viewing.

TABLE 3.1-1 OSI Model Layers and Corresponding Common Protocols

Layer	Protocol
Application	HTTP, SMTP
Presentation	MIME
Session	NFS
Transport	TCP, UDP
Network	IPv4, IPv6
Data Link	PPP
Physical	DSL, ISDN

These requests use application layer protocols, such as Hypertext Transfer Protocol (HTTP) in this case, that utilize TCP/IP to work properly. TCP manages how to partition communications and send network messages from source to destination. TCP is responsible for breaking network messages into smaller packages and frames and then reassembling the messages as they are received at the destination. TCP uses error checking and flow control to ensure network messages get to their destination.

A related protocol in the TCP/IP suite of technologies is the *User Datagram Protocol (UDP)*. UDP is connectionless and is used to transport less important data that does not require the error correction or flow control that TCP provides. UDP is fast and is often used for streaming media to allow content to be transported quickly. The *Internet Protocol (IP)* is used primarily for addressing and routing the network packets from the source to the destination device.

IPv4

Internet Protocol version 4 (IPv4) is the standard for all IP communications today and has been in use since the early 1980s. It is important to note that IP is concerned with logical addressing and routing between local area networks (LANs). Within a LAN, all the hosts adhere to a particular logical addressing scheme. They usually reside on the same logical subnet and communicate with each other without the need for routing to take place. If any hosts need to communicate with a host beyond their subnet to networks that use a different logical IP addressing scheme, then they require a router to send the traffic from their LAN to another LAN. IPv4 is a connectionless protocol where delivery is not guaranteed; it only concerns itself with getting to the next network point between the source and destination network hosts. IPv4 uses 32-bit addressing, which allows for 4,294,967,296 unique IP addresses. These are separated into the different class types (A, B, C, and D), which make use of subnetting and subnet masks to help subdivide networks and facilitate private internal IP addressing.

IPv6

The primary issue affecting IPv4 today is that with the exponential increase in public networks and devices, the number of available IP addresses is running out. *IPv6* is the next generation of the IP protocol that seeks to solve the address space issue and also provide additional network enhancements. IPv6 uses 128-bit addressing, allowing for up to 2^{128} available addresses. Although IPv6 and IPv4 are not interoperable, most modern operating systems, such as Windows 10, now support both IPv6 and IPv4 running concurrently.

With the exhaustion of IPv4 addresses imminent, the push to support IPv6 has resulted in rapid implementation by Internet service providers (ISPs) and large companies. Several technologies are available to aid in the transition from IPv4 to IPv6. For example, you can use the IPSec protocol to tunnel IPv6 traffic. Other technologies, such as the Intra-Site Automatic Tunnel Addressing Protocol (ISATAP) and Teredo, also allow IPv4 and IPv6 clients to communicate with each other over an IPv4 network by tunneling IPv6 packets within IPv4 traffic.

DNSSEC

The *Domain Name System (DNS)* provides a way to translate Internet domain names into IP addresses. For example, the website www.example.com can be translated to an IP address of 93.184.216.34 and is defined as an IANA-managed Reserved Domain under RFC 2606 and RFC 6761, maintained for documentation and illustrative purposes. This allows network applications and services to refer to Internet domains by their fully qualified domain name (FQDN) rather than their IP address, which can be difficult for humans to remember and can often change. If a company changes its system's IP address, it can simply update the DNS tables to reflect this. External users will not see a difference, because they will still be connecting to it by name.

DNS servers perform an extremely valuable function on the Internet, and wide-scale communication interruptions can occur if a network DNS server is disabled. Most client machines use DNS each time they try to connect to a network host. The client's DNS server is configured using its network settings, which can be set manually or automatically through services such as Dynamic Host Configuration Protocol (DHCP). Each time a client tries to access a host, such as a website, the local DNS server is queried for the IP address of the domain name. The DNS server translates the name into an IP address, which the client uses to initiate its connection.

DNS servers can suffer from denial-of-service and malformed-request attacks. In a DoS attack, the DNS server is inundated with DNS or ping requests. The load becomes so much that the DNS server cannot respond to legitimate DNS queries. DNS queries to servers can also be manipulated to include malformed input that could crash the server. Ensure that your DNS server software is the latest version, with the most recent security patches installed, to prevent these types of attacks. *DNS security extensions (DNSSEC)* have been developed to protect this vital tool by ensuring that DNS responses are validated, guarding against many types of DNS-focused attacks.

EXAM TIP DNS uses both TCP and UDP port 53. TCP is used for zone transfers between DNS servers, as well as name resolution responses, whereas UDP is used for DNS queries.

SSH

Secure Shell (SSH) enables a user to log in to a remote machine and execute commands as if they were on the console of that system. SSH is a secure replacement for the older Telnet utility, which is insecure because its data isn't encrypted when communicated. SSH provides a secure, encrypted tunnel to access another system remotely. When a client connects to a system using SSH, an initial handshaking process begins and a special session key is exchanged. This begins the session, and an encrypted secure channel is created to allow the access. SSH can also be used in conjunction with other protocols such as File Transfer Protocol (FTP) to encrypt file transfer communications.

EXAM TIP SSH uses TCP port 22.

S/MIME

Multipurpose Internet Mail Extensions (MIME) is a specification for transferring multimedia and attachments through e-mail. This specification offers a standard way for all mail clients and mail transfer systems to handle certain types of attachments. For example, if a user sends an audio clip to another user through e-mail, the MIME header will include information on the attachment. When the audio clip reaches the destination user, the user's computer will understand what type of file it is and what application can be used to open it. However, MIME, as written in the original specification, offers no security protections for its content.

Secure MIME (S/MIME) is an extension of the MIME standard that is used for digitally signing and encrypting e-mail using certificates. S/MIME is used for sending confidential e-mail that needs to be secured so that other users can't capture the message and read its contents. By the sender encrypting the e-mail, an unauthorized user will be unable to decipher the contents of the message and its attachments. S/MIME requires the use of public key certificates for authentication and provides message confidentiality and integrity via the user's encryption and hashing algorithms.

SRTP

The *Real-time Transport Protocol (RTP)* is used for delivering voice and video services over IP networks. If you've ever used a Voice over IP (VoIP) phone, RTP likely was the underlying protocol that powered it. It is also often used for other services, such as streaming media and teleconferencing. RTP, however, does not inherently integrate encryption, so the *Secure Real-time Transport Protocol (SRTP)* was developed to provide AES encryption, as well as integrity, authentication, and protection from replay attacks. RTP uses UDP across a wide range of ports, usually between 16384 and 32767, depending on the vendor implementation, while SRTP uses port 5004.

LDAPS

A simple Lightweight Directory Access Protocol (LDAP) over SSL service that contains usernames, e-mail addresses, phone numbers, and locations can be a resource for an unauthorized user or malicious hacker looking for an accounting user or an engineering user for purposes of performing corporate espionage. Most LDAP servers support the use of encrypted secure channels to communicate with clients, especially when transferring information such as usernames, passwords, and other sensitive data.

EXAM TIP Remember that LDAP (unencrypted) uses TCP port 389, LDAP over SSL uses TCP port 689, and LDAP over TLS uses TCP port 636.

File Transfer Protocols

Basic types of FTP communications are not encrypted, so any login and password information is sent over the network in clear text and can be easily intercepted by a malicious hacker. *File Transfer Protocol, Secure (FTPS)* software uses encrypted TLS/SSL communications to prevent interception by unauthorized users. FTPS is a secure version of FTP that can be used over an SSL or TLS secure session connection. Using SSL or TLS enables users to perform FTP file transfers securely, using built-in encryption and authentication mechanisms (usually involving public and private keys). Unlike other applications that use SSL or TLS, FTPS uses TCP port 990.

You can also utilize *SSH File Transfer Protocol (SFTP)*, which is used to encrypt FTP sessions with SSH. It functions similarly to normal FTP, but all data is encrypted, so it can't be easily intercepted or read. Other than function, SFTP is *not* the same thing as regular FTP or FTPS, so don't confuse them. SFTP does not use TLS/SSL at all.

NOTE Do not confuse FTPS, which uses TSL/SSL, with SFTP, which uses SSH, to create an FTP tunnel through an SSH connection.

SNMPv3

The *Simple Network Management Protocol (SNMP)* allows you to use network monitoring programs to analyze diagnostic information on network devices. An SNMP agent service runs on the network device, which is accessed by a network monitoring tool. The SNMP agent provides real-time statistics on the device, such as device status, central processing unit (CPU), memory usage, and network activity. The latest release is version 3, *SNMPv3*.

The information available from the SNMP agent is organized into objects that are described by a management information base (MIB) file. Each hardware vendor typically provides its own MIB file unique to the device, which can then be imported into the network monitoring tool.

SNMP has very basic security that makes use of a type of password system called *community strings*, which are simple passphrases for SNMP to access each device. Most administrators leave the default community string *public* as is, but this opens a vulnerability because anyone who knows the community string can connect to the SNMP-enabled device. SNMP passwords should be immediately changed from the default if set up on the switch.

You can also use an access control list to limit SNMP access to the specific IP address of your network monitoring system.

HTTPS

Hypertext Transfer Protocol over SSL/TLS (HTTPS) provides a secure means of communicating HTTP data between a web browser and a web server. All HTTP communications are sent in clear text, so no messages are secure, and they can be easily viewed using a protocol analyzer. This makes HTTP unusable for communications requiring security and privacy, such as web-based banking and other online financial transactions. HTTPS protects the communication channel by using SSL/TLS and certificates to provide encrypted and protected communications. When you're connecting to a website that uses a secured channel, the uniform resource locator (URL) begins with *https* instead of *http*, as in https://secure.website.com. HTTPS is typically used in banking and online shopping transactions, where the transfer of credit card and personal information must be encrypted to prevent an unauthorized user from stealing the information while it's in transit between the client and the server. When a client connects to the secure site, the web server sends a certificate to the web browser to establish its identity. If the browser accepts the certificate and finds no validation issues with the certificate, SSL/TLS is activated between the server and client. This ensures that the website is genuine (it is what it says it is) and that the client is not connecting to a *rogue* site. In many web browsers, a secure site is indicated by a small padlock icon in the application taskbar. HTTPS uses TCP port 443 for communications. Because SSL in all of its versions has been declared as no longer secure, HTTPS uses TLS as its default secure protocol.

EXAM TIP HTTPS should not be confused with S-HTTP, another similar implementation that only encrypts the message headers.

IPSec

IP Security (IPSec) is a standards-based suite of protocols that provides confidentiality, integrity, and authenticity to information transferred across IP networks. It works on the IP network layer to encrypt communications between the sender and receiver. IPSec is most often used to secure virtual private network (VPN) communications over an open network such as the Internet; however, because IPSec operates at lower levels than most application security protocols (such as SSL/TLS), applications do not need to be aware of IPSec to make use of its benefits, which makes its implementation more flexible. IPSec ensures that communications cannot be read by a third party, that traffic has not been modified in transit, and that messages received are from a trusted source.

NOTE IPSec use is mandatory in IPv6.

IPSec uses two types of encryption modes: transport and tunnel. In *transport* mode, IPSec encrypts the data portion of each packet, but not the header. This can be used only in host-to-host communications. *Tunnel* mode, on the other hand, encrypts both the header and the data of the network packet. This is used to host VPN gateway communications, the most common form of virtual private network. The receiver of the packet uses IPSec to decrypt the message. For IPSec to work, each communicating device needs to be running IPSec and share some form of public key. Key management is provided by the Internet Key Exchange (IKE), formerly ISAKMP/Oakley. IKE enables the receiver to obtain a public key and authenticate the sender using digital certificates.

IPSec consists of component protocols, including *authentication header (AH)* and *encapsulating security payload (ESP)* headers. The AH is an IP header that is added to a network packet and provides its cryptographic checksum. This checksum is used to achieve authentication and integrity to ensure that the packet has been sent by a specified source and has not been captured and changed in transit. ESP is a header applied to an IP packet when it is encrypted. It provides data confidentiality so that the packet cannot be viewed in transit. In newer IPSec implementations, the AH functionality is always performed within the ESP header, resulting in a single combined ESP/AH header.

Security associations (SAs) are the basic building blocks of IPSec communications. Before any two devices can communicate using IPSec, they must first establish a set of SAs that specify the cryptographic parameters that must be agreed upon by both devices before data can be transferred securely between them, including the encryption and authentication algorithms and keys.

The primary way of establishing SAs and managing VPN keys is via the Internet Security Association and Key Management Protocol (ISAKMP) and IKE. ISAKMP/IKE is the protocol for performing automated key management for IPSec. The ISAKMP/IKE process automatically negotiates with the remote VPN device to establish the parameters for individual SAs. An SA is established so that all key exchanges can be encrypted and no keys need to be passed over the Internet in clear text. Once the SA is established, a session SA is negotiated for securing normal VPN traffic, referred to as IKE Phase-1 and Phase-2 negotiations. The session SAs are short-lived and are renegotiated at regular intervals, ensuring that the keys are discarded regularly. The same keys are used only for a short period of time and for limited amounts of data.

E-mail Protocols

E-mail servers store incoming mail for users and are responsible for sending outbound mail from local users to their destination. Most e-mail servers are configured to protect user inboxes by requiring users to authenticate to the account. If the user login or password is not valid, the user won't be able to access the contents of the inbox.

Post Office Protocol (POP) is an Internet protocol that provides a way for users to retrieve mail from their inboxes using a POP-enabled e-mail client. The e-mail messages are stored on the server until the user connects to it and downloads messages to the e-mail client. Most POP accounts are set to delete the messages from the server after they've been retrieved.

The *Internet Message Access Protocol (IMAP)* is like POP in that it's used to provide a mechanism for receiving messages from a user's inbox. IMAP has more functionality than POP, however, because it gives users more control over what messages they download and how these messages are stored online.

Both basic POP3 and IMAP send credentials in clear text when authenticating. To protect the transfer of credentials from packet sniffers, you should use Secure POP or Secure IMAP services, which utilize TLS to encrypt the login and passwords.

EXAM TIP POP uses TCP port 110, and IMAP uses TCP port 143. Secure POP uses TCP port 995, and Secure IMAP uses TCP port 993.

The *Simple Mail Transport Protocol (SMTP)* is the e-mail message-exchange standard of the Internet. Whereas POP and IMAP are the Internet protocols used to read e-mail, SMTP is the Internet protocol for delivering e-mail. SMTP is used to navigate an e-mail to its destination server. Mail servers that run SMTP have a relay agent that sends a message from one mail server to another. Because mail servers, as per their function, need to accept and send data through an organization's routers and firewalls, this relay agent can be abused by unauthorized users who relay mail through the server. These e-mails are usually from spammers sending out unsolicited messages while hiding the original sending location of the e-mails through spoofed addresses. The need for e-mail server security becomes even more important when these users send malicious e-mails with attachments that contain viruses, malware, and phishing attempts.

To protect the mail server from this type of abuse, the SMTP relay agent should be configured to send only mail originating from its own network domain. SMTP authentication should also be enabled to allow only authenticated clients to relay through the SMTP server to send mail. A secure version of SMTP, *SMTP Secure (SMTPS)*, uses TLS and is characterized by its use of TCP port 465.

EXAM TIP SMTP uses TCP port 25 for communication, although many ISPs have started to use alternative ports to prevent connections from spammers' relays. It is a security best practice to disable SMTP relay on your SMTP server.

NTP

On a network, hosts often get their time from a central source, such as a network time server or Internet-based time source running the *Network Time Protocol (NTP)* on UDP port 123. An authentic time source is required on a modern network, since so many synchronization and security services rely on consistent, accurate time across the network. Kerberos (discussed in depth in Objective 3.8, later in this domain) is one example of an authentication protocol that requires consistent time set between all hosts if authentication is to work properly. The hosts on the network, if set correctly, take into account time zone differences between the local time zone and Universal Coordinated Time (UTC), which NTP normally uses.

DHCP

The *Dynamic Host Configuration Protocol (DHCP)* is used to allocate IP addresses and other network information on a network automatically, such as DNS and default gateway information, to clients as they access the network. DHCP servers can be deployed instead of having to configure each client on the network manually with specific information. This greatly reduces administrative overhead because, with static manual addressing, if something changes on the network, such as the address of a DNS server, you have to change the information manually on every client. DHCP uses UDP ports 67 and 68 for its back-and-forth communications with the client.

Use Cases

Now that you've reviewed the most critical secure protocols, the following list summarizes how these protocols are most commonly used to power networks and services:

- **Voice and video** RTP and its secure counterpart, SRTP, are used for audio and video transport.
- **Time synchronization** Time is synchronized on networked devices through a central source, such as a network time server or Internet-based time source running NTP on UDP port 123.
- **E-mail and web** To protect the transfer of credentials from packet sniffers, you should use Secure POP or Secure IMAP services, which utilize SSL/TLS to encrypt the login and passwords. HTTPS provides a secure means of communicating HTTP data between a web browser and a web server for sensitive browsing, such as online banking.
- **File transfer** FTPS software uses encrypted TLS/SSL communications to prevent interception by unauthorized users. You can also utilize SFTP, which is used to encrypt FTP sessions within SSH.
- **Directory services** Lightweight Directory Access Protocol (LDAP) provides distributed directory services. LDAP servers use the now-deprecated Secure Sockets Layer (SSL) protocol or the Transport Layer Security (TLS) protocol (also called LDAPS, or sometimes also Secure LDAP) to provide encrypted secure channels for communication with clients, especially when transferring information such as usernames, passwords, and other sensitive data.
- **Remote access** IPSec is most often used to secure VPN communications over an open network such as the Internet.

- **Domain name resolution** DNS security extensions (DNSSEC) have been developed to protect domain name resolution (DNS) services by allowing DNS responses to be validated, guarding against many types of DNS-focused attacks.
- **Routing and switching** The two aspects of the TCP/IP protocol, TCP and IP, manage and route network messages.
- **Network address allocation** DHCP is used to allocate IP addresses and other network information on a network automatically.

REVIEW

3.1: Given a scenario, implement secure protocols You should understand the layers of the OSI model, know the basic protocols, and the major use cases that individual protocols support.

3.1 QUESTIONS

1. Which of the following statements are true regarding TCP/IP? (Choose two.)
   - **A.** TCP/IP protocols are part of the OSI model.
   - **B.** TCP/IP is a protocol stack containing multiple protocols.
   - **C.** TCP/IP closely maps to the OSI model.
   - **D.** TCP/IP protocols are part of the transport and network layers of the OSI model.
2. Which of the following is a true statement regarding IPv6?
   - **A.** IPv6 requires the use of NAT to help conserve IP addresses.
   - **B.** IPv6 has been implemented on the Internet worldwide.
   - **C.** IPv6 has 4,294,967,296 available IP addresses.
   - **D.** IPSec is natively included with IPv6.
3. Which of the following IPSec protocols is used to provide authentication and integrity for an entire IP packet?
   - **A.** Encapsulating Security Payload (ESP)
   - **B.** Authentication Header (AH)
   - **C.** Internet Key Exchange (IKE)
   - **D.** Internet Security Association and Key Management Protocol (ISAKMP)
4. Which of the following IPSec modes should be used within a local area network?
   - **A.** Authentication mode
   - **B.** Tunnel mode
   - **C.** Transport mode
   - **D.** Encryption mode

3.1 ANSWERS

1. **B C** TCP/IP is a protocol suite that has multiple protocols in it and closely maps to the OSI model layers.
2. **D** IPSec is natively included with IPv6.
3. **B** The Authentication Header (AH) protocol is used to provide authentication and integrity for an entire IP packet, regardless of whether it is in transport mode or tunnel mode.
4. **C** Transport mode should be used within a local area network, since the IP header can't be encrypted.

Objective 3.2 Given a scenario, implement host or application security solutions

Although the primary focus of this objective is host and application security, it also mentions connecting technologies as well, since there are so many dependencies throughout the infrastructure to ensure that hosts and applications are locked down and secure. Some of the concepts discussed in this module are expanded upon and explained in greater detail in the next few modules. However, for the CompTIA Security+ exam, you should understand the solutions that are involved with implementing host and application security.

Host and Application Security

For many years in the early era of networking, the focus of security efforts was perimeter security. The prevailing thought was that if you installed a firewall and configured it properly, you could keep out all threats. We now know that strategy definitely does not work, as the threat landscape has changed significantly over the years and more and more modern threats target hosts and applications, whether in a client–server model or a web-based application model. Therefore, understanding host and application security is very important for IT professionals. Many different technologies, security controls, and other efforts go into securing end-user hosts and the varying applications they use.

Endpoint Protection

Endpoint protection is focused on the host level, but it doesn't necessarily start there. It starts throughout the network. This section discusses various solutions to secure the endpoint, both network-based and host-based technologies, beginning with intrusion detection systems.

Intrusion Detection/Prevention Systems

As a first line of defense for your network security, the implementation of an intrusion detection system (IDS) greatly enhances the security of your network. An IDS can monitor your network activity for suspicious behavior that may indicate someone is trying to break in or damage your network. By proactively monitoring the network border, the IDS can immediately notify an administrator of the intrusion. More advanced detection systems, called *intrusion prevention systems (IPSs)*, attempt to deal with the problem autonomously and either disconnect suspicious network connections or turn off network services that are being attacked.

NOTE Network-based intrusion detection systems, as well as firewalls, are discussed in greater depth in the upcoming objective, 3.3; however, a working knowledge of how they function is necessary to understand host-based intrusion detection systems, as well as some other underlying technologies that support host and application security.

A network-based IDS (NIDS) examines network patterns, such as an unusual number of requests destined for a server or service (for example, an FTP server). The headers of network packets can be analyzed for possible spoofing attempts or suspicious code that indicates a malformed packet. Corrupted packets and malformed data can bring down a web server that's vulnerable to such attacks.

A NIDS typically consists of the following components, as shown in Figure 3.2-1:

- **Detection agent** The *detection* agents of an IDS usually are physically installed in a network and are attached to core network devices, such as routers, firewalls, and switches. Detection agents can also be software agents that use network management protocols, such as the Simple Network Management Protocol (SNMP). They simply collect the data passing through the network and send it on to the network monitor for analysis.
- **Monitor** The *network monitor* is fed information from the detection units and analyzes the network activity for suspicious behavior. This is the heart of the IDS, which collects information from the network, analyzes it, and then uses the notification system to warn of any problems. The monitor can utilize several methods, including heuristic-, behavior/anomaly-, rule-, and signature-based scanning, to detect network threats. These are discussed in more detail later, in the "Monitoring Methodologies" section.
- **Notification system** The *notification system* is used for notifications and alarms, which are sent to the administrator. Once the network monitor recognizes a threat, it writes to a log file and uses the notification system to send an alert, such as an e-mail or a Short Message Service (SMS) message, to an administrator. The notification system can usually be configured to allow for a variety of methods of communication.

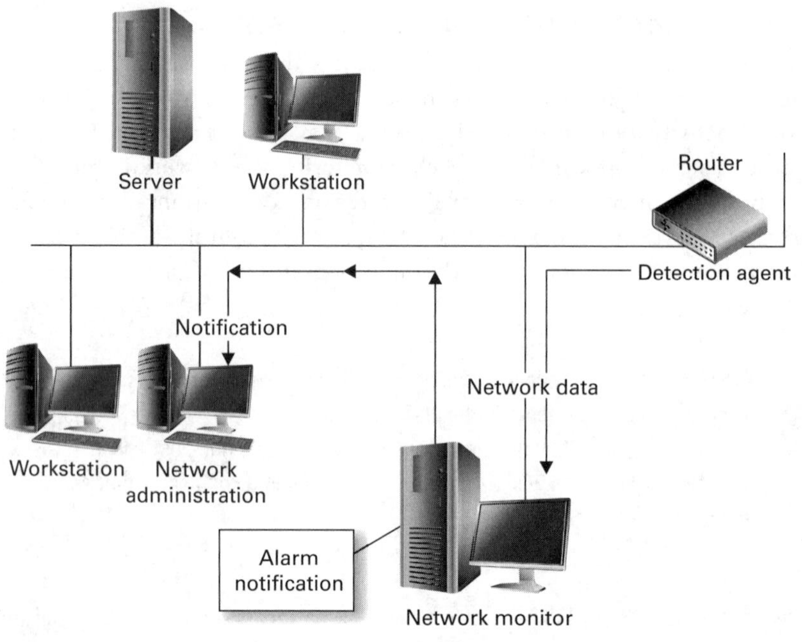

FIGURE 3.2-1 Network intrusion detection system (NIDS)

To protect the entire network, the IDS is usually located at a central point, such as a main router, switch, or firewall system. An IDS can also be deployed either *in-band* (more often referred to as *inline*), where all traffic is analyzed (often at the network edge), or *out-of-band*, where only some traffic is analyzed, often using a passive tap or other collection mechanism. An IDS can only monitor what it sees, so placing it further down in the system lessens the chance of finding intrusions, especially because your firewall and routers are the entry points to the network. Therefore, an inline IDS deployment is more secure. This characteristic makes a network-based system generally more valuable than a host-based system because of its capability to detect intrusions at the entrance to the network. The disadvantage of a network-based system is that it can rarely detect intrusions originating from the internal network. This is where also using a host-based IDS in your overall security model is important.

NOTE Network-based intrusion systems also are not effective in monitoring encrypted communications, such as communications over a virtual private network (VPN).

When an intrusion is detected, the system works in either an active way or a passive way to alert an administrator of the problem. A passive system will only send warnings and alarms through log files, e-mail, instant message, or SMS message. An active system tries to fix the problem by shutting off certain services or preventing connections from a suspicious host.

Active Detection A NIDS that uses active detection methods can take immediate steps to halt an intrusion. These types of systems are also called *network-based intrusion prevention systems (NIPSs)* because they actively attempt to prevent intrusions rather than just detect them. The advantage of this method is that it can attempt to prevent the intrusion from continuing. Active detection prevents the suspicious activity from expanding into actual damage or data loss. This is a great advantage over passive detection systems, which merely log the incident or send an e-mail to the administrator, who might not see the message for many hours before she can perform any preventive actions. By then, it could be too late.

EXAM TIP A network-based intrusion prevention system (NIPS) tries to prevent an intrusion from continuing after detecting it.

Network-based active detection systems can automatically reconfigure logical network topologies to reroute network traffic in case of some form of network attack, such as a DoS attack. They can also detect suspicious activity on a network connection and terminate it, logging the IP address to prevent any further connections from that origin. The active detection system can also sense attacks on certain ports or services, such as an SNMP port on a router, and shut down the port to prevent any more attacks on it.

The disadvantage of active detection systems is that the occurrence of false positives can cause the system to shut down services or network connections for legitimate requests.

Passive Detection Passive detection by a NIDS involves alerting an administrator of the intrusion so that he can take the necessary actions to stop it. The system will not take any active steps to prevent the detected intrusion from continuing. The disadvantage of a passive system is that the administrator might not get the alert immediately, especially if he is offsite and not carrying a smartphone or other mobile device. By the time he gets to the system, the damage of the intrusion could have already been done.

Passive methods of detection usually consist of some form of logging utility that logs events as they happen and stores them for later examination or notifies the administrator of high-level warnings and errors. If no type of messaging alert function is configured, the administrator must scan the log files regularly for suspicious behavior.

EXAM TIP Remember that active intrusion detection takes steps to mitigate an intrusion, whereas a passive system typically logs the event or generates alarms.

Next-Generation Firewalls

Next-generation firewalls (NGFWs) combine the traditional capabilities of a firewall to block traffic at the perimeter with more active NIDS/NIPS technologies, as well as being application aware, meaning that they catalog applications approved for use within the network and examine traffic passing to and from them and can "learn" new applications as they are added to the network. Adopting the qualities of a behavioral device, they can alert to both signatures and anomalies within a network. Many next-generation firewalls also contain active threat intelligence capabilities, meaning that they are being regularly updated with current threat intelligence that enables them to block emerging threats more actively.

Cross-Reference

Firewalls are discussed in depth in Objective 3.3, later in this domain.

Monitoring Methodologies

Monitoring applications such as the various IDS/IPS solutions are used to monitor and analyze traffic—either from the network or from hosts—to detect security threats such as network-based attacks (DoS attacks, ping sweeps, and port scans). When a security threat is detected, the monitoring system logs the event and notifies the administrator or takes immediate steps to mitigate the incoming threat. Different types of monitoring methodologies can be used to detect intrusions and malicious behavior. The following sections describe these monitoring methodologies and their benefits and weaknesses.

EXAM TIP Understand the differences between signature-, behavior/anomaly-, heuristic-, and rule-based monitoring methodologies, including their strengths and weaknesses.

Signature-Based Monitoring Signature-based monitoring systems are like antivirus programs and contain predefined signature databases of known attacks that have appeared previously. Each type of attack can be recognized by its unique characteristics, and a signature is created for that type of attack. For example, signature-based systems can detect popular types of DoS attacks. The signature (if available) can detect this exact information in the network packet and generate an alert to the administrator. These databases are dynamic, and the monitoring program must be continually updated to ensure that it has the latest signatures to identify the latest types of threats.

Signature-based systems are powerful and efficient because they rely on the collective knowledge of security vendors, who analyze and collect information on Internet security threats and trends and update their databases quickly when new threats arise. However, signature-based systems are unable to detect very new attacks whose signatures are not yet available. In this respect, signature-based systems are often used in conjunction with behavior-based systems.

Behavior/Anomaly-Based Monitoring Behavior-based (also referred to as *anomaly-based*) monitoring systems do not use a predefined database of signatures but instead start from a baseline of normal behavior and then monitor network traffic based on these performance profiles and increasingly sophisticated analytics to recognize behavioral anomalies that exceed the thresholds of the normal baseline. Such a monitoring system becomes more effective over time as baseline activity is recorded, allowing the system to detect aberrations to the baseline more efficiently. For example, a sudden burst of incoming connections that is out of character for the network will trigger the monitoring system to generate alerts of the activity and, in some cases, take proactive steps to mitigate the anomalous behavior (which could be a DoS attack) by blocking the attempted connections.

The primary benefit of behavior-based systems is that they easily and quickly adapt to the current environment and can detect new variants of attacks that a signature- or rule-based monitoring system might not recognize. The monitoring system is actively looking for behavior that is inconsistent with the current system baseline profile; therefore, the system recognizes even new types of attacks immediately and can take action. New attacks are often referred to as *zero-day attacks*, and signature-based monitoring systems might not recognize them as threats.

KEY TERM A **zero-day attack** is a type of attack that has rarely or never been encountered (such as an unknown virus or a malicious program) and takes advantage of previously unknown weaknesses and vulnerabilities in a software program or operating system. Because the attack is new, no existing defense or signature has been created to detect it.

The disadvantage of a behavior-based system is that building the baseline profile takes some time, and until the system learns enough information about the current system, it cannot accurately detect anomalies to that profile; efficiency is built over time. False positives can occur, in which normal behavior is flagged as anomalous because the system has not had time to build its baseline profile to recognize it as normal behavior. Also, the anomalous behavior detected can generate an alert, but the monitoring system can only warn the administrator that the thresholds have been exceeded; the administrator must determine whether an actual attack is taking place and what steps to take to mitigate it. The behavior-based monitoring system doesn't always recognize the type of specific attack, only its symptoms.

Heuristic-Based Monitoring Heuristic-based security monitoring continuously trains on network behavior. Heuristics uses an initial database of known attack types but dynamically alters their signatures based on learned behavior of inbound and outbound network traffic. These types of systems are powerful for detecting suspicious behavior that might not be detected by other methods, but they require constant tuning to prevent false positives.

Rule-Based Monitoring Rule-based security monitoring takes more work to match the efficiency and effectiveness of other types of monitoring methods such as signature- and behavior-based systems. Like a firewall, a rule-based security monitoring system relies on the administrator to create rules and determine the actions to take when those rules are transgressed. For example, a rule can be created that will block connections from an IP address if more than 100 connections are attempted from the same IP address within a certain time, such as 30 seconds. This could indicate a DoS attack, and when the rule thresholds are exceeded, the offending connection will be blocked to contain the threat.

Rule-based systems require significant manual initial setup and constant maintenance to keep the rules current and up to date with the latest threats. These factors are handled automatically by a signature-based system, which already contains an up-to-date database of the latest security threats and compares these threats with the behaviors the system is experiencing. The system will then take action as appropriate.

Host-Based Intrusion Detection System

A *host-based intrusion detection system (HIDS)* monitors a specific host for suspicious behavior that could indicate someone is trying to break into the system. A HIDS monitors inbound and outbound network activity, networking service ports, system log files, and timestamps and content of data and configuration files to ensure they have not been changed. The host-based system can only monitor the system on which it is installed and is typically used for critical server systems rather than user workstations. A host-based system can detect an attack by a malicious user who is physically accessing the system console. The unauthorized user may be trying to access an administrator account or trying to copy files to or from the system, for example. The HIDS can also alert the administrator if someone has tried to log in to an account unsuccessfully too many times.

A HIDS using active methods of detection can take immediate steps to halt an intrusion. This is preferable because it prevents the suspicious activity from continuing. Passive methods merely log the incident or alert the administrator, who might not see the message for many hours before she can act. If the intrusion is detected as originating at the system console, the system can shut down and disable that user account or automatically log out the user. Locking accounts is a form of detection used by most network operating systems that disable accounts if a predefined number of unsuccessful logins occurs. The disadvantage of active detection is the case of a false-positive detection, in which the system automatically shuts down services when no attack is occurring; this can cause unnecessary and often costly downtime. Passive detection methods do not take active steps to prevent an intrusion from continuing if it is detected. Passive methods typically include logging events to a system log that can be viewed by an administrator later or, if configured to do so, forwarding the log entries through e-mail, instant messaging, or a text message. This enables the administrator to be notified as the intrusion is happening and gives the administrator a chance to catch the unauthorized user in the act and to prevent damage or data theft. If the administrator is not immediately notified, she must be sure to audit system log files regularly for critical warnings and errors that indicate suspicious activity.

EXAM TIP Make sure you know the difference between network- and host-based intrusion detection systems, as well as the difference between active and passive versions of these systems and how they mitigate threats.

Endpoint Detection and Response

Endpoint detection and response (EDR) refers to an emerging category of tools that use agents to continuously monitor endpoints for potential threat activities and store related data in a centralized repository where it can be analyzed for malicious events to facilitate a more rapid response. While this sounds similar to, say, anti-malware tools, EDR tools are considered more advanced because they employ a higher degree of automation to help facilitate threat hunting and are capable of reacting to a broader set of attacks.

Data Loss Prevention

Data loss prevention (DLP) solutions require the identification of information that is critical to the organization or considered "sensitive" (either PII—personally identifiable information—or identified as such through classification levels) and then work to ensure that this data doesn't leave the network via a USB device, e-mail, or some other method. In DLP, data is tagged and labeled with metadata denoting its security or sensitivity level as well as attributes that may or may not allow it to leave via various means. Some data might be tagged as safe to leave via USB or encrypted e-mail, but not via unencrypted e-mail. For example, DLP solutions would look for mobile devices that are connected and then monitor (or block) any data transfers of data that has been tagged as such. This can be achieved either through dedicated, onsite appliances or through cloud solutions that funnel data requests to the cloud where the analysis is conducted offsite by experts. E-mail filters can also be created to identify certain sensitive data patterns, such as Social Security numbers, and block e-mails containing that data from exiting the organization.

Anti-malware and Anti-spyware Software

To protect your systems from being infected by viruses, malware, spyware, and other types of malicious code, anti-malware systems should be installed in all aspects of the network—from desktop computers to servers and firewalls. Because viruses and malware can enter a company network in a variety of ways, such as via a USB key brought from home by a user, via e-mail attachments, and via Internet downloads, anti-malware protection should be set up for all these different types of access points. Anti-malware protection should be set up on every server, desktop, and laptop in the system and should include scheduled updates of signature files (discussed in more detail later in this section) from a central anti-malware update server. This can protect both the computers and the networks to which they connect, as well as provide a first level of defense to prevent viruses from spreading to the network.

Protecting just the end-user systems is not enough, however. All servers should be protected to prevent malware transmitted from a desktop system from spreading to any of the server systems. The reverse situation is also a great concern: If a server has a common file that is used by all company systems and that file becomes infected, simply accessing the infected server file can infect all the systems. Most viruses and spyware enter a system from e-mail attachments and Internet downloads that come from outside the company. E-mail servers that send and receive mail should be protected with special anti-malware software that can scan incoming e-mail for attachments with viruses. The anti-malware software either cleans or quarantines the virus, or deletes the message, and then sends notification e-mails to the source and recipient to warn about the existence of the virus.

NOTE When installing anti-malware software on an e-mail server, be certain to install the version of the software that examines incoming mail and attachments. Normal anti-malware protection only prevents viruses in normal program files outside the e-mail system.

Many types of network firewalls or other types of network-perimeter devices can be set up with virus-protection software that scans files being downloaded from the Internet. With the amount of traffic that goes through a firewall, this type of protection can slow down the network considerably, so be aware and evaluate your system needs carefully.

Although there are advantages to this all-in-one approach, such as standardization and the ability to update products more efficiently, in some instances it may be better to have different products from different security vendors on a host. As discussed in Domain 2, Objective 2.5, *vendor diversity* is a best practice that assumes similar products from the same manufacturer are often vulnerable to the emerging exploits in a similar manner, so an attacker could take advantage of this scenario and make it through multiple layers of defenses more effectively and efficiently. With vendor diversity, you would not use the same vendor for, say, antivirus and host-based firewalls. Obviously, there are disadvantages to this practice as well, including the previously mentioned standardization that may cause your administrators to spend more time keeping products updated. However, having a few different products installed increases the likelihood that an attack missed by one solution will be caught by another.

Host-Based Firewalls

Most organizations have firewall servers or appliances that protect the perimeters of their network from Internet attacks and hide the details of the internal network. Computer users who connect directly to an Internet connection rarely have any type of hardware-based firewall. Software-based firewall applications, however, have become an absolute necessity for a user connecting directly to the Internet from home or work using a cable modem, digital subscriber line (DSL), or dial-up method. A host-based firewall application (also sometimes referred to as a personal firewall) performs several critical functions to protect a user's host computer:

- **Blocks incoming network connections** The primary purpose of the personal firewall is to block incoming network connections from the Internet. It can hide your system from port-scanning attacks whereby malicious hackers probe network-connected computers for open network ports and vulnerabilities. The firewall software effectively makes your computer invisible to the Internet, and it will not reply to any network probes or diagnostic utilities such as ping or traceroute. Worms and other malware threats that are spread through the Internet will be stopped in their tracks by the firewall software because they will not be able to see your system to connect to it.

- **Watches for suspicious outbound activity** A personal firewall monitors outbound activity and allows the user complete control over what applications are allowed or blocked access to the Internet. For example, when your antivirus software periodically retrieves the latest virus signature file from an Internet site, your personal firewall will alert you that the application is trying to access the Internet. In this case, the activity is acceptable, so you can allow the software to pass through the firewall and to do so automatically on subsequent accesses so you will not receive an alert each time. This type of protection is extremely important to protect against Trojan horse and spyware applications that may be running on your computer and sending private information back to a malicious user. The personal firewall will detect the suspicious outbound activity and alert you. You can block the application if you do not recognize it and then attempt to remove it with your antivirus or anti-spyware software.
- **Provides ability to block/allow programs** All applications that potentially try to communicate out to the Internet can have their access controlled by the personal firewall. The personal firewall allows you to control which applications can send data to the Internet and which cannot. Some applications need to communicate with other servers to work properly, and you must take care not to block critical system or application services. In addition, trusted applications can occasionally visit an Internet site to check for new updates to the software, and this can be considered acceptable activity. Other applications, however, may be secretly sending information out to the Internet, such as personal identification information or data about your activities on your computer, such as lists of websites you have visited.
- **Warns of unpatched software and outdated antivirus files** Many personal firewalls can scan your computer to make sure that your OS and application software are running the latest versions, and they will alert you if your software seems to be out of date. Most personal firewalls will alert you if your antivirus signature files are out of date and will prompt you to run the updated software to get the latest files.
- **Provides web browser security** Personal firewall software can also strengthen the security and privacy of your web browsing sessions. The software can block pop-up and banner ads to prevent you from accessing known phishing or spyware sites and to ensure that your web browsing cookies and web cache are not causing security and privacy issues. Many firewalls will also block websites that run scripting, which is a primary source for browser exploits and security risks. However, scripting and cookies are often necessary for certain websites such as online banking, and it will be necessary to adjust your firewall settings as appropriate to protect your web browsing sessions without impacting functionality.
- **Provides e-mail security** Some personal firewalls monitor your inbound and outbound e-mail and can quarantine suspicious attachments to help prevent the spread of viruses, worms, and Trojan horse software. In some cases, if a worm infects your computer and your e-mail application is attempting to mail the worm to everyone in your address book, the personal firewall can detect this activity and block outbound mail from your computer and prevent you from accidentally infecting other computers.

Boot Integrity

The *Basic Input/Output System (BIOS)* of a host system contains the program code and instructions for starting a computer and loading the OS; because it is so fundamental to the operation of everything it loads, maintaining *boot integrity* is essential. BIOS software can be updated when new hardware support and device drivers are required. BIOS software updates may also contain bug fixes and security enhancements that prevent problems in the BIOS code from being exploited and causing a system to be compromised; the BIOS of servers and clients should be updated to the latest version. Most BIOS programs also contain a basic password feature that allows the network administrator to assign a password to the BIOS that must be entered before any BIOS changes or updates can occur. This provides an additional layer of security to prevent unauthorized access to the BIOS software or the primary system settings. Administrators should be aware that unauthorized users could also boot a system (if they have physical access to it) using a live CD or DVD media that can boot their own OS and bypass the actual BIOS and OS of the computer. The live optical disc contains a minimal OS software environment and does not boot any code from the system hard disk. From the disc's OS, an attacker can access the host system and its hard disk.

Although it's often still referred to as the BIOS, more modern systems, including Mac computers and Windows PCs after Windows 8, use the *Unified Extensible Firmware Interface (UEFI)* to boot, which can be loaded either from flash memory, a network share, or a hard drive. UEFI has several improvements over traditional BIOS, including better performance and increased security features. One of these features is *secure boot*, which is designed to prevent malware from modifying or replacing the boot loader by checking the certificate resident within the bootloader; if it has been tampered with, UEFI secure boot prevents the system from booting. The *Measured Boot* process in Windows 10 uses the UEFI and a trusted platform module (TPM; discussed later in this section) to provide a more secure boot process. Measured Boot also allows for *boot attestation*, where the Measured Boot logs are sent to a remote server for attestation, or evaluation, to allow action or remediation if required.

The process goes as follows:

1. The PC's UEFI firmware stores in the TPM a hash of the firmware, bootloader, boot drivers, and everything that will be loaded before the anti-malware app.
2. At the end of the startup process, Windows starts the non-Microsoft remote attestation client. The trusted attestation server sends the client a unique key.
3. The TPM uses the unique key to digitally sign the log recorded by the UEFI.
4. The client sends the log to the server, possibly with other security information.

Another modern technique used to ensure boot integrity is the *hardware root of trust*, which uses an actual immutable (not capable of being changed) piece of hardware that contains the keys used for cryptographic functions, while also verifying that the BIOS that is being loaded is the known-good, expected version, rather than having been replaced by a corrupted version.

The hardware root of trust will not allow the boot to take place if this has occurred. Once the boot is validated by the hardware root of trust, it is then passed down the line for the secure boot process. Many modern systems have this new feature built in.

Databases

Protecting databases, including password databases, is a primary concern. One method of protecting password databases is called *salting*, which refers to adding a suffix of random characters (called a *salt*) to the password before it is encrypted. Each password has its own salt, which is different for every password in the database, even identical passwords. Salting makes it difficult for a hacker to use brute-force methods to crack the password database. The longer the salt is that is added to the password, the less likely it is to be cracked. Early implementations used 12-bit salts; today 256-bit salts are recommended.

Note that data in a regular database is not normally encrypted during processing and use and is often taken from elsewhere in the database. Another concept to know is *tokenization*, as discussed in Domain 2, Objective 2.1; tokenization is similar to data masking in that sensitive data is replaced, but instead of being replaced by dummy data, the data is replaced with a token that refers back to the actual, sensitive data and represents the data in lieu of the real data element.

Finally, it is common for databases to be protected through *hashing*, where a value is used to create a unique "fingerprint" for a message. This prevents the message from being improperly accessed on its way to its destination. Hashing is used to protect the integrity of a message and is most often used with digital signatures. The most commonly used hashing function is the *one-way hash*, a mathematical function that takes a variable-sized message and transforms it into a fixed-length value referred to as either a *hash value* or a *message digest*. This function is "one-way" because it's difficult to invert the procedure, and the results are never decrypted, only compared to each other when repeating the same function on the same message. The hash value represents the longer message from which it was created. The receiver then performs the same hashing function on the message and compares the resulting hash value with the one sent with the message. If they're identical, the message was not altered.

Database Encryption

Company databases can consist of millions of records and terabytes of data. Data is the heart of a company, and if this data is damaged, lost, or stolen, it could mean the end of that company. Although most security resources are spent on encryption of data in transit, you must also consider the confidentiality of data in storage.

Databases can be encrypted so that even if an attacker were able to gain unauthorized access to a database, she would not be able to read the data without the encryption key. You can encrypt the entire database itself or the actual physical database files (which also protects backups of the database). For more granularity, you can even encrypt individual cells/records in the database that are decrypted as authorized by the user.

As with other encryption methods, key management and authentication can create security issues, and it is a best practice that the encrypted key never be stored with the encrypted data. Encryption keys should be stored and managed by external devices such as an HSM (discussed later in this objective).

Application Security

As previously discussed in Domain 2, Objective 2.3, developers must build their applications from a secure base and use *secure coding practices* to make sure that when an application is deployed, it does not contain security issues and is designed to be resistant to application errors and crashes that can create a condition of vulnerability within the application and potentially expose sensitive data or allow the system to be exploited. This section discusses some critical security concepts that should be considered when developing and implementing applications.

Secure Development Operations

Secure development operations (often shortened to *DevSecOps*) brings together the project and product managers, software developers, and the operations group to better facilitate rapid but secure software development, testing, deployment, and change management through a combination of automation, continuous integration, and secure baselines. As more organizations utilize more rapid software development methodologies, such as the Agile method discussed in Objective 2.3, DevSecOps and its less-security-focused brother, DevOps, have become more important to securely but swiftly release software into production.

Emerging tools available to DevSecOps personnel include immutable infrastructure and infrastructure as code. *Immutable infrastructure*, although not completely standardized as a definition, means the infrastructure can never be changed once instantiated. If a change needs to be made, it must be replaced fully with another instance of the infrastructure that is fully tested and secure. Think about it this way: as software changes are made, the software and its infrastructure are tested and are ready to be deployed and made immutable (or unable to change). The infrastructure is deployed as a single set, and the old iteration is removed and its resources freed for use. This provides both performance and security benefits.

Software applications cannot be considered only in a bubble; you must also consider the surrounding infrastructure that supports them, often called a *data center*. DevSecOps and DevOps personnel are required to work together to consider these aspects and *provision* (appropriately prepare) and *deprovision* (appropriately release or redirect resources) data center assets to support software and user requirements. Whereas this is often done through the configuration of servers, network hardware, and software residing on subsequent software, *infrastructure as code (IaC)* manages and provisions data centers through machine-readable files rather than the physical hardware. The physical equipment is generally a "bare-metal server" with virtual machines and configurations that all come together to be considered the "infrastructure." Infrastructure as code allows DevSecOps and DevOps personnel to be much more agile by automating the process of spinning up or shutting down resources as needed.

Secure Cookies

Cookies are small text files that are saved on your computer to store data for a specific website you have visited. Cookies can contain all types of data specific to that website, such as information to track unique visitors to the website, login information for the user, and information on other websites you have visited. Some cookies are cleared after your session on a specific website ends, other cookies expire over a certain period or time, and still other cookies do not expire at all but stay on your system until you delete them.

Due to the often-sensitive information they contain, cookies can frequently be a security and privacy risk in the event a malicious user accesses a cookie with your credentials for a specific website. Many web users also have privacy concerns about website cookies that track previous websites they have visited.

Most web browsers have a configuration option that lets you examine each cookie on your system. You can keep or delete cookies or clear all the current cookies off your system. Cookies can also be expired after a certain amount of time has passed. When you start web surfing again, new cookies will appear in your cookie directory. You also have the option of blocking third-party cookies, which are typically cookies from advertising sites not related to the current site you are browsing. Blocking third-party cookies can greatly reduce the chance that your private web browsing history will be leaked to third-party sites.

Secure cookies have the Secure attribute set and thus will transmit only over secure channels, such as HTTPS. This helps to ensure that cookies cannot be exploited in attacks such as cross-site scripting (XSS) and that languages such as JavaScript will not have access to your cookies, which they otherwise could if your cookies were not marked as secure.

NOTE To protect your privacy even more and to avoid sending demographic information to websites, most web browsers allow you to disable cookies and to delete any existing ones upon exiting the program. Unfortunately, many websites require cookies to be enabled to function properly.

HTTP Headers

Objective 1.3 of Domain 1 discussed HTTP headers and their manipulation. To recap, HTTP request and response messages have headers that include various HTTP commands, directives, site referral information, and address data. This data is simple text that can be modified by a malicious user. By manipulating this header information, a hacker can then perform a variety of attacks such as XSS, session and web page hijacking, and cookie modification. It is considered more secure for applications to process server-side headers, which are generally safe and cannot be manipulated, and ignore client-side headers in HTTP requests because of the security concern that they are easily manipulated. It is also a great idea, when possible, to force use of HTTPS through the HTTP Strict Transport Security (HSTS) header, which disallows a connection through HTTP and protects against various attacks such as man-in-the-middle.

Code Testing and Verification

Dynamic code analysis is conducted by executing software on a real or virtual processor, with inputs that allow the tester to determine how the software will behave in a potentially negative environment, looking for race conditions, incorrectly handled exceptions, resource and memory release issues, and potential attack vectors. *Fuzzing* is a dynamic technique that can help test input validation and error/exception handling by entering random, unexpected data into application fields to see how the software program reacts. Many application vulnerabilities originate from input validation issues, buffer overflows, and error handling, and fuzzing helps make sure that the software does not crash, lose or manipulate data, or provide unauthorized access based on input validation defects. It is also possible to perform dynamic verification of code at runtime by executing the software and extracting information to determine if it is operating in a secure state and within its modeled specifications.

Static code analysis, conversely, is performed without executing the program, often using an automated tool, as many programs have become so large that having someone (or group of people) manually review the code is not enough.

Stress testing checks the ability of a piece of software to undergo large amounts of stress or extremely heavy operating loads. Stress testing pushes the software beyond its normal or best-scenario operating environments and determines what the behavior would be in a real-world, heavy-load situation. Stress testing is critical for software and supporting infrastructure where resiliency, reliability, and error handling might mean the difference between life and death, such as in industrial control systems or weapons platforms—though large retail outlets also find it important to use stress testing to understand how the holiday rush might affect their systems.

Error and Exception Handling

Developers must be careful when coding applications to determine how the software program should react to error conditions and exceptions. In many cases, an unexpected error condition can reveal security vulnerabilities that can be exploited. For example, a software program may crash and drop to a command line that can be used by a hacker, or error messages may indicate full file and directory paths that the hacker can use as knowledge to further penetrate the system.

Error and exception handling is largely determined by the operating system and the programming language environment in use because they can offer varying levels of tools to deal with software exceptions. Generally, developers must make sure that a program should still be able to retain its state and continue to function in the event of an error condition. The program should be able to roll back to its previous state without interrupting the flow of the application.

Error messages must be informative to the user, but system details should never be revealed unless the software is running in a special debugging mode only available to the developers, where verbose error logging can help them trace a problem to fix a programming issue.

Transitive Access

Transitive access occurs when you have access permissions or systems of trust between different components of a software application that allow users to pass through unexpectedly and without proper authorization to access another software component.

For example, consider an application or operating system that establishes a trust relationship between two software components, A and B, that allows full access for data passing between these components. Another separate trust relationship is set up between components B and C that allows similar full access between those two components. If there is no explicit nontransitive access specified, any user who is authenticated and authorized for component A is allowed access through component B, and then by the separate trust relationship, unauthorized access to component C.

You must be careful when coding software that no software components allow pass-through transitive access by ensuring that trusts between components are nontransitive and require explicit authorization before access is granted.

Input Validation

Input validation refers to the process of coding applications to accept only certain valid input for user-entered fields. For example, many websites allow users to fill in a web form with their name, address, comments, and other information. If proper input validation code has not been included in these types of web forms, in certain cases a malicious user can enter invalid input into a field that may cause the application to crash, corrupt data, or provide the user with additional unauthorized system access. Invalid input often leads to buffer overflow types of errors that can be easily exploited. Encoding proper input validation within an application reduces the risk of a user inadvertently or intentionally entering input that can crash the system or cause some other type of security concern.

As you know by now, validation is a strong mitigation strategy to prevent many attacks. The two main ways to conduct this are client-side validation and server-side validation, and they both have pros and cons.

For example, client-side validation can respond to the user more quickly because the feedback can be generated almost instantaneously; if a user inputs numeric digits in a nonnumeric field, for instance, he can receive instant feedback rather than waiting for the server to respond. This type of validation requires fewer server resources for processing and is generally considered faster.

Server-side validation is more widely compatible; what if the user doesn't have the software installed that you require? A server-based implementation is more software agnostic. It also is generally considered more secure because the server doesn't show its code to the client.

Before implementing a validation technique (and it's incredibly important that you do), consider these benefits and drawbacks, and make the appropriate choice for your situation.

Escaping

Another concept related to input validation is *escaping*. Without proper validation, hackers can input actual commands into input fields that are then run by the operating system. Escaping recognizes specific types of command characters and parses them as simple data rather than executing the text as a command.

Code Reuse and Third-Party Libraries

Code reuse is the use of existing source code for a new purpose, either for a new program or for a new environment. Although code reuse obviously can have some cost- and time-saving benefits by eliminating duplication of effort, there are negative aspects to be considered. Reuse of code that contains weak cipher suites and implementations, often incorporated to better integrate with legacy software, can introduce inherent weaknesses into your new project. Similarly, third-party libraries and software development kits (SDKs) may not have had adequate quality or security vetting and can also introduce unknown weaknesses. One way to mitigate this is by looking for signed code where possible; *code signing* entails using a certificate to digitally sign executables and scripts to confirm that the software was developed by the appropriate author and has not been manipulated in any way, thus providing integrity and a measure of authenticity.

In a similar manner, *stored procedures* are saved subroutines that can be used within applications accessing databases, saving time and memory by combining the execution of several statements into one stored procedure and allowing applications to call that procedure rather than the multiple statements. This also reduces code duplication, thus further allowing for consolidation and centralization of that procedure. Although using stored procedures can provide security benefits through the central management and less code sprawl, you need to be diligent in reviewing any stored procedures to ensure that you understand clearly what they are executing.

Allow and Block/Deny Lists

Allow lists prevent unauthorized applications from executing by checking each potential execution against a list of applications that have been granted execution rights. If an application is included in the allow list, it can execute. If not, it is terminated. Often, allow-listing checks the hash of the potential application against the known-good hash to ensure that an application isn't maliciously claiming to be the legitimate version.

Conversely, most anti-malware vendors use *block lists* or *deny lists*; they require maintaining a list of "known-bad" applications, or just applications that the administrators don't want to have choking the available bandwidth or worse (think video games, bitcoin mining, and so on). Applications that don't appear on the deny list can execute.

There is no definitive answer as to which method is better; you could argue that deny-listing is better because of the intricate nature of enterprise systems and the number of applications required to support daily operations. In a deny-list solution, these applications would be more likely to execute as planned. However, proponents of an allow-list solution argue that it only takes one malicious program slipping through the deny list to wreck an organization, and therefore it is better to put the time and effort into developing a list of allowed applications. It is a good idea to go over both solutions with the leadership of the organization and make an informed choice of how to proceed.

EXAM TIP As information technology and cybersecurity evolves, some terms are replaced in favor of others. The terms *allow-listing* and *deny-listing* (and their variations) replace the older terms *whitelisting* and *blacklisting*, which are being deprecated across the industry. However, the CompTIA Security+ exam objectives previously included the terms whitelisting and blacklisting, so you may encounter those terms on the exam.

Hardening

The operating system is the primary software that controls how your system works and how it interoperates with your hardware. The OS is the most critical part of your computer system. *Operating system hardening* refers to keeping the OS and applications current through regular updates and critical software patches and removing unnecessary software services from the system. This is true no matter the type of operating system, including those residing on your network devices, servers, workstations, appliances, kiosks, and mobile devices. Despite having been tested before being released, every OS experiences some software bugs and security vulnerabilities after release. New versions of the software or bug fixes and patches are released to correct these issues, and you should make sure that these are installed on the OS as soon as possible. You must also be aware of any types of OS vulnerabilities in virtual machines installed in your environment that run multiple types of OSs on the same hardware platform. In addition to staying on top of software updates, you need to examine many other areas of your OS for security vulnerabilities, including examining the registry, configuration options, running services, and file systems.

Trusted Operating System

Some organizations have resorted to using a *trusted OS*, which is an OS that has met a set of standards such as the Common Criteria. These standards validate the security posture of an OS, sometimes only on particular hardware. Trusted OSs are often required within high-security environments such as government systems.

Trusted OS configurations are not necessary in lower-security environments, and using them in such environments may create situations where hardware and OS software are difficult to upgrade on an appropriate schedule. Additionally, trusted OS implementations often cause issues with hardware performance and application functionality, so they should be used only when necessary in high-security environments.

Operating System Updates

As mentioned, your OS software should be operating at the latest release version with the most recent security patches applied. OS vendors regularly release software updates, which are often rolled into larger software packages called *service packs*, *updates*, or *packages*, depending on the OS. Smaller bug fixes or patches that fix critical security vulnerabilities (sometimes called *hot fixes*) are usually released quickly so that administrators can patch their systems before hackers can take advantage of the vulnerability. Vendors usually provide these patches and service packs as downloads from their websites. Some OSs have automatic system update functions that can periodically connect to the vendor's website and download the latest versions of software components. Some vendors release an update disc or Internet download every few months that contains all the latest patches and bug fixes since the last version. It is especially important that you perform this software update procedure just after a new system has been installed. The OS installed on a computer is often the original version that shipped with the hardware; since that time, several service packs and patches have probably been released.

NOTE Even if you just installed a service pack or package update for your OS, you need to install any security patches released after that service pack or update to be completely current and fully protected.

Patch Management

In organizations with hundreds and often thousands of workstations, keeping all the operating systems and application software up to date can be a logistical nightmare. In most cases, OS updates on workstations can be automatically applied via the network. However, administrators must have a clear security policy and baseline plan to ensure that all workstations are running a certain minimum level of software versions. This should include updates both to OSs and updates to third-party applications.

Before you install any update or patch onto networked systems, you should first install it on a server in a lab environment. In some cases, software updates have been known to fix one problem but cause another. If no lab system is available, you can patch a server after business hours, constantly monitoring that server and having a back-out plan in place to remove the update if something should go wrong. While using the auto-update function that is embedded within most modern OSs and critical third-party applications such as browsers can ensure that updates are pushed in the most expeditious manner, you run the risk of having software conflicts, especially with legacy applications that might be dependent on an older version to function.

Services and OS Configuration

After you've installed an OS, configuring the many administrative and security-related options can increase your system security. Other options might make your system more vulnerable to attack, which is why installing or enabling only the necessary options for a system is critical. By enabling unnecessary options, you create potential vulnerabilities for unauthorized users to exploit—broadening your *attack surface*. You should also investigate the OS for ports and services enabled by default that are not required, and this is especially important when you are enabling services to be run on your system. Examples of services that might not be needed but that could be running are file- and print-sharing services and Internet services such as Hypertext Transfer Protocol (HTTP), File Transfer Protocol (FTP), Simple Mail Transfer Protocol (SMTP), Domain Name System (DNS), and Dynamic Host Configuration Protocol (DHCP).

If the system you are configuring does not need to share files, disable the server service so that no one on the network can connect to a network share on that system. Enabled Internet services can cause a variety of security vulnerabilities by opening network ports on your system to which unauthorized users can connect. For example, enabling web server services on your system enables hackers to connect to your system by issuing HTTP requests to the server, where they can attempt a variety of attacks to gain access or to disrupt communications. Remember that it's always better to configure a system to have the least amount of ports and services enabled, or *least functionality*, to minimize the attack surface available to a malicious actor. Also, although backward compatibility with older OSs and software sounds like a safe bet, it exposes your system to *downgrade attacks*, which force a system to revert to an older or less-secure mode of operation. Removing backward compatibility helps prevent these attacks.

EXAM TIP Services that are not required by the system should be disabled or removed, while existing services should be configured to provide maximum security.

File System Security

For file servers that share files with other users and computer systems, the file system in use must properly address security concerns for locking down file sharing. Older types of disk file systems, such as File Allocation Table (FAT), do not provide the same security as NT File System (NTFS) on modern Microsoft systems or ext4 on later Linux systems. Newer file system formats allow for greater access controls, such as specific security permissions for files and directories. Some file systems also provide encryption capabilities so no one can read the contents of a system without the proper key to decrypt it. Another aspect of file system security is how access permissions are configured for files on the server. Without proper access control, users can read or modify files that could be confidential in nature. Protection is critical for OS files that contain administrative programs and sensitive configuration programs. Access to system files should be granted only to system administrators, and user files should be stored on a separate disk or partition to ensure these system files are not accidentally accessed or removed. Each user should have a separate home directory to which only he or she has access. Group or department directories should be set up for files that must be shared among groups.

System User Accounts and Password Threats

Although the most common form of system authentication is a login and password procedure, this is also considered one of the weakest security mechanisms available. Users' passwords tend to be weak because users use common dictionary words or personal information that can be easily guessed by an unauthorized user. Often, a user's password is the name of a spouse or a pet or a birth date. Or the user may reveal passwords to others or write them down in conspicuous locations, such as a note taped to the computer monitor. Most operating systems come with a default administrative account called *admin*, *administrator*, or another similarly obvious name that points to this account as being necessary to manage and administer the system. For example, the *root* account is still the primary account that's been used for decades for full access to a Unix system. Most malicious users and attackers look for the admin or root account of a system or device as the first account to be compromised. It is a best practice for network administrators either to disable or rename default or administrator accounts, or, if that is not possible, to create an alternative administrative account with equal access rights and name it something inconspicuous. This ensures that a malicious user cannot automatically try to log in using the well-known account names for the admin user. It is a regular practice to use separate logins for each administrator to ensure that any admin account actions can be properly logged and audited. Generally, network administrators should never name accounts after their job function, such as *admin*, *backup*, *databaseadmin*, and so on. Enforcing the use of strong passwords, which are not based on dictionary words or personal information but include the use of alphanumeric characters and uppercase and lowercase letters, greatly diminishes an unauthorized user's ability to guess a password.

Passwords are usually attacked either online or offline. In an online attack, the attacker attempts to log in as a user by guessing the user's password. If the attacker has the password already, or can effectively guess the password based on knowledge of the person, an online attack might work. However, this is usually the most ineffective and inefficient type of attack, because most systems are configured to automatically lock the user account after a certain number of unsuccessful login attempts. In an offline attack, the (generally hashed) database of user credentials is usually stolen to be attacked offline by being loaded on to a system where the attacker has a variety of tools. If the attacker has the hashed passwords, he can wage different attacks against them, such as brute-force or dictionary attacks. Remember that hashing is a one-way function that is not intended to be decrypted and that it is mathematically difficult to find two different pieces of plain text that, when subjected to the same hashing algorithm, produce the same identical hash. When this does occur (and, although extremely rare, is theoretically possible), it is called a *collision*, and can be used in a so-called *birthday* attack, which attempts to just find a piece of plain text that supplies the same hashed value, no matter what the original plain text might have been.

A *brute-force attack* is the most basic type of password attack. In this attack's simplest form, an attacker might repeatedly attempt to guess the user's password. A more effective way would be to simply start at the beginning of the character set and try all possible combinations, in order, until the attacker eventually finds the correct combination of characters and password length. This obviously would take a very long time for a person to accomplish on his own; however, improved hardware and software have reduced the time of performing brute-force attacks. Even with the best hardware and software, though, brute-force attacks could theoretically take several hundred or more years to go through every permutation.

More effective and efficient, a *dictionary attack* uses dictionaries, or lists of common words across various types of organizations, languages, and other words that might be used for passwords, as well as common substitutions, such as using the @ symbol in lieu of the letter *a*. A *rainbow attack* is a variation on a dictionary attack that, instead of trying to guess the password, uses precomputed hashes (called *rainbow tables*) developed by software that can process huge lists of words and spit out their hash, which is then added to the rainbow table's file. The attacker then compares the rainbow table to the password hashes she obtained illicitly, looking for matches.

To ensure the usefulness and efficiency of a login and password procedure, you must create and strictly follow account and password policies, such as enforced password expiry and rotation after a specific period.

Host Internet Access

Most users have access to the Internet to send and receive e-mail and instant messages and to access information they need to do their work. Although most networks are secured from outside intrusion through routers and firewalls, several security vulnerabilities can be created by users inside the network. At the office, users often download and install applications that should not be operating on the company network, such as chat, file-sharing, and music-sharing programs. Unfortunately, these applications can contain security vulnerabilities that allow access to unauthorized users outside the company via unique service ports that the company firewall might not be blocking.

Beyond the security vulnerabilities, user interaction with external Internet users can result in viruses or Trojan horse programs being downloaded that allow backdoor access to the user's computer. To protect against the use of these programs, the network administrator should block the service ports accessed by these programs on the main network firewall so that they cannot communicate with the Internet. The administrator can also assign access rights to users on their computers that deny them the ability to install any type of software that is not already loaded on their system.

Some users also download questionable content from the Internet, such as pornographic materials or other objectionable content, onto their office computers. This presents a legal problem for the company, as many companies have been sued for allowing such access. To prevent this activity, network administrators can install special web filter programs that block access to these sites. Similar to the deny list (aka blacklist) mentioned earlier, these filters use a list of known objectionable sites that is compared to the websites users try to access through their web browsers. These lists can also contain well-known phishing, spyware, and malware sites, which can also be blocked accordingly.

Software Access and Privileges

All software on the workstation should be kept current with the most recent patches and upgrades to remove security vulnerabilities from previous versions. The administrator should ensure that users have only the access privileges they need to perform their job functions. For example, any system functions that enable changes to be made to the network address of a computer—or any other type of system change—should be off limits to a regular user and accessible only to the administrator. Regular users should not be able to access any application or configuration programs other than those required for their jobs. The most efficient way of preventing certain system functions from user abuse is to enact network-wide security policies that are automatically set for each workstation on the network. This can save considerable time because an administrator does not have to visit each workstation and block out items one by one.

Securing Peripherals

Although certainly the bulk of your efforts will go toward securing the hosts, don't forget the peripherals that are connected to those hosts. As described in Objective 1.2 of Domain 1, hardware keyloggers can pass your sensitive information almost undetectably, but more benign items, such as wireless keyboards and mice, can pose their own threat of attacks based on their wireless connectivity. Therefore, it is considered a best practice to not use these in a secure environment and instead stick to their wired counterparts. Displays have their own vulnerabilities as well; for example, they can suffer from issues related to leaking electromagnetic emanations, especially the older CRT models; an attacker can use those emanations to "read" the sensitive information on the screen. If this is a concern, special testing can be done to check for emissions. Although more modern displays are less prone to emanation issues, in a highly secure environment, it's a good idea to choose your equipment carefully, such as using National Security Agency– or Canadian TEMPEST–approved equipment, to be sure that an attacker cannot use those emanations to "read" the sensitive information on the screen.

Have you ever considered your printer or multifunction device (MFD) as a threat vector? You should, because an unsecured printer can provide access into your network in the same way an unsecured host might. Printers often connect via Ethernet to the same networks that your more traditional hosts connect to and often have no or very minimal security controls applied. Modern MFDs can be configured to require passwords or two-factor authentication, and if you have implemented this within a more secure environment, it's a great idea that you check out a secure configuration guide for printers. If you see any odd behavior coming from your printer, such as refusing to print or unknown content being printed, don't just assume that your printer is misbehaving; it could be an attack against an accessible printer.

Mobile devices will be covered in Objective 3.5 later in this domain, but other devices that you should be on the lookout for include portable hard drives, SD cards, digital cameras, flash drives, and other external storage devices—some are even Wi-Fi enabled—that can be used to remove your organization's precious data from a host or network device. Make sure your data loss prevention (DLP) solution is scanning, blocking, and reporting these connections.

Disabling Unnecessary Ports and Services

Have you ever started the Task Manager function within Microsoft Windows and viewed how many services are running, even when you really don't seem to be doing much on the system? Most modern operating systems run many unnecessary services, from allowing use of legacy network protocols to using shiny new graphical themes. Each of these services can expose vulnerabilities to an eager intruder. It is worth your time to research the unnecessary services running on your OS of choice and disable them.

Most network devices allow you to secure the device right down to the port level. For example, a network switch might have 24 port connections that link your client workstations. You can configure the switch to only allow certain devices to use specific ports, and even disable ports that aren't in use to prevent an unauthorized user from simply plugging his device into the port.

You can also configure network devices to accept only data from specific MAC address ranges, which limits access to the switch or port based on the hardware address of the connecting client.

Disabling Unnecessary Accounts

The more accounts that are allowed access to a system, the more likely it is that a hacker (or even a malicious insider) could use an account to perform unwanted activities. It's a great idea to audit and then disable accounts that aren't needed; these can be guest accounts or accounts of users who have temporarily or permanently lost access through termination of employment or other changes. This provides a smaller attack surface to secure.

Improving Baseline Configurations

As discussed previously in this objective, *application allow-listing* works off the basic premise that certain programs or applications that are trusted are "good" while others are not trusted and should not be allowed to be loaded or executed. Good applications are "whitelisted." *Application deny-listing*, conversely, involves creating a list of applications that have been established to be malicious or untrustworthy and will therefore not be permitted access. Both are great approaches; however, application allow-listing is the better choice because you can control exactly which applications can run on a system. Deny-listing only allows you to specify a finite number of disallowed applications—where there are probably dozens (if not hundreds) more that you don't know about but wouldn't want to run on your hosts. Think of application allow-listing as a *default deny* type of rule (where anything that is not specifically allowed is denied by default) and deny-listing as a sort of *default allow* rule (anything not specifically denied can run).

Data Execution Prevention (DEP) debuted within Windows XP and Windows Server 2003 operating systems natively; it is a Windows feature that attempts to protect your computer from malicious code by disallowing the ability to execute code from memory locations that are reserved for Windows and other programs that are known to be good. If an application does attempt to run code from one of these locations, a memory violation occurs and the process is terminated. If this occurs, an administrator should look to determine what the offending application is; it could be a truly malicious situation, or an internal application that has not been coded properly. Be mindful that applications using dynamic code generation often have issues with DEP-enabled systems.

Trusted Platform Module

A *trusted platform module (TPM)* is a special hardware chip that is typically installed within a computer system or device, such as on the system motherboard of a computer desktop or laptop. This module provides authentication by storing security mechanisms such as passwords, certificates, and encryption keys that are specific to that system hardware. The chip itself contains a built-in RSA (Rivest, Shamir, and Adleman) key that is used for encryption and authentication. In the past, hardware-based passwords on desktops and laptops were typically stored in clear text and, therefore, vulnerable to unauthorized access. With the advent of TPM, any system passwords are now stored and encrypted on the TPM chip. The TPM provides greater security benefits over software-based solutions because it runs in a closed hardware subsystem that mitigates external threats. TPM-based systems are compatible with most popular operating systems.

Laptops are especially prone to physical theft because of their portability, and if the hard drive contents are not encrypted, an unauthorized user can easily access these files. The TPM allows the contents of the hard drive to be encrypted; the user simply generates a key that is stored on the TPM chip. When the user needs to access the hard drive, she uses OS software, such as Windows, to send the key to the TPM chip for authentication. This prevents an unauthorized user from accessing the hard drive contents of equipment. As previously mentioned, the Measured Boot process within Windows 10 uses the UEFI and TPM together to provide a more secure boot process.

Hardware Security Module

A *hardware security module (HSM)* is a specialized hardware appliance used to provide onboard cryptographic functions and processing. This physical hardware device can be a stand-alone device attached to a network or connected directly to a server as a plug-in card. HSMs are primarily used to host integrated cryptographic functions, such as a Public Key Infrastructure server for encryption, decryption, and secure key generation and management, but they can also be used to provide onboard secure storage of encrypted data. With their processing speed and security, HSMs are often used for banking applications (such as ATMs) that require scalable, performance-based solutions for critical key management and security.

Full-Disk Encryption

With *full-disk encryption (FDE)*, the entire contents of a computer system's hard drive are encrypted, typically by encrypting the disk volume that contains all the operating system data; this does not include the booting instructions located in a boot volume or master boot record (MBR). By encrypting all files, including temporary and swap space files, you ensure that no unauthorized user can access this data if the system is compromised or stolen.

Many operating systems come with their own proprietary whole-disk encryption mechanisms that encrypt and decrypt data on the fly as the user is operating the computer. You can encrypt a system's OS volume on the hard drive and provide authentication for the boot process (which cannot be encrypted). It is critical that disk encryption systems use some form of authentication for the boot process, such as a locked-down mini OS or a TPM mechanism whose only function is to authenticate the user before booting the system. Otherwise, an unauthorized user can still boot the system and access user files as if he were the original user. To authenticate the user, a combination of passwords, passphrases, personal identification numbers (PINs), or hardware tokens can be used before allowing access to the encrypted disk volumes. A related concept is the *self-encrypting drive (SED)*, which employs full disk encryption but, without user input, encrypts itself fully and continuously. The SED then requires an authentication key (essentially a password) to decrypt, even if the drive is moved into a different system. The industry standard for these drives is the Opal Storage Specification.

Individual File Encryption

Data encryption can also be taken to a very granular level where only individual files and folders are encrypted by the file system itself, rather than the contents of entire partitions or a whole disk. This type of encryption has the benefit that each encrypted file or folder will have a different encryption key. This approach provides stricter access control; however, it requires efficient key management to properly oversee different keys with different user authorizations.

Removable Media and Mobile Devices

The ability to transfer information easily from one computer device to another has been made easier with removable media and mobile devices. Technologies such as removable hard drives, USB keys, and flash memory in mobile devices give users flexibility in moving data from one system to another.

Removable media can contain critical and confidential data that must be protected from unauthorized access and physical damage or destruction. The portable nature of many types of computer media means more opportunities for an unauthorized user to obtain or damage the information they contain. Security must be a priority to protect the confidentially and integrity of data, especially when this information is being physically moved from one place to another. This involves the use of encryption and authentication to secure access to the data, as well as physical and environmental protection of the removable media itself.

While the data is protected by encryption, there are security concerns with the methods used to access and decrypt data. A user must authenticate using a password, passphrase, or some other identifier before he can decrypt the contents of the device. If the authentication process is weak, the strong encryption techniques can be easily subverted. More advanced USB flash drives can store the actual encryption key on a separate controller part of the USB device that is protected from the main flash drive where the data is encrypted.

Sandboxing

As discussed in Objective 2.2 of Domain 2, sandboxing is a common function of virtual machines. To recap, with sandboxing, the underlying machine layer theoretically is unharmed in the event of a malware outbreak or other security breach. Sandboxing is often used to open e-mail attachments or other high-risk files in an environment that will be less harmful if they do indeed turn out to be malicious. Many modern browsers, e-mail clients, and security tools include some level of sandboxing to reduce these risks. Newer versions of Windows 10 include built-in sandboxing that can be used to run unknown or potentially malicious executables.

REVIEW

Objective 3.2: Given a scenario, implement host or application security solutions Use antivirus and anti-malware software to protect hosts and applications against a wide variety of malware programs. Firewalls can monitor the inbound and outbound network activity of your system and notify you of abnormal behavior. They can also provide the ability to block or allow access. Use passwords and encryption to protect the data of mobile devices. Use security baselines and policies to establish a strong, secure foundation for your OS, applications, and web browsers for all your systems, including mobile devices.

Applications must be designed and developed with security in place. Use input validation to make sure hackers cannot insert malformed input or command requests in application input forms. Escape out special characters and command characters so that they are processed as data, not actual commands. Software should be developed to combat resource exhaustion and memory leaks. Use fuzzing to test input validation by entering random, unexpected characters into application input forms. Don't display filename and directory paths in error messages. Make sure your application handles exceptions without crashing or providing unauthorized access. Make sure applications have secure configuration baselines and that all software is up to date with all security patches installed.

Use data loss prevention concepts such as outbound content filtering and encryption to prevent confidential data loss and interception. Use TPMs for secure storage of encryption keys and certificates for hardware platforms. HSMs are used for high-end security applications that require secure key generation and management on a separate hardware appliance. Full-disk encryption and self-encrypting drives encrypt an entire disk or volume based on the choices made. Database encryption can secure data in storage on a database server. You can encrypt the physical database files, or you can encrypt data cells/records within those files for granular protection that includes user authorization for accessing specific encrypted data.

3.2 QUESTIONS

1. An executive is traveling with his laptop computer to a conference. The contents of his laptop contain very confidential product information, including development specifications and product road maps. Which of the following techniques can be implemented to protect the confidentiality of the data on the laptop?
   A. Make sure all software is up to date.
   B. Password-protect the laptop BIOS.

C. Move the confidential documents to a USB key.

D. Encrypt the hard drive using a TPM.

2. A security patch for your OS was released about a week after you applied the latest OS service pack. What should you do?

A. Wait until the release of the next full service pack.

B. Download the patch only if you experience problems with the OS.

C. Do nothing—the security patch was probably included with the service pack.

D. Download and install the security patch.

3. As part of your security baselining and OS hardening, you want to make sure that you protect your organization from vulnerabilities in its operating system software. Which one of the following tasks should you perform?

A. Update antivirus signature files.

B. Install any patches or OS updates.

C. Use an encrypted file system.

D. Use a host-based intrusion detection system.

4. The __________ process in Windows 10 uses the UEFI and a trusted platform module to provide a more secure boot process, also allowing for boot attestation.

A. Boot management

B. Secure boot

C. Measured boot

D. Safe mode

5. Which of the following is *not* commonly used to secure a database?

A. Salting

B. Synchronization

C. Tokenization

D. Hashing

3.2 ANSWERS

1. **D** A trusted platform module (TPM) allows the contents of the hard drive to be encrypted with encryption keys that are stored on the TPM chip, which can be accessed only by the end user. This prevents an unauthorized user from accessing the hard drive contents of equipment.

2. **D** Even though you just installed the latest service pack, a security vulnerability might have recently been discovered, requiring that you install a new security patch. You will not be protected from the vulnerability if you do not install the security patch, and waiting for it to be included in the next service pack might be too dangerous.

3. **B** The most recent software updates and patches for your operating system will contain the latest bug and exploit fixes. This prevents known bugs and weakness in the OS from being exploited.
4. **C** The Measured Boot process in Windows 10 uses the UEFI and a TPM to provide a more secure boot process, also allowing for boot attestation.
5. **B** Tokenization, salting, and hashing are often used to secure databases, including password databases.

Given a scenario, implement secure network designs

Network security devices and secure network design provide a first line of defense for detection and prevention of attacks at your network border. These security threats could be low-level, network-based threats such as TCP/IP protocol attacks, or they could be high-level application threats such as application content downloaded from the Internet via a web browser. Several network security tools are available, such as firewalls, routers, switches, proxy servers, filters, intrusion detection systems, virtual private networking, and monitoring devices, that not only detect network threats but also take proactive steps to stop them from entering or leaving your network.

Secure Network Design

Setting up your network securely requires planning to make sure that your network is safely partitioned into network security zones. By splitting your network into public, private, and high-security zones and then regulating access between these zones with other types of networking techniques, you provide several lines of defense against incoming network attacks. Understanding the areas within your network that need to be defended allows for the implementation of layered security (also known as defense-in-depth), or the application of a combination of different solutions to provide more comprehensive coverage of assets. As the different technologies are discussed, be thinking of how they could be combined to more effectively secure a network than using one device alone.

The following sections discuss the network security devices and secure network design principles that can maximize the ability to detect and prevent network security threats at your network's borders.

Load Balancing

A *load balancer* is a network device that helps evenly distribute the flow of network traffic to other network devices, either in an *active/active mode* (two or more load balancers distributing the load) or an *active/passive mode* (where one or more nodes remain on standby until needed). In larger networks that process thousands of network transactions per minute, the load balancer spreads the network load between each network device to ensure that network congestion and bottlenecks do not occur, using at least one *virtual IP address* that is publicly available.

Your organization may have several routers on the network border to process incoming network connections and route them to their required destinations. If a specific router receives too many network requests at one time, it can cause a bottleneck in processing requests and cause network delays. Other routers may not be receiving enough network traffic, running at only partial capacity compared with what their resources are capable of.

Large organizations use load balancers with web services distributed among several web servers to provide their customers with enough processing power and resources to respond to thousands of web requests per hour. The load balancer is required to analyze the incoming requests and route the requests evenly between these servers. Also, many load balancers also function as SSL/TLS accelerators, offloading the resource-intensive process of accepting SSL/TLS requests, unencrypting the traffic, and passing the unencrypted traffic on to its destination. This allows for a more robust implementation of SSL/TLS across large networks with minimal performance degradation.

Load balancers can perform their functions through scheduling algorithms, such as round-robin techniques where each server in turn is sent a request, or they can use intelligent load-balancing methods (for example, current number of connections and response times) to detect which servers are overloaded and which servers have enough resource capacity to handle incoming requests. Many high-end load balancers work at the application layer to properly load-balance specific protocols and network application services.

Load balancers possess the network security awareness to help prevent denial-of-service (DoS) network attacks by detecting floods of network packets and preventing them from overloading the devices for which they are balancing network traffic. Modern load balancers support the concept of *persistence*, meaning that sessions can be "sticky" and follow the individual user. Also, note that some applications do not work well when load balanced; in this case, session affinity subverts the load balancer and sends client requests directly to the specific application server, binding the user's session to that server.

As discussed previously in Objective 2.5 of Domain 2, for more advanced high-availability purposes, the use of *clustering* technology enables you to use several servers to perform the services of one. Clustering greatly enhances load balancing, as the resources of all the servers can be used to perform the same task as one server. For fault tolerance purposes, if one system goes down, one of the other servers in the cluster can take over seamlessly without any interruption to the clients.

Network Segmentation

Securing a network infrastructure can be a daunting task for a network administrator. Depending on the size and complexity of the network, the administrator must examine the security implications of several interconnected communication systems, from the internal networking equipment of an organization, such as routers, firewalls, and switches, to users who access the organization's network remotely via a VPN.

Compounding the problem are the several types of Internet services that most companies and organizations need to run their business: web services, e-mail, and file transfer servers. These types of applications require special attention regarding security. At the same time, you need to protect your internal network hosts and servers from unauthorized access from the public Internet.

To provide maximum security with the least amount of administrative overhead, the use of security zones is recommended. Security zones are created when parts of your network are divided into special separated areas where similar systems and servers reside. By putting all your Internet servers in one zone and your internal network in another zone, you create a protective wall to regulate access between them. This type of topology is created using a firewall, which controls access to the various zones through a rules-based access system.

Dividing your network into separate security zones lets you create physical and logical barriers between the different areas of your network. These zones enable you to allocate different types of security, depending on the sensitivity of the data and network equipment within that zone. This is the equivalent of setting up fences or walls between different buildings in a facility, which prevent users of one building from entering another building for which they are not authorized. A *firewall*, as discussed later within this section, is used to set up these zones on the network. The firewall uses a special set of rules to admit or deny network access, as appropriate, such as only allowing FTP traffic to a specific server. By setting up the firewall to split the network into different zones, you can more easily create firewall rules to allow access to servers in those zones.

There are two further important topics to consider regarding different security zones and how to maintain separation between them:

- **East-west traffic** Lateral movement between different elements and zones of the network, be it server-server, web-server, or application-server. Generally, it is assumed that once an adversary gains access to a part of the network, they will attempt to move laterally, or east-west.
- **Zero trust** Validates and enforces access control to all elements and zones of the network at the time of access to attempt full segmentation; no assumptions are made based on zones, and instead are made based on user, device, and application identities.

The three main zones into which networks are commonly divided are the external public network, the internal private network, and a screened subnet, as shown in Figure 3.3-1.

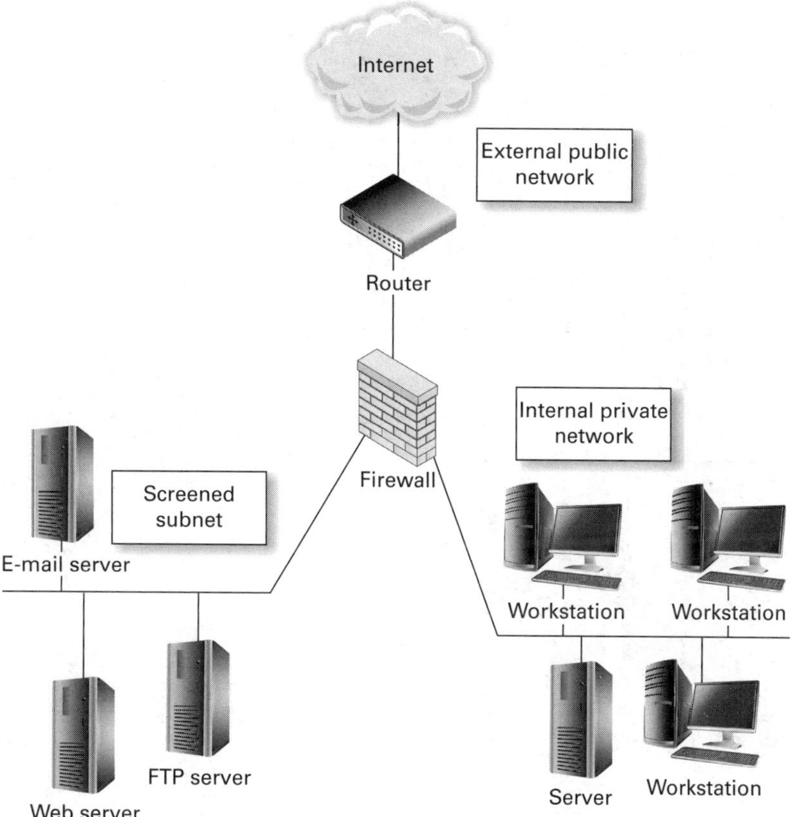

FIGURE 3.3-1 Network security zones

Screened Subnet

The *screened subnet* is an area of the network where a high number of publicly accessed Internet systems should be located. In an overall network security topology, the screened subnet is situated between the public and protected zones (private network), as shown in Figure 3.3-2.

The screened subnet provides a buffer zone between your external network devices and the internal network that comprises your servers and user workstations. The screened subnet usually contains popular Internet services—web servers, mail servers, and FTP servers. These services may need to be accessed by those on the public network, the Internet. Your company might use a website that hosts certain services and information for both current and potential clients. A public FTP server on the screened subnet might serve files to all users or only to certain clients. Your mail server needs to allow a connection from the Internet to let e-mail be relayed to and from your site and to provide mail access for your own users who might be using the system remotely.

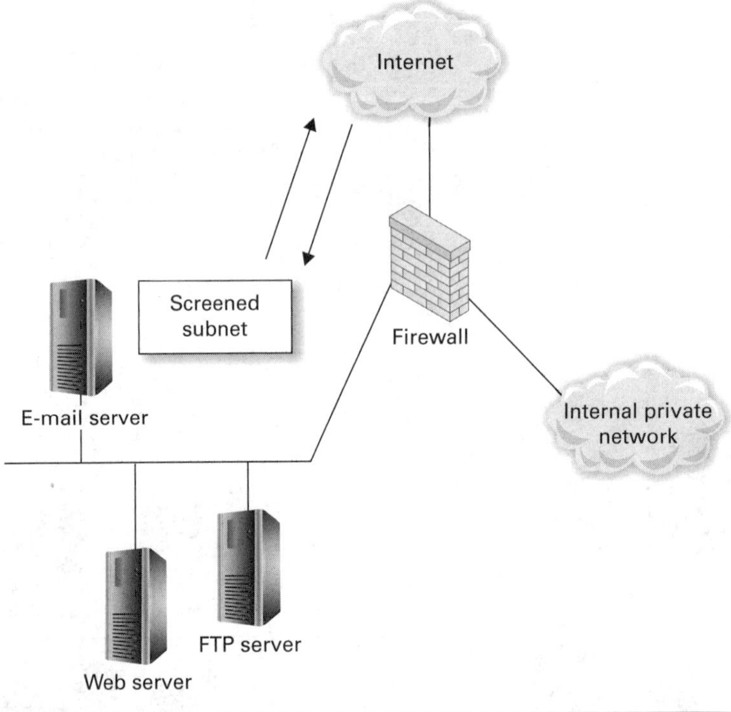

FIGURE 3.3-2 The screened subnet

EXAM TIP Know the purpose of the screened subnet and how a firewall can be configured to separate the Internet servers within it from the internal network.

These Internet services, however, should be separated from your internal local area network (LAN). If you were to host a web server on your internal LAN that is accessible from the Internet, you would create vulnerabilities in your network because an unauthorized user might be able to compromise the web server and then have full access to your internal LAN. If the web server is on your screened subnet and is somehow compromised, the hacker could only get as far as the screened subnet because the internal LAN is on another network, protected by the firewall.

EXAM TIP The previous term used for a screened subnet was a demilitarized zone (DMZ). You may see this term used on the exam as well, so be prepared for it.

NOTE Many web servers act as a front end for access to database servers, which need to be located on the internal LAN. Make sure that only those ports needed for access to the database are opened by the firewall and that access can only be granted from that web server. If a hacker were to compromise the security of the web server, she might be able to use that as a jumping point to get to the database server on the internal LAN.

Intranet

An *intranet*, or internal network, is a locally available web network that is not accessible from the public Internet. The prefix "intra" specifies this is an internal network. Many companies provide web services that are relevant to their internal employees only and not to the public or the company's customers. These web pages usually contain such services as a directory of contact information for everyone in the company, or they are dedicated to specific departments (for example, human resources or engineering) or are finance web pages dealing with the company's stock and financial plans. Web-enabled applications for internal use give employees access to internal services via a web browser.

The intranet only lets internal employees have access to these web pages because the information they provide can be confidential and shouldn't be accessed by the public, especially rival companies. The web servers that host intranet services are located on the private internal LAN in the overall security zone model to prevent access from both the public and screened subnet zones.

Extranet

An *extranet* is an extension of your private network or intranet. An extranet extends outside the body of your local network to enable other companies or networks to share information. For example, an automobile manufacturing company could have an extranet that connects selected business partners so they can access and share specific information on availability and inventories between the networks. These are often referred to as *business-to-business (B2B)* communications or networks because one company uses the internal resources and services of another.

Extranets can open security vulnerabilities in your network unless they are configured properly. Older types of extranets used dedicated communications links between the companies, which are much more difficult for an unauthorized user to penetrate. Now, most extranets use VPN tunnels over the Internet to communicate, which makes them more susceptible to intrusion. To ensure extranet communications are secure, your VPN, encryption, and firewall configuration must be carefully planned to limit the access of an intruder.

Virtual Local Area Network

A virtual local area network (VLAN, or *virtual LAN)* is a type of logical network that exists as a subset of a larger physical network. Smaller networks can be divided into segments easily, with little administrative overhead. Splitting the network into segments allows network data and broadcast traffic to stay on the local segment, without broadcasting data to the entire network.

Segmentation of LANs also provides extra security because a user on one LAN will not have access to another one without special permission.

Unfortunately, segmenting a larger network into smaller networks can be tedious and might involve the purchase of extra networking equipment, such as switches and routers, and extra cabling to separate them. This is where VLANs can help because the network segmentation is performed through software rather than hardware. VLANs have the capability to isolate network traffic on specific segments, and even provide crossover functionality to enable certain VLANs to overlap and allow access between them.

EXAM TIP Know how VLANs can increase security and performance in a network, as well as the different ways they can be implemented.

The capability to create VLANs is dependent on the capabilities of your network equipment. Most modern switches and routers support the use of VLANs, which can be enabled simply through changing the configuration of the network device. There are three basic types of VLANs:

- **Port-based VLAN** The port-based VLAN uses the specific port of a network switch to configure VLANs. Each port is configured as part of a specific VLAN. In order for a client workstation to be assigned to that VLAN, it needs to be plugged into that port.
- **MAC address–based VLAN** The MAC address–based VLAN tracks clients and their respective VLAN memberships through the MAC address of their network card. The switches maintain a list of MAC addresses and VLAN memberships, and they route the network packets to their destination, as appropriate. The advantage of MAC address–based VLANs is if clients' VLAN membership changes, they needn't be physically moved to another port. One drawback of this method is that being part of multiple VLANs can cause confusion with the switch's MAC address tables. Thus, this model is recommended for single VLAN memberships.
- **Protocol-based VLAN** A protocol-based VLAN is the most flexible and logical type of VLAN. It uses the addresses of the IP layer to assign VLAN settings, and an entire IP subnet can be assigned a certain VLAN membership.

Figure 3.3-3 shows an example of a typical VLAN configuration. This network is divided by network subnets configured as part of a certain VLAN. The switches use a port-based VLAN configuration across two floors of a building.

Virtual Private Network

A *virtual private network (VPN)* is a special, encrypted communications tunnel between one system and another. VPNs are used to secure remote access in most modern networks, as shown in Figure 3.3-4.

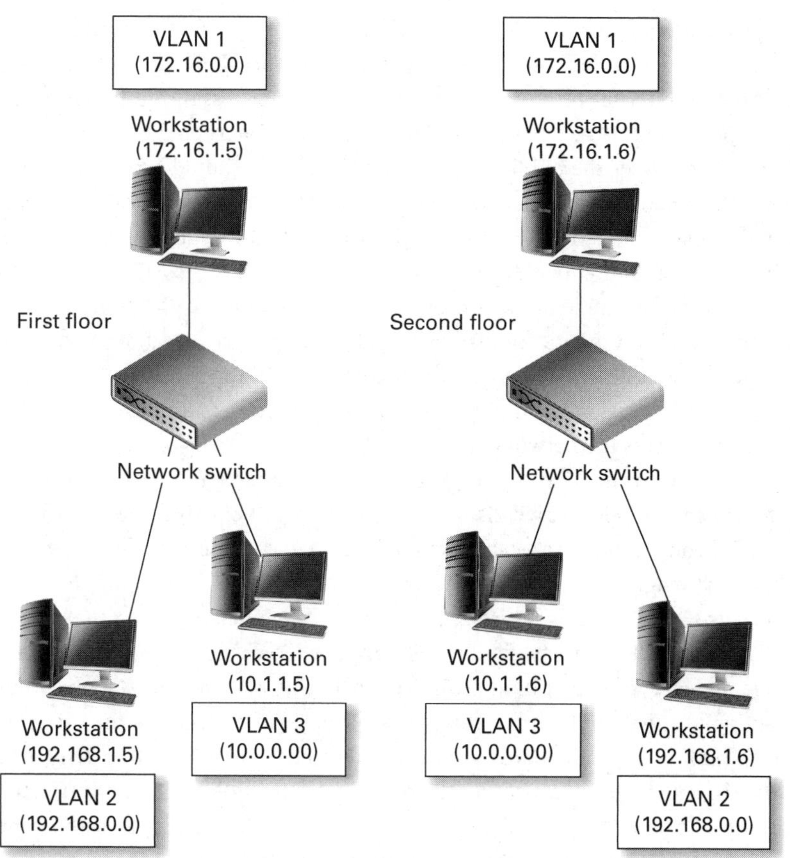

FIGURE 3.3-3 A typical VLAN configuration

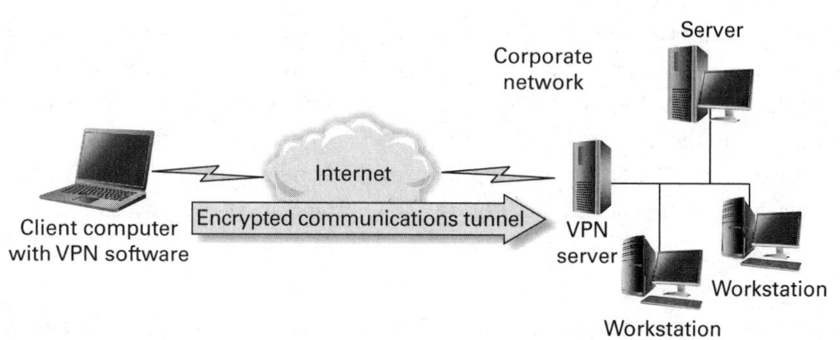

FIGURE 3.3-4 VPN (virtual private network)

A VPN makes use of an encrypted tunneling protocol, such as IPSec, Secure Sockets Layer (SSL), or Transport Layer Security (TLS), to connect networks together. A tunneling protocol allows an existing internal protocol, such as private IP addressing, to be encapsulated and relayed over the Internet to its destination. This VPN link is encrypted to provide secure access to a private network over the public Internet. The VPN link should be protected with strong encryption and authentication mechanisms to ensure its security. VPNs can be integrated with a wide variety of authentication systems, such as IPSec, Lightweight Directory Access Protocol (LDAP), Remote Authentication Dial-In User Service (RADIUS), Kerberos, and digital certificates. A common implementation of VPN uses the *Layer 2 Tunneling Protocol (L2TP)* along with IPSec for its authentication and encryption, which is compatible on many operating systems, including mobile device OSs. Another common way to protect VPN communications is to allow the VPN to assign IP addresses as the user connects and to allow only these blocks of IP addresses to access the network.

After connecting to the VPN server, users have a secure channel between them and the network to which the VPN server is attached, enabling them to remotely access network resources. VPN endpoints are typically secured by a VPN concentrator device or server that is responsible for managing the encrypted VPN tunnel between a client computer and the main network, or *site-to-site*, such as between two branch office networks in different geographic locations. A VPN server consists of a typical network server running VPN software services that manage the encrypted communications tunnel. The VPN server can run other services (such as authentication), but it may connect to other external servers for these services. A VPN concentrator is a specific hardware device dedicated to VPN connectivity. It is an integrated device that manages all aspects of the connection, including the encryption tunnels and authentication of the VPN client. Authentication can be integrated within the concentrator, but it can also connect to external services, such as an organization's LDAP server, to authenticate clients. Newer VPN configurations now automatically connect users to the VPN server rather than requiring a login to the VPN server, and they are *always on*, which reduces the risk of users attempting to connect to internal resources without the protections of the VPN and allows for a more seamless user experience.

VPN concentrators can allow for *split tunneling*, meaning that users can access content in different security domains at the same time (for example, intranet resources and the Internet), by only routing the traffic to internal resources through the VPN connection while not allowing connections to the Internet to pass through the VPN. Conversely, *full tunneling* routes all traffic through the VPN. Split tunneling reduces the bandwidth used by the VPN but also reduces the ability to use content monitoring and to protect users over insecure connections.

DNS

As discussed in Objective 3.1 earlier in this domain, the *Domain Name System (DNS)* provides a way to translate Internet domain names into IP addresses. This allows network applications and services to refer to Internet domains by their fully qualified domain name (FQDN) rather than their IP address, which can be difficult to remember and can often change. If a company changes its system's IP address, it can simply update the DNS tables to reflect this. External users will not see a difference, because they will still be connecting to it by name.

DNS servers perform an extremely valuable function on the Internet, and wide-scale communication interruptions can occur if a network DNS server is disabled. Most client machines use DNS each time they try to connect to a network host. The client's DNS server is configured using its network settings, which can be set manually or automatically through services such as Dynamic Host Configuration Protocol (DHCP). Each time a client tries to access a host, such as a website, the local DNS server is queried for the IP address of the domain name. The DNS server translates the name into an IP address, which the client uses to initiate its connection. As discussed previously, it is recommended that DNSSEC be used to validate DNS responses, guarding against many types of DNS-focused attacks.

Network Access Control

Any network is often at its most vulnerable from internal attacks from hosts on its own network rather than malicious entities attacking from outside the network. *Network access control (NAC)* enables your network devices to allow or deny access to clients based on predefined access policies in a permanent method using persistent agents that are installed on the device or using a dissolvable agent that authenticates and then is deleted or "dissolved." NAC policies set out rules for what clients can access on the network and define a minimum set of parameters that clients must have configured to ensure they are properly configured and "healthy." This helps prevent viruses and worms that have infected a client on your network from infecting other systems by denying the client access to the network based on its status.

NAC policies can assess a connecting host and examine several factors: for example, the computer's operating system and applications patch update level, the existence of antivirus software and the date of its signature files, the existence of network vulnerabilities, and the access rights of the user who is logged in. The policy then decides whether to limit access to network resources based on these factors. Any clients that do not meet the minimum policy guidelines can be denied access or have severe restrictions imposed on their access, such as the inability to see and use network resources such as file servers.

NAC-aware appliances are typically inserted into the network before major access switches and routers. Ideally, NAC-aware routers and switches can be deployed on your network that remove the need for separate devices and allow your routers and switches to control access policies for your network. With multiple vendors, each with its own NAC support, successful implementations of NAC on your network require that all network infrastructure devices such as routers and switches be from the same vendor, as interoperability with other types of NAC systems may result in incompatibility and blocked access for major portions of your network.

Most NAC methods require an agent to be running on the client. This agent can be permanently installed as a service on the client system; in some cases, *agentless* solutions, often using Active Directory, can verify the access policy as the user logs in and out of the domain. If someone brings an unauthorized client into your network, these solutions can enforce your network policies, even though the client does not have permanent NAC client software installed.

These methods require some administrative overhead, especially regarding access for other devices (such as printers and other network-aware devices) that do not have operating systems or antivirus software running. Most NAC systems allow you to whitelist (allow full access without scanning the device) based on the system IP address or hardware MAC address.

Out-of-Band Management

Objective 3.2 earlier in this domain discussed the concepts of in-band and out-of-band within the context of intrusion detection systems. To recap, an IDS can be deployed either *in-band* (more often referred to as *inline*), where all traffic is analyzed (often at the network edge), or *out-of-band*, where only some traffic is analyzed. This is a helpful analogy to consider when thinking of how out-of-band management works, as the network or system management is done not "inline" or on the same primary network connection that is used to conduct operations. This creates a natural physical access control to the management interface because, when configured properly, there is no access to the out-of-band management connection from the primary network. Think of it as a "one-way" door that can only be exited, not entered. Out-of-band management can be used to conduct critical administrative tasks such as powering on or rebooting network-connected devices remotely in the event of a crash, for example.

Port Security

For network devices, such as switches and routers, *port security* involves not only securing the physical ports that allow hosts to plug into a network device but also logically securing those ports. Ports on networking devices can be configured such that only specified hosts can connect to them, based on MAC address or other criteria. Ports should also be completely turned off if they are not being used, so that unauthorized hosts can't plug into them and attempt network connections or attacks. Properly configured port security is a key measure to prevent *broadcast storms* (aka network storms), where broadcast or multicast traffic begins overwhelming the network as it is broadcasted and rebroadcasted between systems. This can lead to a devastating network failure.

From a logical perspective, disabling unused ports and enforcing criteria that hosts must meet in order to connect to the network via a switch port are good practices, but there are also other things you can do regarding port security. One key security control that can be used is a port-based authentication system, such as the IEEE standard 802.1X. This standard provides for port-based authentication and can be used on both wired and wireless networks. It is most commonly seen on wireless networks, however, and then only when a more robust security method, such as WPA/WPA2 Enterprise, is used. 802.1X can use a wide variety of authentication protocols, including the Extensible Authentication Protocol (EAP), and supports both user authentication and device authentication. Additionally, 802.1X provides for mutual authentication between users, hosts, and the network.

In wired networks, 802.1X can be implemented on network devices to provide for authentication of plug-in devices. This ensures that only authorized devices can connect to the network.

Any unauthorized host attempting to connect is denied access, and is even unable to detect any traffic.

The *Media Access Control (MAC)* address is a unique "calling card" identifying a specific network card. For wireless security, for example, access points can hold a list of MAC addresses associated with the clients (computers, mobile devices, and so on) that can access the wireless network. If a client's MAC address isn't listed, the client isn't allowed to connect. Because each MAC address is unique, it can be used as the basis for a port security technique known as *MAC filtering*. In wired implementations, both VLANs and 802.1X methods use MAC filtering. VLANs base membership on MAC addresses when wired clients are plugged into switches and can place the wired host in the correct VLAN, or even deny access to the network based on MAC address (as can regular switch port security). MAC filtering, although better than nothing, isn't considered terribly secure and can be easily defeated through spoofing. If port security is turned on in a switch, only specified MAC addresses can plug into a switch port and connect to the network. Any unauthorized hosts will not be allowed to connect, and the connection can be logged and an alert sent to an administrator.

While MAC filtering (generally through use of VLANs or 802.1X) is the most common measure you'll see used for port security, some other port security measures you need to know include

- **Bridge Protocol Data Unit (BDPU) guard** The BDPU guard feature is used to prevent BDPU-related attacks, as well as misconfigurations such as improperly connected switches. A BDPU is a message that travels around a LAN to detect and prevent loops within the network topology. BDPU guard helps enforce secure configurations when enabled on a port by forcing administrators to put an interface back into place manually after a misconfiguration.
- **Dynamic Host Configuration Protocol (DHCP) snooping** DHCP snooping works at Layer 2 to protect against DoS attacks from malicious (or even just improperly configured or unknown) DHCP servers that can compete with the official DHCP server by offering IP addresses. Even a benign situation such as a user unknowingly connecting an off-the-shelf wireless router with DHCP enabled can create this situation, and DHCP snooping helps mitigate this by dropping DHCP traffic that is not trusted.

Network Appliances

With the surge in network attacks as well as ransomware and malware directed at both servers and user desktops, not only from traditional phishing but also from malicious websites, peer-to-peer file sharing, and social media networks, there is a greater need for network appliances that can offer several layers of security protection against incoming messages from a wide scope of communications mediums. This section discusses several important network appliances that you need to understand.

Jump Server

A *jump server* (sometimes referred to as a *jumpbox*) is used to manage systems and devices across security zones. This allows an administrator to manage, say, a device within the screened subnet from the internal network rather than requiring her to log in to that system directly. Jump servers, therefore, must be hardened sufficiently to withstand any attempts at using them to move across security zones. Jump servers often use Secure Shell (SSH) tunneling to provide their connectivity across zones.

Proxy Server

A *forward proxy server* is an application, network server, or multipurpose device that accepts and forwards requests from clients to other servers. The proxy server performs this function on behalf of the client. The proxy is typically situated between the clients and the Internet, and it can be used to forward requests for many types of traffic and data transfers, such as web and FTP. This protects the specific addresses of internal clients from being revealed to external servers and allows the proxy server to filter incoming and outgoing requests to prevent attacks and malware from reaching the client systems.

The most commonly used type of forward proxy server is for web browsing. A web client requests a specific uniform resource locator (URL) in its web browser that is sent to the proxy server. The web proxy server forwards the request to the destination website using its own IP address as the source of the request. When the data is retrieved, the proxy server may cache or content-filter the data and then return it to the requesting client. Web proxy servers are used primarily for their caching capability, which boosts web browsing performance by storing content retrieved from an external web server. The next time a client retrieves the same web data, the web proxy can serve the information to the client without sending another request to the external web server. This greatly reduces the amount of bandwidth required to retrieve numerous web requests from an organization and provides significant cost savings. Proxies that do not modify requests and simply redirect them are called *transparent proxies*, whereas those that do make modifications are called *nontransparent proxies*. Clients should not be aware of the presence of a transparent proxy—after all, it is meant to be "transparent"—whereas a nontransparent proxy often adds elements to the request.

Conversely, a *reverse proxy server* works on behalf of servers to accept requests from external clients, forwarding them on to the servers behind it. An example of how this might work is if an external client wants to gain access to your web server. Rather than allow that traffic direct access to the web server, the reverse proxy acts as a "go-between," providing cached content for high-demand content, as well as increased protection in the event your web server does not have appropriate security configurations for public use.

NIDS/NIPS

Intrusion detection and prevention systems were covered in Objective 3.2 earlier in this domain, but here's a recap for purposes of their role as network appliances: IDSs can be either active or passive. In an *active detection system*, intrusion attempts are dealt with immediately by shutting down network connections or services that are being attacked. A *passive detection system*, on the other hand, relies on notifications to alert administrators of an intrusion. Active detection deals more swiftly with situations but can cause unwanted behavior if false positives (blocking legitimate traffic) arise. What's more, false negatives can allow unauthorized traffic to flow with an administrator unaware. It is critical to make sure, no matter which type of system you use, that your IDS or IPS is tuned carefully.

A network-based IDS (NIDS) examines network patterns, such as an unusual number of requests destined for a server or service (for example, an FTP server). The headers of network packets can be analyzed for possible spoofing attempts or suspicious code that indicates a malformed packet. Corrupted packets and malformed data can bring down a web server that's vulnerable to such attacks. Some more advanced detection systems, called *intrusion prevention systems (IPSs)*, can attempt to deal with the problem autonomously and either disconnect suspicious network connections or turn off network services that are being attacked.

To protect the entire network, the IDS is usually located at a central point, such as a main router, switch, or firewall system. An IDS can also be deployed either *in-band* (more often referred to as *inline*), where all traffic is analyzed (often at the network edge), or *out-of-band*, or passive, where only some traffic is analyzed. An IDS can only monitor what it sees, so placing it further down in the system lessens the chance of finding intrusions, especially because your firewall and routers are the entry points to the network.

Network monitoring applications such as a NIDS/NIPS are used to monitor and analyze network traffic to detect security threats such as network-based attacks (DoS attacks, ping sweeps, and port scans). When a security threat is detected, the monitoring system logs the event and notifies the administrator or takes immediate steps to mitigate the incoming threat. Different types of monitoring methodologies can be used to detect intrusions and malicious behavior. The following sections describe these monitoring methodologies and their benefits and weaknesses.

Signature-Based Monitoring

Signature-based monitoring systems are like antivirus programs and contain predefined signature databases of known attacks that have appeared previously. Each type of attack can be recognized by its unique characteristics, and a signature is created for that type of attack. For example, signature-based systems can detect popular types of DoS attacks. The signature (if available) can detect this exact information in the network packet and generate an alert to the administrator. These databases are dynamic, and the monitoring program must be continually updated to ensure that it has the latest signatures to identify the latest types of threats.

Signature-based systems are powerful and efficient because they rely on the collective knowledge of security vendors, who analyze and collect information on Internet security threats and trends and update their databases quickly when new threats arise. However, signature-based systems are unable to detect very new attacks whose signatures are not yet available. In this respect, signature-based systems are often used in conjunction with behavior-based systems.

Behavior/Anomaly-Based Monitoring

Behavior-based (also referred to as *anomaly-based*) monitoring systems do not use a predefined database of signatures but instead start from a baseline of normal behavior and then monitor network traffic based on these performance profiles and increasingly sophisticated analytics to recognize behavioral anomalies that exceed the thresholds of the normal baseline. Such a monitoring system becomes more effective over time as baseline activity is recorded, allowing the system to detect aberrations to the baseline more efficiently. For example, a sudden burst of incoming connections that is out of character for the network will trigger the monitoring system to generate alerts of the activity and, in some cases, take proactive steps to mitigate the anomalous behavior (which could be a DoS attack) by blocking the attempted connections.

The primary benefit of behavior-based systems is that they easily and quickly adapt to the current environment and can detect new variants of attacks that a signature- or rule-based monitoring system might not recognize. The monitoring system is actively looking for behavior that is inconsistent with the current system baseline profile; therefore, the system recognizes even new types of attacks immediately and can take action. New attacks are often referred to as *zero-day attacks*, and signature-based monitoring systems might not recognize them as threats.

The disadvantage of a behavior-based system is that building the baseline profile takes some time, and until the system learns enough information about the current system, it cannot accurately detect anomalies to that profile; efficiency is built over time. False positives can occur, in which normal behavior is flagged as anomalous because the system has not had time to build its baseline profile to recognize it as normal behavior. Also, the anomalous behavior detected can generate an alert, but the monitoring system can only warn the administrator that the thresholds have been exceeded; the administrator must determine whether an actual attack is taking place and what steps to take to mitigate it. The behavior-based monitoring system doesn't always recognize the type of specific attack, only its symptoms.

Heuristic-Based Monitoring

Heuristic-based security monitoring continuously trains on network behavior. Heuristics uses an initial database of known attack types, but dynamically alters their signatures based on learned behavior of inbound and outbound network traffic. These types of systems are powerful for detecting suspicious behavior that might not be detected by other methods, but they require constant tuning to prevent false positives.

Rule-Based Monitoring

Rule-based security monitoring takes more work to match the efficiency and effectiveness of other types of monitoring methods such as signature- and behavior-based systems. Like a firewall, a rule-based security monitoring system relies on the administrator to create rules and determine the actions to take when those rules are transgressed. For example, a rule can be created that will block connections from an IP address if more than 100 connections are attempted from the same IP address within a certain time, such as 30 seconds. This could indicate a DoS attack, and when the rule thresholds are exceeded, the offending connection will be blocked to contain the threat.

Rule-based systems require significant manual initial setup and constant maintenance to keep the rules current and up to date with the latest threats. These factors are handled automatically by a signature-based system, which already contains an up-to-date database of the latest security threats and compares these threats with the behaviors the system is experiencing. The system will then take action as appropriate.

Hardware Security Modules

As discussed in Objective 3.2 earlier in this domain, a *hardware security module (HSM)* is a specialized hardware appliance used to provide onboard cryptographic functions and processing. This physical hardware device can be a stand-alone device attached to a network or connected directly to a server as a plug-in card. HSMs are primarily used to host integrated cryptographic functions, such as a Public Key Infrastructure server for encryption, decryption, and secure key generation and management, but they can also be used to provide onboard secure storage of encrypted data. With their processing speed and security, HSMs are often used for banking applications (such as ATMs) that require scalable, performance-based solutions for critical key management and security.

Sensors

Monitoring schemes must be built on the foundation of timely and relevant data collection mechanisms. *Sensors* are one way of collecting this data, either through a network test access point (TAP) or through a passive device that then passes the data on to a security information and event management (SIEM) solution or other appliance for analysis and action. To this end, almost anything can be considered a sensor, so it's important to carefully think through what data you're trying to capture and analyze to make sense of the events taking place across your network. A combination of network-based and host-based sensors provides the most comprehensive approach, as they each have their pros and cons. For example, depending on the placement of a network sensor, you may miss critical data if it doesn't traverse the segment of the network that the sensor has access to. Also, network sensors can't decrypt the traffic from a host, so they might give you an idea that something's happening, but not the "what" that you need. The host-based sensor comes in and provides more context about the events taking place on individual hosts. As you determine the best setup to monitor your network and systems for activity, it's important that you remove redundancy and attempt to find complementary solutions wherever possible, in order to ease the possibility of information overload or, even worse, sensors that are working against each other.

Collectors

Collectors are generally Simple Network Management Protocol (SNMP)–based tools that gather information on the IP-based devices across the network for reporting purposes. Recall from the previous objective (3.2) that SNMP is the mechanism many IDSs use to collect data passing through the network and send it to the network monitor for analysis. Similarly, a solution like the Cisco Common Service Platform Collector (CSPC) gathers information that is then used for holistic care of the network devices and reporting on configurations, product life cycle, and current inventory.

Aggregators

As the name indicates, *aggregators* aggregate, but instead of aggregating only logs and events for analysis, as discussed previously, they also aggregate the traffic coming from network TAPs and switched port analyzers (SPANs), allowing a single view into the information traversing the network. This provides the optimal place to monitor all traffic, not just an individual segment. Aggregators are passive, meaning they do not interfere with the traffic flow, but instead copy the information passively and merge it all together for monitoring and analysis.

Firewalls

Firewalls are like physical security walls situated between an organization's internal network and any external public networks such as the Internet, as shown in Figure 3.3-5. The firewall protects an internal network from access by unauthorized users on an external network.

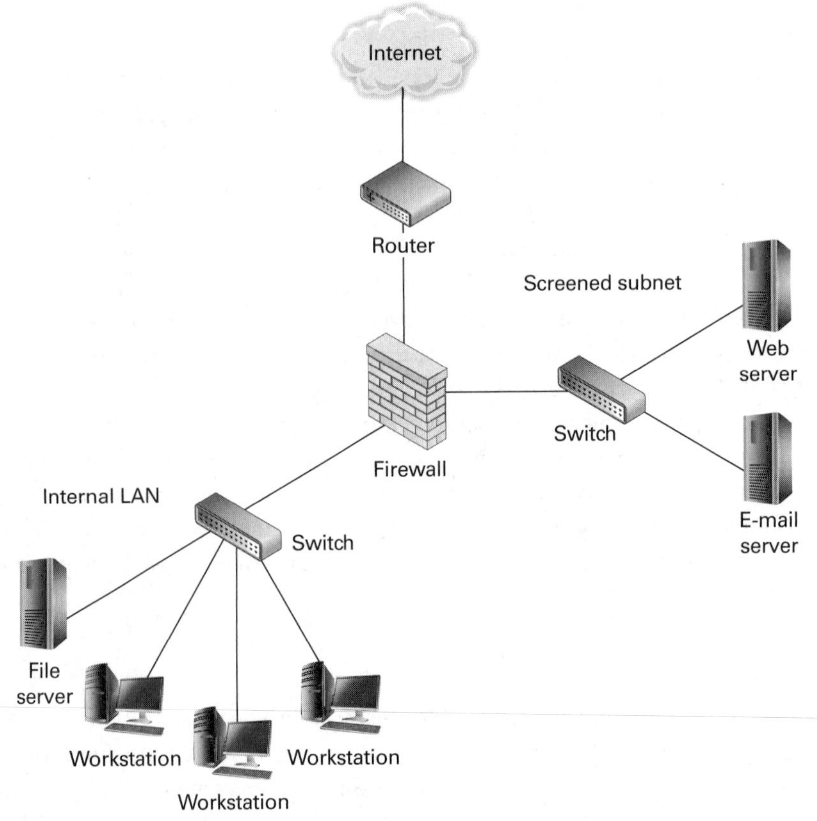

FIGURE 3.3-5 Network firewall deployment

The external network can be located on the Internet or may even be another network within the same organization. A network firewall is a critical system in an organization's overall security architecture. The firewall controls and monitors access between different networks by filtering inbound and outbound traffic, manages access controls to requested locations, and typically blocks all services except those explicitly permitted by the administrator.

To configure the firewall, an administrator must set up several rules to use each time on incoming and outgoing network communications. These rules can be general or specific. For example, a firewall can be configured with a rule that states that any Hypertext Transfer Protocol (HTTP) traffic can come and go on a specific network. A rule can also be much more detailed and state that a Simple Mail Transfer Protocol (SMTP) packet destined for a mail server can only come from a specific host. The best practice to use when configuring a firewall for the first time is to implicitly deny everything by default and then create rules to allow the access you need. This ensures you're starting off with the most secure model and working backward to configure the firewall to accept certain types of communications.

Most firewalls log network traffic and activity and activate alarms if anomalous situations are detected. The firewall implements security, authentication, and access controls at multiple levels while remaining completely transparent to internal users. Most firewalls provide the following services and security features:

- **Packet filtering** The firewall analyzes each network packet destined for inside or outside the network; it can filter out dangerous malformed packets, attacks, and spoofed IP addresses to prevent unauthorized access. Packets are also analyzed and acted upon based on the rules enabled by the administrator.
- **Stateful and stateless inspection** Stateful inspection of packets ensures that the firewall maintains a record of the connections that pass through and monitors their state from when they are connected to when they close. This ensures that the firewall is not only tracing packets but also analyzing the state of the entire connection. Stateless inspection, conversely, does not maintain a record and uses an access control list (ACL) to allow or deny traffic. Depending on the configuration of the access rules, certain actions can be taken when an anomalous change of state occurs (such as a connection hijack).
- **Access and authentication control** The firewall can restrict access to networking services based on source and destination IP addresses, type of service, and time/day of the week, and through authenticated access. Most firewalls have very flexible access control policies that can be fine-tuned by the administrator to secure access for specific users and networks.
- **Application layer filtering** Firewalls can be aware of specific applications and services such as DNS and SMTP e-mail. This allows a firewall to analyze network traffic and apply access rules that are specific to that application. For example, the firewall can act as an application gateway for e-mail servers to help secure the connections between external e-mail servers and your local e-mail servers and clients that send and receive messages. The firewall can detect if these services are trying to be accessed on unauthorized ports for that specific application.

- **Network address translation (NAT) gateway** Most firewalls utilize NAT to map source IP addresses of outbound connections so that those connections appear to have originated from the firewall's address. This allows internal networks to be hidden behind a single Internet IP address with no additional registered addresses required.

Some firewalls now have the capability to decrypt sessions; although this is helpful from a malware prevention or data loss prevention (DLP) perspective, it also can present privacy concerns and should be assessed through a cost/benefit analysis.

Firewalls come in hardware (appliance), software (host-based), and virtual varieties, and both proprietary and open-source firewall solutions are available. There are pros and cons to each, and ideally you'll use some combination of these solutions to best meet your needs. For example, the traditional hardware firewall can be placed at the perimeter of the network to provide overwatch and action on the traffic coming in and out of the network. This enables the firewall to block and report on potentially malicious traffic rapidly. However, many hardware firewalls have issues with inspecting encrypted traffic, meaning they can tell you something might be happening but not exactly what it is. Software, or host-based, firewalls are installed on each respective device, and the number of software firewall solutions has grown exponentially over the last few years. Even Microsoft Windows and macOS have software firewalls built in natively. Software firewalls, because they function on the respective host, provide much more granularity and context and are great for blocking specific content at the keyword level, not just at the URL level. These features make them great for home use, for example. However, they can have a negative effect on system performance.

Finally, virtual firewalls can be deployed much like software or as a virtual appliance, and provide a firewall service within a virtualized environment. Virtual firewalls can both monitor traffic going and coming to/from just as a hardware firewall (bridge mode) or as a kernel process at the hypervisor level (hypervisor mode). Virtual firewalls are ideal for monitoring and filtering virtualized environments and can be more easily managed from a centralized location.

Web Application Firewall

An increasingly important type of firewall to implement within a security-focused configuration is the *web application firewall (WAF)*, which can filter and monitor HTTP traffic between web applications and the Internet, helping to mitigate many common web attacks such as cross-site scripting (XSS), SQL injection, and cross-site request forgery (XSRF/CSRF). The WAF essentially acts as a reverse proxy to the web server by having the client pass through the WAF before it can reach the server.

Content Filtering

To address privacy concerns and data loss prevention, certain types of organizations (such as financial and medical companies) must now adhere to specific government regulations regarding the release of private data. This means that organizations must take greater control over the outbound content that is transmitted outside their networks.

Several types of rules and standards are in place that financial organizations must comply with to protect the security and privacy of data, such as the Payment Card Industry Data Security Standard (PCI DSS). PCI DSS is a compliance standard that defines the minimum amount of security that is required for credit card, debit card, automated teller machine (ATM) system, and other financial transactions. Most major credit card and banking companies are PCI DSS compliant. These compliance rules are primarily based on the storage and transmission of sensitive financial information. For example, a bank must ensure that a private customer's credit card or banking details are not transmitted outside of its networks, or if they must be transmitted, that they are encrypted.

Medical and health providers must adhere to strict rules, such as the Health Insurance Portability and Accountability Act (HIPAA). These rules ensure that healthcare organizations are accountable for the privacy and security of their patients' medical records. Outbound content filtering can ensure that messages with specific identifying information can be blocked from being sent outside of the organization.

An outbound content filter on a proxy server can monitor outgoing e-mails (including deep content scanning of e-mail attachments and web file uploads) and scan the content for patterns of credit card or account numbers. If they are encountered in the message, they can be blocked or quarantined, or policies can be put in place to automatically encrypt the message before it leaves the organization.

URL Filtering

Organizations can filter specific URLs or file types (such as .mp3, .exe, and .zip) to prevent them from being accessed. Examples are adult sites and other types of content that should not be viewed or used on a corporate or public network. URL-filtering software uses a predefined list of sites that are allowed or blocked as required via policies. If a client tries to access a blocked website or file, that client will receive a warning message and will not be allowed access to that website.

There are also third-party public URL-filtering products that contain a list of categorized websites that are most commonly blocked because of their content. These are configurable by the administrator to block specific types of content, such as offensive sites, gambling sites, or even sites that reduce productivity such as shopping sites and social media.

Unified Threat Management

Unified threat management (UTM) is the evolution of the traditional firewall concept into an all-in-one device designed to act as a firewall, IDS, load balancer, DLP device, and filter for spam and malware. Although combining these functions into one device eases the management load on administrators, it is also a single point of potential compromise or network latency.

Next-Generation Firewalls

As discussed in the previous objective (3.2), *next-generation firewalls* (NGFW) combine the traditional capabilities of a firewall to block traffic at the perimeter with more active NIDS/NIPS technologies, and they are application aware. Many next-generation firewalls also contain active threat intelligence capabilities, meaning that they are being regularly updated with current threat intelligence that enables them to block emerging threats more actively.

Access Control Lists

Access control lists (ACLs) are used by network devices to control traffic in and out of your network and can be general in nature or specific to certain types of communications. ACLs are typically used in firewalls to control communications between public and private networks, but they can also be used on internal routers and switches to regulate traffic within the network. An ACL entry usually includes the origin of the network packet, the destination, the protocol used (TCP or UDP), the TCP/IP port used, and whether access is allowed or denied.

The following types of parameters can be controlled using an access control list:

- **Source IP address** Specifies the originating source IP address of a packet, whether an internal or external machine or an internal address that it proxies to an external address.
- **Destination IP address** Specifies the IP address where the packet is going, which can be internal or external to the network.
- **Port number** Specifies the TCP/IP port number the communication is using. Each type of TCP/IP service uses a standard port.
- **Protocol** Identifies the protocol being used in the transmission, such as FTP, HTTP, or DHCP, and is usually used in conjunction with a port number that's standard to that protocol or service. This parameter can also be used to define whether the protocol is using TCP or UDP.
- **Permit or deny** Permits or denies the communication specified in the ACL entry.

The following is an example of code for an ACL entry for a router:

```
permit source 192.168.13.2 destination 10.1.5.25 tcp port 80
```

The syntax used by your network device will be like this entry, but the specific syntax varies from vendor to vendor. In this example, the ACL entry permits TCP traffic on port 80 (the default port for HTTP) from the host 192.168.13.2 to a host on network 10.1.5.25. The destination might be some type of secured web server that needs to be accessed from a web browser client on the source host. This prevents any other system—internal or external—from connecting to that web server, as shown in Figure 3.3-6.

Route Security

Source routing is a feature that allows the sender of a packet to specify the route that the packet will take to reach the recipient. It can be used to trick victims into routing their traffic through a network device of the attacker's choosing, so the traffic can be intercepted and possibly read on its way to the intended receiver. Source routing also allows an attacker to spoof

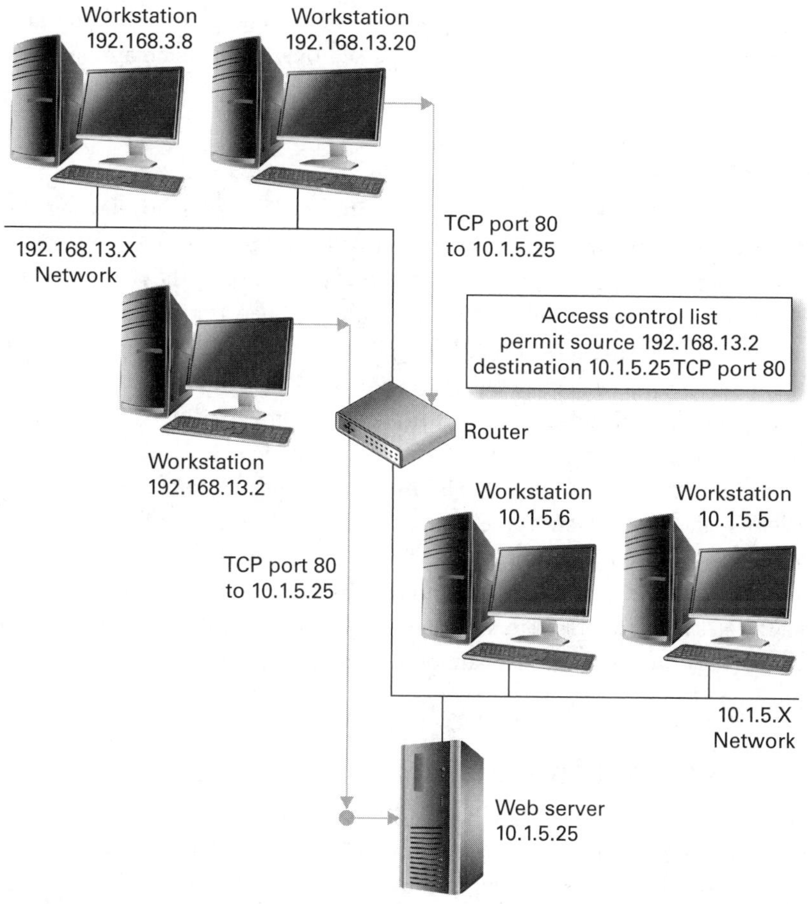

FIGURE 3.3-6 Using an access control list to prevent other systems from connecting to a web server

an IP address when sending packets and still receive the response, even though they have used a fake IP address. Most modern networking equipment can be set to prevent source routing, though this option should be weighed against the advantages that source routing brings, such as improved troubleshooting capabilities.

Quality of Service

Quality of service (QoS), much as the name suggests, is the measurement of the overall quality of a service. Within a network context, data quality metrics such as throughput, availability, and packet loss are considered, and adjustments are made to the traffic prioritization—some traffic, such as streaming video services, might be set as a lower priority to improve the service given to more essential traffic. As Voice over IP (VoIP) and web conferencing solutions—which are particularly sensitive to lag or dropped packets—are becoming extremely prevalent within business environments to conduct globally dispersed operations, maintaining QoS is more important than ever.

Implications of IPv6

As discussed in Objective 3.1 earlier in this domain, the primary issue affecting IPv4 today is that with the exponential increase in public networks and devices, the number of available IP addresses is running out. To recap, IPv6 is the next generation of the IP protocol that seeks to solve the address space issue and also provide additional network enhancements. IPv6 uses 128-bit addressing, allowing for up to 2^{128} available addresses. Although IPv6 and IPv4 are not interoperable, most modern operating systems, such as Windows 10, now support both IPv6 and IPv4 running concurrently, as well as allow for some transition mechanisms, such as Teredo, to allow for interoperability between them.

With the exhaustion of IPv4 addresses imminent, the push to support IPv6 has resulted in rapid implementation by ISPs and large companies. IPv4 addresses are almost exhausted, and technology has evolved to incorporate the new standard, so your ISP and other providers have likely already incorporated the standard, though the transition may have been transparent to customers. Network administrators should address this transition to IPv6 by identifying and cataloging legacy equipment that cannot be migrated and prioritize it for replacement if deemed incompatible.

Port Spanning/Monitoring

We briefly discussed switched port analyzers (SPANs) earlier in this objective; *port mirroring* (also known as *port spanning*) sends the packets that traverse a switch port (or even a VLAN) to another port that is used for monitoring. By default, switched networks do not allow for traffic monitoring, so this is the ideal place to set up your analysis solution that ingests traffic, such as your IDS, or anything that requires packet capture for review. The port mirroring process should be completely transparent to the systems and devices on the network. However, a SPAN can drop packets and add overhead to the network device, while a TAP, as a dedicated hardware device, is passive and does not add overhead. Therefore, many network administrators prefer to use a TAP when possible.

Monitoring Services

Several monitoring tools can help administrators collect data on system and network performance and usage and compare these statistics against measured baselines of typical system and network behavior. By analyzing performance trends over time, administrators can discover anomalies in the behavior of the system that differ greatly from the performance baselines; such anomalies can indicate a security issue such as a network attack or virus/worm infections. The following sections describe some of the common concepts and security tools for monitoring your systems and networks for security-related issues.

System and Performance Monitoring

System and performance monitors examine how much CPU, memory, disk input and output, and network bandwidth are being consumed at any time or during a specified period. Administrators can examine the resulting data for trends that might indicate anomalous behavior. For example, if a web server is infected with a virus or worm, it may be unresponsive to client requests or fail to respond in a timely manner. Several unrecognized processes might be running on the system and taking up most of the CPU processing time (with levels of 90 percent or more), memory usage might be unusually high, and network usage may have jumped as the worm tries to replicate itself to other servers. In other cases, excessive network usage (especially a large amount of network connections from external systems) often indicates a DoS attempt.

EXAM TIP Recognize what types of performance behaviors can indicate security issues when using system and performance monitors. High processor, memory, or network usage could indicate potential DoS attacks or virus and worm activity.

You can establish performance baselines and then track performance data to look for thresholds that surpass the baselines. This information allows you to recognize anomalous system behaviors and perform a closer examination to discover the source of the anomalies that affect system performance, such as misconfigured devices. To establish a good performance baseline, you must measure your system activity for 24 hours a day for at least seven days. Data should be collected during working hours, nonworking hours, and weekends to provide an accurate view of your system performance at different times of the day and days of the week. Simply sampling performance data for a few hours during the day will not provide an adequate overview of system performance trends. Likewise, measuring performance for only a few days during the week will not produce a sufficient baseline for activity during off-work hours and weekends.

The performance baseline should indicate that most primary activity occurs during normal working hours, with lighter activity during nonworking hours. Occasional spikes in activity in off-hours can also indicate normal behavior; system backup or archiving processes, for example, will increase CPU, memory, disk, and network activity during the times the processes are taking place. Your baseline will include this information as well so that you can anticipate that performance spike. Performance spikes that you cannot account for may indicate unauthorized activities or other security-related issues.

After you have recorded a system baseline, many performance monitors allow you to set alarm thresholds for parts of the system. For example, the system can notify you when CPU or memory usage exceeds a specific threshold (such as 90 percent).

Take care when setting thresholds, however, to be sure that you don't receive alarm notifications for slightly above-average behaviors or for very short spikes in activity. For example, you might set your performance monitor to send an alert when CPU usage exceeds 90 percent for at least 30 minutes; this ensures that each momentary processing spike will not generate an alert and that prolonged usage at a high rate will generate a notification.

Protocol Analyzers

A protocol analyzer is a device or application that can intercept, log, and analyze network traffic. Each individual network packet can be examined to decode its header information (which contains the packet's origin and destination) and its contents. Protocol analyzers are not used continually to monitor every packet that passes through the network. Because of the huge amounts of data flowing across a network, this would be an impossible task. Instead, protocol analyzers are used to troubleshoot specific network segments or traffic to and from a specific host on the network. Administrators can use an analyzer to track specific network protocols as they send out queries and receive responses; this helps narrow down sources of communications issues. Protocol analyzers are also useful for helping spot any unencrypted, or clear text, credentials that might be passed.

In terms of monitoring for security issues, protocol analyzers are very useful for viewing the source, destination, and content of specific network packets. For example, a network administrator might suspect that a specific workstation on the network is infected with a Trojan that is exfiltrating data from the workstation to an attacker's computer over the Internet. By using the protocol analyzer, the administrator can watch every single network packet that leaves the workstation and narrow down the search using the ports specifically used by Trojans. Examining the workstation will show communications to and from these ports to a specific external IP address on the network. At this point, the administrator can confirm the type of Trojan being used and attempt to clean it off the infected workstation. The external IP address to which the Trojan is communicating can also be blocked at the firewall to prevent any future occurrences of data being transmitted to that address.

Protocol analyzers and similar network monitoring tools can also be used to track general trends in networking bandwidth. For example, suppose you hear complaints from users that a specific web server is responding too slowly. By enabling the protocol analyzer to analyze network packets going to and from the web server, you discover massive amounts of network traffic originating externally from the network. By analyzing the network packets, you discover ping messages from multiple IP addresses. This indicates that your web server could be suffering from a distributed denial-of-service (DDoS) attack in which multiple computers on the Internet are sending a flood of ping requests to the web server to slow it down or crash it. You can then take steps to mitigate the attack, such as disabling the ping service on the web server.

Network Monitor

Network monitoring applications allow administrators to take a real-time view of current network activity on the entire network. Network monitors display a map of the network and indicate bandwidth usage and network trends, similar to how a traffic congestion map would depict a major expressway. Network monitors are usually located in full view of administrators so that they can constantly monitor the health of the network with a quick glance, as well as provide asset management through alerts when new assets have been joined, reducing asset sprawl and unauthorized device use.

A network monitoring application can alert administrators if a specific section of the network has lost connectivity due to a failed switch or network cable. The display will indicate that section of the network in a warning color (such as red) that can be noticed immediately by the monitoring administrator. Alerts can also be sent via e-mail, text message, and pager to notify administrators of critical network errors.

Beyond general network troubleshooting issues, network monitors can be a valuable resource for alerting administrators to network problems that result from security-related issues. For example, if one of the organization's Internet web servers is experiencing a DoS attack, the network monitor will indicate severe congestion on the network between the primary router/firewall and the web server. In many cases, the network monitor may show the web server as completely unavailable, as the server cannot respond to the diagnostic queries from the monitor due to the attack. Network monitors can also be configured to alert if new access points are set up that might indicate unapproved wireless connectivity.

Abnormal network activity can also be detected by the monitor on specific hosts on the network that could be infected with a worm, virus, or Trojan horse program that is trying to replicate itself to other systems on the network. This allows the administrators to pinpoint the source of the anomalous network activity quickly and take immediate steps to shut down the server or workstation and run diagnostics and antivirus scans to try to clean the infected host.

File Integrity Monitors

With any type of monitoring or measurement over time, you must initially start with a baseline of current activity and then measure this against future activity. The initial baseline provides you with a level of activity that is considered "normal" for your environment. When you have your baseline and continue to monitor further activity, any anomalies that go beyond your measured baseline thresholds will be easily apparent. This is done through *file integrity monitoring*, which alerts administrators on baseline deviations, allowing them to determine if the issue is malicious or a result of a misconfiguration. Several leading security compliance regulations and standards, such as the Sarbanes-Oxley Act (SOX) and HIPAA, require file integrity monitoring.

REVIEW

Objective 3.3: Given a scenario, implement secure network designs Appropriate network design is critical to securing your network infrastructure. Differentiate your network into security zones to create logical and physical barriers between your networks. Put high-security servers such as web servers and e-mail servers in the screened subnet to protect the private network. Use network security techniques such as private addressing, NAT, subnetting, and VLANs to separate networks. Secure remote access with authentication and encrypted VPNs. Firewalls can monitor the inbound and outbound network activity of your system and notify you of abnormal behavior. They can also provide the ability to block or allow access. HSMs are used for high-end security applications that require secure key generation and management on a separate hardware appliance. A variety of methods can be used to effectively monitor a network, to include SPAN and TAPs. Understand the differences among the methods and where they should be deployed.

3.3 QUESTIONS

1. After a security review, Tom has recommended that his organization install a network-based intrusion prevention system (NIPS). Based on the current budget, his manager recommended that he install a less costly network-based intrusion detection system (NIDS). What are the primary security differences between a NIDS and a NIPS that Tom could use to justify the additional costs? (Choose two.)
   - **A.** A NIDS only detects TCP/IP attacks.
   - **B.** A NIPS actively tries to mitigate an incoming intrusion rather than just detect it.
   - **C.** A NIDS can raise alarms when it detects an intrusion.
   - **D.** A NIPS is only host based, not network based.
2. Lauren must install and secure her organization's Internet services, including web, FTP, and e-mail servers, within the current network topology, which uses a network firewall to protect the organization's internal networks. In which security zone of the network should Lauren install these servers to isolate them from the Internet and the organization's internal networks?
   - **A.** Screened subnet
   - **B.** VLAN
   - **C.** Internal network
   - **D.** Intranet
3. Max's organization is growing fast, and the number of clients and devices on the organization's network has doubled in size over the last year. Max has been tasked with partitioning the network. Which of the following would best help partition and secure the network?
   - **A.** MAC
   - **B.** NAC
   - **C.** VPN
   - **D.** VLAN
4. Bobby is the network administrator for a company whose users are streaming too much video and using up the company's valuable bandwidth resources. Which technology would be best for Bobby to implement to help save resources?
   - **A.** Content/URL filter
   - **B.** Anti-spam filter
   - **C.** Protocol analyzer
   - **D.** IDS

3.3 ANSWERS

1. **A B** A NIPS actively tries to mitigate an incoming intrusion rather than just detect it. A NIDS actively monitors for intrusions and alerts the administrator when it detects one. A NIPS goes a step further and tries to actively prevent the intrusion as it is occurring.
2. **A** The screened subnet is a network that typically contains Internet servers and services that are accessible from the outside world but need to be isolated from your internal network. The screened subnet ensures incoming connections for these services are routed to the screened subnet and never reach the internal LAN.
3. **D** A virtual LAN (VLAN) is used to segment a network into smaller logical units to aid in security and performance. VLANs are logically isolated from each other to prevent network traffic and unauthorized access.
4. **A** Bobby could use content/URL filtering to analyze network traffic and block specific sites, such as the main streaming video sites, from being accessed. The end users will receive an error when they try to access those sites.

Objective 3.4 Given a scenario, install and configure wireless security settings

An aspect of network security that is often ignored but can provide direct access to your organization's networks is the use of wireless communications. Without proper security procedures, any person with a wireless device can connect to your network and eavesdrop or access private data by bypassing the traditional security defenses used in wired local area networks (LANs). A firewall or router with maximum security configured for your wired LAN will not stop a hacker who is able to access your network from an unencrypted and insecure wireless access point (WAP).

From the end-user perspective, the popularity of wireless devices and the wide availability of free and open public wireless access mean that users can access the Internet anywhere at any time. Enabling users to check their e-mail, manage their finances, perform their work, or just browse the Web can be an incredible boost to personal and business productivity, but this easy access to the Internet can also create the potential for deep security and privacy threats. Using your wireless device, such as a laptop, on an open, unencrypted network could mean your passwords and private data are being transmitted in clear text and could be captured by hackers monitoring these networks.

Wireless security is an important part of your overall network security strategy and design. Strong wireless security not only protects your networks from unauthorized intrusion but also protects your users from having their authentication credentials and sensitive data intercepted when they use wireless devices.

This objective provides an overview of wireless and encryption protocols and the design of wireless networks.

Wireless Security

One of the greatest changes in networking technology is the phenomenal growth and penetration of wireless communications. Wireless networks use radio frequency technology to transmit data through the air, effectively bridging the gap between data connectivity and user mobility. Wireless networks allow the mobile world to reach the Internet, not only with laptop computers but also with other telecommunication devices, such as smartphones, wireless-enabled tablets, and many other devices.

Wireless connectivity lets users perform their daily computing functions, such as checking e-mail, scheduling the calendar, and browsing the Internet, without physically plugging into a network. Wireless applications also extend into the business world, where inventories are taken by handheld devices and entire floors of a building are set up with wireless networks to enable mobile users to move their laptops and other wireless devices from room to room without the encumbrance of wires.

The popularity and explosive growth of wireless networks, however, have also introduced increased concerns for the security of wireless data. More so than for traditional wired networks, wireless security heavily involves the use of encryption technologies, coupled with traditional security mechanisms such as access control and authentication.

Wireless security depends on the different types of wireless network configurations available and the types of devices that will connect to them. The following sections discuss the various wireless network technologies and their topologies, as well as the protocols, hardware, and software that make them work.

Cryptographic Protocols

For a historical primer on wireless security protocols, it's important to consider the grandfather of the group, *Wired Equivalent Privacy (WEP)*. WEP was an IEEE 802.11 standard for encrypted communication between wireless clients and access points. WEP used the RC4 key encryption algorithm, along with a weak 40-bit initialization vector (IV) as a seed, to encrypt communications before they were transmitted over the wireless network. Because WEP repeated the same IV at various times, it was relatively easy to capture it and decrypt WEP traffic.

After the WEP standard was deprecated in 2004, the industry moved on to *Wi-Fi Protected Access (WPA)*. WPA was created as a stopgap to fix several weaknesses in its predecessor, WEP, until WPA2 could be fully implemented. WPA could use either a pre-shared key (PSK) or an authentication server that distributes the keys. With WPA, data was encrypted using a 128-bit key that was routinely changed during sessions using the *Temporal Key Integrity Protocol (TKIP)*. WPA also provided improved integrity checking of data traversing the wireless network to ensure it could not be intercepted and changed on the way to its destination.

This provided much more protection than the original WEP protocol; however, because TKIP was cryptographically like WEP and thus vulnerable to many of the same attacks, WPA was deprecated in favor of WPA2.

WPA2

Wi-Fi Protected Access 2 (WPA2) replaced WPA with a stronger 256-bit encryption and added Robust Security Network (RSN) support that includes added protection for ad hoc networks, key caching, pre-roaming authentication, and the Counter-Mode/CBC-MAC Protocol (CCMP). CCMP utilizes the Advanced Encryption Standard (AES) cipher to replace TKIP. It is a block cipher using a 128-bit key and is secure against the bulk of attacks currently directed against wireless networks.

All currently manufactured devices support WPA2, while some still support WPA, using AES. If your network devices support only WPA or WPA2, you should always choose to use WPA2.

WPA3

Wi-Fi Protected Access 3 (WPA3) was announced in January 2018 as a replacement to WPA2 to incorporate increased cryptographic strength, increased authentication, and ease of use. As announced by the Wi-Fi Alliance, WPA3 includes the following two modes of operation:

- **WPA3-Personal** Offers more resilient, password-based authentication even when users choose passwords that fall short of typical complexity recommendations. WPA3 leverages Simultaneous Authentication of Equals (SAE), a secure key establishment protocol between devices, to provide stronger protections for users against password-guessing attempts by third parties.
- **WPA3-Enterprise** Offers the equivalent of 192-bit cryptographic strength, providing additional protections for networks transmitting sensitive data, such as government or finance. The 192-bit security suite ensures that a consistent combination of cryptographic tools are deployed across WPA3 networks.

CCMP

With the advent of WPA2 replacing its predecessor, WPA, the use of *Counter-Mode/CBC-MAC Protocol (CCMP)* was introduced, which uses the AES cipher to replace the previously used TKIP. It is a block cipher using a 128-bit key and is secure against the bulk of attacks currently directed against wireless networks. CCMP is the standard for encryption within WPA2 and provides confidentiality, access control, and authentication.

SAE

Simultaneous Authentication of Equals (SAE) was originally developed for mesh networks but was subsequently implemented within WPA3 and defined by IEEE as "a simple protocol for authentication using only a password." SAE was developed to provide a secure alternative for certificates or when a centralized authority is unavailable. It is peer-to-peer in nature and can facilitate simultaneous initiation. SAE uses the Diffie-Hellman key exchange, with the addition of an authentication mechanism to provide forward secrecy (PFS).

Authentication Protocols

While encryption protocols such as WPA2 support the encryption of the communications link and data for wireless networks, they do not provide a secure authentication function for accessing wireless networks. The protocols in the following sections are popular methods for the transmission and security of authentication data within standard wireless encryption protocols.

Extensible Authentication Protocol

The *Extensible Authentication Protocol (EAP)*, specified in Internet Engineering Task Force (IETF) RFC 3748, is used primarily in WPA- and WPA2-based wireless networks for securely transporting authentication data, but it has also been used previously for remote access authentication to local area networks.

EAP separates the message exchange from the authentication process by using a different exchange layer, and it provides a module-based infrastructure that supports several different types of authentication methods. Microsoft Windows uses EAP to authenticate remote access, VPN, and site-to-site connections over Point-to-Point Protocol (PPP). With this method, you can use most standard authentication servers, such as Remote Authentication Dial-In User Service (RADIUS) or Kerberos (described in Objective 3.8, later in this domain), to authenticate connections.

Although EAP provides a very flexible authentication infrastructure, one of the major issues with EAP is that part of the initial exchange is transmitted in clear text, including authentication credentials and results. For WPA and WPA2 wireless networks, EAP authentication occurs before any wireless transmissions are encrypted.

EAP has been extended with other protocols to help improve security, such as EAP-FAST, EAP-TLS, and EAP-TTLS (discussed in upcoming sections), which utilize Transport Layer Security (TLS). EAP can also be used in combination with RADIUS and 802.1X to provide a federated wireless network; this has been implemented widely across the educational sector via eduroam, allowing wireless users across a campus to roam freely across more than 10,000 locations globally. Table 3.4-1 provides a comparison of 802.1X EAP derivations for review.

Protected Extensible Authentication Protocol

Protected Extensible Authentication Protocol (PEAP) uses TLS to transport EAP within an encrypted communications tunnel over a wireless connection. This has advantages over EAP-TLS, a similar protocol (discussed shortly), because there is no need for a client certificate.

With PEAP, an encrypted tunnel is formed to a server using TLS and a server-side certificate. This provides for secure key exchange between the client and the server, which then allows for normal EAP authentication methods for the client authentication stage.

TABLE 3.4-1 Comparison of 802.1X EAP Derivations (adapted from Intel; https://www.intel.com/content/www/us/en/support/articles/000006999/network-and-i-o/wireless-networking.html)

	EAP-TLS (Transport Layer Security)	EAP-TTLS (Tunneled TLS)	PEAP (Protected EAP)	EAP-FAST (Flexible Authentication via Secure Tunneling)	LEAP (Lightweight EAP)
Client-side certificate required	Yes	No	No	No (PAC)	No
Server-side certificate required	Yes	Yes	Yes	No (PAC)	No
WEP key management	Yes	Yes	Yes	Yes	Yes
Rogue AP detection	No	No	No	Yes	Yes
Provider	Microsoft	Funk Software	Microsoft	Cisco	Cisco
Authentication attributes	Mutual	Mutual	Mutual	Mutual	Mutual
Deployment difficulty	Difficult (because of client certificate deployment)	Moderate	Moderate	Moderate	Moderate
Wi-Fi security	Very high	High	High	High	High when strong passwords are used

EAP-FAST

EAP Flexible Authentication via Secure Tunneling (EAP-FAST) was one of the standards (along with PEAP and EAP-TLS) specifically created by Cisco Systems to replace the *Lightweight Extensible Authentication Protocol (LEAP)*, which had been in turn developed to address security issues with EAP. EAP-FAST establishes a secure tunnel through the use of a Protected Access Credential (PAC) and has three phases:

- **0** In-band provisioning, providing the peer with a shared secret
- **1** Tunnel establishment, authenticating the PAC and establishing a key
- **2** Authentication, authenticating the peer

EAP-TLS

EAP Transport Layer Security (EAP-TLS), established in IETF RFC 2716 (obsoleted by RFC 5216), is the original, and still widely used, wireless LAN EAP protocol. EAP-TLS improved on the original EAP through support for certificate-based mutual authentication. Because it uses TLS, it facilitates both dynamic session key generation and certificates for user and server authentication.

EAP-TTLS

EAP Tunneled Transport Layer Security (EAP-TTLS) extends EAP-TLS. As described in IETF RFC 5281, "EAP-TTLS allows legacy password-based authentication protocols to be used against existing authentication databases, while protecting the security of these legacy protocols against eavesdropping, man-in-the-middle, and other attacks." EAP-TTLS does away with the client-side (aka supplicant) certificate, meaning only the authentication server requires a digital certificate. Once the authentication server is authenticated using its digital certificate, an encrypted tunnel is established between the client and the server. Only requiring the server-side certificate improves ease of management.

IEEE 802.1X

802.1X is an IEEE standard, just like the 802.3 Ethernet standards and 802.11 wireless networking standards, but it is not a wireless standard per se. Although 802.1X is probably most commonly implemented on corporate wireless networks as the preferred form of authentication, it can be used in wired networks as well. This makes it easier for wireless and wired networks to interoperate, because they can use the same authentication methods and can connect to each other quite easily. 802.1X is called a *port-based* access control method and can use a wide variety of different security protocols. In that respect, 802.1X is more of a security authentication framework than a protocol itself, because it allows various protocols to be used for authentication.

WPA2 uses pre-shared keys for the personal version of its implementation and uses 802.1X for the enterprise implementation (the context discussed here). When using this type of enterprise implementation, not only can you authenticate WPA2 devices but you can also require the users themselves to authenticate with the network they are connecting to. This ensures not only that unauthorized devices can't connect to the network but also that users of network-connected devices are authorized. 802.1X can use several different types of authentication protocols, including EAP and its variants, discussed previously.

Using 802.1X, when a client connects to a wireless access point, the wireless port is initially set to an unauthorized state so that it can't perform any network functions, which include receiving an IP address from a Dynamic Host Configuration Protocol (DHCP) server. The WAP then asks the client for authentication credentials. Once received, this data is forwarded to an authentication server running a service such as RADIUS (discussed in the next section). If the client is accepted as an authorized user, then the client port on the WAP is switched to an authorized state and normal communications can commence.

802.1X can be helpful in allowing WLANs to scale upward in size easily while maintaining a centralized authentication system. This authentication, however, should be coupled with a strong communications encryption mechanism to provide full security. Note that networks that use 802.1X not only can authenticate devices such as laptops and workstations but also users and can easily be integrated into an authentication or directory service such as Active Directory.

RADIUS

Remote Authentication Dial-In User Service (RADIUS) is the most common Internet standard used for authenticating clients in a client–server environment. When the remote user accesses a network through a remote access device, the user is authenticated by a RADIUS server that compares the user's authentication credentials against those of the server's database. If the credentials match, the user is granted access to the rest of the network. The client's credentials that are sent to the RADIUS server are encrypted to prevent someone from capturing the transmission. RADIUS servers also include accounting and reporting functions that can monitor and log data on each connection, such as packet and protocol types, as well as the length of time connected. Note that RADIUS weakly encrypts passwords during the authentication process, but not usernames. Figure 3.4-1 shows an example of how a RADIUS server authenticates a remote access client.

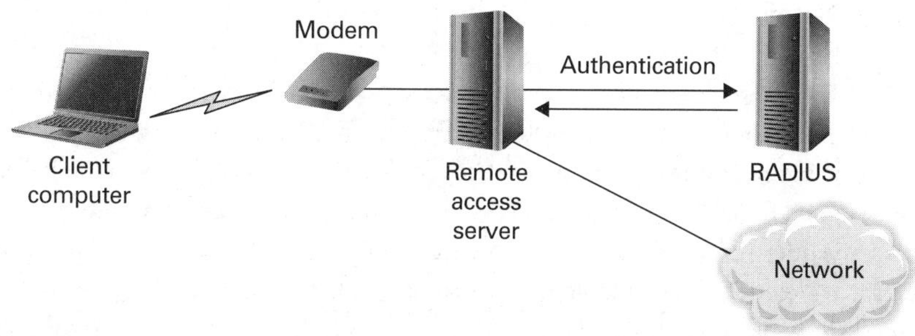

FIGURE 3.4-1 RADIUS server authentication

Methods

Wireless security protocols use different methods of operation, depending on factors such as whether the protocol is deployed for personal use (such as in-home networking or small businesses) or is deployed for use in an enterprise environment. Authentication methods range from simply using a pre-shared key (PSK) to using more sophisticated methods and protocols. The following sections describe various methods of implementing wireless security protocols.

Pre-shared Key vs. Enterprise vs. Open

The original WPA protocol required either no authentication (open), authentication to a RADIUS server (WPA-Enterprise), or the use of a pre-shared key (WPA-PSK, aka WPA-Personal). WPA's successors, WPA2 and WPA3, have implemented similar modes:

- **WPA-PSK/Personal** Originally conceived for personal or small business networks, personal authentication can be used to mutually authenticate wireless client devices and WAPs. The pre-shared key method means that all devices on the WLAN must use the same passphrase key to access the network.
- **WPA-Enterprise** Enterprise mode is more robust but is complex and hard to use. It was developed for larger infrastructures, more suited for environments with hundreds of clients, where using a single passphrase key for each device is not scalable. The authentication server takes care of key management between the wireless devices on the network.

Wi-Fi Protected Setup

Although not a security standard, the role of *Wi-Fi Protected Setup (WPS)* within a wireless network is important to understand. WPS was designed to allow users with less technical savvy to easily set up a wireless network and associated peripheral devices. For example, a WPS-enabled router might only require the home administrator to hold down a button combination on the device to sync to the network. This is perceived as easier for an inexperienced user to implement than a passphrase. However, as noted in Objective 1.4 of Domain 1, many devices that are enabled for WPS also use Near Field Communication (NFC), making attacks against WPS-enabled networks easy to accomplish. It is recommended to disable WPS unless it is absolutely necessary.

Captive Portals

Have you ever tried to access a hotel website and been presented with a page asking you to log in with your name and room number? If so, you've experienced a captive portal. *Captive portals* are designed to halt a user before accessing a wireless network by trapping packets until a web browser is opened, where the portal opens for entering credentials or payment information. The user will generally be unable to perform any functions, such as web browsing, until she has successfully passed the portal.

Installation Considerations

There are a number of things you should consider when constructing your wireless network. For example, your physical environment can greatly affect the performance of your wireless network:

- Clear or open areas provide better radio range than filled or closed areas.
- Metal or other physical obstructions can hinder the performance of wireless devices. Avoid placing these devices in a location where a metal barrier is situated between the sending and receiving antennas.
- Radio penetration is affected by the materials used in the building construction. Drywall construction allows greater range than concrete blocks, whereas metal construction can hinder and block radio signals.

The following sections contain other important installation considerations and tools to best design and implement your network.

Site Surveys

A *site survey* is a physical examination and review of your current network environment. An initial site survey should be performed before installation of a wireless network to ensure the environment will be conducive to wireless communications. The site survey can also help determine the best placement and coverage for your wireless access points. When your wireless network is in place, you can use software to scan and test your wireless network to examine its power and range.

Wi-Fi Analyzers

A *Wi-Fi analyzer* is specialized software that scans your wireless network and WAPs and records signal strength and interference levels, depending on your location within your premises. You can run the software on a laptop and walk around your building to look for zones with a low signal strength or high interference. Using this information, you can rearrange your WAP and antenna placement, as well as modify your wireless network settings to increase range and power to these low-signal zones. Some examples of these analyzers include WiFi Analyzer and Netcut.

Heat Maps

A *heat map* is a visual representation of the wireless signal strength as you move from place to place. Software such as SolarWinds can be used to estimate signal coverage, considering where WAPs are placed physically and how they interact. This visual can be used to find dead zones, or areas that need further coverage from current or new WAPs.

Channel Overlap

Choosing the correct channel for your wireless network to communicate on is critical. A 2.6-GHz router has 11 channels, with channel 1 being the lowest frequency and then moving slightly higher for each channel. The most commonly used channels are 1, 6, and 11, because they are sufficiently far apart as to be less likely to overlap and interfere with each other. The default on many wireless routers is channel 6. Be aware that various wireless technologies are in the 5-GHz range, with many more nonoverlapping channels, ranging from 7 through 196.

Wireless Access Point Placement

Wireless access points are limited by range—from 100 meters indoors to 500 meters outdoors—depending on the physical environment. In large wireless environments, multiple WAPs are needed to provide a wide coverage area for the clients. The WAP ranges must overlap so that network connectivity is not lost when roaming from one WAP to another.

Antenna and WAP placement are important to consider, to make sure they are not close to any other electrical wires or devices (especially those that broadcast on a similar frequency) where interference can cause a loss of wireless signal. WAPs should be positioned at a high, central point of the area that they are servicing to ensure the widest, most unobstructed coverage. In smaller LAN-based WAPs, the antenna is attached directly to the device and cannot be moved away from the device. Extend the antenna to its maximum length to ensure a strong signal. Antennas that can be attached to WAPs with a cable should still be located as close as possible to the WAP. The longer the cable, the higher the chance that signal attenuation or electromagnetic interference (EMI) can occur.

KEY TERM **Attenuation** describes how an electronic signal becomes weaker over greater distances. This applies to both cable and wireless signals.

Many WAPs use dipole antennas that split the signal wire into two wires that provide omnidirectional coverage, with the wireless signal radiating outward in all directions. With 802.11n networks, you can use Multiple-Input Multiple-Output (MIMO) technology, which uses multiple sending and receiving antennas to boost the power and range of the network. All devices on the network must support MIMO to use its multipath benefits. Older hardware uses only a single in/out path.

EXAM TIP Antenna placement is a key factor in ensuring maximum range and power for your wireless network. Be aware of the different issues that affect antenna placement and how to improve wireless network reception.

Controller and Access Point Security

Just as with any physical security measure, your first line of defense in wireless security is the physical security of the devices—controllers and WAPs—themselves. Unauthorized people must be prevented from accessing these devices to potentially make changes, whether incidental or malicious. These devices should be stored within locked rooms accessible only to authorized personnel, and regular scans should be made for rogue access points across the organization.

REVIEW

Objective 3.4: Given a scenario, install and configure wireless security settings Even more so than security for wired networks, wireless security heavily involves the use of encryption technologies, coupled with traditional (wired) security mechanisms such as access control and authentication. Wireless networks should use WPA2 and WPA3 encryption whenever possible. Understand the various authentication protocols and how they have evolved since EAP. Understand what pre-shared key and enterprise implementations are best suited for. In addition, ensure that wireless access points are properly physically secured. Understand the use for WPS and that it should be removed unless needed. Captive portals require a user to authenticate (and often pay) through a web browser before they can use the network. Understand how site surveys, heat maps, Wi-Fi analyzers, and WAP placement are used to best implement a secure and strong wireless network.

3.4 QUESTIONS

1. After creating a heat map of a specific floor of his building, Rich realizes that two of the farthest offices on his floor have very poor signal strength. Which of the following actions can Rich perform to provide the *best* solution to increase signal strength to that part of the building?
   - **A.** Disable encryption to speed up the network
   - **B.** Add another wireless access point
   - **C.** Change from channel 1 to channel 6
   - **D.** Disable authentication
2. Tim has set up a wireless network for his small office of 50 users. Which of the following encryption protocols should he implement to ensure the highest level of encryption security?
   - **A.** WAP
   - **B.** WPA
   - **C.** WEP 128 bit
   - **D.** WPA3

3. Tara is installing a wireless network in a manufacturing facility. Which of the following aspects of the wireless network should she concentrate on to prevent security issues with EMI?
   - **A.** Use of WPA3 encryption
   - **B.** Use of 802.11g or 802.11n
   - **C.** Network name
   - **D.** WAP and antenna placement

3.4 ANSWERS

1. **B** It sounds like Rich has some offices in a dead zone, so it would be best for him to install another wireless access point to make sure the offices have appropriate coverage.
2. **D** WPA3 is currently the strongest level of encryption security available for a wireless network. WPA3 replaces the weaker WPA and WPA2.
3. **D** Tara needs to make sure that the antenna and wireless access point are not placed close to any other electrical wires or devices (especially those that broadcast on a similar frequency) that can cause electrical interference and a loss of wireless signal.

Objective 3.5 Given a scenario, implement secure mobile solutions

Mobile devices are everywhere! Consider that smartphones, tablet devices, laptop computers, e-readers, and even car stereos now contain the computing power of many traditional desktop machines only a few years ago; the proliferation of mobile devices has far exceeded the adoption of those desktop machines. The concern with mobile devices, however, is their care and maintenance from a security perspective. Have you considered patching your car recently?

Mobile Security Solutions

Security concerns for mobile devices derive from the nature of their portability, which makes them susceptible to theft, vandalism, and unauthorized access to data. The following sections describe additional security precautions to consider for mobile devices.

Connection Methods and Receivers

As discussed throughout this book, connectivity allows you to transfer information from one point to another using conventional means such as cellular or Wi-Fi networks or using less conventional means such as Bluetooth or NFC. Each of these connection methods has its own nuances that must be considered when you're looking to apply security controls, but there are often commonalities, such as minimizing your attack surface by disabling unneeded capabilities and keeping your devices patched.

Cellular

The general cellular infrastructure is made up of mobile devices, towers, and infrastructure nodes that assist in connecting mobile devices to the public switched telephone network (PSTN). Simple cellular service, while often considered more secure than using random Wi-Fi hotspots, is still vulnerable to eavesdropping by several parties, not least of which is the cellular provider itself. When using a cellular device, it's a smart idea to disable any geolocation services that could allow you to be tracked and to turn off other communications methods that might be in discovery mode (such as Wi-Fi, Bluetooth, and NFC) unless needed at that moment.

Wi-Fi

Wireless networks have been discussed at length in this book, particularly in the previous objective, 3.4. The core tenets remain the same: when possible, use the highest level of encryption available to you, such as WPA3. Do not connect to SSIDs that you are unfamiliar with, such as free airport or coffee shop wireless access points. Use a VPN whenever possible, even on mobile devices.

Bluetooth

Bluetooth is an open standard for short-range radio frequency (RF) communication, used primarily in the consumer market space and, to a lesser extent, in the commercial market space. Bluetooth is used mainly to establish ad hoc wireless personal area networks between devices such as cell phones, laptops, automobiles, medical devices, printers, keyboards, mice, and headsets. Bluetooth allows easy file sharing, elimination of messy cables in small spaces, and even Internet connectivity sharing between devices. However, without proper authentication, an unauthorized user can connect to an unprotected Bluetooth device and access any data stored on the device. If you choose to use Bluetooth, see if your device allows discovery mode to be disabled when not required.

NFC

Near Field Communication (NFC) is a standard used primarily in mobile devices to facilitate easy communications between two or more devices simply by bringing them into proximity (likely touching them together). NFC technology is often used within applications to send pictures, contact cards, and other media between compatible devices. However, while the range of NFC is limited to the immediate proximity of the devices, the standard itself is essentially an emanation, making it quite vulnerable. Because NFC uses RFID technologies (discussed in an upcoming section), it is vulnerable to eavesdropping by another NFC device, man-in-the-middle attacks, and relay attacks (relaying modified information back and forth from the victim's device, impersonating one of the devices). Unless required, do not enable NFC, and if you do choose to use it as a connection method, disable it when not in use.

Cross-Reference

Securing wireless networks, including the use of Wi-Fi, Bluetooth, and NFC, is covered in more depth in Objective 3.4, earlier in this domain.

Infrared

Radio is part of the electromagnetic (EM) spectrum, which comprises a wide range of electromagnetic radiation and energies with different characteristics, including infrared, visible, and ultraviolet light; microwaves; X-rays; and many others. A personal area network (PAN) is created when two or more devices, some using older infrared technologies, are connected and exchange data. These devices have been standard for several years now but are being replaced by those that use other technologies, such as Bluetooth and 802.11 wireless. As with other capabilities, if infrared is available but is not being used, it's a good idea to disable it.

USB

Various previous objectives have described different uses for the common Universal Serial Bus (USB) port, including the use of USB storage devices. Another use that you should understand is the capability to use USB to network-enable a device, such as a laptop, via a USB network card. While this is increasingly less common now because almost everything comes network-enabled by default, clients can have wireless network cards that connect via USB. If this functionality is not required for a device, it's a good idea to disable it to prevent personal networking cards to be used to network-connect devices, such as laptops that are meant to be air gapped (that is, have no network connectivity with anything).

Point-to-Point

Point-to-point, in the strictest sense, refers to one host or station communicating directly with another distinct host. The hosts could be two computers, a computer and a wireless access point, two infrastructure devices, and so on. Point-to-point connections allow the two hosts to share data without necessarily traversing the Internet and can provide a more secure mechanism to share files between two authorized parties. However, point-to-point connections can also be used to share files and other content for less noble reasons, so on devices carrying secure or proprietary information, it's best to keep an eye on this setting and disable it if possible.

Point-to-Multipoint

Point-to-multipoint means that a host can simultaneously communicate with multiple hosts. You typically see point-to-multipoint implementations in both wired and wireless networks, such as a star network topology. Generally, a point-to-multipoint configuration has a centralized base and then a number of points that do not connect directly to each other but instead use the base to relay information back and forth among the hosts.

Global Positioning System

Many mobile devices, primarily smartphones, contain Global Positioning System (GPS) chips so that they can be tracked by and use the services of GPS satellites. If your device is ever lost or stolen, you can track the location of the device via its GPS coordinates and attempt to recover it. However, having GPS enabled can lead to geo-tagging of images, for example, as well as the ability to geolocate devices within secure areas. Again, if this is not an end state you desire, it's a good security practice to disable GPS entirely. (GPS tagging is discussed later in this objective.)

RFID

Radio-frequency identification (RFID) uses RF to identify and track "tagged" items. Passive RFID tags have no batteries and draw power from the RFID reader itself, while active RFID tags have batteries attached and can continuously send a signal out as a beacon. Active tags have a much longer range but are more expensive. A common use of RFID is to tag cargo that is being moved from Location A to Location B and track its movement and provide reports; it also reduces the risk of theft, since RFID technology can track the amount of cargo. Mobile RFID readers can be installed on smartphones, for example, to allow the phone to read an RFID tag and serve as a reader on-the-go. RFID is also used within NFC communications, as noted previously.

Mobile Device Management

Mobile device management (MDM) requires an organization to develop an infrastructure that can account for all the different types of mobile devices used to process, store, transmit, and receive organizational data in the same way that more traditional devices do. MDM often includes software that manages applications on these mobile devices (called *mobile application management*, or *MAM*, discussed in more depth later in this objective). MDM manages many of the same considerations you would have within a more traditional infrastructure, such as patch management, access control, antivirus, and authentication, along with the more mobile-specific requirements such as context-aware authentication and remote wipe in the event of loss or theft. A related concept you should know is *Unified Endpoint Management (UEM)*, which evolves the MDM concept to include management of all endpoints, including desktops, printers, and other more traditional enterprise devices, within a single management interface.

Organizations that distribute mobile devices to their users may choose to control not only the applications that are installed or executed on the devices but also the content that can be present or loaded on the devices. For example, an organization could choose to remove or disable the games, instant messaging features, or the ability to stream videos while connected to the corporate network. Another control that should be considered is blocking third-party app stores. Be mindful of the ability of users to potentially "root" or "jailbreak" their devices (covered in more depth later in this objective); this process uses mobile device software exploits to allow third-party apps to be loaded, as well as features that aren't approved to be used. Similarly, apps and custom firmware can be sideloaded on Android devices using external media (such as via USB drive or other mechanism).

Many companies, particularly those operating in sensitive environments, choose to also disable unused features or those that could present security concerns. These might include Bluetooth, Wi-Fi, cameras, voice or video recording, over-the-air (OTA) updates, use of external media or devices (using technologies such as USB On-The-Go [OTG]), the ability to connect to wireless ad hoc networks, tethering (use of the data plan to create a WAP), and the use of NFC payment methods such as Apple Pay or Google Pay. Each of these features can create its own security concerns and potentially compromise both the company data and personal data resident on the mobile device.

After a policy has been created, the IT staff should implement that policy, whether it involves application control, disabling features, or both, using a group policy for mobile devices. Some mobile OSs are better suited for this; it is worth investigating what the implications will be and then determine the implementation and maintenance costs for a mobile rollout.

Application Management

Modern mobile devices have a wealth of application options at the user's fingertips, allowing access to everything from banking apps to gaming apps. These can be both vendor-supplied apps and apps purchased and licensed through a third-party provider, controlled by the enterprise app store in conjunction with or as part of the application management system. In the case of vendor or third-party apps, application management could centrally manage which users and devices get which apps, of course, but could also be useful in maintaining multiple versions of apps if they are required to support business processes. The solution could also be used to maintain changes and updates for vendor apps and ensure that devices get the most current version when they need it, through either push or on-demand distribution methods. The system could also assist in managing licensing requirements, as there may be limitations on the number of licenses in use based on the organization's agreement with the vendor.

Content Management

In addition to managing aspects of content that include storage, security, and delivery to the user, content management also includes controlling the content on the mobile device itself. This functionality covers content change and updates, as well as versioning control between those changes. This ensures not only that files are kept up to date and records of changes are maintained (either as metadata or as a separate record) but also that file inconsistency and concurrent use issues are prevented and resolved when they occur. Content management could be implemented using permissions, file locks, or other mechanisms.

Remote Wipe

If your device is lost or stolen, an unauthorized person may be able to access your data if your device has no authentication or encryption mechanisms in use. As a protection against such unauthorized access, many mobile devices have the capability to remotely delete their contents, commonly called *remote wipe*. Your mobile device can be tracked by its hardware address, and you can use a management application or a web browser application to initiate a remote wipe of the device so that all your data is deleted. You may have lost the hardware, but your private data is protected by removing it from the device.

Geofencing

You'd never dream of allowing someone to casually walk out of your building with a desktop PC unless authorized. In fact, your organization might implement regular scans to determine equipment inventory and location.

Mobile devices require the same consideration, with the added challenge that they're often meant to walk out of the building. It's still a good idea to know who has what and where it is. You might implement inventory control through those same regular scans, as well as use stickers that have the organization name, a phone number to contact if lost, and a tracking number. You might also implement measures to turn on GPS onboard the device for tracking, or *geolocation*. This type of asset tracking allows for potential recovery if the device is lost, as well as device access control. Perhaps you don't want any mobile devices within sensitive areas of your building, like executive conference rooms or secure laboratories. In this case, you could use the GPS to *geofence* the area and implement access control measures that track where devices are located within the facility, alerting you when mobile devices enter unapproved areas.

Geolocation

As discussed previously in this objective, many mobile devices, primarily phones, now contain GPS chips so that they can be tracked by and use the services of GPS satellites. If your device is ever lost or stolen, you can track the location of the device via its GPS coordinates and attempt to recover it. Understand that GPS functionality also allows pictures and other objects to be "geo-tagged," so a user's whereabouts can be tracked, as discussed later in this objective.

Screen Locks, Passwords, and PINs

If a mobile device is stolen, a simple authentication scheme can deter the unauthorized user from accessing any sensitive information on the device. The thief may simply want the hardware rather than the data that resides within, but any device that contains confidential information may be stolen and have its valuable content discovered, such as company data or personal identity information. This section combines the discussion of passwords, PINs, and screen locks because they are the most common methods of authenticating a user into their phone and preventing unauthorized access to the contents within. A simple screen lock password can block access to the device until the password is properly entered. On laptops, you can enable a BIOS password that is required at boot time before the operating system loads, which prevents anyone from starting up the laptop unless the password is entered. Further, a lockout will disable the device after a certain number of attempts. For example, a mobile phone could be wiped remotely after five attempts; in the event of a lost or stolen phone, this could save the organization from any number of issues.

Push Notifications

Push notifications are small messages sent to a device from a central server, often as alerts or notices. Notifications require that the device have a network connection. While push technology has been used for some time to deliver personal alerts such as news and sports scores, MDM now uses push notifications to perform a wide variety of management functions, including changes in policies or configurations. Notifications can also force applications to schedule an update at a given time or when reconnected to the corporate infrastructure.

Push notifications aren't the only way to send control messages and management commands to devices; the Short Message Service (SMS) that is typically used over cellular services to send text messages can also be used for many of the same purposes. Because SMS doesn't require the robustness of data services, it can be used to send messages to the device if the infrastructure can't easily communicate with it, such as when there is a weak cellular connection.

Biometrics

Objective 2.4 in Domain 2 discussed organizational biometrics in general terms, but biometrics can also be used for mobile device security. Biometric controls on a mobile device often rely on physical features such as fingerprints or face identification (such as used in Apple's Face ID). Combined with other authentication factors such as a PIN or password, biometric elements can provide a very secure authentication mechanism and are increasingly used for authentication into sensitive applications, such as password managers and online banking.

Context-Aware Authentication

Objective 2.4 also discussed two-factor and multifactor authentication, and mobile devices are often used to provide the "something you have" factor (often through an authenticator app, such as Google Authenticator). However, *context-aware authentication* takes that a bit further by requiring different authentication based on the context in which access to a data asset is attempted. For example, a user attempting access within the geofenced proximity of the organization might require less stringent authentication than a user who is not within that location. The data to be accessed can also be a factor used to make a context-aware authentication decision.

Containerization

Data *containerization*, often referred to as *mobile sandboxing*, creates containers within a mobile device that separate different types of data from each another, such as corporate and personal data. This is often used in BYOD (discussed later in this objective) implementations and allows the different types of data to be managed according to the organization's policy.

For example, containers can be created that allow corporate data to be encrypted and only accessible by certain applications and to disable the ability to copy and paste between personal and corporate applications. Data containerization also allows a remote administrator to remove corporate data selectively from the mobile device, in the case of a data leak or other negative event, while not touching personal data.

Storage Segmentation

Mobile devices now have quite a bit of storage space; in fact, today's cellular phones have as much (or more) storage available for use as desktop computers did ten years ago. Mobile devices also can function as removable storage devices, generally by plugging in through a USB interface. However, this also allows sensitive information to be offloaded to the device easily, either for malicious purposes or just for the user's convenience. A good data loss prevention (DLP) solution looks for mobile devices that are connected and monitors (or blocks) any data transfer.

Mobile devices, like more traditional computer systems, can also support *storage segmentation*, which allows more performance-intensive applications to be executed in a segment that increases the performance of that application. Because mobile devices are somewhat less powerful than desktop or laptop computing systems, this can improve performance noticeably.

Full Device Encryption

Beyond authentication, devices can be protected using encryption. When the contents of a mobile device are encrypted, the corresponding encryption key is required before any user can read any data. If the user does not have the key, no access is granted. This is useful for password files that users sometimes keep on their smartphones' flash memory cards and other mobile devices. Many OSs now come with encrypted file systems that provide *full device encryption*, such as BitLocker for Windows and FileVault for macOS. Users can selectively encrypt partitions or entire hard drives that require a password key for access. The files are encrypted and decrypted "on the fly" as the authorized user accesses them. The drive encryption typically employs Advanced Encryption Standard (AES) 128- or 256-bit encryption technology. This encryption slows down performance but provides excellent security for laptops and prevents an unauthorized user from accessing any contents of the hard drive.

Mobile Devices

The following sections describe various other key concepts to understand about mobile devices.

MicroSD HSM

As discussed in Objectives 3.2 and 3.3 earlier in this domain, a hardware security module (HSM) is a specialized hardware appliance used to provide onboard cryptographic functions and processing. This physical hardware device can be a stand-alone device attached to a network or it can be connected directly to a server as a plug-in card—a *MicroSD HSM* in the case of mobile devices. As with more traditional HSMs, MicroSD HSMs support integrated cryptographic functions, such as use of Public Key Infrastructure for encryption, decryption, and secure key generation and management.

Mobile Application Management

Mobile application management (MAM) is a concept related to MDM, as discussed previously, but on a different scale. With MDM, the idea is to reach out and control a device in its entirety through the corporate infrastructure and policy. MAM is limited to simply controlling the applications on the device itself, whether it is owned by the organization or owned by the employee. MAM can be implemented in several different ways, including controlling individual apps, controlling the source of the apps, controlling the security features of the apps, and controlling the apps' data. MAM usually isn't a solution by itself; it's typically used in conjunction with MDM to varying degrees.

EXAM TIP Remember that MAM is application-specific, while MDM can control the entire device.

SEAndroid

SEAndroid, otherwise known as Security Enhanced Linux for Android, was initially developed by the U.S. National Security Agency to enable SELinux for use with Android in order to implement more stringent security practices that improved gaps within Android's security posture, such as the separation between applications and the ability to limit the damage that a malicious application can do. It was such a successful project that SELinux was subsequently implemented as a core part of the Android OS by the Android Open Source Project (AOSP), a good-news story for a historically less-than-secure mobile platform.

Enforcement and Monitoring

When deploying the various mobile solutions discussed in this objective, there are more questions to answer than what provider and plan to choose. In fact, as mobile devices become infinitely more capable and complex, numerous enforcement and monitoring considerations must addressed to properly secure mobile devices that connect to the organization's network, as discussed in the following sections.

Third-Party Application Stores

Enforcement and monitoring of the use of third-party app stores by users are essential for limiting the organization's attack surface. Consider, for example, a personally owned iPhone. After obtaining and registering the iPhone, the user immediately has access to the Apple-managed App Store to download any number of applications, as discussed earlier. However, if the iPhone is corporate owned or the user is permitted to connect it to the corporate network through a BYOD policy, network administrators need to restrict and monitor what the user is allowed to download from the App Store. For example, even apps that are present in the iTunes store for download may not be authorized for use on corporate devices or on some BYOD devices that contain corporate data (depending upon the corporate policy) simply because they may represent a security risk. Further, the organization may have its preferred e-mail app and not authorize a user to download, install, and use a different third-party e-mail app from the App Store. This is where mobile device policies pushed down from the corporate MDM infrastructure would serve to control and limit apps and their use on the devices.

As far as corporate app stores go, keep in mind that an app store really is just a centralized place from which users can download apps. This could be a share on a server that the user accesses from a browser or a function of MDM/MAM that pushes apps to the device. Apps that come from corporate stores are usually those specially developed by the enterprise and are provided for use with corporate data. App stores that are not vendor specific or that are provided by the corporate enterprise network are considered independent or *third-party app stores* and may or may not be authorized as sources from which users can obtain apps. Enterprise-level policies can be implemented and pushed down to the users' devices, which prevents users from accessing these independent app stores, but in some cases they may be authorized.

Rooting/Jailbreaking

Broadly stated, the terms *rooting* and *jailbreaking* refer to bypassing a mobile device's restrictions to use it in ways that were not intended by the manufacturer or mobile service carrier. *Jailbreaking* specifically refers to bypassing software restrictions on an iOS device to run apps that are not approved by Apple and not available on the official App Store. Jailbreaking also allows a user to unlock functionality on the device. Jailbreaking an iPhone can unlock that functionality and allow other devices to use the iPhone's connection to the Internet. Jailbreaking is normally not supported by the manufacturer at all; in fact, jailbreaking typically voids the warranty on a device. Additionally, the manufacturer or the service provider, if they detect that jailbreaking has taken place on the device, can prevent the device from connecting to their services.

Rooting is similar to jailbreaking but is specific to Android. When an Android device is rooted, it means that the user now has full administrative access to the lower-level functionality of the device. Rooting is useful in that it allows the user to perform functions on the device that they would not normally be able to perform and access functions that may be prohibited by the device manufacturer. Again, as in the case of jailbreaking, this is done to install software that otherwise could not be used on the device or to unlock functionality on the device. Although none of the popular Android device vendors condone rooting, in most cases, since the device belongs to the user, the vendors really have no recourse against this practice.

EXAM TIP Be sure to understand the vendor-specific differences between jailbreaking (specific to iOS devices) and rooting (Android devices).

Sideloading

While Apple tightly controls its App Store and how apps are introduced into the Apple marketplace, for instance, Android users can install apps from other sources in addition to the Google Play store (a process known as *sideloading*). These apps may come from independent app developers or enterprise-specific app stores created to develop applications specifically for the mobile users of a particular organization. Sideloading can also refer to the loading of apps through a nonstandard process, such as via USB drive or other mechanism, rather than through the more traditional download process.

Custom Firmware

Custom firmware refers to firmware that is nonstandard, such as an older version that's not the current one, a more secure version such as GrapheneOS, or a customized version specific to a manufacturer, such as Fire OS by Amazon. Android phones in particular are more open to the use of custom firmware and operating systems. While this capability to use custom firmware supports an environment that is much more flexible and open-source friendly, it is important from a security perspective that this capability be disabled within an organizational environment to prevent a custom firmware or OS implementation from being used to inadvertently or purposefully subvert security controls or MDM usage.

Carrier Unlocking

Carriers, such as AT&T and Verizon, often "lock" to their network the mobile devices that they sell to customers. This means that if a customer wants to switch to a competing carrier but keep the same mobile device, the device must first be "unlocked." Generally this requires calling the current carrier directly and giving them the account holder's information and the IMEI number that is tied to the device (the International Mobile Equipment Identity number is a 15-digit number used to uniquely identify a mobile device, typically a smartphone or other device that connects to a cellular network). Note that not all mobile phones are compatible with all carriers due to differences in their specific cellular technologies.

NOTE Some carriers unlock their devices automatically after they are fully paid off, and some don't. Check your specific carrier's policy for unlocking mobile devices.

Firmware Over-the-Air Updates

A critical part of the mobile device life cycle, just as with any host, includes updating the device's firmware or software with new versions, as well as applying patches between updates. These can sometimes be quite large and lengthy to download, which on a mobile device is a practical consideration. To save cell data usage, an organization could choose to allow *firmware over-the-air (OTA) updates* to be downloaded via Wi-Fi only (with exceptions if an update is extremely critical). That raises the issue of what to do if a user doesn't connect to the

Wi-Fi network and has critical updates waiting for an unacceptable period of time. In this case, MDM can be used to force the update or lock access to the device's functionality, much as can be done with a laptop that hasn't followed update policy.

Camera Use

Many devices now have embedded cameras and video recording devices. Within high-security situations, these are often unacceptable. Even within lower-security workplaces, you may be uncomfortable with employees having the ability to record activities (think of a meeting discussing HR actions, for example). Some organizations who are especially concerned about camera use even order their corporate-owned mobile devices without cameras installed to completely prevent the possibility of their use. Alternatively, cameras can be disabled via the MDM.

Short Message Service/Multimedia Messaging Service/ Rich Communication Services

Short Message Service (SMS), Multimedia Messaging Service (MMS), and Rich Communication Services (RCS), often known collectively as *texting*, are some of the primary communications mechanisms on mobile devices. Because SMS doesn't require robust data services, it can be used to send messages to the device in the event that the infrastructure can't easily communicate with the device, which might be the case in the event that Wi-Fi data services, for example, are turned off; a device has a very weak cellular connection; or between incompatible services, such as messages between Android and Apple devices. MMS and RCS were developed to provide richer multimedia experiences to include video and audio recordings. While texting services are often used to communicate within business environments, they are also a potential source of spam over instant messaging (SPIM, previously introduced in Domain 1, Objective 1.1) and present the risk of audio and video recordings being sent from secure environments.

External Media

Disabling unused media ports helps support the defense-in-depth concept by minimizing the attack surface in conjunction with other security measures. If external media is not permitted or is restricted, disabling USB ports and media slots should be considered. Endpoint protection can, for example, disable USB ports for use by all devices except explicitly approved ones, such as USB keyboard and mice. Also, many secure organizations disallow burning to optical discs to remove another way for data to be exfiltrated from a laptop.

USB On-The-Go

USB On-The-Go (OTG) was developed as a mechanism to plug devices such as external drives, cameras, keyboards, and mice into smartphones or tablets. For example, when an external storage drive is connected via USB OTG, it then presents on the compatible mobile device as a drive that can be read from and written to. It's a very cool way to add functionality to a mobile device but presents security concerns just as any USB drive would if plugged into a desktop system, including the ability to transmit malware. If USB OTG is not a functionality needed for your organizational devices, especially corporate owned, it's best to disable it.

Recording Microphone

Voice communications over mobile phones can be intercepted and captured just like any other network communication. For high-security environments and for personal confidentiality, you can encrypt voice communications between users. Software encryption programs are available that run on your mobile device and, when activated, encrypt the voice communication between two users. The other user requires the same software to decrypt and encrypt the communication.

GPS Tagging

As discussed earlier in this objective, the increasing inclusion of GPS within mobile devices, especially smartphones, presents concerns for security-minded professionals. One of those concerns is that GPS functionality allows pictures and other objects to be geo-tagged, which reveals a user's whereabouts and allows them to be tracked. Although geo-tagging might be appealing for personal social media, it has inherent privacy concerns, especially when sensitive work-related mobile communications that should remain private are geo-tagged.

Wi-Fi Direct/Ad Hoc

An *ad hoc network* (called *Wi-Fi Direct* by some vendors, like Microsoft) usually consists of just a few devices that are connected together for the purpose of sharing files, gaming, or Internet connection sharing. Ad hoc networks are typically characterized by low security settings and devices that are relatively close to each other. Ad hoc networks are usually found in places where one user wants to connect to another user's device for a short period of time. This functionality can also be used by threat actors looking to gain access to a mobile device; say, for example, that a user connects to what they believe to be a Wi-Fi hotspot that is instead an ad hoc connection to another user. That user has at least limited access to the files present on the device. Unless this feature is explicitly necessary, it is best to disable this within the MDM.

Tethering

Tethering simply refers to a device sharing its Internet connection with another device. Tethering has been an option for mobile phones for years, albeit sometimes against carrier wishes; for example, some iPhones that used AT&T as a service provider historically weren't able to be used to tether without jailbreaking the iPhone to unlock that functionality. However, more carriers are allowing this functionality natively, but do be aware that while tethering might be a more secure option than connecting to, say, an open airport Wi-Fi, it does use the data plan for the mobile phone and, if not kept in check, can run up hefty fees.

Hotspot

A portable *hotspot* is typically a small device that has access to cellular technologies such as 3G and 4G and provides access to these networks for Wi-Fi devices. This is similar to tethering a mobile phone, as it uses the device's cellular connection, but is instead a dedicated hardware device. These devices can be purchased from wireless providers such as Verizon, Sprint, AT&T, T-Mobile, and other carriers, and are usually specific to the carrier's type of broadband network. These devices can provide wireless access for up to five or ten devices at a time. Many of these devices can be purchased as dedicated hotspots. A hotspot has many of the same considerations that a tethered mobile phone does, in that while it is more secure than an untrusted Wi-Fi connection, it does use a data plan and needs to be monitored for usage.

Payment Methods

Increasingly, mobile phones use NFC communications, as discussed previously, to conduct wireless payment transactions through services such as Chase Pay, Apple Pay, and Google Pay. The devices must be very close to or touching each other and can be used for payment through a mobile application that has the payment card information stored. Using the phone's authentication, this allows payment to be made without ever touching a credit card. This is a very new technology and is just starting to see widespread adoption in newer mobile devices, as well as the infrastructures and applications that support them. Obviously, due to the access to sensitive banking information, the use of these services should be monitored.

Deployment Models

With the proliferation of mobile devices within the workforce, more organizations have begun allowing employees to use their own devices (such as mobile phones and tablets) for work purposes, requiring them to access the corporate information using their personally owned devices. Although this may seem to be logical (employees already have the device, requiring less up-front cost for equipment), several practical considerations should be addressed. Regardless of the deployment model in the organization, there are challenges that must be dealt with, some of which this objective has already touched on. An organization must determine if or how personal mobile devices will be used within its facilities and on its network, what level of control the organization seeks over the devices, and what rights to content and privacy the employee has. This should be expressed in a formal policy that is distributed to and signed by all employees. The following sections describe a variety of deployment model options that can be used, varying in levels of organizational control.

Bring Your Own Device

Once ownership of mobile devices became the norm, people began carrying both personal and corporate mobile devices, which is unwieldy. The *bring your own device (BYOD)* deployment model allows users to join their personal device to the corporate network and use it for official purposes. This creates many difficult scenarios, however, revolving around ownership of content, patching and antivirus, and loss or theft of the device.

Ownership

- **Data ownership** BYOD entails the employee using his or her own device to perform work. However, who owns the data on the device? Does the organization have policies supporting this?
- **Support ownership** Who is responsible for performing technical support on an employee-owned device? Should the IT staff be responsible for supporting any device configuration?
- **Carrier unlocking** Smartphones often are locked to a particular carrier and can only be used on that carrier unless they are purchased specially or the contract has expired. Carrier unlocking outside of these parameters can often incur additional costs. Furthermore, all phones likely will not work on all carriers, so consider this when making choices about a carrier change.

Security Management

- **Patches and antimalware** Patches, antimalware, and other security-related solutions are almost universally accepted on company-owned devices. However, when the device is employee owned, will the user accept this software being loaded on his or her device? Is there a policy in place to require acceptance, and how will it be enforced?
- **Acceptable use policies and adherence** Acceptable use policies (AUP) are designed to list the things that are not allowed on company devices or traffic that is not allowed to traverse the company infrastructure. This generally includes things like pornography, gaming, and stock trading. However, can you force a user to not conduct these activities on a device they own?
- **Onboard camera/video** Many devices now have embedded cameras and video recording devices. Within high-security situations, these are often unacceptable. Even within lower-security workplaces, you may be uncomfortable with employees having the ability to record activities (think of a meeting discussing HR actions, for example).
- **Onboarding/offboarding** If a BYOD policy is implemented, there will need to be procedures for adding new devices to the infrastructure. However, there should also be procedures for removing devices when employees leave. Just as you should remove user accounts across the enterprise, you should also have a plan to remove company accounts and data from employee-owned devices.
- **Architecture/infrastructure considerations** These concerns have implications for your IT staff and potentially your architecture as well. Can your staff be expected to support a wide variety of devices? What software solutions will you implement on devices, and are they compatible with multiple mobile OSs? Will you need more or newer infrastructure to support the load?

- **Device loss or theft** If a device used in a BYOD scenario is lost or stolen, who is it reported to in addition to the corporate security office? The police? The vendor's or user's insurance company? And who pays the replacement cost for the device? Some personal insurance policies and device warranties do not cover a personal device that is also used for work purposes. In addition, in the interests of protecting corporate data, can the device be remotely wiped? If the user has not backed up his or her personal data, it will be wiped as well. Is this acceptable to the user?

Legal

- **Privacy issues** Employees may have concerns that their private data is not so private when their devices are connected to the company network. What will be the policies controlling access to this data, and what are the procedures in place for dealing with situations when private data is compromised?
- **Data protection** As discussed previously, the device may be employee owned, but the company data should belong to the company, no matter where it resides. However, this issue needs to be intricately examined by the legal staff and codified clearly in a manner that strengthens the company's position in the event of a lawsuit or other legal action.
- **Forensic examinations** Forensic analysis is often relied upon to uncover unapproved or illegal behaviors, even those that occurred some time ago and have been (mostly) erased. Much like more traditional computing systems, mobile devices can be a treasure trove of information regarding user activities, particularly for user movement (GPS) and contacts (text and e-mail messages); however, the tricky part can be distinguishing employee data from company data. Further, forensic analysis can uncover activities that, while unapproved on company time, are legal and legitimate during personal hours. Again, policies should be in place considering these situations and how they will be handled.

Corporate-Owned Personally Enabled

An alternative for organizations that are wary of allowing users to bring their own devices is the *COPE* model, or *corporate-owned personally enabled*. This means that the company purchases the device but allows the user to use it both as a personal device and a corporate device. This loosens the restrictions somewhat on what can be installed and what content can be resident on a device but gives to the company greater standardization and more control than the BYOD model.

Choose Your Own Device

With the *choose your own device (CYOD)* deployment model, the organization has a list of approved devices that it will supply a user, and the user chooses the one that is best for his or her needs. Although this model does allow some flexibility for the user, the company benefits from much more standardization and control than with the BYOD model.

Corporate-Owned

As the name indicates, with the *corporate-owned* model, the company chooses the model and supplies it to the user, with no ability to customize. Although this might not be the most flexible for the user, it does provide the company with the highest levels of control. Generally, users must sign a policy on the acceptable use of this technology, which can be then controlled more tightly through the MDM. It is important to also consider the offboarding of these devices, as you don't want them going home with a former employee.

Virtual Desktop Infrastructure

Finally, one solution you should also be aware of is *virtual desktop infrastructure (VDI)*, which allows legacy applications to be run on mobile devices, like how a virtual machine runs on a more traditional workstation. Certainly this does present some positive security considerations, but device capabilities, bandwidth, and general speed and ease of use must be considered to ensure that a user gets a workable experience connecting to virtual devices via mobile devices.

REVIEW

Objective 3.5: Given a scenario, implement secure mobile solutions Mobile devices present both opportunities and challenges to organizations. Strong policies should be implemented that consider measures such as full device encryption, screen locks and device lockout, use of cameras and video, and remote wiping. Understand how MDM can implement those policies. Understand the differences between the various deployment models. If your company chooses to allow personal devices to connect to the corporate network, understand that there are issues with data and support ownership, patch and antivirus management, and acceptable use within the network. Also, be aware that there are many legal and privacy concerns that are inherent with personal and company data residing on employee-owned devices.

3.5 QUESTIONS

1. On a mobile device, __________ allow(s) more performance-intensive applications to execute within their own segment to improve performance.
   A. Storage segmentation
   B. VDI
   C. Remote access controls
   D. MDM

2. You are creating a standard security baseline for all users who use company mobile phones. Which of the following is the most effective security measure to protect against unauthorized access to the mobile device?
   - **A.** Enforce the use of a screen lock password.
   - **B.** Enable the GPS chip.
   - **C.** Install personal firewall software.
   - **D.** Automatically perform a daily remote wipe.
3. __________ is a term that is similar to jailbreaking but is Android specific.
   - **A.** Segmentation
   - **B.** Virtualization
   - **C.** Rooting
   - **D.** Wiping
4. Apple's Face ID is an example of using what?
   - **A.** VDI
   - **B.** Biometrics
   - **C.** Containerization
   - **D.** Segmentation

3.5 ANSWERS

1. **A** Storage segmentation allows more performance-intensive applications to be executed in a segment that increases the performance of those applications. Because mobile devices are somewhat less powerful than desktop or laptop computing systems, this can improve performance noticeably.
2. **A** To prevent unauthorized access to the device in the event it is lost or stolen, you can enable a screen lock password. The user will not be able to access the device until he enters the password.
3. **C** Rooting is a term that is similar to jailbreaking but is Android specific.
4. **B** Apple's Face ID is an example of using biometrics and is commonly used for authentication into newer Apple iPhones and iPads.

Objective 3.6 Given a scenario, apply cybersecurity solutions to the cloud

Earlier objectives have briefly touched on emerging attacks within the cloud environment; this objective covers the implementation of the controls and associated tools to mitigate those attacks.

Cloud Security

Ah, the cloud! We'll just put all of our data in the hands of a trusted cloud service provider, check in occasionally to be sure that our account is paid up, and we'll be safe and secure! Right? Well…perhaps not. Just as there are many different options for on-premises networks, there are many different options for cloud infrastructures, and even more considerations for how to secure them. The following sections discuss the cloud cybersecurity solutions that you need to consider to optimize your organization's cloud experience.

Cloud Security Controls

When considering the variety of cloud security controls, a good starting point is to define what constitutes "cloud computing." The U.S. National Institutes of Standards and Technology (NIST) Special Publication 800-145 provides a good working definition: "Cloud computing is a model for enabling ubiquitous, convenient, on-demand network access to a shared pool of configurable computing resources (e.g., networks, servers, storage, applications, and services) that can be rapidly provisioned and released with minimal management effort or service provider interaction." Meeting these ends securely takes additional time and careful consideration to select the controls that need to be put into place to achieve a balance of efficiency, usability, and security.

High Availability Across Zones

High availability across zones describes a key cloud feature that limits the ability for a single incident, say a natural disaster, to spill over into the surrounding zones and the associated data. Microsoft, with their Azure platform, for example, describes the "blast radius" of a failure that can impact applications and data, with high availability across zones helping to protect the organization by limiting outages and other incidents to one zone. Many cloud service providers (CSPs) tout their high availability as being in the 99.999 percent (known as the "five nines") range. To maintain this level of availability, if one region has an event, such as a flood, tornado, or hurricane, that event will then be limited to that zone and resources shifted to the other zones, allowing business operations to continue.

Resource Policies

As discussed in Objective 5.3 of Domain 5 with regard to written policies such as onboarding and offboarding, organizational policies attempt to control an organization's resources. This is particularly critical with cloud resources, as they are often dynamically allocated to ebb and flow with the organization's needs, as discussed later in this objective, and can cost the organization a significant amount of money if not managed properly. *Cloud resource policies* help to control these unforeseen costs by defining and enforcing limits on how cloud resources are used across the organization as a whole, across specific projects, and by user.

Secrets Management

Within an on-premises infrastructure, there are secrets to manage, such as the keys used to provide PKI services across the organization. Again, cloud computing has its own requirements for management of these secrets, but with its own nuance. For example, many cloud service providers will allow you to choose between encryption keys that are provided and managed by the CSP, encryption keys that are supplied by the CSP and managed by your organization, or encryption keys that are both supplied and managed by your organization. Companies like Google, for example, allow you to conduct secrets management across all of your public and private clouds and revoke access as needed to any and all of the respective parts. Google's Cloud Identity and Access Management (IAM) allows you to share access to encryption keys, secrets, and other security tools via a single pane of control.

Integration and Auditing

It is important that teams both internal and external to an organization be able to integrate, not only with each other, but also with third parties, such as a CSP, who are playing critical supporting roles to conduct daily business. While this integration is critical within a traditional infrastructure, it is also key within the cloud environment, as one wrong configuration—sometimes facilitated by a cloud service provider managing your assets—can open the organizational data assets to a variety of attacks. To this end, it is important to have clear and stringent auditing, especially if you are entrusting your cloud resources to a third-party company. Cloud audit logs help your organization maintain the same level of transparency as it would have with an on-premises instance, which will help you not only maintain your security requirements but also keep third parties in check based on their own service level agreements (you *do* have those defined, right?). Different CSPs have different pricing for audit logs and different default retention periods. Therefore, it is important that, before you choose a CSP, you understand what auditing options it has available, cross reference them against your organizational requirements defined within your security policy, and calculate how much that will cost you in the end.

Storage

Before you choose a cloud services provider, it is critical to understand what assets you'll be storing in the cloud, what groups will need access to those assets, and what their permissions will need to be to get their jobs done.

Permissions generally come in two types of access, which can be broadly defined as follows (terms vary between providers):

- **Uniform access** Allows you to manage permissions to all objects within a bucket or a container
- **Fine-grained access** Allows you to have much more stringent controls per object within a bucket or container

As with any type of access control, getting down into the nitty-gritty, fine-grained access controls will end up being much more time consuming to configure and maintain, and likely will generate many more logs, so it's best not to go crazy with these settings, lest you offset the efficiencies that you've saved by moving to the cloud with the extra time required to manage the permissions. Again, make sure that these permission decisions line up with your organization's security policy, no matter whether it's in the cloud or on premises.

Many cloud service providers automatically encrypt your data within the server, often at no additional charge; however, it is important to review your security requirements—based on the needs of your organization (e.g., regulatory requirements), data sensitivity levels (e.g., PII, HIPAA), and the organizational security policy—to determine if additional encryption is needed. We talked about secrets management earlier and how encryption keys can be stored and managed by the CSP or the customer, but also bear in mind that there is a client-side encryption need, even if you are working predominantly within the cloud. Don't forget that any data stored on the desktop, laptop, or other device is not necessarily encrypted and as safe as the data that has been encrypted within the cloud. As discussed in Objective 2.1 of Domain 2, data at rest, data in transit, and data in processing must all be considered and secured to meet defense-in-depth requirements.

Replication allows cloud storage to be replicated, or essentially copied, from one zone to another. Replication builds on the concept of hot sites (discussed in Domain 2, Objective 2.1) by allowing another availability zone to be essentially a hot site—an exact replica—of your production or primary site, again supporting high availability requirements. A factor to bear in mind, however, is that replication is not a traditional backup: replication is essentially a one-for-one copy of the data, and if bad data is replicated, it is still bad data, without the ability to roll back natively from the replication. Because there is little to no rollback feature with replication directly, it is a good idea to still have more traditional backup mechanisms (tested and known good), and those in turn can be replicated as well, to meet defense-in-depth properties.

Network

Virtual networks give an organization a highly secure environment operating in the same way that a traditional data center would, with public and private subnets, access control policies, virtual machines, and associated hosted applications. Within a virtual network, the network appliances are, as the name suggests, virtual. However, you can still have all of your favorite tools—load balancers, firewalls, and so on. Virtual networks also allow you to extend your existing data center into the cloud, much as you would extend a traditional LAN across regions as a WLAN. You can even tap and monitor network traffic within this virtual network, much as within traditional networks (as discussed in Objective 3.3, earlier in this domain), to incorporate network monitoring through log collection, aggregation, and analysis to protect your cloud assets.

A *virtual private cloud (VPC)* allows the option of having both a public subnet and a private subnet. This is a great option if you want to run a public-facing web application but still maintain a private backend with servers that aren't publicly accessible. In this scenario, the *public subnet* sends its outbound traffic directly to the Internet, and the *private subnet* accesses the Internet by using a network address translation (NAT) gateway residing within the public subnet. This helps provide security to the backend, because the database servers can connect to the Internet using the NAT gateway, but the Internet, in turn, cannot connect back to the database servers.

Network segmentation is just a great idea, no matter whether the network is on premises or in the cloud. Traditional network segmentation uses firewalls to segment different trust zones, often between the public Internet, a screened subnet, and different classifications of data or access requirements within the network. Network segmentation is very similar within the cloud, though many cloud infrastructures use software-defined networking (SDN) in conjunction with virtual firewalls to provide this segmentation. The basics remain the same, however: you should identify the most critical systems and data repositories within your virtual network, make sure those are segmented from less-critical systems and data repositories, and then ensure those are secured from more public-facing segments.

API inspection and integration allows a cloud security provider to assess and improve the security of a consumer's applications in much the same way that code review assesses and improves the security of traditional applications. Amazon Web Services, for example, offers the Amazon Inspector tool that "automatically assesses applications for exposure, vulnerabilities, and deviations from best practices," while Microsoft Cloud App Security can assess the following (see https://docs.microsoft.com/en-us/cloud-app-security/enable-instant-visibility-protection-and-governance-actions-for-your-apps):

- **Account information** Visibility into users, accounts, profile information, status (suspended, active, disabled) groups, and privileges
- **Audit trail** Visibility into user activities, admin activities, sign-in activities
- **Data scan** Scanning of unstructured data using two processes—periodically (every 12 hours) and a real-time scan (triggered each time a change is detected)
- **App permissions** Visibility into issued tokens and their permissions
- **Account governance** Ability to suspend users, revoke passwords, etc.
- **Data governance** Ability to quarantine files, including files in trash, and overwrite files
- **App permission governance** Ability to remove tokens

Compute

Security groups can be used to filter network traffic and confirm resource usage within a virtual network. Very similar to traditional network security rules that deny or allow traffic between resources, filtering by security group can be done within the cloud as well.

For example, Microsoft Azure allows the following attributes to promote filtering of network traffic (see https://github.com/MicrosoftDocs/azure-docs/commit/ee0b4ac3fc0885cf410d-8c805a392e0e0de68dc6):

Property	Explanation
Name	A unique name within the network security group.
Priority	A number between 100 and 4096. Rules are processed in priority order, with lower numbers processed before higher numbers, because lower numbers have higher priority. Once traffic matches a rule, processing stops. As a result, any rules that exist with lower priorities (higher numbers) that have the same attributes as rules with higher priorities are not processed.
Source or destination	Any, or an individual IP address, classless inter-domain routing (CIDR) block (10.0.0.0/24, for example), service tag, or application security group. If you specify an address for an Azure resource, specify the private IP address assigned to the resource. Network security groups are processed after Azure translates a public IP address to a private IP address for inbound traffic, and before Azure translates a private IP address to a public IP address for outbound traffic. Specifying a range, a service tag, or application security group enables you to create fewer security rules. The ability to specify multiple individual IP addresses and ranges (you cannot specify multiple service tags or application groups) in a rule is referred to as augmented security rules. Augmented security rules can only be created in network security groups created through the Resource Manager deployment model. You cannot specify multiple IP addresses and IP address ranges in network security groups created through the classic deployment model.
Protocol	TCP, UDP, ICMP, or Any.
Direction	Whether the rule applies to inbound or outbound traffic.
Port range	You can specify an individual or range of ports. For example, you could specify 80 or 10000–10005. Specifying ranges enables you to create fewer security rules. Augmented security rules can only be created in network security groups created through the Resource Manager deployment model. You cannot specify multiple ports or port ranges in the same security rule in network security groups created through the classic deployment model.
Action	Allow or deny.

Within this particular tool, security groups are evaluated by source, source port, destination, destination port, and protocol, and then it is determined whether to deny or allow the traffic.

Dynamic resource allocation is one of the most exciting properties of cloud computing. Resources can be dynamically allocated within the cloud environment to increase the number of resources allowed in crunch times, and then can be lowered back when operations return to normal. This provides the attribute of on-demand scalability, a characteristic of cloud computing as defined by NIST SP 800-145. However, the cloud resource policy, introduced earlier, is a factor to consider in the context of dynamic resource allocation. Without a stringent resource policy that considers the organizational needs, the projects within the organization, and how resources are allocated by the respective cloud service provider, dynamic resource allocation can mean hefty fees associated with an unexpected increase in allocated resources. It is important for cloud-dependent organizations to monitor and provide metrics on their cloud storage and computing usage and the costs associated, and be on the lookout for any ways to balance requirements, efficiencies, and cost savings.

A *virtual private cloud (VPC) endpoint* allows you to connect a VPC privately to supported services without requiring a NAT device, a virtual private network (VPN), or an Internet gateway. In this scenario, instances in your VPC would not require public IP addresses to communicate with resources in the service. Again, using the example of Amazon Web Services, when a VPC endpoint is connected to a supported AWS service, traffic does not leave the Amazon network, leading to more efficiency and more security. The VPC endpoint is a virtual device, and there are two types: an interface endpoint and a gateway endpoint. Different services require different types of endpoints. As defined by Amazon (https://docs.aws.amazon.com/vpc/latest/userguide/vpc-endpoints.html), an *interface endpoint* is "an elastic network interface with a private IP address from the IP address range of your subnet that serves as an entry point for traffic destined to a supported service," whereas a *gateway endpoint* is "a gateway that you specify as a target for a route in your route table for traffic destined to a supported AWS service."

Container security is essentially, as the name suggests, the security of containers, a popular cloud application packaging mechanism. The security of containers must include not only the containers themselves but also the applications that are relying on them and the infrastructure supporting them. Containers within a cloud environment are very popular because they can hold the entire structure of an application, and its supporting dependencies, and be deployed across various types of target environments in a very streamlined manner. There are a number of tools, such as Cloud Foundry, that allow for security checks of containerized applications as they are developed and deployed.

Solutions

Now that you are familiar with the different security controls that you can implement within a cloud environment, this section discusses some solutions that you can use to implement those controls.

CASB

As discussed in Objective 2.1 of Domain 2, a *cloud access security broker (CASB)* acts as an intermediary between the user of the cloud service and the cloud provider, enforces the enterprise security policy, and helps ensure that the appropriate levels of visibility and security are met. CASBs are (generally, but not always) on-premises services. Some security policies that might be enforced by a CASB include authorization, authentication, encryption, logging, malware prevention, and so on. CASBs are often used in Software as a Service (SaaS), Platform as a Service (PaaS), and Infrastructure as a Service (IaaS) environments.

Application Security

Application security is a top priority across any infrastructure, including the cloud. Especially if an in-house application is going to be deployed into a cloud (within a container or otherwise), it is important to balance the positive attributes that access to the cloud brings with the need for robust security. This objective previously introduced API inspection and integration across different cloud providers, which is an important part of the application security solution, but even in a cloud that you have limited management of, it is important to assess the compliance and security of not only applications already deployed within that environment but also applications that you intend to deploy within that environment before you deploy them. This is often done through enforcement of service level agreements (SLAs) and other third-party security agreements. Take application security within the cloud environment as seriously as you would on-premises.

Next-Generation Secure Web Gateway

Traditional secure web gateways (SWGs) act inline to screen and either block or allow incoming or outgoing web traffic to and from the network. SWGs are often used to prevent users from accessing unapproved websites and to help guard against malware and other external threats attempting to enter the network. For an SWG to be effective, all end-user web browser clients must be configured to use the gateway as their web proxy. Some SWGs can even serve as data loss prevention (DLP) tools, screening for PII and organizational intellectual property that might otherwise leave the network. *Next-generation SWGs* extend this concept by integrating a traditional SWG to cover a CASB and DLP tools within a single pane of control.

EXAM TIP An SWG is a more complex device than a simple web proxy caching server. Beyond performing the basic tasks of a web proxy, an SWG provides content filtering and application-level security to protect end users from accessing dangerous websites and downloading files that are infected with worms, spyware, or malware and from connecting to servers that host phishing and fraud sites. An SWG also differs from a web application firewall (WAF), which acts as a reverse proxy to the web server by having the client pass through the WAF before it can reach the server.

Firewall Considerations in a Cloud Environment

A firewall is a firewall is a firewall, right? Well, mostly. Cloud firewalls attempt to block attacks targeting cloud assets by forming a virtual barrier around those cloud assets, much like how a traditional firewall forms a barrier around on-premises assets. One option is a Firewall as a Service (FWaaS), which runs in the cloud and is managed, updated, and maintained by a third party. The cost of such a service should be weighed against the cost of an organizationally managed cloud-based firewall, or even a so-called next-generation firewall that can protect cloud services as a resident solution.

Reference to the Open Systems Interconnection (OSI) model is helpful for understanding how next-generation firewalls work. They generally operate at both Layer 3 and Layer 7 of the

OSI model. Whereas Layer 3 of the OSI model evaluates the traffic by IP address, protocol, or port, Layer 7 can be much more granular and evaluate information based on the content that's being accessed, the accessing user, and even the application that's being used to access the resource. This provides the next level of granularity available to both on-premises and cloud resources.

Segmentation within the cloud is equally as important as on-premises segmentation. Cloud firewalls can be used to create this segmentation by dividing a cloud network into subnets—as discussed previously—that contain their respective components and potentially interact publicly, privately, or both. As with its on-premises counterpart, this segmentation can help contain breaches, improve compliance, and enforce access control rules within departments, across systems, accounting for data requirements and other security zone–related issues.

Cloud Native Controls vs. Third-Party Solutions

Some of the cloud security controls previously introduced are *cloud native controls*, meaning that they are inherently integrated within the services offered by the cloud service provider (such as the solutions from Amazon, Google, and Microsoft sprinkled throughout this objective). Cloud native controls are important to consider when choosing a CSP. Which CSP provides the most bang for the buck? Maybe you prefer a particular CSP for its containerization, or its application security approach? Cost, of course, is another consideration when developing your approach.

Third-party cloud security solutions have been developed by esteemed Internet security companies such as McAfee, Symantec, and Forcepoint to integrate with existing, more traditional, on-premises solutions. These third-party tools often promise to provide a more cohesive, seamless experience that allows an organization to manage both its on-premises infrastructure and cloud infrastructure in one interface. Again, cost is a factor, but so is the efficiency that the cloud purports to provide. There is no one right solution; compare the capability of your current third-party tools to protect cloud services (and your team's skill level using them) to the capability of the native controls the cloud provider offers. A mix of both could do the trick.

REVIEW

Objective 3.6: Given a scenario, apply cybersecurity solutions to the cloud The cloud presents both opportunities and challenges to organizations, as many emerging capabilities do. One opportunity of cloud computing is to ensure high availability of service for your organization by contracting with CSPs that offer high availability across zones. Strong resource policies should be implemented and enforced. Understand how secrets management and auditing are approached within a cloud environment. Solutions for securing the cloud include CASB, next-generation secure web gateways, and firewalls. Finally, a determination must be made to use either cloud native controls or third-party solutions, or some mixture thereof.

3.6 QUESTIONS

1. A VPC __________ allows you to privately connect a VPC to supported services without requiring a NAT device, a VPN, or an Internet gateway.
   A. endpoint
   B. encryptor
   C. firewall
   D. zone
2. Which of the following acts inline to screen and either block or allow incoming or outgoing web traffic to and from a virtual network?
   A. CASB
   B. API inspection tool
   C. Next-generation SWG
   D. Container security tool
3. Cloud storage permissions can be defined as which of the following types? (Choose two.)
   A. Uniform
   B. Mandatory
   C. Fine-grained
   D. Discretionary

3.6 ANSWERS

1. **A** A virtual private cloud (VPC) endpoint allows you to privately connect a VPC to supported services without requiring a network address translation (NAT) device, a virtual private network (VPN), or an Internet gateway.
2. **C** A next-generation secure web gateway (SWG) acts inline to screen and either block or allow incoming or outgoing web traffic to and from a virtual network.
3. **A C** Cloud storage permissions can be defined within two broad types: uniform and fine-grained.

Objective 3.7 Given a scenario, implement identity and account management controls

Two simple and often overlooked aspects of security are access control and authentication (authentication controls are discussed in far more depth in the next objective, 3.8). In many business environments, access involves a single login to a computer or a network of computer systems that provides the user access to all resources on the network. This access includes rights to personal and shared folders on a network server, company intranets, printers, and other network resources and devices. These same resources can be quickly exploited by unauthorized users if the access control and subsequent authentication procedures aren't set up properly.

Identity and Account Management

An important component of account management is *access control*, which refers to permissions applied to resources that determine which users can access those resources. Essentially, access control ensures that users who are authorized to access certain resources can access them, while users who are not authorized to access those same resources cannot access them. To this end, logical access controls are technical components that control user access to resources. These access controls are typically an integral part of an operating system, network security device, or software application to provide user account, password, and access privileges management. By using a strong user account policy, you can greatly diminish the ability of a hacker to break into a user's account. *Account management*, then, is the application and management of access controls, based on a user's verified identity, to protect organizational assets.

Identity

Identity can be defined as the condition of being a specific person or, in the case of service accounts (accounts that a specific application or service uses to interact with the system), a specific thing. *Identification* means presenting credentials that assert that you are uniquely an individual or entity. An *entity* may be an individual or another host on the network. An entity could also be a process or service running on a host; since many of these services require different access than others, they must be uniquely identified as well. Access control encompasses all the techniques, policies, and programs designed to ensure that only those identities with a verified need and clearance level for a system or data in question are able to access it.

Authentication goes hand in hand with access control by verifying the identities of users to be sure they are exactly who they claim to be. After a user has been authenticated, the resources for which the user has appropriate permissions become accessible. Authentication is a step that comes after a person or entity has presented their identity to the system. The following sections discuss the various ways identities are presented for authentication.

Identity Provider

An *identity provider (IdP)* creates, maintains, and manages identity information for an organization. When users log in to a new organizational service, an IdP often provides a seamless experience of gathering the credentials and passing them on to determine the users' access level. Identity providers often work within a framework such as the Security Assertion Markup Language (SAML, described in Objective 3.8) to allow the transfer of information about an individual—specifically, who they are (authentication) and what they have access rights to (authorization)—between the identity and service providers. This is just an example of how an IdP works to capture and process identity information securely.

Attributes

Attributes apply to subjects and objects and allow or disallow access to objects based on their attributes. This is known as *attribute-based access control (ABAC)*. For instance, if Susie works in human resources, she would have attributes associated with her as a subject (Susie Brown, HR Specialist, HR Department). An object might be, for example, the HR database, with attributes covering its personally identifiable information (PII) data on prospective, current, and former employees. ABAC enables the creation of rules allowing certain subjects (for example, HR Generalists, Specialists, and Managers) to view, edit, or delete PII from the HR database, while others can only update non-PII data.

Certificates

Objective 3.9 will discuss Public Key Infrastructure (PKI) in much more depth, but as a short primer, a *digital certificate* is an electronic credential required by PKI systems that can securely identify an individual, as well as create an association between the individual's authenticated identity and public keys. A trusted party, called a certificate authority (CA), is used to sign and issue certificates. The CA is responsible for verifying the identity of a key owner and binding the owner to a public key. This enables users who have never met to exchange encrypted communications because the authentication is performed by the CA.

Tokens

To provide additional access control and authentication protection, many organizations utilize a system requiring two forms of authentication: in addition to an account name and password, the user requires a hardware or software *token*, such as a special Universal Serial Bus (USB) key, that must be connected to her computer before she is allowed access. Certain types of physical tokens, such as RSA SecurID, provide a logical token number that is generated in conjunction with the access control server and must be entered, along with a username and password, before access is granted.

Tokens provide an extra layer of security, because even if an unauthorized user has access to a physical token (if it was stolen from the user, for example), he still requires a username and password to access the system. Similarly, if the unauthorized user knows a username and password he can use, he still needs the physical token to complete the authentication and access control process.

SSH Keys

As discussed in Objective 3.1 earlier in this domain, Secure Shell (SHH) is a mechanism to enable a user to log in to a remote machine and execute commands as if they were on the console of that system. An *SSH key* can be used within a managed PKI to identify a user and grant access to an asset. A public and private key pair is generated, with the public key installed on the asset that will be requiring access and the private key given to the user that will require access. SSH keys can also be used in an unmanaged infrastructure; typically, all host machines and the user will generate and exchange keys as part of the SSH communications session, if they have not already done so previously.

Smart Cards

As discussed in Objective 2.7 of Domain 2, more advanced personnel-access control techniques include the use of personal identification verification (PIV) cards. The ID card provides photo identification that can immediately identify the wearer as an authorized user. ID cards should be worn where they can always be seen by other employees. The card should identify the person and his job function. By listing job function, the ID card can be used to quickly determine that person's access clearance into a certain part of the facility.

Building on the PIV is the *smart card,* as discussed in Objective 2.4 of Domain 2. To recap, each employee receives a card with a magnetic strip or computer chip that contains her access information. These cards are swiped in magnetic card readers that are stationed outside important access points, such as doors and elevators. If the card uses a chip, the card is inserted into a card reader. The information on the card is then compared with the security access of the area the person is about to enter. If she doesn't have access to that area, the door won't open. The card can also be used as a requirement to log in to sensitive networks and computers. Using a card reader, the computer will not allow you to log in until you have inserted your smart card to verify your identity and access level.

Account Types

Access control methods determine how users interact with resources and computer systems, and even the most basic methods begin by determining the different types of users and their required level of access. Access controls must be enforced on a network to ensure that unauthorized users cannot access its resources or the network and computer system infrastructure and that users receive the minimum access necessary to do their business. The following sections discuss different types of accounts.

User Account

Your first task is to define who the *users* are and to what resources they need access. A "user" in this sense doesn't always mean a specific person. A computer might act as a user when it tries to connect to the resource of another computer system. A resource can be anything from a simple text file on a file server, to a network laser printer, to an Internet proxy server. A user of a resource might also be a computer account used by a system to back up other computer systems' resources and data to a tape drive. This backup user account must also have its access control defined properly so that it can securely perform its job function.

Users who perform the same job functions will most likely need access to the same resources. For example, financial analysts might need access to the same data directory on a specific file server. By grouping these users into one entity, you can assign the resulting group access to the data without needing to perform this configuration for each user.

Users who belong to the same department in an organization will probably need access to the same data and resources. All employees within a department aren't always working in the same physical location. Because of the virtual nature of many large corporate networks, a sales employee in the United States might need access to the same sales database used by a sales employee in Japan. All users from the sales department can be assigned to the same group: Sales. The network administrator needs to configure access to the sales database only once for the entire Sales group, without having to assign access for each individual salesperson.

Shared and Generic Accounts/Credentials

Shared accounts are often used by groups, such as those at a departmental level, to log in to specific applications or data assets. This is a bad idea for many reasons, one of which is the inability to log which specific user is tied to each access. For example, if you have a group account for HR that shows an improper access to sensitive data, because it is a group account, determining which actual user was the perpetrator is very difficult.

Generic accounts are often resident on a system or application when it is set up; these should be disabled or removed, and at the very least their default passwords changed to something much stronger and more complex. It is very easy to search the Internet for generic credentials for different hardware and software, so leaving them present has the almost immediate effect of an attacker having the proverbial keys to the kingdom.

Service accounts are accounts that specific applications or services use to interact with the system. For example, if you have an FTP server that interacts with an FTP service, you might use a service account with limited permissions to allow that service to access the system. This enables you to apply very tight security controls to the service account, rather than using a general user account to perform the activity (a poor security practice). Finally, policies that require users who have access to so-called generic accounts, such as "root," to only execute single processes using their elevated privileges will mitigate some of the risk of having these types of accounts.

Guest Accounts

Guest accounts are a good idea if you need to allow someone access to your system or network for a limited amount of time but do not want to give them a full user account (or your user account information—a very bad idea). Guest accounts generally allow limited access to specific resources that the guest needs, such as access to networked printers or intranet access for filling out timesheets. When the guest feature is not being used, it's a good idea to turn it off because it can provide a point of unauthorized entry into a system. These accounts should only have the bare minimum access to organizational assets, if they have access to them at all, and they should be audited regularly to ensure that they don't stick around after the guests have left the premises.

Account Policies

As an administrator, you must carefully consider system and network security when creating account policies. Basic security practices such as login IDs and passwords must be augmented with advanced logical access control techniques, such as the use of long, nondictionary, alphanumeric passwords; password rotation and expiration; and password aging. You must maintain the protection of personal and shared data resources on network file servers by using directory and file access control permissions on a per-user or per-group basis. In the following sections, we will discuss in more detail some of the more important policies to implement to protect an organization.

Password Complexity

The minimum length for a password can be enforced by the network administrator. This prevents users from using easy-to-guess passwords of only a few characters in length. To enforce *password complexity*, the password should be at least 8 characters, with 10 to 12 being preferable for a standard user account (15 for an administrator/root account), and contain a mix of uppercase and lowercase letters, numbers, and special characters. Historically best practices have required changing passwords roughly every 90 days at a minimum; many modern password best-practice documents are now suggesting that it is better to not change passwords unless breached in order to support the use of truly strong, complex passwords that can then be more readily remembered.

NOTE A password manager, such as LastPass, can create complex passwords on the fly, making it much easier for a user to use distinct, complex passwords.

Password History/Password Reuse

Most login and password authentication systems can recall a user's last several passwords (*password history*) and prevent the user from using the same one repeatedly (known as *password reuse*). This technique is often referred to as *password aging*. If this option is available, it should be enabled so that a user's password will always be different. Without the use of password history, often users will change their password and immediately change it back to the previous one that they can easily recall. Once passwords are breached, they are often uploaded to a paste site or the dark web, and attackers will quickly attempt those breached passwords. If password reuse has occurred, it is then quite easy to gain access to your organizational resources.

Network Location/Geolocation

The next objective (3.8) discusses different types of access control schemes, but one account policy to be aware of for this objective is the ability to control access to organizational assets by network location, based on either where the system is physically connected to the network or where the GPS-enabled geolocation places the system or user. For example, a user can have a different level of access, or no access at all, based on where the user is logging in from. In fact, it is very common, especially within organizations processing secure or classified data, to alert based on unclassified systems logging in on classified networks, and vice versa. Very often, a company could be located in a single building, in several buildings, or in different cities and countries. Many companies divide their resources among physical locations; for example, an office in New York might not need access to resources on a file server in Los Angeles. In this way, the security model can be set up by physical location.

Geofencing/Geotagging

As discussed in the context of mobile devices in Objective 3.5 earlier in this domain, *geofencing* allows a GPS-enabled system to provide a different level of access, or no access at all, based on the physical location of that device as provided by the GPS. For example, a user with a GPS-enabled laptop could receive access to the network if GPS indicates that the laptop is within the boundaries of the organization's physical space, or be denied access to those same assets if GPS indicates the laptop is not located within that boundary. Again, as discussed previously in regard to mobile devices, *geotagging* allows for an automatic tag to be applied based on time and location, for example. This also can be used as a mechanism to determine access levels and controls associated with the location and identity of a user.

Time of Day/Time-Based Logins

If your company operates only during certain hours each day, you can set time restrictions for access to the network. After hours, only a select few users might need access. You can set time restrictions on other users' accounts so that they are able to log in only during operating hours. This reduces the risk of unauthorized users trying to use an employee's account during off-hours to break into the system. Think about a group of system administrators; a role can be applied to that group to designate certain conditions. For example, a day-shift system administrator might have permissions to access resources only between 8:00 A.M. and 5:00 P.M.

Access Policies

In Objective 2.7 of Domain 2, we discussed physical access policies and securing access to physical spaces and systems; logical access policies are very similar in concept, only logical in nature. The access policy defines who has access to organizational assets, be it systems or data, what level of access they have, and often (in the case of time-based controls, for example) when and how long they can have access to that asset. Access policies go hand in hand with permissions, discussed in the next section.

Implicit deny refers to the security principle of starting a user out with no access rights and granting permissions to resources as required. This principle states that an access policy must implicitly deny all access to provide a fully secure baseline. Only then can the administrator grant a user access to resources.

The implicit deny principle is more secure than starting out with a policy that grants a user default access to all resources and then denies access permissions to certain resources. It is too easy for administrators to overlook several aspects of resources that require access to be controlled and denied as appropriate.

The implicit deny policy should be applied to all aspects of an organization's security, from physical security and access control, to file and resources permissions on a file server, to network firewall and router rules. By starting out with the strongest security policy and then creating access permissions, administrators know that all access is denied by default and each access control permission granted is an exception to that policy.

Explicit deny, as opposed to implicit deny, means that access to a certain resource is explicitly denied to a user or group of users and that access to that resource cannot be granted to those users even though access could be inherited from another policy. For example, if the Human Resources directory has an explicit deny for all users in the Finance group, access to that directory will be denied across that group even if some or all of the users have gained access through another policy.

Account Permissions

Permissions are technical access controls that are commonly used to determine what an individual user is authorized to do on a system or with specific data. Permissions can apply to entire systems or to data objects such as files and folders. Different operating systems approach permissions in different ways; for example, Linux- and Unix-based systems follow basic permissions for a file or directory, including read, write, and execute, while Microsoft Windows systems provide a wider variety of granular permissions for both folders and files.

Permissions are assigned based upon the access control model in effect on the system (as discussed in more detail in the next objective, 3.8). As discussed in the previous section, access can be explicitly assigned, which ensures that an individual or group will be able to access a data object and perform the tasks they need, or denied explicitly, so that an individual will never get permission to the data object, regardless of other permissions they may have. Permissions should be audited on a periodic basis to ensure that they are still required for an individual to perform their job.

Account Audits

Conducting a recertification of user rights is key; this type of review validates a user's rights to access areas (physical or logical) based on his or her roles and responsibilities. For example, a user account audit could find that a group of users assigned to a different area of an organization no longer needs access to a sensitive file share; revoking this access helps mitigate insider threats. Continuous monitoring of accounts also helps ensure that external threats do not create new accounts for their own nefarious use.

Also, the following events connected with user accounts should be regularly audited:

- **Account creation** Knowing when an account was created can help you identify unauthorized accounts, such as those created by malicious intruders looking to gain persistent access to a system.
- **Assignment of rights, privileges, and permissions** That same intruder might be looking to gain elevated privileges within his new account. Perhaps he is looking to use his privileges to move laterally within your network. Understanding who has privileged access (and why) and reviewing this frequently will help sort out the accounts that need that level of access and those that don't. You should also be sure that an account with privileged access is not shared across multiple users.

- **Disabling accounts** Accounts should be disabled after a certain number of days without use or when a user has gone into a status where she temporarily doesn't need access (such as long-term leave).
- **Deleting accounts** Users who have left the organization for any reason, or accounts that have been disabled due to nonuse, should be deleted within a set period of time to ensure that they can't be used—either by that user, who might be attempting to gain unauthorized access, or by a hacker who is looking to hide his activities using a legitimate account.

Impossible Travel Time/Risky Login

Even in organizations where personnel travel globally frequently, it is extremely unlikely that a user will log in from Brazil and China in the same day, for example. Keeping an eye on where failed login attempts are coming from and associated times can help you spot potential brute-force attacks against your systems. Further, security vendors, such as Microsoft on their Azure Active Directory platform, have implemented analytics to determine risky logins and minimize access to those logins automatically. This determination is made using a number of inputs, including login location, previous user behavior, and activities that have been flagged for known attack behaviors. If the risk is calculated to be high, policy can be enforced to block access completely, allow access, or only allow access with successful multifactor authentication.

Lockout

Just as discussed in Objective 3.5 regarding mobile lockouts, it is best practice to lock out a system or user account after a certain number of failed login attempts. Often this lockout threshold is three or so failed logins, after which point the user account must be subsequently unlocked by an administrator, who should verify the identity of the user and force a password reset. Locking the account help helps prevent brute-force attacks, but just know that it also can create a type of denial of service if an attacker is "walking" a directory of accounts looking to find one that can be accessed.

Disablement

When an employee leaves the company, her account should be immediately disabled. This is especially important for any employee who is suddenly terminated for any reason. By immediately disabling the account, you deny access to further attempts by that user to access her account. Another best practice is to disable accounts you don't recognize as valid. Unauthorized users could have broken into the system and created their own "dummy" accounts to perform malicious activities unnoticed. If the account is valid, the user will contact you because he can't log in. You can then verify whether the user should have access to the system.

EXAM TIP It is often considered better to disable, rather than completely delete, accounts in the case an investigation needs to be conducted after an employee leaves an organization.

REVIEW

Objective 3.7: Given a scenario, implement identity and account management controls Understand the role of an identity provider and how attributes, certificates, tokens, SSH keys, and smart cards are used to establish identity. Some of the most effective account restrictions include limiting logon attempts, using expiry dates, disabling unused accounts, setting time restrictions, and using tokens. Use password policies such as strong passwords, password rotation, and employing password aging to prevent password weaknesses. Permissions to create, delete, and modify the files and directories within your file structures should be applied carefully based on the user's role, especially for accounts such as guest, shared, and service accounts. It is best to start with a clean slate and add access permissions based on the needs of the user or group, giving them only enough access permissions to perform their job function.

3.7 QUESTIONS

1. Rowan works for a company that has had a string of incidents where weak employee passwords have been hacked through brute-force methods and then used by unauthorized users to gain access to the network. Which of the following security policies would be *best* for Rowan to implement to prevent brute-force hacking attempts on employee passwords?
   - **A.** Password rotation
   - **B.** Password length and complexity restrictions
   - **C.** Password expiration
   - **D.** Password lockout
2. Alex has already implemented a password expiration and rotation policy that forces his organization's users to change their password every 60 days. However, he is finding that many users are simply using their same password again. Which of the following can Alex implement to improve security?
   - **A.** Password history
   - **B.** Password complexity
   - **C.** Password lockout
   - **D.** Password expiry
3. An __________ creates, maintains, and manages identity information for an organization.
   - **A.** Identity manager
   - **B.** Identity provider
   - **C.** Identity validator
   - **D.** Identity authority

3.7 ANSWERS

1. **D** Rowan can lock out an account if an incorrect password has been entered too many times. Although password length, complexity, rotation, and expiration are helpful security measures, brute-force attacks can most efficiently be stopped by limiting the number of attempted logons.
2. **A** When password history is enabled, the system can remember a user's former passwords. When the current password expires, the system forces the user to use a new password that is not the same as one of her previous passwords, preventing password reuse.
3. **B** An identity provider (IdP) creates, maintains, and manages identity information for an organization.

Given a scenario, implement authentication and authorization solutions

As previously discussed in Objective 2.4 of Domain 2, to use the resources of a computer system or network or to enter a secure facility, a user must first be authenticated. Identification and authentication verify that the user is who he says he is and has the credentials to access these resources. The most common form of authentication requires a username and password. More secure schemes use multiple factors to strengthen the authentication process and confidence in the identity and credentials of a user.

Methods such as security cards, tokens, and personal identification numbers (PINs), as well as more advanced techniques such as biometric voice and fingerprint recognition, offer additional forms of authentication. When a user logs in to a system, he supplies a set of credentials or login identifiers that must be matched against credentials stored in an authentication database. If any of the information doesn't match, the user is refused entry or access to the system. Authentication and access control methods are only as efficient as the amount of time and planning spent setting up and configuring the system. The more complex the login process, the more difficult it will be for an unauthorized user to gain access to a system.

This objective covers the different management and access control schemes and concepts that you need to know.

Authentication and Authorization

As a refresher of the authentication concepts introduced in Objective 2.4, before a user is allowed access to a facility or resource, the user must pass three primary levels of security:

- **Identification** The user must initially identify herself as a valid user for that network, usually with a login username or account name. *Identification*, also referred to as *identity proofing*, ensures that a user (which could also be an application program or process) is who she claims to be. For example, before performing any type of online banking, a customer must identify who she is and have sufficient physical identification, such as a bank card, password, PIN, and so on, to be able to prove her identity before the process goes any further.
- **Authentication** *Authentication* is the process of validating the user's identification. This means that the user is verified as being the person whose identity she has claimed to be. After presenting identifying credentials, the user must then pass the authentication phase. If the credentials she provided match entries in the global database of login usernames and passwords stored on the network, the user is authenticated and is granted access to the network. To be authenticated properly, the user must provide proof that she should be using the login name by supplying a password, PIN, or token. If the identity and password or PIN match the central database, the user is authenticated.
- **Authorization** When a user tries to access a resource, the system must check to see if that user ID is authorized for that resource and what permissions or privileges the user has when using it. Just because a user has been identified and authenticated to a network doesn't mean she should be able to access all resources. If the system determines that the user may access the resource, the user is authorized and allowed access with the privileges she has been granted.

EXAM TIP It is critical for the exam to understand the differences between identification, authentication, and authorization and how they work together.

The following sections describe how these activities take place.

Authentication Management

Several of the following concepts have been introduced in previous objectives, but they are reiterated here because you are required to understand how to implement them effectively to support authentication management within an organizational infrastructure, another layer of a defense-in-depth approach.

Password Vaults/Key Vaults

Password vaults, otherwise known as *password managers*, help to ensure that strong authentication is used by making it much easier for a user to use strong, random passwords through integration within the operating system (OS) or browser. Password vaults are built into many popular operating systems and web browsers, such as Apple iOS and Google Chrome, and are available as stand-alone applications, such as LastPass. While some password vaults simply store a user's passwords and allow the user to quickly authenticate into applications and websites through the single click of a button, thus not requiring the user to remember her passwords, other password vaults like LastPass take it a step further by incorporating the ability to generate strong passwords automatically, compare all the stored passwords, and provide reports on the strength and reuse of stored passwords. Some solutions even allow you to share passwords securely with other users of that particular password vault software; in the event that you want to share a password with a friend or family member, you don't have to send it via an e-mail or text message or even make a phone call. The best password managers do not actually store the passwords in their own storage, but instead store them on the user's device and make use of hashes, meaning that if the password vault site is breached, your passwords are not also breached. *Key vaults* serve much the same purpose but manage cryptographic keys in such a fashion that keys can be generated, imported, provisioned, and stored in the cloud without applications having direct access to them.

TPM

As a recap of the coverage in Objectives 2.1 and 3.2, a *trusted platform module (TPM)* is a special hardware chip that is typically installed within a computer system or device, such as on the system motherboard of a computer desktop or laptop. A TPM provides authentication by storing security mechanisms such as passwords, certificates, and encryption keys that are specific to that system hardware. The chip itself contains a built-in RSA key that is used for encryption and authentication. In the past, hardware-based passwords on desktops and laptops were typically stored in clear text and, therefore, vulnerable to unauthorized access. With the advent of TPM, any system passwords are now stored and encrypted on the TPM chip. The TPM provides greater security benefits over software-based solutions because it runs in a closed hardware subsystem that mitigates external threats. TPM-based systems are compatible with most popular operating systems.

HSM

Also discussed previously in several objectives, a *hardware security module (HSM)* is a specialized hardware appliance used to provide onboard cryptographic functions and processing. This physical hardware device can be a stand-alone device attached to a network or connected directly to a server as a plug-in card. HSMs are primarily used to host integrated cryptographic functions, such as a Public Key Infrastructure server for encryption, decryption, and secure key generation and management, but they can also be used to provide onboard secure storage of encrypted data. With their processing speed and security, HSMs are often used for banking applications (such as ATMs) that require scalable, performance-based solutions for critical key management and security.

Knowledge-Based Authentication

You'll often see knowledge-based authentication used in conjunction with other forms of authentication, such as username and password, particularly on banking or other sensitive websites and applications. An example of knowledge-based authentication is a website that requires you to answer a challenge question such as "What was your first car's make and model?" Knowledge-based authentication helps to ensure that the person that is attempting to gain access to that particular site is who they say they are, through ensuring that they know critical pieces of information about that person's life. A great reminder of how social media can be exploited is that attackers will often comb social media sites looking to see if users have given bits of personal information within their posts about their daily lives that can be harvested for future use. You'll even sometimes see quizzes being shared online that ask many of these questions to see if an unsuspecting user will answer them and give up the sensitive challenge responses.

Authentication

Authentication solutions protect your networks not only for internal users on your wired LAN but also remote access users who access your network resources over an Internet VPN or wireless network. Protection of the authentication phase of your communications is vital to prevent your users' logins and passwords from being captured. The following sections describe several popular authentication solutions, some of which were introduced previously in the context of wireless authentication in Objective 3.4, earlier in this domain.

Password Authentication Protocol

The *Password Authentication Protocol (PAP)* is the most basic type of authentication that consists of comparing a set of credentials, such as a username and a password, to a central table of authentication data. If the credentials match, the user is granted access. PAP is most often used with dial-up remote access methods.

Although the password tables used by PAP are encrypted, the actual communications between the client and authentication server are not, allowing the username and password to be sent over the network in clear text. This can easily be captured by an unauthorized user monitoring the network. Typically used for dial-up authentication, PAP is also the default authentication protocol within Hypertext Transfer Protocol (HTTP). Because of PAP's weaknesses, CHAP is usually used in place of PAP.

Extensible Authentication Protocol

The *Extensible Authentication Protocol (EAP)* is primarily used in wireless networks, but it can also be used in traditional LANs and remote access methods. The EAP framework provides an extension of the types of authentication protocols that are typically used in PAP and CHAP methods. For example, instead of a simple username and password, additional methods can be used, such as tokens, Kerberos, biometrics, and Transport Layer Security (TLS).

Challenge Handshake Authentication Protocol

The *Challenge-Handshake Authentication Protocol (CHAP)* is much more secure than PAP. Once the communications link is completed, the authenticating server sends a random value to the client. The client sends back the value combined with the username and password credentials, plus a predefined secret, calculated using a one-way hash function. The server compares the response against its own calculation of the expected hash value. If the values match, the client is granted access.

CHAP provides protection against replay attacks, which are used by hackers to capture data and then send it again. To prevent this type of attack, CHAP uses an incrementally changing identifier and a variable challenge value, and the authentication can be repeated any time while the connection is open using the new identifiers.

IEEE 802.1X

The *IEEE 802.1X* standard is a port-based authentication mechanism for devices connecting to wired or wireless networks. Its goal is to provide a centralized authentication framework for LANs and wireless LANs (WLANs) that includes wired clients, wireless clients, and the wireless access points (WAPs) that connect them to the network.

For wired LANs, 802.1X is implemented on network devices such as switches to provide access control by authenticating connecting clients based on the user or system identity. You can then allow or block network connectivity and apply network access policies based on this authentication.

In WLANs, a client automatically connects to the closest WAP and then authenticates to the network by directly communicating with the network's native authentication. Unfortunately, unless the LAN is protected with a strong encryption method, the client can perform certain network functions without authentication, such as ping requests.

Using 802.1X, when a client connects to a WAP, the wireless port is set to an unauthorized state so it can't perform any network functions. The WAP then asks the client for authentication credentials. Once received, this data is forwarded to an authentication server running a service such as RADIUS (discussed in the next section). If the client is accepted as an authorized user, then the client port on the WAP is switched to an authorized state and normal communications can commence.

802.1X can be helpful in allowing WLANs to scale upward in size easily while maintaining a centralized authentication system. This authentication, however, should be coupled with a strong communications encryption mechanism to provide full security. Note that networks that use 802.1X can authenticate not only devices such as laptops and workstations but also users and can easily be integrated into an authentication or directory service such as Microsoft Active Directory.

Remote Authentication Dial-In User Service

Remote Authentication Dial-In User Service (RADIUS) is the most common Internet standard used for authenticating clients in a client–server environment. When the remote user accesses a network through a remote access device, the user is authenticated by a RADIUS server that compares the user's authentication credentials against those of the server's database. If the credentials match, the user is granted access to the rest of the network. The client's credentials that are sent to the RADIUS server are encrypted to prevent someone from capturing the transmission. RADIUS servers also include accounting and reporting functions that can monitor and log data on each connection, such as packet and protocol types, as well as length of time connected.

Single Sign-On

In early computer systems, when networking wasn't as available as it is today, each computer contained a set of resources the user could access. To access the resources of a computer system, the user typed a specific login and password for that computer. Each specific computer required a separate login and password. This was tedious for computer users and administrators alike because of the frequency with which login accounts and passwords needed to be reset for each computer if a user forgot them.

Nowadays, modern networks provide resources that are spread throughout the computer network and that can be accessed by any user from any location. The user can be onsite on her own computer, or she can be logged in from home or on the road by using dial-up methods or via the Internet. With the vast amount of resources that can be contained on a large computer network, the concept of different logins and passwords for each resource has been eliminated in favor of a *single sign-on (SSO)* to the network; the user must be authenticated only once on the network to access the resources on it. This type of centralized administration is a much more efficient way for a network administrator to control access to the network. User account policy templates can be created and used network-wide to remove the need to configure each user's account settings individually, except for a unique login and password.

An example of single sign-on is a Microsoft Active Directory username and password required for accessing directories, files, and printers on a network, along with Microsoft Exchange mail servers and SQL database servers. Lightweight Directory Access Protocol (LDAP), discussed previously in Domain 2, Objective 2.4, is also a popular authentication protocol incorporated in most directory services and used for single sign-on purposes.

Security Assertion Markup Language

The *Security Assertion Markup Language (SAML)* allows the transfer of information about an individual—specifically, who they are (authentication) and what they have access rights to (authorization)—between identity and service providers. The SAML standard provides three general roles: the principal (typically a user), the identity provider, and the service provider (such as an ISP or an application service provider). The service provider requests information from the identity provider; SAML 2.0 supplies a token containing assertions, or a packet of information about a principal upon receipt. The service provider then decides to allow or deny access to the requested service. If authenticated, the service is provided to the identity (user). Shibboleth, developed as an improvement on SAML 2.0, furthers it to provide federated single sign-on across organizations and to control privacy for users through attribute management.

Terminal Access Controller Access Control System Plus

The Terminal Access Controller Access-Control System (TACACS) is an older type of authentication protocol that's like RADIUS. A remote access user connects to a network and is authenticated by the TACACS server before being allowed access to the network's resources. Three versions of TACACS have been used, with TACACS+ being the current standard:

- **TACACS** The original protocol, which performs both authentication and authorization.
- **XTACACS** Extended TACACS, which builds on TACACS by separating the functions of authentication, authorization, and accounting.
- **TACACS+** A completely different protocol version that is proprietary to Cisco and adds the use of both a username and password for authentication or other authentication methods, such as Kerberos and dynamic passwords, through security tokens. All communications are encrypted.

Unfortunately, the TACACS protocols have several security vulnerabilities, including a weak encryption algorithm. This has decreased its use in favor of the standards-based RADIUS authentication protocol.

OAuth

OAuth, originally specified in IETF RFC 5849 and superseded in IETF RFC 6749, is an authorization framework designed to use secure tokens to allow clients to gain access to resource owners to request authorization to use resources, as well as authorization servers that enable the resource owners to allow or deny the authorization request.

OpenID

OpenID, also known as OpenID Connect, builds on the OAuth 2.0 family of specifications, allowing a client to perform identity verification and receive information about both the end users and their sessions. To quote the official website (https://openid.net/connect/):

> OpenID Connect is an interoperable authentication protocol based on the OAuth 2.0 family of specifications.... It's uniquely easy for developers to integrate, compared to any preceding Identity protocol. OpenID Connect lets developers authenticate their users across websites and apps without having to own and manage password files. For the app builder, it provides a secure, verifiable answer to the question: "What is the identity of the person currently using the browser or native app that is connected to me?"

Kerberos

Kerberos is a network authentication protocol, prominently used in Microsoft Windows Active Directory (AD) implementations. It is an open standard, supported officially as an Internet standard by RFC 4120. The most current version of Kerberos widely in use is version 5.

Kerberos uses a system based on authentication tickets issued to the authenticated user, as well as timestamps. Timestamps help prevent replay attacks because the tickets expire after a short time and must be refreshed, requiring that the user be reauthenticated and the ticket be reissued. Kerberos's timestamps rely heavily on authoritative time sources throughout the network architecture, so many implementations also include a network time server. If clients are outside a certain tolerance for time difference (generally five minutes) between them and the Kerberos server, the users logging in to those clients will not be authenticated.

Kerberos uses several components that you should be familiar with for the exam. First, the Key Distribution Center (KDC) is responsible for authenticating users and issuing session keys and tickets. In AD implementations, the domain controller serves as the KDC. Next are two services, an Authentication Service (AS) and a Ticket-Granting Service (TGS). Although these services are not required to be on the same host, they frequently are on AD domain controllers in a Windows environment (for simplicity and efficiency's sake) and are part of the KDC implementation.

When a user logs in to the system, the AS verifies the user's identity using the credentials stored in AD. The user is then issued a Ticket-Granting Ticket (TGT) by the AS, which can be used to access resources throughout the domain. The TGT expires after a certain amount of time, so it must be periodically reissued. When a user wants to access a resource in the domain, the client presents the TGT to the TGS for authentication, and the TGS generates a session key for the communications session between the user and the resource server. This is known as a *service ticket*, and it's used for the duration of the access to the resource. When a user later needs access to the same resource again, or a different resource, the older ticket is not reused; instead, a new service ticket is generated.

Note that the process just described is specific to Windows AD implementations of Kerberos, but the principles are the same regardless of what operating system and LDAP-based implementation are in use. A network that uses Kerberos as its authentication protocol is called a *Kerberos realm*. Kerberos uses both TCP port 88 and UDP port 88 and uses symmetric key cryptography. Figure 3.8-1 illustrates the Kerberos process in Windows AD.

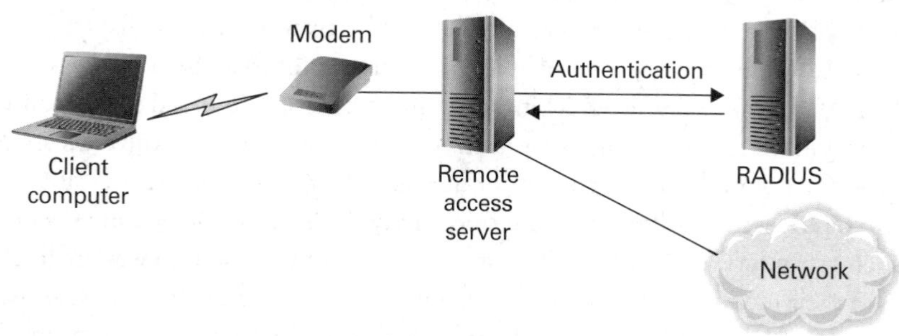

FIGURE 3.8-1 Kerberos implemented within a Windows environment

Access Control Schemes

Access control schemes are policies that define how users access data. Access control schemes also determine the extent or degree to which a user can further allow others access to the data. These policies form a framework based on the security and business goals of the organization. The rules of the framework are enforced through access control technologies. This section covers the main access control types.

Role-Based Access Control

Role-based access control (RBAC), also referred to as *nondiscretionary access control*, is a centrally controlled model that allows access based on the role the user holds within the organization. Instead of access being given to individual users, access control is granted to groups of users who perform a common function. For example, many organizations have special "contractor" roles comprising employees who work on a contract basis and are not full-salaried employees; these workers are given less access to certain resources or parts of the network. In an IT department, for example, a user given the role of backup administrator might have access to controlling backup and restore operations, but he would not have privileges to add users or assign access permissions, which are reserved for the role of system administrator. No matter who is assigned the backup administrator role, the access permissions are the same. Database servers such as SQL servers often use role-based permissions to restrict access to certain portions of the database. Note that role-based access control is often confused with the use of groups in a discretionary access control (DAC) model; they aren't quite the same. The use of roles is mandatory in an RBAC scheme; there aren't any individual access permissions or rights granted. In a DAC scheme, the use of groups (often thought of as roles) is purely for the sake of convenience for the administrator; there are still some individuals who can have their own access permissions.

Rule-Based Access Control

Rule-based access control provides enhanced granularity when specifying access control policies and indicates specifically what can and cannot happen between a user and the resource. This type of access control policy is typically defined by an access control list (ACL), such as TCP Wrappers, which specifies a set of rules that must be followed before access is granted. Unlike the DAC method (discussed in an upcoming section), rule-based access control does not necessarily have to be tied to an authorized identity and could involve access permissions based on network location, content of messages (such as e-mail text or attachments), and other types of content filtering. These rules are typically implemented in network access devices such as routers, firewalls, and content-filtering systems, and they apply to all users, regardless of their identity. Rule-based access control can also use elements such as username or ID, time of day, location, type of access, and so on. For example, user Bob from accounting may only be able to access a certain file between 8 A.M. and noon, but not after that, or is only able to write to one document and only read another one during that same timeframe.

Rule elements are typically very specific and restrictive in a well-implemented rule-based access control model.

Mandatory Access Control

In a *mandatory access control (MAC)* model, the operating system is in control of access to data. Most data owners can assign permissions to their own files and share them however they see fit, but OS access controls override any data owner settings. Users have little freedom to adjust access controls, except for specific data under their control. When defined on the system, users are given certain access rights representing a certain level of trust. The data resources themselves also have security classifications that define the level of trust a user must have to access the data. If a user doesn't have the appropriate access rights to use the data, he is denied access. This type of model is centralized and is often used in high-security environments, such as the military or government offices, where access control is tightly guarded through strict OS security policies. Military classification levels such as Confidential, Secret, and Top Secret are examples of MAC in which specific security access is restricted, depending on the classification of the data, the user's security clearance (or access) level, and the user's need to know.

Discretionary Access Control

Discretionary access control (DAC) enables data creators and owners to specify which users can access certain data. Access to resources is allowed only for authorized users through permissions on the resource. This is the most common model used in Windows and Unix environments in which administrators create a hierarchy of files, directories, and other resources that are accessed based on user privileges and access rights. Resource owners are typically allowed to control who accesses their resources. For example, an individual user can share specific files or directories with users he or she authorizes. This model is a less centralized version of the mandatory access control.

Attribute-Based Access Control

Attribute-based access control (ABAC) is considered the evolution from the previous generations of access control, even though it has been around for several years. ABAC applies attributes to subjects and objects and allows or disallows access to objects based on their attributes. For instance, if Susie works in Human Resources, she would have attributes associated with her as a subject (Susie Brown, HR Specialist, HR Department). An object might be, for example, the HR database, with attributes covering its PII data on prospective, current, and former employees. ABAC enables the creation of rules allowing certain subjects (HR Generalists, Specialists, and Managers) to view, edit, or delete PII from the HR database, while others can only update non-PII data. ABAC provides even more granularity and flexibility than role-based access control because attributes can be updated, and their relationships are modified automatically. New subjects can be added without new rules.

Conditional Access

Conditional access is a more thoughtful approach to securing critical assets that considers who is attempting to access, what asset they're attempting to access, and other conditions to determine another level of authentication that might be required. This access can require such policies as

- Requiring multifactor authentication for administrative users
- Requiring multifactor authentication when behavior is deemed abnormal (e.g., after normal business hours)
- Requiring organization-owned devices to access specific systems (e.g., budget, HR systems)
- Rejecting logins by legacy protocols
- Rejecting logins from locations that are considered risky

Conditional access shouldn't be used as the only access control model, but instead as a way to ensure that the most critical assets are protected at a higher level based on the conditions that are in place in real time.

Privileged Access Management

As discussed in Objective 3.7, your administrative or root accounts can be considered the proverbial keys to the kingdom, meaning that if they are compromised, the effects can be much more damaging than simply having a breach of a standard user account. Therefore, it is important to consider how privileged access, whether it be full access to systems or networks, is monitored and managed to ensure that these accounts are not compromised or, in the worst case scenario, can be recovered if they are compromised. In order to properly manage privileged access, consider which groups have significant access and then set up authentication, preferably multifactor. Once that's done, audit and alert on privileged access requests. You should know who has privileged access and why. One administrator should not have the sole responsibility (meaning a single point of failure) for this monitoring; instead, multiple personnel should have the ability to identify who is gaining access to what assets. This is an important step to identify potentially malicious insiders and to maintain accountability.

Filesystem Permissions

Objective 3.7 discussed account permissions, and filesystem permissions work hand in hand with the account permissions to determine who can have access to what resource. To recap, permissions can apply to entire systems or to data objects such as files and folders (this is the filesystem). Different operating systems approach permissions in different ways; for example, Linux- and Unix-based systems follow basic permissions for a file or directory, including read, write, and execute, while Microsoft Windows systems provide a wider variety of granular permissions for both folders and files.

REVIEW

Objective 3.8: Given a scenario, implement authentication and authorization solutions Understand how authentication management solutions can help your organization allow secure access to assets. Authentication services such as PAP, CHAP, EAP, 802.1X, RADIUS, and so on have their rightful places in authentication management, but their pros and cons should be considered before adopting them for a particular organization. Understand password keys, password vaults, TPM, HSM, and knowledge-based authentication. Recognize the differences in the various access control schemes. In a MAC model, the OS of the network is in control of access to data. DAC allows the data owners to specify what users can access certain data. Privileges can be assigned by user, group, or role in the company. Role-based access control allows access to be based on the role the user holds within an organization. Rule-based access control is based on ACLs and is not necessarily tied to the identity of a user; it provides access rules that are applied to all users in the organization, based on elements such as desired action, location, time of day, role, user ID, and other factors. Attribute-based access control provides more granularity and scalability by assigning attributes to subjects and objects. Finally, understand the concepts of conditional access, privileged access management, and filesystems permissions.

3.8 QUESTIONS

1. SAML implementations have three basic roles: the identity, the identity provider, and the __________.
   A. Internet provider
   B. service provider
   C. authentication provider
   D. authorization provider
2. Your organization has several home users with Internet access who require remote access to your organization's network. Which of the following remote access and authentication technologies would be the most secure?
   A. Dial-up access to a Kerberos server
   B. A VPN authenticated to a RADIUS server
   C. Telnet access to a local password database
   D. Wireless access to an LDAPS server
3. You are creating an access control model that will allow you to assign specific access policies depending on which network a user is on and not necessarily on the actual identity of the specific user. Which privilege management access control model would you use?
   A. Rule-based access control
   B. Discretionary access control
   C. Attribute-based access control
   D. Mandatory access control

3.8 ANSWERS

1. **B** The service provider takes the token passed from the identity provider and either accepts the request and provides services to the user or denies the request and does not.
2. **B** By using a VPN authenticated to a RADIUS server, you ensure that your communications are encrypted and that secure authentication takes place to the RADIUS server.
3. **A** Rule-based access control is defined with an access control list (ACL), which specifies a set of rules that must be followed before access is granted. Rule-based access control does not necessarily have to be tied to an authorized identity and could involve access permissions based on network location, content of messages (such as e-mail text or attachments), and other types of content filtering.

Objective 3.9 Given a scenario, implement public key infrastructure

Traditional cryptography methods based on symmetric key cryptography use the same secret key by both the sender (to encrypt the message) and the receiver (to decrypt the message). Unfortunately, it can be difficult to transmit the secret key securely from one user to another. If an unauthorized user intercepts the key, he can decrypt, read, forge, and modify all messages encrypted using that key. Key management is a challenge for these systems, especially for systems that serve large numbers of users.

Public key cryptography was introduced in 1976 by Whitfield Diffie and Martin Hellman, whose public key protocol was created to solve the key management problem. In public key cryptography, each user receives two keys: the public key and the private key. The private key is kept secret, while the public key can be published for any user to see or use. The problem faced using symmetric keys is solved because no need exists to share a secret key. All transmissions involve only the public keys; no private key is ever transmitted or shared. With public key cryptography, *asymmetric cryptography* is used to exchange symmetric keys. The sender encrypts the message with the receiver's public key. The receiver then decrypts the message with his own private key, as shown in Figure 3.9-1. The security mechanism is safe if the private keys aren't compromised.

Public key cryptography is efficient and secure, and it scales well with a large number of users, making it ideal for all types of critical personal and business communications and transactions. It is at the heart of Public Key Infrastructure, the focus of this objective.

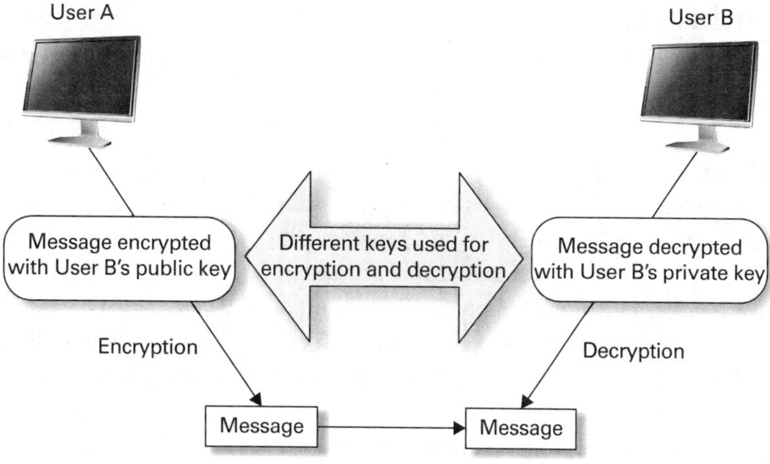

FIGURE 3.9-1 Public key cryptography

Public Key Infrastructure

The *Public Key Infrastructure (PKI)* is a standard infrastructure consisting of a framework of procedures, standards, and protocols, based on public key cryptography. A hybrid of asymmetric and symmetric key algorithms, PKI provides the full range of information assurance objectives for confidentiality, integrity, authentication, and nonrepudiation. The asymmetric keys are used for authentication, and then one or more symmetric keys are generated and exchanged using asymmetric encryption.

Cross-Reference

See Domain 2, Objective 2.8 for more information on the differences between asymmetric and symmetric cryptography.

A message is encrypted with a symmetric algorithm, and that message is then encrypted asymmetrically using the recipient's public key. The entire message (symmetrically encrypted body and asymmetrically encrypted key) is sent to the recipient. The message can also be digitally signed using digital certificates.

EXAM TIP Public key cryptography uses a hybrid of symmetric and asymmetric encryption systems. A message is encrypted using a symmetric algorithm, and that message is then encrypted asymmetrically using the recipient's public key. The entire message (symmetrically encrypted body and asymmetrically encrypted key) is sent to the recipient.

PKI Fundamentals

The following sections discuss the core concepts needed to securely manage a PKI system from start to finish.

Key Management

Encryption key management deals with the generation, distribution, storage, and backup of keys. Securing encryption keys is an extremely important aspect of encryption and cryptography. Once a key is generated, it must be secured to prevent an unauthorized user from discovering the key. Attacks on public key systems are typically focused on the key management system rather than on attempts to break the encryption algorithm itself. No matter how secure or difficult a cryptographic algorithm, the entire process can be compromised by poor key management.

Keys need to be generated and securely sent to the correct user. The user must then store the key in a secure place so that it can't be accessed by another user. The key can be encrypted and stored on a hard drive, an optical disc, a flash device, a USB key, or a trusted platform module (TPM). The keys should also be recoverable if they're lost or damaged, or if passwords to use them are forgotten. Key storage is an important aspect of secure key management, which can be centralized either to a server or a third-party service. Key storage can involve both hardware and software storage methods.

In the early days of encryption key management, cryptographic keys were stored in secure boxes and delivered to users by hand. The keys were given to the systems administrator, who distributed them from a main server or by visiting each workstation. This type of administrative overhead for key management could almost be a job itself, and it obviously didn't scale well in large enterprise networks. In today's networks, key distribution and storage are typically performed automatically through a special key management system, such as a key management server, or through a third-party service such as Verisign or Entrust. Key management can be an extremely time-consuming process for network administrators in a large enterprise network.

Once a key pair has been generated, the private key must be safely stored to protect it from being compromised, lost, or damaged. The type of security used to encrypt and protect the private key should be as strong as the security used to encrypt and protect the actual message or files. A few methods for protecting the private key can be used, including both hardware and software methods.

The most important aspect of hardware key protection is the ability to protect the hardware itself. Many users store their private keys on their computers' hard disks. Their computers might be part of a network, potentially allowing access to anyone on that network. To prevent this sort of access, private keys are usually stored on removable media that can be more easily protected and can be physically carried with the user. This hardware can be typical media, such as a DVD or a USB device. However, these small media devices can be easily lost or stolen, which is why the stored key should always be encrypted. As previously mentioned, you can also use a TPM, which is a special hardware chip that is installed within a computer system or device, such as on the system motherboard of a computer desktop or laptop. This protected, encrypted module can store encryption keys that are specific to that system hardware.

Cross-Reference

Trusted platform modules are discussed in more detail in Objectives 3.2 and 3.8, earlier in this domain.

A private key should never be stored in its plaintext form. If an unauthorized user manages to find the file or steals the device in which the file is located, that user could uncover the private key. The simplest method of protection is to secure the encrypted private key with a password and store it locally on disk or a USB key. The password should be as carefully crafted as your network password so that it can't be guessed easily or discovered through brute-force attack methods.

EXAM TIP A private key should never be stored in plaintext form. It needs to be encrypted and protected with a password.

For enterprise-level networks, the installation of a key management system takes the burden of key storage and protection away from the user and lets the OS or application manage key storage on a centralized server.

An additional method of protection includes the generation of another key pair to be used to encrypt the private key. This key is usually kept with a third party using a type of key escrow service (discussed later within this objective.)

Certificate Authority

A *certificate authority (CA)* is an organization or entity that issues and manages digital certificates and is responsible for authenticating and identifying users who participate in the PKI. This service doesn't necessarily involve a third party; it can be internal to an organization. A CA server can be set up to act as the manager of certificates and the user's public keys.

Third-party CAs are special organizations dedicated to certificate management. Some of the larger companies that offer this service, such as Verisign and Entrust, have their functionality built into popular web browsers to perform certificate services automatically.

EXAM TIP A certificate authority is an organization or entity that issues and manages digital certificates. The CA is responsible for authenticating and identifying users who participate in the PKI.

Intermediate CA

The root certificate and root CA are typically used to issue certificates to *intermediate CAs* (or *subordinate CAs*). These CAs are used in larger organizations to manage the daily workload of issuing the actual user entity certificates. Later in this objective intermediate CAs are discussed further in the context of how online and offline CAs work with intermediate CAs in a certificate chain of trust.

Registration Authority

Some of the actual authentication and identification services for certificates are managed by other organizations called *registration authorities (RAs)*. These organizations offload some of the work from CAs by confirming the identities of users, issuing key pairs, and initiating the certificate process with a CA on behalf of the user. The RA acts as a middleman between the user and the CA and doesn't issue certificates on its own.

Certificate Revocation List

When a certificate is revoked, it's placed on a CA's *certificate revocation list (CRL)*, which includes certificates that have been revoked before their expiration date by the CA. A CRL is used by other users and organizations to identify certificates that are no longer valid.

CRLs can be distributed in two main ways:

- **Pull model** The CRL is downloaded from the CA by those who want to see it to verify a certificate. In this model, the user or organization is responsible for regularly downloading the latest CRL for the most recent list.
- **Push model** In this model, the CA automatically sends the CRL out to verifiers at regular intervals.

These models can also be hierarchical in nature, in which a specific CRL of a CA is pushed to other sites, where other users and organizations can download it. CRLs are maintained in a distributed manner, but various central repositories contain the latest CRLs from many CAs. Websites and companies that deal with large numbers of secure transactions might need their own local version of a CRL that can quickly be compared to the large number of certificates accepted.

To check the status of a certificate, the CRL can be obtained from the specific CA or from a centralized database of CRLs released by a collection of authorities. To help automate this process, certificate status checks have been built into software applications, such as e-mail programs and web browsers, that automatically check the status of a received certificate. Status checks can also be made manually by checking the website of a CA and entering the serial number of a certificate.

Certificate Attributes

Digital certificates typically meet the International Telecommunication Union Telecommunication Standardization Sector (ITU-T) X.509 standard, which dictates how digital certificates are constructed. In addition to the public keys of the user and the digital signature of the issuer, digital certificates also contain other *certificate attributes*, such as the certificate serial number, the algorithm used to create the digital signature of the issuer, identifying information for both the user and the issuer, validity dates of the certificate, the purpose for which the certificate is intended to be used, and the thumbprint of the certificate (a hash of the certificate itself).

Table 3.9-1 shows common attributes associated with X.509 certificates.

TABLE 3.9-1 Common Attributes Associated with X.509 Certificates

Common Attribute	Description
C	The country
CN	The common name (fully qualified domain name)
DC	The domain component
DNQ	The distinguished name qualifier
L	The locality name
MAIL	The e-mail address
O	The organization's name
OU	The organizational unit name
PC	The postal or ZIP code
SERIALNUMBER	The certificate serial number
STREET	The street address of the organization
ST (or SP or S)	The state or province name
T	The title
UID or USERID	The user identifier
UNSTRUCTUREDADDRESS	The IP address
UNSTRUCTUREDNAME	The host name

Online Certificate Status Protocol

The *Online Certificate Status Protocol (OCSP)* was developed as a more resource-efficient alternative to CRLs. In a similar fashion, a client contacts an OCSP responder that refers to a CA. The OCSP responder returns a signed response to the client ("good," "revoked," or "unknown"); that response contains less information than a typical CRL response, hence the resource savings. OCSP also allows a grace period that enables a user with expired certificates to continue accessing resources for a time after their official expiration. A potential concern regarding OCSP is that it can be vulnerable to attacks through replay; a signed, valid "good" response can be captured and sent later in lieu of a valid response. Also, while more resource efficient than a CRL, OCSP does still require that the remote responder be queried for each request, which can slow down the browsing process, particularly for high-volume sites. A CRL can still be preferred over the use of OCSP if a server has issued many certificates to be validated within a single revocation period. It may be more efficient for the organization to download a CRL at the beginning of the revocation period than to utilize the OCSP standard, necessitating an OCSP response every time a certificate requires validation.

EXAM TIP Know the purpose of a CRL and how it can be used to verify certificates. Understand the strengths OCSP brings as compared to a traditional CRL.

Certificate Signing Request

A user sends a *certificate signing request (CSR)* to a CA to apply for a certificate. To verify the user's identity, the CA and RA usually require some form of identification, such as a driver's license, Social Security number, address, or phone number. For an organization, the CSR often requires the fully qualified domain name (FQDN) of the server, the name of the organization, and the public key for the organization. Once the identification is established, the CA generates public and private keys for the user. A certificate is then generated with the identification and public key information embedded within it.

EXAM TIP A certificate contains the authenticated identification of a user or organization and their public key information.

Expiration

Within each certificate is a specific date for the beginning and ending of that certificate's life cycle. Most certificates are valid for approximately one to three years. The length of time for which the certificate is valid depends on the type of certificate issued and its purpose. A high-security defense contractor might switch its key pairs on a regular basis, meaning the certificates it uses could be valid for a short time.

The purpose of certificate expiry is to protect certificates from brute-force attacks. The longer certificates are in use, the greater the risk that they will be cracked. This is like a password expiry and retention scheme for a network in which users must regularly change their passwords to prevent them from being compromised.

If the certificate will be allowed to expire and not renewed, users should take actions to decrypt any data encrypted with the private key, as well as take any other actions necessary to ensure an "orderly" expiration. Otherwise, if you want to use a certificate after its time of validity is complete, you'll need to renew the certificate.

EXAM TIP Once a certificate has expired, it can't be renewed. A new certificate and key pair need to be generated.

Types of Certificates

A *digital certificate* is an electronic credential required by PKI systems that can securely identify an individual, as well as create an association between the individual's authenticated identity and public keys. Common certificate extensions include .der, .pem, .cer, .p12, .p7b, and .pfx, all of which are covered in the next section. The CA, as discussed previously, signs and issues certificates. The CA is responsible for verifying the identity of a key owner and binding the owner to a public key. This enables users who have never met to exchange encrypted communications because the authentication is performed by the CA.

TABLE 3.9-2 Commonly Used Certificate Types

Name	Description
Wildcard	Used to secure multiple first-level subdomains within one domain; one certificate can be used for *.mheducation.com, for example. Cannot be used for both *.mheducation.com and *.mheducation.net.
Subject Alternative Name (SAN)	Used to specify multiple hosts to use the same certificate. Can be used for www.mheducation.com and www.mheducation.net.
Code signing	Used to validate the integrity of code to ensure that it has not been tampered with.
Self-signed	A certificate that is signed by the same organization that it is certifying.
Machine/computer	Used for identifying and controlling which machines/computers are allowed to access network resources within an organization.
E-mail	Used to provide both confidentiality and integrity of e-mail when used with S/MIME.
User	Used for client authentication and encrypting user files.
Root	Used to validate the authenticity of other certificates; sometimes referred to as "trust anchors" and self-signed.
Domain validation	Used within X.509 to validate control of a domain.
Extended validation (EV)	Used within HTTPS to validate domains; obtaining an EV requires a request be made to a CA to prove identity. Can be used for multiple domains but not wildcards.

Each certificate contains a unique serial number, an identity, and public key information for the user, as well as the validity dates for the life of the certificate. Table 3.9-2 lists different types and descriptions of commonly used certificates.

Certificate Formats

The X.509 standard defines some of the infrastructure involved in requesting, processing, and issuing a certificate. For example, a certificate can have a different file extension depending upon how it is encoded and the information it contains. Additionally, individual vendors, such as Microsoft, Apple, Verisign, and so on, each have their own proprietary way of managing certificates, although for the most part they are X.509 compliant. Depending on the server the certificate will be used with, you'll need to be mindful of the file extension that is required; for example, Windows and Apache web servers don't use the same extensions.

International Telecommunications Union, "Information technology – ASN.1 encoding rules: Specification of Basic Encoding Rules (BER), Canonical Encoding Rules (CER) and Distinguished Encoding Rules (DER)," ITU-T Recommendation X.690, ISO/IEC 8825-1:2008 (what a mouthful!) was published in November 2008. We're not going to dive deeply into the topic of encoding, but what you need to know is that you'll see .cer and .der as common extensions used by binary encoded certificates.

The Privacy Enhanced Mail (PEM) format improves on the DER standard by incorporating Base64 (otherwise known as ASCII) encoding rather than binary. This makes PEM more universally usable, and PEM files can contain many different types of data formats inside. PEM as a mail concept never took off, but it's widely used by CAs.

RSA Security, Inc., also published a series of file types and formats, called Public Key Cryptography Standards (PKCS), which are used throughout the industry, although considered proprietary by RSA. For example, a PKCS#7 file is a certificate used to sign or encrypt digital messages, such as e-mail, and has a .p7b extension. A PKCS#12 file contains both public and private keys and is encrypted via asymmetric algorithm; it used for secure key storage and has a .p12 or .pfx extension. While these extensions are sometimes discussed interchangeably, .pfx (Personal Information Exchange) is a Microsoft standard that was the predecessor of the PKCS #12 file. Both are able to archive multiple cryptographic objects.

NOTE Certificate extensions are not always interchangeable, due to the different formats and encodings used. Some can be converted from one format to another, however, if required.

Other Important Concepts

Finally, the following concepts extend the information we've covered in the previous sections and are important to know for both the exam as well as your own PKI implementations.

Online vs. Offline CA

Root CAs are so critical to the trust model that they are often kept disconnected from any network and are sometimes powered down (offline). Once intermediate CAs have the ability to issue, validate, and revoke certificates, the need to have the root CA available is outweighed by the damage that would be caused by its compromise (potentially requiring revocation of all issued certificates). Keeping the root CA offline minimizes this potential, and the root CA can be brought back online for important tasks such as issuing and reissuing intermediate CA certificates.

Stapling

The TLS Certificate Status Request extension, more commonly known as *OCSP stapling*, further improves on OCSP efficiency by including ("stapling") the signed response with the TLS/SSL handshake, rather than querying the OCSP responder each time. The stapled response is signed by the CA to minimize fraud at the server level.

Pinning

Certificate pinning was defined in IETF RFC 7469 to "[allow] web host operators to instruct user agents to remember ("pin") the hosts' cryptographic identities over a period of time.

During that time, user agents (UAs) will require that the host presents a certificate chain including at least one Subject Public Key Info structure whose fingerprint matches one of the pinned fingerprints for that host."

Essentially, certificate pinning is designed to create a trust relationship between you and the site, rather than relying solely on the CA's trustworthiness. However, over the last few years, concerns with the pinning concept being exploited have emerged and pinning has fallen out of favor as a security measure. While Google, for example, was an early adopter of pinning within its Chrome browser, it has removed support for it in favor of a newer technology, Certificate Transparency.

Trust Model

A *trust model* defines how users trust other users, companies, CAs, and RAs within the PKI. Trust models provide a chain of trust from a user's public key to the root key of a CA. The validated chain then implies authenticity of all the certificates. The following are the most common trust models used in PKI:

- **Web of trust** This simplistic trust model relies on each user creating and signing his or her own certificate. This is the basis for encryption applications where no central authority exists, such as Pretty Good Privacy (PGP) or Gnu Privacy Guard (GPG. With this model, each user is responsible for authentication and trust, and anyone can sign someone else's public key. When User A signs User B's key, User A is introducing User B's key to anyone who trusts User A. Each user is then considered a trusted introducer in the model. Technically, neither PGP nor web of trust is PKI, since it is all peer-to-peer certificate trust and management, versus a centralized CA, but it's an important concept to understand for the exam.
- **Third-party (single authority) trust** A third-party central certifying agency signs a given key and authenticates the owner of the key. Trusting that authority means, by association, that you trust all keys issued by that authority. Each user authenticates the other through the exchange of certificates. The users know the CA has performed all the necessary identification of the owner of the certificate and can therefore trust the owner of the message.
- **Hierarchical model** An extension of the third-party model, root CAs issue certificates to other lower-level CAs and RAs. Each user's most trusted key is the root CA's public key. The trust inheritance can be followed from the certificate back to the root CA. This model allows enforcement of policies and standards throughout the infrastructure, producing a higher level of overall assurance than other trust models. A root certificate is trusted by software applications on behalf of the user. Intermediate CAs are subordinate to root CAs and trusted much like the root CAs in that they are delegated authority to issue and validate certificates.

KEY TERM A **root certificate** is the highest certificate in the hierarchical tree. A root certificate is used to sign other, lower-level certificates, which inherit the trust of the root certificate.

Key Escrow

Key escrow involves a trusted third party, such as a government agency or an authorized organization, that holds a special third key on top of your private and public key pair. The third key is used to encrypt the private key, which is then stored in a secure location. This third key can be used to unlock the encrypted copy of the private key in case of loss or theft of the original key. The concept of key escrow has been heavily overshadowed over the years by debates between privacy groups and the government because it concerns the issue of data privacy versus national security. Although the main concern of privacy activists is the possible abuse by the government regarding individual data privacy, the main security issue for most companies is the idea of a third-party entity controlling a crucial part of the company's security infrastructure.

Another common key escrow entity is the CA, which is responsible for authorizing and distributing certificates and encryption key pairs. As part of your overall security plan, the ability for the CA to protect your information is crucial. CAs are a popular target of malicious hacker attacks because of the valuable information they store. Attacks are usually targeted at the CA's own private keys.

The CA's key pairs are common targets of cryptanalytic attacks that attempt to break weak keys through brute force. CAs should be both secure and practical because their public key might be written into software used by many users. If the key needs to be changed, every user's software will need to be updated to accept the new key.

NOTE When examining a key escrow service, pay careful attention to its methods of security, including the secure storage and transfer of keys and certificates.

Certificate Chaining

As discussed previously, for security purposes, the root CA is usually taken offline and not used to issue certificates to users. If the root CA is ever compromised, the *certificate chain*, or the certificates that are issued from it, including subordinate CA certificates and any user certificates, are rendered untrustworthy. This affects the entire chain, depending upon which key within the chain was compromised. If the root certificate or private key is ever compromised, this could conceivably render the entire certificate chain invalid. The entire chain of certificates may have to be revoked and reissued.

REVIEW

Objective 3.9: Given a scenario, implement public key infrastructure Private keys need to be stored securely and, preferably, encrypted with a password. Key escrow companies can store the encryption key that can unlock the encryption on your private key, which is stored at your location. Certificates need to be renewed before expiry; otherwise, a new certificate must be generated. A certificate should be suspended or revoked if the keys related to that certificate are compromised. Check the CRL for certificates that have been revoked and understand the strengths and weaknesses of using OCSP and new extensions such as OCSP stapling and pinning. Finally, it is important to understand the different trust models and how certificate chains operate and can be compromised.

3.9 QUESTIONS

1. To improve the integrity and authentication of your encryption systems, you have contacted a CA to generate which of the following items for you?
   A. Digital certificate and public/private key pair
   B. Public key and a private hash
   C. Private key and a certificate
   D. Secret key for the local encryption server
2. You have been tasked with contacting your CA and revoking your company's current web server certificate. Which of the following is the most likely reason to revoke the certificate?
   A. You renewed your certificate after it expired.
   B. The previous network administrator who created the certificate was fired.
   C. You installed a new web server.
   D. Your current certificate expires in less than 30 days.
3. You need to look up the details of a certificate that was revoked. Where can you find this information?
   A. Certificate expiry list
   B. Registration suspension list
   C. Certificate revocation list
   D. Registration expiry list
4. You need to renew your company's certificate for its public web server. When should you renew the certificate?
   A. On its expiry date
   B. After it expires
   C. After it's revoked
   D. Thirty days before expiry

5. OCSP __________ improves upon the original OCSP efficiency by including a time-stamped, signed response with the TLS/SSL handshake.
   - **A.** pinning
   - **B.** stapling
   - **C.** assigning
   - **D.** synchronization

3.9 ANSWERS

1. **A** When a user's identification is established, the certificate authority (CA) generates public and private keys for the user. A certificate is then generated with the identification and public key information embedded within it. Once the user is registered and receives his certificate, he can begin using it to send encrypted messages.
2. **B** The certificate should be revoked because the user assigned to that certificate is no longer with the company. This prevents the user from continuing to use that certificate for encryption and authentication.
3. **C** A certificate revocation list (CRL) is published by a CA to show certificates that have been revoked. A verifier can examine the list to check the validity of another user's certificate.
4. **D** Most certificate authorities require that a certificate be renewed within a certain amount of time before the actual expiry date. This provides the CA with enough time to renew the certificate and deliver it back to the client for distribution.
5. **B** The TLS Certificate Status Request extension, more commonly known as *OCSP stapling*, further improves efficiency by allowing the certificate holder to query the Online Certificate Status Protocol (OCSP) responder itself at set intervals and including ("stapling") the signed response with the TLS/SSL handshake, rather than query the OCSP responder each time.

Operations and Incident Response

Domain Objectives

- **4.1** Given a scenario, use the appropriate tool to assess organizational security
- **4.2** Summarize the importance of policies, processes, and procedures for incident response
- **4.3** Given an incident, utilize appropriate data sources to support an investigation
- **4.4** Given an incident, apply mitigation techniques or controls to secure an environment
- **4.5** Explain the key aspects of digital forensics

Objective 4.1 Given a scenario, use the appropriate tool to assess organizational security

Objectives 1.7 and 1.8 in Domain 1 discussed the basics of different assessments, such as vulnerability assessments and penetration tests, and the pros and cons of each. This objective builds on that information by providing different tools that you can use to conduct these activities effectively and efficiently within an organization.

Assessing Organizational Security

A variety of tools are available to the network administrator and security professional to test networks and systems for vulnerabilities and weaknesses; unfortunately, these tools are also available to unethical hackers who use them to exploit specific vulnerabilities. By proactively monitoring your network for vulnerabilities and taking immediate steps to rectify them, you ensure that hackers using the same tools will not find vulnerabilities to exploit. You must routinely scan your network for vulnerabilities, whether they be unpatched operating systems and application software (such as web servers and database servers) or unused open ports and services that are actively listening for requests.

Network Reconnaissance and Discovery

Attackers generally follow a certain pattern to achieve their goals: they perform reconnaissance of the organization to determine potential vulnerabilities, extensive scanning to determine software versions and other pertinent information, and then determine how to exploit those vulnerabilities, all without triggering alerts or autonomous systems. The thorough tester will follow these same steps to determine the system's vulnerabilities most realistically. The following tools are essential parts of the testing toolkit.

EXAM TIP While you might be more familiar with one OS (e.g., Microsoft Windows) than others (e.g., macOS), it's important to know all of the following commands and tools for the exam, even if they are used within an OS you don't regularly use.

tracert/traceroute

tracert, a Microsoft Windows command (also known as *traceroute* on Unix-based systems), displays the route of packets and timing between point A and point B. It's very useful to help an administrator understand where along a route potential delays are arising. tracert uses ICMP

```
dawn@Dawns-MacBook-Pro-2 ~ % traceroute mheducation.com
traceroute to mheducation.com (204.74.99.100), 64 hops max, 52 byte packets
 1  192.168.7.1 (192.168.7.1)  6.511 ms  4.674 ms  6.901 ms
 2  192.168.0.1 (192.168.0.1)  6.390 ms  7.478 ms  7.957 ms
 3  24.96.117.1 (24.96.117.1)  20.422 ms  19.647 ms  17.236 ms
 4  10.52.130.60 (10.52.130.60)  16.917 ms  20.082 ms  31.327 ms
 5  user-24-96-198-229.knology.net (24.96.198.229)  20.704 ms  25.426 ms  18.956 ms
 6  static-69-73-17-237.knology.net (69.73.17.237)  22.790 ms  21.027 ms  20.280 ms
 7  static-216-186-189-254.knology.net (216.186.189.254)  29.742 ms  26.467 ms  40.239 ms
 8  dynamic-75-76-35-117.knology.net (75.76.35.117)  30.706 ms  36.383 ms  27.073 ms
 9  68.142.89.204 (68.142.89.204)  41.062 ms  33.152 ms  25.693 ms
10  lag27.fr4.iad.llnw.net (68.142.88.132)  41.451 ms  70.647 ms  42.035 ms
11  ultradns.p1-13-10g.fr3.iad.llnw.net (208.111.132.1)  43.484 ms  43.376 ms  43.142 ms
12  * * *
13  * * *
14  * * *
15  * * *
```

FIGURE 4.1-1 traceroute

packets with the time-to-live (TTL) decremented by 1 for each "hop" (typically a router or other network device) encountered along the route from the source host to the destination host.

Figure 4.1-1 shows an example of traceroute output from macOS.

nslookup/dig

Both *nslookup* and *dig* are command-line tools used to search the Domain Name System (DNS) to determine the mapping of domain names to IP addresses. nslookup comes natively on Windows systems (dig can be installed after the fact), while newer Linux systems include both natively. Although nslookup is still widely used, it has been deprecated and may be removed in future distributions.

ipconfig/ifconfig

ipconfig (used primarily in Windows systems) and *ifconfig* (used in Unix-based systems) are used to view the current configuration of IP interfaces at the command line; ifconfig also permits the enabling and disabling of interfaces.

Figure 4.1-2 shows an example of ifconfig output from macOS.

nmap

One of the most popular tools used for network mapping is an open-source and publicly available utility called *nmap*. It is used by hackers to scan and map networks and is used by administrators to audit their networks for security weaknesses. The nmap command-line utility uses simple text commands with switch options to perform tasks.

nmap can scan a particular host, or an entire logical network segment if given the proper network address and subnet mask. nmap can also output to a wide variety of formats, including

```
dawn@Dawns-MacBook-Pro-2 ~ % ifconfig
lo0: flags=8049<UP,LOOPBACK,RUNNING,MULTICAST> mtu 16384
        options=1203<RXCSUM,TXCSUM,TXSTATUS,SW_TIMESTAMP>
        inet 127.0.0.1 netmask 0xff000000
        inet6 ::1 prefixlen 128
        inet6 fe80::1%lo0 prefixlen 64 scopeid 0x1
        nd6 options=201<PERFORMNUD,DAD>
gif0: flags=8010<POINTOPOINT,MULTICAST> mtu 1280
stf0: flags=0<> mtu 1280
en5: flags=8863<UP,BROADCAST,SMART,RUNNING,SIMPLEX,MULTICAST> mtu 1500
        ether ac:de:48:00:11:22
        inet6 fe80::aede:48ff:fe00:1122%en5 prefixlen 64 scopeid 0x4
        nd6 options=201<PERFORMNUD,DAD>
        media: autoselect (100baseTX <full-duplex>)
        status: active
ap1: flags=8802<BROADCAST,SIMPLEX,MULTICAST> mtu 1500
        options=400<CHANNEL_IO>
        ether b2:9c:4a:be:ce:eb
        media: autoselect
        status: inactive
en0: flags=8863<UP,BROADCAST,SMART,RUNNING,SIMPLEX,MULTICAST> mtu 1500
        options=400<CHANNEL_IO>
        ether 90:9c:4a:be:ce:eb
        inet6 fe80::1ce0:46d5:33c0:9eee%en0 prefixlen 64 secured scopeid 0x6
        inet 192.168.7.141 netmask 0xffffff00 broadcast 192.168.7.255
        nd6 options=201<PERFORMNUD,DAD>
        media: autoselect
        status: active
```

FIGURE 4.1-2 ifconfig

the ubiquitous CSV format. Table 4.1-1 lists some of the more commonly used command-line options for various scanning techniques.

Figure 4.1-3 shows example nmap output from macOS, using the Zenmap graphical user interface (GUI).

ping/pathping

As the Internet Control Message Protocol (ICMP) is built natively into every TCP/IP device, and the follow-on responses provide invaluable information about the target, ICMP makes a good place to start when you begin network scanning. A good example is the Echo Request—Type 8—that when sent to a host, returns a Type 3. This could mean the host is down, or the network route is missing or corrupt in your local route tables—Type 0—or that something is preventing ICMP messages altogether—Type 13.

TABLE 4.1-1 nmap Command-Line Switches for Various Scanning Techniques

Switch	Type of Scan
-sT	Full TCP connect scan
-sn	Ping scan
-sU	UDP scan
-sA	Ack scan
-sN/sF/sX	TCP Null, FIN, and Xmas scans

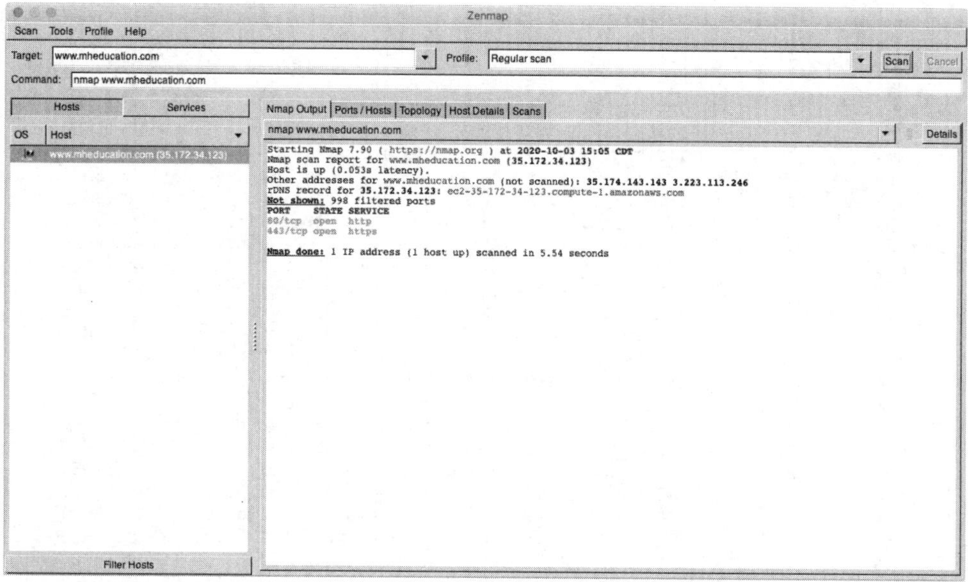

FIGURE 4.1-3 nmap scan of www.mheducation.com with the Zenmap GUI

This process, called a *ping*, has been part of networking from the beginning, and combining these pings to all the addresses within a subnet range is otherwise known as a *ping sweep*. A ping sweep is often the easiest way to identify active machines on a network, but it's often not the best way. While ICMP is a part of the TCP/IP stack, it's not always enabled on each device as a matter of security. Many administrators purposefully disable ping responses on devices and configure firewalls to block them. *pathping* is an evolution that essentially combines the functionality of ping and traceroute to discover spots where there is network latency or loss.

hping

hping (also known as hping3, its current version) is a Windows and Linux packet generator and analyzer that can be used to conduct both ping sweeps and port scans and can act as a packet builder. Similar to nmap, hping has specific syntax for what you're trying to accomplish, with many switches and options. hping is a reliable tool to send specifically crafted packets to a host to elicit a specific response, but it also can potentially be used to initiate an attack. hping is often used by security professionals to help determine how a network host will react to certain traffic during a vulnerability assessment or penetration test.

netstat

netstat is a command-line tool that displays any active TCP connections that are present. With parameters, netstat can display the ports where you are listening as well as the routing table, and it can be used to determine if there are problems in the network and if any traffic is present.

Figure 4.1-4 shows an example of netstat output from macOS.

```
dawn@Dawns-MacBook-Pro-2 ~ % netstat
Active Internet connections
Proto Recv-Q Send-Q  Local Address          Foreign Address        (state)
tcp4       0      0  192.168.7.141.50172    192.168.7.1.ssdp       ESTABLISHED
tcp4       0      0  192.168.7.141.50171    192.168.7.1.ssdp       ESTABLISHED
tcp4       0      0  192.168.7.141.50170    192.168.7.1.ssdp       ESTABLISHED
tcp4       0      0  192.168.7.141.50169    192.168.7.1.ssdp       ESTABLISHED
tcp4       0      0  192.168.7.141.50168    192.168.7.1.ssdp       ESTABLISHED
tcp4       0      0  192.168.7.141.50167    192.168.7.1.ssdp       ESTABLISHED
tcp4       0      0  192.168.7.141.50166    192.168.7.105.49178    ESTABLISHED
tcp4       0      0  192.168.7.141.50165    ord37s07-in-f34..https ESTABLISHED
tcp4       0      0  192.168.7.141.50164    nycp-hlb08.doubl.https ESTABLISHED
tcp4       0      0  192.168.7.141.50163    nycp-hlb08.doubl.https ESTABLISHED
tcp4       0      0  192.168.7.141.50161    daldt.adsafeprot.https ESTABLISHED
tcp4       0      0  192.168.7.141.50160    nycp-hlb08.doubl.https ESTABLISHED
tcp4       0      0  192.168.7.141.50159    nycp-hlb08.doubl.https ESTABLISHED
tcp4       0      0  192.168.7.141.50158    nycp-hlb08.doubl.https ESTABLISHED
tcp4       0      0  192.168.7.141.50157    nycp-hlb08.doubl.https ESTABLISHED
tcp4       0      0  192.168.7.141.50156    a23-212-148-171..https ESTABLISHED
tcp4       0      0  192.168.7.141.50154    a23-212-148-171..https ESTABLISHED
tcp4       0      0  192.168.7.141.50153    nycp-hlb08.doubl.https ESTABLISHED
tcp4       0      0  192.168.7.141.50152    nycp-hlb08.doubl.https ESTABLISHED
tcp4       0      0  192.168.7.141.50151    nycp-hlb08.doubl.https ESTABLISHED
tcp4       0      0  192.168.7.141.50150    nycp-hlb08.doubl.https ESTABLISHED
tcp4       0      0  192.168.7.141.50149    ec2-52-41-253-59.https ESTABLISHED
tcp4       0      0  192.168.7.141.50148    ec2-34-194-237-4.https ESTABLISHED
tcp4       0      0  192.168.7.141.50147    server-52-85-83-.https ESTABLISHED
tcp4       0      0  192.168.7.141.50146    ec2-44-238-224-2.https ESTABLISHED
```

FIGURE 4.1-4 Example netstat output

netcat

netcat is a multifunctional command-line utility that allows read/write access across the network from the command line and is the back end that "powers" a number of other tools. netcat can do everything from a port scan across the network to allowing chat (albeit crude) functionality between users. ncat is the "next generation" netcat integrated with nmap.

IP Scanners

IP scanners (such as the popular open-source Angry IP Scanner) scan an entire IP range and report back active devices. Generally an IP scanner does this by using a simple ping sweep, pinging machines to see how they respond, and gathering what information it can about the host. Many IP scanners can also do port scans. IP scanners can be either command line or graphical in nature. These are great tools for testing, but also for an administrator who wants to see what's on her network, as especially large networks can get out of hand quickly.

arp

Address Resolution Protocol (ARP) is used by systems on a network to associate an IP address of a system with its hardware MAC address. This information is stored within a table called an ARP cache. The *arp* command is used to view and make changes to the ARP cache.

route

On Unix-like operating systems, such as Linux, the *route* command allows modification of the IP routing table. It is primarily used to set static routes for traffic to be sent to specific networks or hosts. Note that on Linux, you can show the routing table, but on macOS, you use the netstat command (discussed previously) with the -rn options.

curl

The *curl* (sometimes displayed as cURL) command within Unix and Linux allows the user to transfer data to or from a server using a variety of protocols, including HTTP, HTTPS, and FTP.

theHarvester

theHarvester is a Python-based tool used to collect open-source intelligence (OSINT) and can be very useful to a penetration tester in the early stages of testing. The tool gathers OSINT available about an organization's data, including names, e-mail addresses, and IP addresses, both actively and passively from a variety of online sources, including LinkedIn, Twitter, Google, and DNS lookups.

NOTE You can download theHarvester from https://github.com/laramies/theHarvester?

sn1per

sn1per is an automated scanner available for Unix and Linux that is often used during penetration tests to enumerate a network and perform a vulnerability scan. Among its capabilities is the capability to conduct ping sweeps, DNS lookups, and WHOIS lookups for reconnaissance before moving to more advanced, intrusive measures such as attempting exploits, running targeted nmap scans, and enumerating shares.

scanless

scanless is a Unix/Linux-based command-line tool that can perform anonymous port scans on a target, meaning that the scan will not be conducted from your IP address. To do this, scanless utilizes a number of exploitation websites to conduct the scan.

dnsenum

dnsenum is a penetration-testing Perl script, available through the popular Kali Linux distribution, that enumerates a target's DNS information. In doing so, dnsenum gathers information such as the target's address (A record), name servers, and MX records. It can also do more intrusive activities such as brute forcing subdomains.

Nessus

Nessus (available at www.tenable.com) is a popular commercial vulnerability scanner, available in both Linux and Unix versions, that scans systems for thousands of vulnerabilities and provides an exhaustive report about the vulnerabilities that exist on your system. Nessus is highly configurable and can allow you to use a wide range of plug-ins (scanning signatures based on vulnerability or operating system). Nessus can scan a wide variety of operating systems and applications, including all flavors of Windows, macOS, and most Linux distributions. Nessus reports provide information on missing patches and updates, configuration issues, and so on. It can break those down into OS, network segment, vulnerability severity, and many other categories. Nessus can output its results in a variety of report formats, including its native Nessus (XML) format, PDF reports, and CSV format.

Cuckoo

Cuckoo, available for Unix- and Linux-based systems, is an automated malware analysis tool that provides a sandboxed environment where an analyst can safely execute Windows, Unix, macOS, and even Android malware and receive a report regarding the behavior of the malware when executed.

File Manipulation

Being able to manipulate files at the command line is an essential skill for the Unix/Linux user, and mastering these functions is important not only for the exam but also for daily operations and the use of many of the more powerful command line–based tools discussed in this objective.

EXAM TIP While many security professionals prefer one operating system over others (e.g., Windows over Linux), you are expected to know the basics of file manipulation in both for the exam.

Table 4.1-2 lists some of the more commonly used command-line utilities for file manipulation.

TABLE 4.1-2 Command-Line Utilities for File Manipulation

Utility	Function
head	Output the first part of files
tail	Output the last part of files
cat	Concatenate files and print on the standard output
grep	Print lines that match patterns
chmod	Change file mode bits (used to change permissions)
logger	Enter messages into the system log

Shell and Script Environments

Understanding the shells available within various operating systems, as well as the popular scripting languages that are used within exploitation frameworks, is key not only for the exam but also for general security principles. The following sections discuss the most important shell and script environments to know.

SSH

As discussed in Domain 3, Objective 3.1, *Secure Shell (SSH)* enables a user to log in to a remote machine and execute commands as if they were on the console of that system. SSH is a secure replacement for the older Telnet, which is insecure because its data isn't encrypted when communicated. SSH provides a secure, encrypted tunnel to access another system remotely. When a client connects to a system using SSH, an initial handshaking process begins, and a special session key is exchanged. This begins the session, and an encrypted secure channel is created to allow the access. SSH can also be used in conjunction with other protocols such as FTP to encrypt file transfer communications.

PowerShell

Ah, what is there to say about PowerShell that most of the current breach reports and global threat trend documents haven't already described? PowerShell exploits have become a really big deal. To take a page out of Microsoft's own book, "PowerShell is a cross-platform task automation and configuration management framework, consisting of a command-line shell and scripting language." PowerShell is now the default command shell as of Windows 10, and it has proven ripe for exploit, as being able to overtake PowerShell and execute commands inside of it often can evade security tools through the guise of being an administrative task.

Python

Python is a powerful scripting language that's also known as a quite easy-to-use language, and there are many scripts (check out Kali Linux for examples) that will help penetration testers and other curious professionals to automate their activities. However, to paraphrase OWASP (discussed in Domain 2, Objective 2.3), you need to make sure you not only secure systems with Python (using the great scripts available) but also secure your scripts (using appropriate application security techniques) and secure the interpreter and the area around it through appropriate permissions and other best practices.

Packet Capture and Replay

One of the most powerful types of tools available for determining the who, what, when, where, why, and how of an event are packet capture and replay tools. They enable you to "play back" an event, just as it happened, for analysis. The following sections describe the most important packet capture and replay tools for you to know.

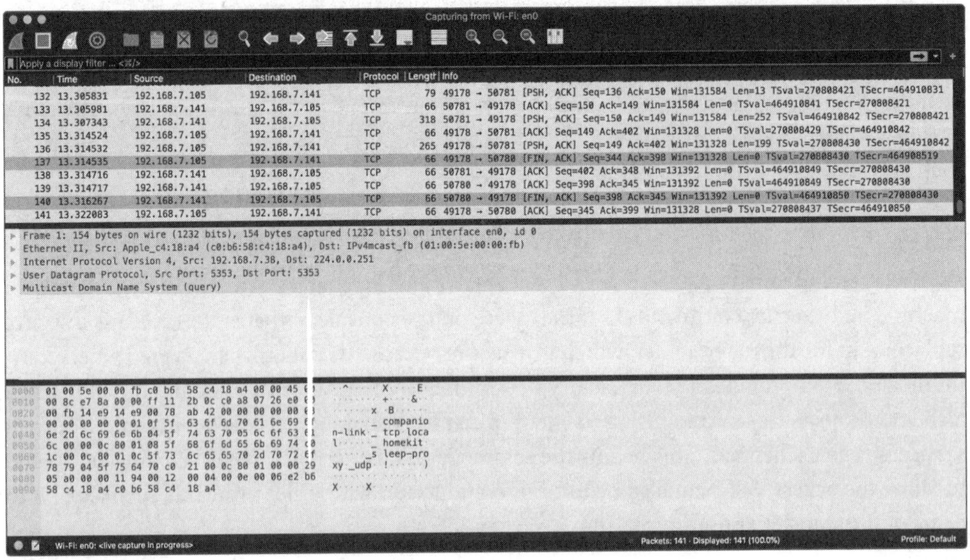

FIGURE 4.1-5 Example Wireshark capture

Wireshark

Wireshark is the ubiquitous traffic-capture and analysis tool used by cybersecurity analysts. Wireshark is available not only in a graphical version but also a command-line version, called tshark, which makes scripting easier. Wireshark is available for Windows, Linux, and macOS platforms. It is open source and free to use but does exist as a commercial version as well. Wireshark can be used on both wired and wireless networks. For wireless networks, however, it requires a network card that has been put into monitor or promiscuous mode, so that it can capture all wireless traffic on a network. For wired traffic, the machine serving as the host running Wireshark must be able to capture all traffic on a segment, including the ability to span a switch for switched traffic.

Wireshark uses a capture format called a pcap (for *packet capture*) file. Note that this is a binary file and not a text-based (such as a CSV format) file. Wireshark can read files from other packet-capture tools as well, such as tcpdump, discussed next. Note that packet captures contain huge volumes of data and can grow in size quickly, so organizations that perform a lot of packet captures must have a lot of space to store them. Packet captures can also be very unwieldy to analyze in large sizes.

Figure 4.1-5 shows an example Wireshark capture from macOS.

Tcpreplay

Tcpreplay is a suite of free utilities on the Unix/Linux platforms, available through open source, that enables you to edit and replay previously captured network traffic. As noted, it's a suite, so it has many different functions available:

- **tcpreplay** Replay pcap files at arbitrary speeds onto a network
- **tcprewrite** Edit pcap files and create a new pcap file
- **tcpreplay-edit** Edit pcap files and replay onto a network
- **tcpprep** Create client/server definition cache files used by tcpreplay and tcprewrite
- **tcpbridge** Bridge two network segments with the power of tcprewrite
- **tcpliveplay** Replay a TCP pcap file in a manner that a server will recognize
- **tcpcapinfo** Raw pcap file decoder and debugger

tcpdump

tcpdump is a packet-capture utility built into most modern Linux distributions, but it is also found in some macOS and Windows ports. It's used to view network packets and to output to a file. tcpdump essentially monitors all network traffic and sends it to a file or allows an operator to monitor it in real time on the screen. Because it cannot display and filter as elegantly as Wireshark, it's more useful as a capture tool than as an analysis tool. Its output can be imported into a variety of packet-analysis tools, including Wireshark. Because it is a command-line tool with a variety of options, it's very useful in scripts that require very specific capture filters.

Forensics

There are several popular forensic tools available to capture system images, ranging from commercial tools to free Linux tools like dd that can obtain a system image. Additionally, there are hardware imaging devices specifically designed for forensic use that can capture system images from different types of media and create their hash values at the same time. The following sections discuss the most important tools to know for the CompTIA Security+ exam.

Cross-Reference

Digital forensics is covered in more depth in Objective 4.5, later in this domain.

dd

The *dd* command is the granddaddy of forensic imaging tools. It's part of the GNU Core Utilities, which are the basic file, shell, and text manipulation utilities of the GNU operating system. Essentially, dd copies a file (from standard input to standard output, by default) while optionally performing conversions on it.

memdump

When capturing data for forensics, especially in the initial stages directly after an incident, you must consider the levels of volatility and focus the priority efforts on preserving the most volatile types of data before moving on to less-volatile data. The early focus should be on system memory or crash dump files, error messages on the screen, and log files, before moving on to less-volatile data. Within Unix/Linux systems, the *memdump* command-line tool dumps those contents of physical memory as a raw dump that can be analyzed for forensic purposes.

WinHex

WinHex is a hexadecimal editor for the Windows family of operating systems that is frequently used for forensic purposes. Its main functions include the ability to inspect files and recover data from corrupted disk drives. WinHex is available in multiple license types with a variety of added features based on the license purchased.

FTK Imager

Forensic Toolkit (FTK) from Access Data is one of the titans in the field of computer forensics, allowing for investigation-quality imaging and analysis of systems. One key part of this suite is *FTK Imager*, a data preview and imaging tool that lets you quickly assess electronic evidence to determine if further analysis with FTK is needed. FTK Imager officially includes the following functionality:

- Parse XFS file systems when investigating and collecting from Red Hat Linux environments
- Capture and view APFS images from macOS hard drives
- Create forensic images of local hard drives, optical discs, thumb drives or other USB devices, entire folders, or individual files from various places within the media
- Preview files and folders on local hard drives, network drives, optical discs, and thumb drives or other USB devices
- Preview the contents of forensic images stored on the local machine or on a network drive
- Mount an image for a read-only view that leverages Windows Internet Explorer to see the content of the image exactly as the user saw it on the original drive
- Export files and folders from forensic images
- See and recover files that have been deleted from the Recycle Bin but have not yet been overwritten on the drive
- Create hashes of files to check the integrity of the data by using either of the two hash functions available in FTK Imager: Message Digest 5 (MD5) and Secure Hash Algorithm (SHA-1)

Autopsy

Autopsy is a free digital forensic tool, available for Windows, macOS, and Linux, that is modular, meaning that it comes with a standard set of capabilities, and more can be added through selecting modules from third parties. Some of these modules include the following:

- Timeline Analysis: Advanced graphical event viewing interface
- Hash Filtering: Flag known bad files and ignore known good
- Keyword Search: Indexed keyword search to find files that mention relevant terms
- Web Artifacts: Extract history, bookmarks, and cookies from Firefox, Chrome, and Internet Explorer

- Data Carving: Recover deleted files from unallocated space using PhotoRec
- Multimedia: Extract EXIF from pictures and watch videos
- Indicators of Compromise: Scan a computer using STIX

Exploitation Frameworks

Exploitation frameworks are platforms that can be used to craft and execute exploits against targets. They generally contain suites of tools and serve as a "Swiss Army knife" of exploitation, a one-stop shop for hackers and security professionals alike. There are both paid and free exploitation frameworks, and each has its pros and cons. The following are the most important frameworks to know for the exam:

- **Metasploit Framework** Managed by the security firm Rapid7, "[Metasploit] provides the infrastructure, content, and tools to perform penetration tests and extensive security auditing." Metasploit is updated regularly with new modules to exploit new vulnerabilities, and installers are available for Windows, Linux, and macOS. There is also a paid version available, Metasploit Pro.
- **Core Impact** Developed by Core Security, Core Impact is a commercial product that has introduced a quite automated approach to the penetration testing process. Core Impact can even exploit a machine and automatically attempt to use it to move laterally across a network. It also provides tight integration with other Core Security vulnerability-management tools.
- **CANVAS** Developed by Immunity, CANVAS has many of the same zero-day exploit features of the previously discussed tools, but historically has had more focus on industrial control system (ICS) exploits.

Password Crackers

Password cracker programs (also referred to as *password auditing tools*) are used by hackers to attack a system's authentication structure (such as its password database) and attempt to retrieve passwords for user accounts. The programs are also used by security administrators to proactively audit their password database to look for weak passwords.

NOTE Examples of password-cracking programs include classic standbys such as John the Ripper and Cain & Abel.

Password crackers use a variety of methods:

- **Dictionary attack** This type of attack employs a list of dictionary words that are tried against the authentication database. Because users often use known dictionary words as passwords, this attack can succeed in cracking many passwords.

- **Brute-force attack** This attack uses a calculated combination of characters to guess the password. The brute-force method will keep trying every single combination until it gets the password right.
- **Hybrid attack** Many programs use a combination of dictionary and brute-force attacks to add numbers and special characters (such as the @ symbol for *a*) to the dictionary words to crack more-difficult passwords.

Cross-Reference

Domain 1, Objective 1.2 discussed the different types of password attacks in more depth.

After the attacker cracks a specific password, she will be able to access that user account. The administrator account for a system is most commonly attacked because it has full access privileges.

Many older computer authentication schemes stored the passwords in clear text, making it easy for any hacker who was able to access the password database file to crack an account. Most modern operating systems, at the very least, provide some type of one-way hashing function to protect the password database. If the password database file is accessed by a hacker, it will be of no use because the contents are encrypted. However, many sophisticated password-cracking programs can analyze the database and attack weak encryption methods repeatedly to crack passwords over time. For example, the LANMAN hash used in older Windows-based systems to protect passwords was weak and could be cracked easily if the hacker could gain access to the password database.

Protecting against online password-cracking programs relies on a strong password policy, as discussed in Domain 3, Objective 3.7. Setting maximum login attempts will lock out an account if the password has been unsuccessfully entered a set number of times. It is important to discern here between online attacks and offline attacks: Online attacks (conducted against passwords as they reside on a live system) can be mitigated through lockouts and password policies resident on the affected system. Hackers conducting offline attacks generally move the file (or files) they wish to use to their own system, where they can run a password cracker or other tool against it without being locked out. The same mitigations for the online attack aren't effective here; strong passwords are the key to slowing down this type of attack, as well as the obvious solution: don't let the file leave your system!

Data Sanitization

Domain 2, Objective 2.1 covered the fundamentals of data sanitization (to the point of media destruction), but here is a recap of the different methods:

- **Wiping** The use of a program to conduct "passes" of random or nonrandom data, overwriting a file or an entire drive. This is generally done in one or more passes, with the larger number of passes taking more time, but considered more secure. Reuse is possible after wiping.

- **Burning** Tossing whatever media you wish to destroy into an incinerator that burns it beyond recovery.
- **Shredding** Commonly used with paper or optical media to shred the item beyond recovery, generally in strips or further into small, confetti-style pieces; it is important when employing the shredding technique that your chosen shredding solution creates such small pieces that they cannot be pieced back together.
- **Pulverizing** Much like shredding but reduces the media to dust.
- **Pulping** Mixing water and special chemicals with the paper to remove any ink; the paper can then be recycled.
- **Degaussing** Involves running a strong magnet over magnetic storage (such as a non–solid-state hard drive) to erase the contents and restore it to a blank and generally unusable state.

REVIEW

Objective 4.1: Given a scenario, use the appropriate tool to assess organizational security Different types of assessment tools can be used by network administrators to find and mitigate vulnerabilities. Understand how the major network reconnaissance and discovery tools are used to identify active systems, enumerate them, and determine vulnerabilities that can be exploited. Understand the key file-manipulation commands and their use. Know the major shell and scripting environments. Understand packet-capture and replay tools and why and when to use them. Know the major forensic tools and their platforms. Exploitation frameworks are available as platforms for both attackers and security professionals to guard against attacks. Finally, various methods are available to sanitize media to protect sensitive data.

4.1 QUESTIONS

1. Which of the following choices is *not* considered an exploitation framework?
   - **A.** Metasploit
   - **B.** Nessus
   - **C.** CANVAS
   - **D.** Core Impact
2. Within Unix/Linux systems, the __________ tool dumps the contents of physical memory.
   - **A.** coredump
   - **B.** fulldump
   - **C.** sysdump
   - **D.** memdump

3. Which file-manipulation command is used to print lines that match patterns?
   A. grep
   B. cat
   C. head
   D. chmod
4. Which of the following is a Windows and Linux tool that can be used to conduct both ping sweeps and port scans, as well as acting as a packet builder?
   A. nmap
   B. Nessus
   C. hping
   D. tcpdump

4.1 ANSWERS

1. **B** Metasploit, Core Impact, and CANVAS are exploitation frameworks. Nessus is a vulnerability scanner.
2. **D** Within Unix/Linux systems, the memdump tool dumps the contents of physical memory.
3. **A** The grep command is used to print lines that match patterns.
4. **C** hping (also known as hping3, its current version) is a Windows and Linux tool that can be used to conduct both ping sweeps and port scans, can act as a packet builder, and can run many scans.

Objective 4.2 Summarize the importance of policies, processes, and procedures for incident response

As much as you try to prevent them, incidents (such as data breaches, information spillage, or ransomware) or disasters will occur. The best way to handle them is fastidious preparation to promote a smooth response and recovery. This objective covers the policies, processes, and procedures that you should consider as part of your organization's preparation.

Incident Response

When a security incident (or disaster scenario) occurs, the initial incident response can make all the difference—either it quickly mitigates a threat, preventing it from spreading and causing further issues, or it fails to prevent the incident from spinning out of control, causing irreparable damage to your organization's ability to function. The following sections detail the critical aspects of incident response that you should know to recover from a variety of natural or person-made events.

Incident Response Plans

Incident response must be planned to ensure that your front-line employees are prepared in the event of a security incident to quickly contain the incident, preserve any evidence in the event of a security breach, and escalate issues as appropriate to company management or third-party authorities. Without a plan (in writing, not memory), those who discover an incident are likely to take incorrect steps, or no steps at all. Spend the time to put a plan in writing, signed by a member of management, and you will save time and money in the event of an incident. A comprehensive plan should include the roles and responsibilities of all the stakeholders who will execute the plan. This should include the incident response team and first responders, the reporting and incident escalation requirements and associated timeframes, and the specific steps that will be taken to handle different incident types and categories of crisis effectively and efficiently, while appropriately preserving precious evidence. For example, the reporting for a personally identifiable information (PII) breach sent by e-mail will have different reporting and escalation thresholds than finding child pornography on a company system, and there should be no guessing about what to do in the heat of the moment. The plan must be clear, simple, and understood by all stakeholders.

Further, any plans should be exercised (discussed further in the next section) to ensure that the parties involved feel comfortable executing the steps. Remember that in a time of crisis, people can "freeze up" and feel unsure of what to do. Having a written, exercised set of plans takes the burden of memory off your organization's staff and allows them to have confidence that they are doing the right thing at the right time.

Incident Response Process

Incident response is not a single event; it's a life cycle that should iteratively improve based on the findings from previous incidents. The following sections describe the crucial steps to prepare for, deal with, and learn from incidents toward continuous improvement.

Preparation

Preparation could quite possibly be the most essential phase of the incident response life cycle. During the preparation phase, a number of activities must be carefully planned and executed; the different plans that should be pursued are discussed later in this objective, but as part of preparation these plans must be documented and agreed upon with the key stakeholders, both internal and external to the IT/cybersecurity staff.

Identification

After the discovery of an incident, company personnel must report it to the appropriate person, and this person should be identified ahead of time (you did this during preparation, right?).

The incident could have been discovered by a security guard, an employee working late, or, in many cases, the network or security administrator. The company's incident response plan should have defined the first responders from the incident response team who can be deployed to respond to the incident and start the process of collecting and retaining potential evidence properly. In other words, the specifics of the incident must be identified first to contain, eradicate, and recover from it.

Containment

The containment phase stops damage from escalating further and helps preserve evidence for any possible future action. The number-one priority is to stop the progress of any unwanted activity, be it malware, a hacking action, or even equipment failure. Often, this entails a quarantine of affected systems from unaffected systems to prevent the spread of the incident, or removal of affected devices from the network. At this point, the system(s) may undergo forensic analysis or be wiped clean, depending on policy and type of incident.

Eradication

Eradication will consider the required actions to mitigate any lingering negative elements, the effect of isolation on normal business operation, the damage that has occurred, and then the organizational policies to stop unwanted activity and get back to business. Perhaps the affected machines will be reimaged and put back on the network, or more advanced forensic analysis will occur. These decisions should take into consideration the nature and scope of the incident and the organizational policies and resources available to implement the eradication, including the time, cost, and scope of the proposed countermeasures.

Recovery

Ideally, the affected systems or segments will be recovered and reconstituted, the steps appropriately documented throughout each phase, and there will be a good sense of how many resources—time, money, and lost data—have been expended on the effort. When a security incident is being investigated, every single detail should be meticulously documented to ensure that every aspect of the incident, from the specific details of the security breach to every step taken during the incident response process, is recorded. This should include, at a minimum, the date and time of the action or event, a list of personnel involved, the event itself, and any data or equipment involved. This is especially important in an incident that may potentially lead to criminal or civil litigation.

During the recovery, keep careful track of the number of person-hours and expenses required to respond to, investigate, and eradicate the security incident. These statistics are very useful for future risk analysis and security budgeting, and they help assign a real dollar value as a cost for the incident beyond the costs incurred for loss of data and system downtime. Other departments, such as accounting and human resources, may have to provide the data (such as labor rates of personnel involved) to help substantiate this portion of the incident report.

Lessons Learned

Even in the worst scenarios, it is important to take stock of the lessons learned. It is rare to have an incident and accompanying response take place with no hiccups; these should be documented. Was the team adequately prepared? Did they have sufficient resources at their disposal to fully investigate and contain the incident? Were organizational policies not followed? Were the policies not sufficient to cover the scope of the incident?

Conversely, good can often be found in a negative situation. For example, did the team operate smoothly because the procedures were practiced ahead of time? This should be noted also.

EXAM TIP Knowing the steps and order of the incident response process is important.

Exercises

To complete your incident response plan, you must fully test and exercise it to ensure all parts of the plan work as they should. Re-creating an event without affecting the current operations of your company might be difficult, but some form of exercise should be performed at least once a year.

One common type of test is a *tabletop exercise*, which requires the involved parties to sit around a—you guessed it—table and step through a scenario to discern weaknesses in the plan. Tabletop exercises are generally paper based, meaning that no actual steps are undertaken. Conducting this type of test several times will make participants more comfortable in the event they must conduct the plan, almost like muscle memory. The next step up from the tabletop exercise in terms of realistic testing of a plan is a *walkthrough*, where the team does "walk through" the steps of an incident response, but not in a real-world scenario where the tasks must be performed or equipment utilized.

Many effective disaster recovery or incident response exercises involve the choice of a *simulation*, or simulated scenario, such as a fire in a certain part of the building. In the exercise, your team must consult the recovery plan documentation and execute it accordingly. Depending on the size of the company, it might be feasible to involve only certain departments, but the IT department should always be included because its main responsibilities are the network infrastructure and data recovery. During the exercise, every phase should be fully documented using a checklist. Any exceptions or problems encountered during the procedure should be thoroughly documented.

When the exercise has been completed, the original plan that was tested should be reviewed for any findings of procedures that didn't work correctly or that need to be modified because of the test. The plan should be updated with any new information emerging from the event. Any changes to the existing facilities or infrastructure should initiate a review of the response or recovery procedure, and any necessary changes to the recovery procedures should be made immediately to reflect the new environment.

Attack Frameworks

Attack frameworks help a professional to think like a hacker in order to improve the organization's security and are often used when conducting different types of tests or exercises. Attack frameworks help enrich scenarios and make them more realistic by providing detail regarding how adversaries prepare for, execute, and behave during and after cybersecurity incidents based on their tactics, techniques, and procedures (TTPs), which are defined here:

- **Tactics** The end state or states that the adversary is attempting to accomplish (e.g., lateral movement through a network)
- **Techniques** How the adversary accomplishes their tactics (e.g., lateral tool transfer to accomplish lateral movement)
- **Procedures** The tools and steps used to accomplish the techniques (e.g., an advanced persistent threat actor has a history of deploying tools after moving laterally using administrative accounts)

In the following sections, we'll discuss the most important frameworks you should know for the exam.

MITRE ATT&CK

MITRE supervises and provides oversight of U.S. federally funded research and development corporations (FFRDCs), meaning that MITRE supports R&D for the U.S. government; however, many of the tools MITRE develops are also released for public use within an open-source format. In 2013, MITRE created the ATT&CK framework to help catalog emerging tactics, techniques, and procedures being used in attacks globally. The MITRE ATT&CK Matrix for Enterprise (see https://attack.mitre.org/) divides enterprise attack tactics into the following categories, each of which is broken down into techniques, which in turn are subdivided into procedures:

- Initial Access
- Execution
- Persistence
- Privilege Escalation
- Defense Evasion
- Credential Access
- Discovery
- Lateral Movement
- Collection
- Command and Control
- Exfiltration
- Impact

The MITRE ATT&CK framework has also been extended to include a PRE-ATT&CK Matrix, an ATT&CK for Industrial Control Systems (ICS) Matrix, and two ATT&CK Matrices for Mobile (Android and iOS), and has been integrated into other MITRE products, such as CALDERA, which can be used to automate penetration testing.

The Diamond Model of Intrusion Analysis

The Diamond Model of Intrusion Analysis was developed in 2013 by a group of leading intrusion analysts who built it around the underlying question, "What is the underlying method of our work?" Using this as the starting foundation, the Diamond Model categorizes the relationships and characteristics of an attack's four main components: an *adversary* deploys a *capability* over some *infrastructure* against a *victim*. These are known as *events* and form the diamond. Analysts then populate each part of the diamond with the information they gather during the analysis process.

Lockheed Martin Cyber Kill Chain

The term "kill chain" was originally used within the military to describe the stages of attacks against enemies. It was applied to an organization's cybersecurity by the major defense contractor Lockheed Martin, with the end state of portraying how attackers step through their actions to reach their final goal. Attackers succeed only if they complete steps 1–6 in order to get to the final seventh step. Table 4.2-1 provides a summary.

Communication Plan

An organization's *communication plan* is a critical part of the overall incident response plan, as it defines how, within an incident scenario, communications such as reporting will flow up and down the organization's chain of command for decision-making, laterally within the

TABLE 4.2-1 The Lockheed Martin Cyber Kill Chain

Step Number	Attack Name	Description
1	Reconnaissance	The adversary conducts research to understand their target.
2	Weaponization	The adversary crafts the malware that will be used against their target.
3	Delivery	The adversary launches malware against their target.
4	Exploitation	The adversary exploits a vulnerability to gain access to their target.
5	Installation	The adversary installs a backdoor or implant in the target environment.
6	Command and Control (C2)	The malware opens a command channel for the adversary to use.
7	Actions on Objectives	The adversary accomplishes the mission's goal.

organization to execute actions as required, and even externally to communicate with external agencies (this is often a key action, especially in situations where reporting must be done within a certain time period after, say, a breach of customer data). The communication plan should include steps on when and how an organization must disclose details of an incident to regulatory agencies. Often this will be tied directly to the type of data affected and how many records were lost, in a tiered model, with less extensive or damaging breaches requiring no notification and larger ones requiring notification within a certain time period.

Following a data breach or other negative security incident that potentially affects customer, health, or other sensitive data, the decision will need to be made whether to release this information publicly. In some cases, doing so is mandatory, but in other cases, doing so just makes good business sense. The latter is often the case, for example, when a phishing or spam incident leads to client e-mail addresses being harvested, with them in turn receiving the same offending e-mail. In this scenario, while the client e-mail addresses might not be considered sensitive data, alerting the affected clients and offering to share remediation tips with their respective IT staffs might engender goodwill. The communication plan should include steps on who would be involved in making the decision to contact these external entities, the information that should be released, and who will send the notification.

Communication plans should be kept current with the current contact information for all supporting personnel, and each person involved should have a current copy in printed format. This allows the staff who will be involved in the communications to know, no matter how dire the cyber event, what, when, where, and why information should be shared (or not) and who it should (or shouldn't) be shared with.

Business Continuity Plan

Although the chances of a large disaster, whatever the cause, interrupting or halting business operations are slim, all companies should be prepared for negative events, whether cyber-related or not. The *business continuity plan (BCP)* is a detailed, comprehensive document that provides an initial analysis of the potential risks to the business because of a disaster, an analysis of the potential business impact, a *disaster recovery plan (DRP)* for restoring full operations after a disaster strikes, and a *continuity of operations plan* for best continuing operations if disrupted from normal activities by any situation, from a simple outage to an attack.

The process of creating a business continuity plan includes the following phases:

- *Creating a disaster recovery team.* Defining the personnel, internal and external, who will be essential to respond and recover from a disaster.
- *Performing a risk analysis.* Understanding the organization's threats and vulnerabilities.
- *Performing a business impact analysis (BIA).* Understanding the resulting impact to the business.
- *Performing a privacy impact assessment (PIA).* Understanding what privacy information is stored and how it is protected.

- *Creating a disaster recovery plan (DRP).* Defining the procedures to recover critical capabilities after a disaster.
- *Preparing documentation.* Documenting and staffing procedures through the chain of command.
- *Testing the plan.* Conducting tests and exercises to measure effectiveness.
- *After-action reporting.* Using test and exercise results to continually improve the plan.

Cross-Reference

The BIA and PIA are discussed in Domain 5, Objectives 5.4 and 5.5, respectively.

Disaster Recovery Plan

Organizations must devise a *disaster recovery plan* to establish the procedures to quickly recover critical systems after a service disruption. This includes defining and prioritizing specific tasks to aid in the process and defining clear objectives that must be met during the recovery phase.

Responsibilities must be clearly defined for individuals participating in the recovery as part of the disaster recovery team. Tasks should be divided and assigned to the appropriate people and departments. Everyone must be trained on the specific procedures, and those procedures must be properly documented. Team leaders must be established, and central authorities can guide the recovery process through each of its critical steps.

Every organization also needs to decide which aspect of the business is the most critical and must be up and running first if a disaster occurs. Different departments in the company have unique objectives and priorities, but certain functions can be delayed if they don't immediately impact the company's ability to function.

The most important part of the company to get operational is basic communications, such as desk phones, mobile phones, networking connectivity, and e-mail. Until these communication lines are functional, the company's ability to coordinate the disaster recovery effort will be greatly reduced, causing much confusion and chaos. Business-critical items should come next, such as file servers, database servers, and Internet servers that run the company's main applications or anything specifically needed by customers. Most of these responsibilities are defined in the IT department's contingency plan.

The company's ability to restore full operations as quickly as possible depends on the efficiency with which it meets the objectives and goals outlined in the disaster recovery plan.

Your organization's disaster recovery plan must also contain information on succession planning for key employees. Depending on the type of disaster, specific employees might not be available or could be directly affected by the disaster. You must identify key positions that can be filled in by other employees who can take over and execute the same responsibilities. These positions can be very technical in nature, such as a network administrator, or at the executive level to provide direction during a disaster.

Continuity of Operations Planning

As discussed earlier in this book, the ability to provide continuity of operations is the goal of maintaining a high-availability system. This initially requires that you identify systems that need to provide services always. Keep in mind that although they are parts of the same process as a whole, continuity of operations planning (COOP) and disaster recovery planning are actually two separate activities with distinct goals. Continuity of operations means that the business is functioning and operating to perform its mission, while disaster recovery is more focused on saving lives, preventing injury, and preserving equipment, data, and facilities. COOP helps ensure that the business has the right systems, equipment, data, infrastructure, and, of course, people to maintain operations. This means that considerations such as backups, redundant equipment, alternate processing sites (hot, cold, warm), and extra supplies are equally important in keeping the business up and running. The following questions should be considered to help you in this planning:

- What is the monetary cost of an extended service downtime?
- What is the cost to a customer relationship that can occur because of an extended service downtime directly affecting that customer?
- Which services must be available always? Rank them in order of priority.

If your company hosts several services that are required by customers, these services should be given higher priority than your own systems because the service level promised to customers must be maintained always.

EXAM TIP Be sure to understand the differences between continuity of operations plans and disaster recovery plans; even though they are often used together in a contingency situation, they have different missions.

Incident Response Team

An *incident response team* is responsible for creating the incident response plan and executing the plan and associated procedures as quickly as possible following an incident.

The team should include stakeholders from all departments, including management. Designated backup team members should also be assigned in case an original member isn't available to perform the appropriate function. In an incident scenario, each team member is responsible for certain priorities and tasks, which could include coordination of other department personnel (such as HR or legal) and contact with outside reporting agencies, as well as equipment and service vendors as required. However, the bulk of the work will likely be the responsibility of the IT staff, which needs to coordinate the technical response and conduct any follow-on analysis, such as forensics.

Stakeholder Management

After any negative cyber event or disaster has occurred that has affected an organization's systems, all stakeholders in the process—those parties both inside and outside of the cybersecurity organization—must be efficiently and effectively managed. During a negative cyber event or disaster, often everyone from employees to the CEO, and even potentially clients or customers, is a stakeholder in the organization's success. This objective previously discussed communications planning, and this is a key aspect of stakeholder management.

Another way stakeholder management is accomplished is through reporting submitted to the chain of command that describes the ongoing incident response efforts. This reporting is a joint responsibility between the lead of the incident response or disaster recovery effort, the senior manager of the IT and/or cybersecurity organization, team members who have contributed to the effort, and any other stakeholders (e.g., legal or HR) whose input is deemed critical to the report due to the nature of the event. All available information about the incident should be collected, organized, and summarized in the report. Any technical details required should be included as attachments or appendices; this helps streamline the communications for leadership while still allowing an "in the weeds" level of detail should it be desired.

Retention Policies

Collecting and preserving potential evidence for forensic analysis is an essential function of post-incident activities, but it can't wait until the end of the process; in fact, ensuring that potential evidence is gathered and handled properly should be a priority from the very beginning of an event, to ensure that potential evidence isn't overwritten by remediation activities. The team performing incident response activities should be trained to identify what should be prioritized for collection and should have documented steps for ensuring that it is gathered and preserved properly within *retention policies*. Proper handling of evidence is required for it to be admissible in a court proceeding.

Cross-Reference

Forensic response is described in more detail in Objective 4.5, later in this domain.

However, forensic analysis isn't the only reason you should have documented retention policies. An example of a situation where these polices are also used is for public government e-mails and written documents that must be stored to comply with "sunshine laws" that allow the public to file freedom of information requests for the documentation. These laws are meant to promote transparency and openness within the government and reduce corruption. Many of these laws require that all documents pertaining to public official activities (with limited exceptions) be stored for a period of five to ten years. In this scenario, a retention policy must be set to comply with the requirement, and all personnel must be regularly trained on how to follow the procedures. Further, IT or cybersecurity personnel must take steps to ensure that this data is backed up as a critical asset so that, should the worst-case scenario occur, the data can be retrieved even years down the road.

REVIEW

Objective 4.2: Summarize the importance of policies, processes, and procedures for incident response Organizations should have detailed procedures for identification of and response to incidents; these should be written down and thoroughly tested before an incident ever occurs. It is important that first responders know their roles and responsibilities for isolating incidents and performing damage control, communications that must occur, and implementing mitigation solutions. These steps should all be documented, and the lessons learned should be cataloged for refinement of the procedures. Understand the major attack frameworks that can help inform your planning and testing. Create a disaster recovery plan that documents your organization's risks, an analysis of the potential business impact of a disaster, a contingency plan, succession planning, and network and facility documentation. Don't forget to identify mission-essential functions and associated critical systems. Exercise your business continuity and disaster recovery plans on a regular basis and conduct any applicable privacy impact assessments if privacy data is being processed.

4.2 QUESTIONS

1. Which of the following is not a step of the incident response process?
   - **A.** Eradication
   - **B.** Preparation
   - **C.** Formulation
   - **D.** Lessons learned
2. An organization's __________ must also contain information on succession planning for key employees.
   - **A.** Disaster recovery plan
   - **B.** Incident response plan
   - **C.** Communication plan
   - **D.** Lessons learned
3. According to the Diamond Model of Intrusion Analysis, which of the following is not a component of an attack?
   - **A.** Victim
   - **B.** Adversary
   - **C.** Environment
   - **D.** Capabilities

4.2 ANSWERS

1. **C** Eradication, preparation, and lessons learned are all formal steps of the incident response process.
2. **A** Your disaster recovery plan must also contain information on succession planning for key employees.
3. **C** The Diamond Model underscores the relationships and characteristics of an attack's four main components: adversary, capabilities, infrastructure, and victim.

Objective 4.3 Given an incident, utilize appropriate data sources to support an investigation

Previous domains have discussed the different hardware and software solutions that your organization can put into place to collect data, from logs to NetFlow, as examples. These are vital elements to support an investigation when that time inevitably comes. This objective explores how the different data sources support a robust post-incident investigatory approach.

Data Sources

As noted, there are many different types of data sources, all of which must be identified, collected, and retained correctly to support an effective investigation. This section dives into those different types of data sources.

Vulnerability Scan Output

As discussed in Domain 1, Objective 1.7, vulnerability scanners typically include a few scanning and security assessment capabilities, such as port scanning, network scanning and mapping, and OS and application server scanning. The vulnerability scanner accesses a database of known OS weaknesses and application program vulnerabilities (such as web and database servers). It scans the target system to determine whether any of the vulnerabilities listed in its database exist. The output of a vulnerability scan provides a list of vulnerabilities, generally prioritized by criticality, that need to be remediated. Figure 4.3-1 shows an SSL scan generated by ImmuniWeb; note how it lists its different tests and how the website scored in response to those tests.

SIEM Dashboards

As introduced in Domain 1, Objective 1.7, security information and event management (SIEM) tools are used to gather and analyze multiple sources of data to enable cybersecurity analysists to understand trends better and make decisions. A *SIEM dashboard* provides a

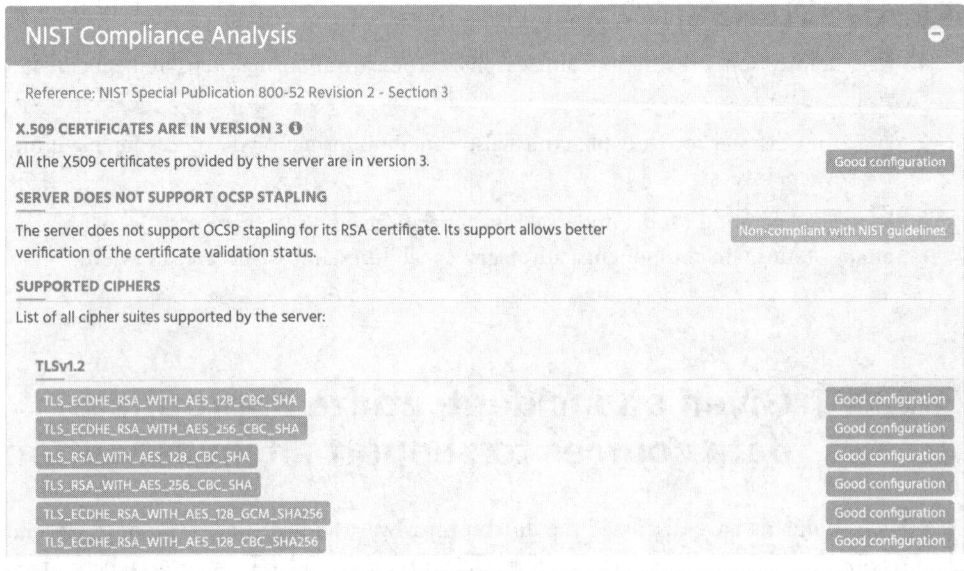

FIGURE 4.3-1 SSL vulnerability scan from ImmuniWeb

one-stop shop so that cybersecurity analysts don't have to use numerous tools. The dashboard presents, in one consolidated view, the correlated information that the analyst needs. Generally, the dashboard also enables the analyst to develop queries to filter and simplify the data that is presented. The following sections discuss different aspects of how the SIEM dashboard can be configured for optimal success when investigating an incident.

Sensors and Data Correlation

Optimal SIEM usage must be built on the foundation of timely, relevant, and correlated data. *Sensors* are an ideal way to collect this data, either through a network tap or through a passive device that then passes the data on to a SIEM for analysis and action. Almost anything can be considered a sensor, including endpoints themselves, so it's essential to carefully think through what data you're trying to capture and analyze to make sense of the events taking place across your network.

As a cybersecurity analyst, *data correlation* is crucial because you're looking to make a statistically significant tie between data to determine what an event means. A combination of host-based and network-based sensors provides the most comprehensive approach, but they each have their pros and cons that you should consider. For example, depending on the placement of a network sensor, you may miss critical data if it doesn't traverse the segment of the network where the sensor has access. The host-based sensor provides more context about the events taking place on individual hosts, but not for the network.

Sensitivity

Sensitivity is an important consideration when setting up your SIEM, as you need to avoid false positives and false negatives in order to know the truth about what's happening within your enterprise. The first step is to develop a known-good baseline. With any type of monitoring or measurement over time, you must initially start with a baseline of current activity and then measure this against the future activity. The initial baseline provides you with a level of activity that is considered "normal" for your environment. After you have established your baseline and begin to monitor further activity, any anomalies beyond your measured baseline thresholds will be readily apparent. For example, baselining your organization for higher levels of network traffic during regular business hours, say, 8 A.M. to 5 P.M. in your time zone, will help you spot the anomaly of large amounts of data leaving the network at midnight. However, a baseline needs to be revisited often, as data is continually being collected and fed into the SIEM, and operating environments can be changed. For example, perhaps a new office is opened in a different time zone, which could affect the scenario discussed previously. The differing hours of operation could begin to cause false-positive alerts.

Trends

Understanding *trends* as they are occurring is a crucial feature of SIEM usage. Once you have your baseline set and have adjusted sensitivity correctly, as discussed previously, you can collect and examine data across a period of time, looking for patterns. When you look for patterns in data that you've seen previously, this is known as *historical analysis*. This historical analysis of trends can also be used to create analytics to predict future events better. This is a more proactive approach than merely sitting back and waiting on alerts (discussed in the next section). Most security monitoring applications can fuse information from several log sources into one database that can be easily searched and analyzed using the logging application. They can generate reports on log entries for specific services or overall trends in the log data; this is much easier and more efficient than scanning through individual log files. Important reporting information to ingest includes the following items:

- **Antivirus and anti-malware reports** Show how many inbound viruses and malware programs were blocked and can also show how many virus- or malware-infected messages were sent outbound from systems internal to your network.
- **Firewall reports** Analyze trends in the total amount of network activity inbound and outbound. These reports can also highlight the top types of attacks that were blocked by the firewall.
- **Anti-spam and e-mail content filtering** Reports on the number of spam messages blocked by your anti-spam filter and any specific content blocked inbound or outbound from deep content scanning of e-mail messages and their attachments.
- **System reports** Indicate the amount of disk space used; CPU, memory, and network usage; and other hardware-related trends. These reports are essential for capacity planning and identifying servers that need to be upgraded or identifying where additional servers are required.

Reports should be created, at minimum, weekly. By comparing reports on a week-to-week basis, you are more likely to spot short-term spikes and abnormal behavior that can indicate a security issue. At the same time, other trends, such as network usage, can be monitored for a longer term for capacity planning. For the executive level, you can create monthly and yearly reports to analyze overall trends that have a longer-term impact on your systems for capacity planning and expansion.

Alerts

Once a SIEM is appropriately configured, one of its most important features is to alert on anomalies. For example, a larger-than-usual volume of traffic leaving the network could be the result of a data breach or other malicious activity. At the same time, something as seemingly innocuous as an increase in failed logins can indicate an attempt to brute force into the network. Most security logging applications and monitors can scan current activity and the system log files and generate alerts and notifications of specific critical errors. Alerts can be sent in various ways, including an onscreen alert (from your monitoring application or personal computer), e-mail message, or SMS.

Alerts should be triggered by any monitoring function that exceeds a threshold. For example, you want to receive an immediate alert notification if one of your critical disk drives is running out of space, or if your network-based intrusion detection system has detected a security intrusion. You must be careful to fine-tune sensitivity levels (as previously noted) so that you are not receiving too many alarms for issues that are noncritical. If you receive too many, you will eventually stop paying attention to them, and critical alerts may go ignored. Alert notifications need to be flexible to allow you to fine-tune the results of your monitoring applications to view and report only on serious or critical errors. Informational data, such as general notifications or low-level warnings, are usually ignored.

Log Files

Your organization should carefully collect, analyze, and preserve security and access logs in case of a security compromise or policy violation. For example, there may be evidence of attempts at network intrusion that go completely unnoticed because notifications and alerts in the security logs went unnoticed or unheeded. In this case, you must review your IT incident response policies and procedures to understand why these activities went unnoticed and the risk continued. Recording and collecting logs of security activity aren't helpful unless you are able to review and analyze the data and compare it to your organization's current policies and the level of incidents that occur. The following sections discuss various different types of log files that you should collect and preserve.

Network

Because all inbound and outbound network traffic passes through the network firewall, the firewall logs are a critical resource when you're examining network trends and analyzing for anomalous behavior. A firewall is the first line of defense at the network's perimeter, and network attacks are often first detected and discovered in the firewall logs. For example, when new worms infect Internet servers and then try to spread to other Internet servers, the connections must pass through an organization's firewall. The network administrator who monitors the firewall is the first to notice and report these worm outbreaks. The administrator will notice hundreds of denied connections to servers on the network, as the firewall is blocking these connections from entering. DoS attacks are also detected in a similar manner.

The most common types of anomalous network behaviors that can be detected at the firewall are port scans. Hackers often use port-scanning software to scan a specific network address to probe for open ports or to perform a scan of all IP addresses on the network to see which systems respond. Hackers can then use this information to target systems they know are alive on the network and to listen for requests on specific ports. Firewalls (if they are implemented properly) will protect the details of the internal network and will not allow port and IP scanners to glean any information from the network.

Firewall logs can be scanned for patterns of port-scanning behaviors, such as a single network address trying to connect to consecutive port numbers on the same system from port 1 to 65525, or an IP range scan in which a single network address is scanning banks of IP addresses such as 192.168.1.1 to 192.168.255.255. For example, the following log trace shows an example behavior of a port scan from a specific IP address:

```
Source: 172.16.1.12 Destination: 192.168.1.128 TCP Port 21
Source: 172.16.1.12 Destination: 192.168.1.128 TCP Port 22
Source: 172.16.1.12 Destination: 192.168.1.128 TCP Port 23
Source: 172.16.1.12 Destination: 192.168.1.128 TCP Port 24
Source: 172.16.1.12 Destination: 192.168.1.128 TCP Port 25
Source: 172.16.1.12 Destination: 192.168.1.128 TCP Port 26
Source: 172.16.1.12 Destination: 192.168.1.128 TCP Port 27
```

The port scan will continue until it reaches port 65525 to find open ports that can be accessed and potentially attacked.

Firewall logs (including personal software firewalls) are also an important tool for exposing Trojans or other types of malicious software installed on client computers that are trying to communicate through the firewall back to the hacker's computer. An administrator can see the source and destination IP addresses of the request and identify which computers might be infected on the network and then take immediate steps to clean the Trojan.

Systems, Applications, and Users

In addition to logging network traffic, you should log the activities of systems and applications. When establishing baselines, discussed previously in this objective, gathering logs is essential. As a reminder, good baselines enable you to determine what is baseline behavior and what is anomalous behavior. Both systems and applications can be tracked, whether it's the amount of traffic they generate, files they access, or the amount of memory they use. Anomalous behavior could be a malicious act, a user issue, or an issue with the hardware or software itself. Regardless of the source, this behavior is a notable event that you'll be glad you tracked.

Next we'll discuss some of the most important types of events for you to log.

System-Level Events *System-level events* are events specific to a certain system or a network of systems, including the following:

- **Login and logout times** The logs of users that entered and exited a system can be helpful in determining which user was accessing the system at the time a security event occurred.
- **Login attempts** If a user seems to be trying to access an account too many times with the wrong password, this could indicate someone is trying to hack into that account. Many network operating systems can limit the login attempts by disabling the account if too many unsuccessful logins occur.
- **Password and account changes** By analyzing account and password changes, you can monitor whether a user had suddenly gained privileges she never had before and that weren't entered by the network administrator.

Privileged-User Events *Privileged-user events* include events performed only by users with elevated privileges, such as the following:

- **Account creation** Knowing when an account was created can help you identify unauthorized accounts, such as those created by a malicious intruder looking to gain persistent access to a system.
- **Assignment of rights, privileges, and permissions** That same intruder might be looking to gain elevated privileges within his new account. Perhaps he is looking to use his privileges to move laterally within your network. Understanding who has privileged access (and why) and reviewing this access frequently will help sort out the accounts that need that level of access and those that don't. You should also be sure that an account with privileged access is not shared across multiple users.
- **Disabling accounts** Accounts should be disabled after a certain number of days without use or when a user has gone into a status where she temporarily doesn't need access (such as long-term leave).
- **Deleting accounts** Users who have left the organization for any reason, or accounts that have been disabled due to nonuse, should be deleted within a set period of time to ensure that they can't be used—either by that user who might be attempting to gain unauthorized access or a hacker who is looking to hide his activities using a legitimate account.
- **Changes to critical files and logs** Losing files that have been determined to be particularly important, such as executables and dynamic-link libraries (DLLs), as well as security logs, could be devastating. Logging any changes to those files and then alerting administrators is a good idea.

Application-Level Events These events happen at the *application level* (for example, when a user is using an application to view or manipulate data). The amount of information that can be collected with this type of monitoring can be overwhelming, so only certain key elements should be recorded:

- **File access** The application logs can record which files were accessed and what times certain files were modified from their original form. Monitoring critical system files for this type of activity is especially important.
- **Error messages** By recording error messages that occur during the use of an application, you can analyze whether the user is intentionally trying to use the application in a manner for which it wasn't designed.
- **Security violations** Any attempts at using an application to compromise access permissions should be recorded. Repeated security violations of the same resource can indicate improper behaviors.

EXAM TIP Know what types of networking and system activities beyond everyday use can be considered suspicious.

User-Level Events *User-level events* can be recorded to monitor activities performed by users. Like application-level events, a large list of activities can be recorded. The following are the most common user-level events that should be recorded:

- **Use of resources** The administrator can record what resources a user accessed during a login session, such as files, servers, printers, and any other network services. This will help indicate whether users are accessing information to which they should not have access or information that is inappropriate to their job and security level.
- **Commands and keystrokes** At a granular level, the keystrokes and commands used by a user while logged in can be recorded and analyzed for unusual activity. This sort of logging can be the most time consuming to analyze.
- **Security violations** Each time a user attempts to access a resource for which he doesn't have the necessary privileges, an entry can be written to a log. Too many attempts at inappropriately accessing resources can indicate attempted unauthorized activity.

Security

Because a specific system or network device can contain log files for a variety of operating system processes, system services, and application programs, several different log files might need to be analyzed by the security administrator. Many of these logs are extremely large and can generate gigabytes of data within a single day of operation. It would be very difficult for the administrator to be proactive and manually monitor and analyze each of these logs every single day.

Access logs provide information on user logins and logouts from specific servers and network resources. Access logs are a valuable audit tool because they provide information on when a specific user has logged in or out of the network and can be used to pinpoint not only malicious behaviors but also authentication issues. If security anomalies occur during a certain time, you might be able to narrow down which users were logged in at the time of the incident.

Access logs also record failed attempts at logging in, and patterns of behavior can be detected by checking the access logs for numerous attempts at trying to access an account. For example, suppose the access logs show that someone has tried to access the administrator account over the network during nonworking hours. After several attempts at guessing the password, the account was locked out to prevent further brute-force attempts. The access logs will show the IP address from which the attempted logins originated, and the administrator can determine whose workstation is the source of the attempted unauthorized access.

A typical access log can display information like the following:

```
08:33 Login: admin 192.168.1.110 Success
08:52 Logout: admin 192.168.1.110
10:45 Login: admin 192.168.1.110 Success
11:50 Logout: admin 192.168.1.110
15:20 Login: admin 192.168.1.110 Success
17:10 Logout: admin 192.168.1.110
23:11 Login: admin 192.168.1.99 Failure
23:57 Login: admin 192.168.1.99 Failure
23:59 Login: admin 192.168.1.99 Failure
```

This indicates normal login and logout behavior for the admin user from his or her workstation during normal work hours. However, starting at 11:11 P.M., a user attempted to log in as the admin user from a different workstation on the network and failed three times. In most cases, if automatic account lockout is enabled, the admin user account can be locked out after the third unsuccessful attempt, depending on the configuration.

Web

As discussed in Domain 3, Objective 3.3, a web application firewall (WAF) can filter and monitor HTTP traffic between web applications and the Internet, helping to mitigate many common web attacks such as cross-site scripting (XSS), SQL injection, and cross-site request forgery (XSRF/CSRF). The WAF essentially acts as a reverse-proxy to the web server by having the client pass through the WAF before it can reach the server.

WAF logs can be helpful in determining what type of activities transpired in a specific user session that may have ended in a compromise. Further, WAF logs can include more information on the traffic that moved between the client and the server.

Another type of web log that should be considered is the proxy log. A web proxy server forwards its requests to the destination website using its own IP address as the source of the individual request. When the specific data is retrieved, the proxy server may cache or even content filter the data in question and then return it to the requesting client. Proxy logs can be highly useful, as they can provide details regarding the session between a user and their destination. Logs should tell you about the content that was transferred, if applicable, a most important finding.

DNS

DNS logs typically contain information on Domain Name Service (DNS) queries to the server, including the source IP address of the request and the domain name of the destination IP address that the DNS server will return in the response. DNS logs can also contain error messages and notifications for regular processes, such as failed zone transfers that occur when the DNS server cannot update zone information to another system.

This information can help administrators track the source of possible DNS poisoning attempts, in which the DNS tables of IP addresses and hostnames are compromised by replacing the IP address of a host with another IP address that resolves to an attacker's system. If authentication measures are in place to protect against DNS poisoning attacks, you might see several failed attempts to update the zone information on your DNS server in the DNS logs. These logs can help you track down the IP address of the attacker's server, which will be indicated in the DNS queries.

In a DoS attack, DNS logs will indicate that a specific host is sending large amounts of queries to your DNS server. If you determine the IP address source of the queries, you can take steps to block that address from connecting to your DNS server.

NOTE Typically, DNS logging is enabled only while you're trying to troubleshoot an issue. If the DNS server is logging every single query from clients, the massive amounts of DNS lookup queries that occur in a large organization can cause performance issues.

Authentication

Authentication logs are a goldmine of information in the event of a suspected or confirmed intrusion, but they also are useful to see who within the organization is being targeted. They allow you to investigate brute-force attempts, for example; think of the scenario where a user has had an inordinate number of failed login attempts during a certain time period. Having this level of insight can help you understand which accounts might need a higher level of visibility or IP ranges to block. Further, "impossible" login attempts that occur—say, a user is physically in Chile but attempts to log in from Tokyo—can alert you to nefarious activity as well.

Dump Files

When collecting forensic data evidence, it is important to realize that any type of digital data has a specific volatility. Some data is more persistent and less volatile; for example, a printout of a log file or a copy of the file on backup tape is less volatile than a live data log file on a disk that is constantly being modified and overwritten. The RAM of a computer system is extremely volatile because the data is not persistent and can change at any time within a matter of seconds. When capturing data for forensics, especially in the initial stages directly after an incident, you must consider the levels of volatility and focus your efforts on preserving the most volatile types of data before moving on to less-volatile data. Your early focus should be on system memory or crash *dump files*, error messages on the screen, and log files before moving on to less-volatile data. Any memory dumps should be saved to make sure you have evidence of all activity during the time of the incident. If you reboot the server to get it functioning again, you can lose valuable data residing in memory.

VoIP, Call Managers, and SIP Traffic

The last several years have seen an exponential growth in VoIP (or Voice over IP) communications, where clients use the TCP/IP protocol to communicate over traditional computer networks. VoIP clients include basic phone services, as well as video conferencing and other types of multimedia applications that are communicated over a network. Similarly, the Session Initiation Protocol (SIP) was developed as a text-based mechanism to coordinate multimedia communications. SIP issues the signaling commands between parties but doesn't actually handle the protocols.

The advantage for VoIP services is that the long-distance costs associated with traditional phone networks practically disappear, as phone services can be deployed globally and users can communicate over existing Internet communication lines. A user in an office in New York can call an office associate located in Tokyo using a VoIP phone that communicates over existing Internet and VPN connections between their offices, completely bypassing the traditional phone system network.

Security concerns over VoIP and SIP have also grown because they use the same computer networks as other Internet traffic and are open to the same types of computer vulnerabilities, such as denial-of-service attacks, spoofing, eavesdropping, call interception, man-in-the-middle attacks, and even voicemail spam.

A call manager allows data to be logged and gathered about VOIP and SIP calls that might be useful for investigation. This includes any inbound or outbound calls that are made by a user, inbound calls that resulted in a voicemail, and patterns of usage by user, including calls made and bandwidth used.

EXAM TIP Recognize how different log types and logging solutions work together to support the cybersecurity program.

syslog/rsyslog/syslog-ng

For Unix-based systems, the *syslog* (system logger) functionality allows all systems on a network to forward their logs to a central syslog server. The syslog server stores these log entries in one large log file. The administrator can perform simple text and pattern searches on this log to pinpoint specific information required from all the server logs on the network.

rsyslog and *syslog-ng* both extend the simpler syslog to an enterprise-level functionality with a more robust feature set, including additional configuration options and filtering capabilities.

journalctl

Within Linux operating systems, *journalctl* is used to review logs that are generated by the journald service; not only does journald gather logs for the system, but most applications that run as a service within Linux use it for logging as well. Because journald generates the logs in a binary format, journalctl is used to view them in a readable format. As with most commands, it has a variety of parameters that can be used to tailor the query. If executed without any parameters, journalctl shows the full contents of the journal, starting with the oldest entry collected. The following are a few important parameters to know:

- **-n** Shows the most recent journal events and limits the number (without a further argument, the default is 10)
- **-f** Shows only the most recent journal events and continuously prints new events as they are added to the journal
- **-p** Filters messages by priority as based on syslog levels ["alert" (1), "crit" (2), "err" (3), "warning" (4), "notice" (5), "info" (6), and "debug" (7)]

NXLog

NXLog is meant to be an open-source, universal log collector across many popular operating systems, such as Windows, Unix, and Linux. After the logs have been collected, NXLog can then forward them to a database or file, making it a solid choice for backing up logs. The following are a few important parameters to know:

- **-c conffile** Specifies an alternate configuration file, conffile. On Windows, this option must be used with -f.
- **-f** Runs in the foreground and does not daemonize, or run in the background.
- **-v** Verifies the configuration file syntax.

Bandwidth Monitors

In addition to using network monitoring tools to monitor network traffic moving to and fro, as previously discussed, administrators can use *bandwidth monitors* to better understand network usage, including the current average download and upload speeds across the network, where a bottleneck might exist in the network that needs to be addressed, and the availability of the network equipment, including switches and routers. Bandwidth monitors can provide reports to the analyst on trends within the network usage.

Metadata

Metadata is meta, meaning that it's literally "data about data." Metadata can provide additional insight or context about collected data, above and beyond the actual content itself. The following sections lay out some important bits of metadata that can be used to get the fuller picture during an investigation.

E-mail

Metadata from e-mail is often among the most critical information collected in an investigation. The following are some of the most important fields to consider:

- **To** Who the e-mail was sent to
- **From** Who the e-mail said it was sent from
- **CC** Anyone on the carbon copy (CC)
- **BCC** Anyone on the blind carbon copy (BCC); these recipients' e-mail addresses aren't visible to the other recipients
- **Timestamp** The date/time group for the e-mail synced with your time server

Mobile

As mobile devices are almost ubiquitous, chances are good that one or more mobile devices may have metadata relevant to an incident. In such cases, a mobile device may provide a wealth of metadata for analysis during an investigation, including important items such as the following:

- **Photos and video** Photos and videos themselves have metadata, often tied to the GPS location where they were taken and the time/date they were taken.
- **Social media** Social media sites such as Pinterest generate their own unique metadata based on tags.
- **Phone calls** Metadata related to a phone call includes the time at which the call was made and its duration, the GPS location from which the call was made, the phone number that was called, and the GPS location of the corresponding device.

Web

When web metadata is described, it's usually in the context of the content of a web page that's visible to search engines. While the user interacts with the web page and the visible contents, search engines interact with the metadata to understand and catalog the site. Some of the most important fields containing metadata to consider are

- **Title** This is the actual title of the page that will be displayed in your search results.

- **Description** The descriptive text that will be shown under the title within your search results.
- **Keywords** This is where you put the main themes of what your page is about. Note that this was once how search engines ranked their results, but it is less important now.

File

File metadata contains information about the file itself that can be very useful during an investigation. For example, you might have a Word document that says it was created by one author, but the metadata can actually tell who initially created the document. The following are some of the most important file metadata fields to consider:

- **Title** The title of the file
- **Created** The date and time that the file was initially created
- **Modified** The date and time that the file was last modified in any way

NetFlow/sFlow

As defined in NIST Special Publication 800-61 Rev. 2, "[a] network flow is a particular communication session occurring between hosts. Routers and other networking devices can provide network flow information, which can be used to find anomalous network activity caused by malware, data exfiltration, and other malicious acts." Flow analysis is a very powerful technique to analyze network traffic, and one of the most ubiquitous examples of a flow analysis tool is Cisco's NetFlow, which groups traffic into flows. Other standards include sFlow, echo, and IPFIX. sFlow, short for "sampled flow," does not separate traffic into flows, but instead conducts a random sampling of packets to achieve scalability. NetFlow has been superseded by IPFIX.

The IP Flow Information Export (IPFIX) protocol is defined in IETF RFC 7011 as a common representation of flow data and a standard means of communicating, as required for transmitting traffic flow information over a network for collection. Like NetFlow, IPFIX groups traffic into flows to then send on to a centralized collection point. IPFIX is based on NetFlow v9.

Protocol Analyzer Output

As discussed in Domain 3, Objective 3.3, a *protocol analyzer* is a device or application that can intercept, log, and analyze network traffic. Within the protocol analyzer, each individual network packet can be examined to decode its header information (which contains the packet's origin and destination) and its contents. This captured traffic is essential to conducting an investigation. Earlier in this domain, Objective 4.1 discussed the popular analyzer Wireshark, and Figure 4.3-2 shows a typical protocol analyzer display from Wireshark, which shows each inbound and outbound network packet and the exact details of each packet's contents.

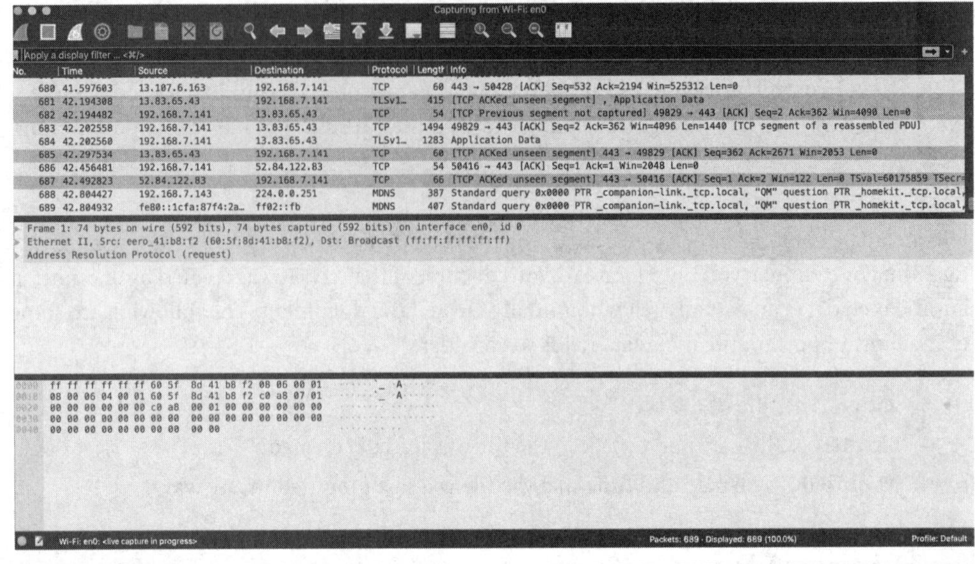

FIGURE 4.3-2 Wireshark output

REVIEW

Objective 4.3: Given an incident, utilize appropriate data sources to support an investigation This objective covered some important types of data that can be used within an investigation, as well as some different tools to analyze that data. It discussed different elements within a SIEM that need to be addressed for the SIEM to function optimally. It also discussed different types of metadata that can be gathered and analyzed.

4.3 QUESTIONS

1. Which of the following is used to analyze logs generated by journald?
   - **A.** syslog
   - **B.** sFlow
   - **C.** journalctl
   - **D.** rsyslog
2. Which of the following is based on NetFlow version 9?
   - **A.** IPFIX
   - **B.** sFlow
   - **C.** syslog
   - **D.** syslog-ng

3. What is the term for "data about data" that provides a rich investigatory source?
   A. Analysis
   B. Logging
   C. Scanning
   D. Metadata

4.3 ANSWERS

1. **C** journalctl is used to analyze logs generated by journald.
2. **A** IPFIX is based on NetFlow version 9, which has since been deprecated.
3. **D** Metadata literally means "data about data" and provides insight regarding things like the creation date/time of a file, keywords, and other pertinent information.

Objective 4.4 Given an incident, apply mitigation techniques or controls to secure an environment

Previous objectives (for example, Objective 3.2 in Domain 3) have discussed at length the application of controls to mitigate security risks. This objective covers many of the same concepts but within the context of remediating and improving your organization's environment after an incident.

Incident Mitigation

Earlier in this domain, Objectives 4.2 and 4.3 described in depth incident response plans and processes and the appropriate data to collect and retain for purposes of dealing with incidents when they occur. However, once the dust has settled somewhat and you can begin the remediation process, you need to identify the priorities of the effort. Obviously, this depends heavily on how the specific incident occurred and your organization's particular configuration, so for the purposes of exam preparation, this objective focuses on several important remediation techniques that are commonly implemented regardless of the specifics of the incident or configuration.

Reconfigure Endpoint Security Solutions

Objective 3.2 of Domain 3 discussed endpoint protection in depth. Despite your best efforts to protect the endpoints in your organization, you may find weaknesses in your endpoint armor after an incident occurs, requiring that you reconfigure your endpoint security solutions to ensure that a similar incident does not occur. This section discusses three options that you can tweak in your endpoint security solutions to strengthen your organization's security posture.

Application Approved Lists

Application approved lists (also known as *allow lists* and *whitelists*) prevent unauthorized applications from executing by checking each potential execution against a list of applications that have been granted execution rights. If the application is approved to execute, it can proceed as planned. If not, it is terminated. Often, approved-listing solutions check the hash of the potential application against the known-good hash to ensure that the application isn't maliciously claiming to be the legitimate version.

In the post-incident scenario, if the organization uses an application approved list, it is critical to review any applications that were involved in the incident to be sure they aren't inadvertently included in the approved list. This can often happen if an older application previously added to the list should have been removed but was not.

Application Block Lists/Deny Lists

Conversely, *application deny lists* (also known as *block lists* and *blacklists*) are the method used by most anti-malware vendors; they require maintaining a list of "known-bad" applications, or just applications that the administrators don't wish to have choking the available bandwidth or worse (think video games, bitcoin mining, and so on). Applications that don't appear on the deny list can execute. In the post-incident scenario, you would add to the deny list any applications that are unneeded and contributed to the incident.

EXAM TIP The terms *application approved list* and *deny list* (and their variations) replace the older *whitelisting* and *blacklisting* terms, which are being deprecated for use across the industry. However, you may still see the older terms in the CompTIA objectives and on the exam.

Quarantine

As discussed in Domain 3, Objective 3.2, antivirus protection should be set up on every server, desktop, and laptop in the system and should include scheduled updates of virus signature files from a central antivirus update server. This can protect both the computers and the networks to which they connect, as well as provide a first level of defense to prevent viruses from spreading to the network.

E-mail servers that send and receive mail should be protected with special antivirus software that can scan incoming e-mail for attachments with viruses. When the antivirus software detects a virus, the virus is either cleaned or quarantined, or the message is deleted, and then notification e-mails are sent to the source and recipient to warn about the existence of the virus. Remember that quarantining a message or its attachments effectively isolates that message from the system and disables its ability to execute, just in case it has any malicious properties. Post-incident, check the quarantined messages for possible entry vectors, and also tune the quarantine function to include any potential messages that may have been missed.

Cross-Reference

Application approved listing, deny listing, and quarantining are also discussed in Domain 3, Objective 3.2.

Configuration Changes

Reconfiguring your organization's endpoint security solutions to address weaknesses discovered after an incident is a good start to your remediation efforts, but you also have to consider whether you need to make configuration changes to other security solutions protecting your organization, as discussed in this section.

Firewall Rules

Post-incident, properly configuring the firewall is often one of the first steps, especially if inadequate rules enabled an intruder to infiltrate the network or exfiltrate data from the network. To properly configure the firewall, you must set up many rules to allow incoming and outgoing network communications for specific ports and protocols. These rules can be general or specific. For example, a firewall can be updated with a rule that states that any HTTP traffic can come and go on a specific network, but the rule can also be much more detailed and state that an SMTP packet destined for a mail server can come only from a specific host IP address. Further, you can configure firewall rules that allow all traffic access to any part of the network unless explicitly denied; however, this can create huge headaches once the list gets large! Make sure you understand the pros and cons of the different methods of denying traffic, described in Domain 3, Objective 3.2.

Mobile Device Management

As discussed in Domain 3, Objective 3.5, permitting employees to connect their mobile devices to the organization's network increases direct access to organizational intellectual property. Mobile device management (MDM) solutions are designed to ensure that an organization can manage that access. When an incident involves one or more employee mobile devices, the organization needs to make configuration changes to its MDM solution. To reduce the potential for these devices to be exploited, consider disabling unused features or those that could present security concerns. These might include Bluetooth, Wi-Fi, cameras, voice or video recording, over-the-air (OTA) updates, use of external media or devices (using technologies such as USB On-The-Go), the ability to connect to wireless ad hoc networks, tethering (use of the data plan to create a wireless access point), and the use of NFC payment methods, such as Apple Pay or Google Pay. Each of these features can create its own security concerns and potentially compromise both the company data and personal data resident on the mobile device.

Another control that should be considered when using MDM is blocking third-party application stores. After a policy has been created, the staff should implement that policy, whether it involves application control, disabling features, or both, using a group policy for mobile devices.

Data Loss Prevention

As covered previously in Domain 3, Objective 3.2, *data loss prevention (DLP)* solutions require the identification of information that is critical to the organization or considered "sensitive" (either PII—personally identifiable information—or identified as such through classification levels) and then work to ensure that this data doesn't leave the network via a USB device, e-mail, or some other method. In DLP, data is tagged and labeled with metadata denoting its security or sensitivity level as well as attributes that may or may not allow it to leave via various means. After an incident, especially one where data left the enterprise and wasn't properly blocked via the DLP solution, consider tuning the DLP to better monitor which data is covered and how it can properly leave the network. E-mail filters can also be created to identify certain sensitive data patterns, such as Social Security numbers, and block e-mails containing that data from exiting the organization.

Content Filter/URL Filter

Some users download questionable content from the Internet, which can lead to malware spreading across your enterprise or other issues. Post-incident, network administrators can reconfigure content filtering or URL filtering to block access to these sites as needed. Similar to the deny list mentioned earlier, these filters use a list of known objectionable sites or content that is compared to the websites or content users try to access through their web browsers. These lists can also contain well-known phishing, spyware, and malware sites, which can also be blocked accordingly.

Update or Revoke Certificates

As mentioned in Domain 3, Objective 3.9, which discussed certificates at length, a certificate can be suspended or revoked before its expiration date for several reasons. The most common reason for *revocation* is that the user of that certificate is no longer authorized to use it, as in the case of a company employee who quits his job or is fired. Other reasons for revocation include the problem of a key pair or certificate being compromised in an incident. If the private key is lost or compromised, the details in the corresponding certificate will no longer be valid. Post-incident, immediately revoking the certificate means it can't be used for any authentication, encryption, or digital signature purposes. Alternatively, *suspension* is a temporary revocation of the certificate until the problem concerning the certificate or the certificate owner's identity can be corrected. A suspension also might be appropriate if, for example, the certificate holder is on extended vacation or perhaps under investigation and shouldn't be allowed to use the certificate during this time.

Suspension of a certificate can be undone, but revocation is permanent. When a certificate is revoked, it's placed on a certificate authority's certificate revocation list (CRL), which includes certificates that have been revoked before their expiration date by the CA. A CRL is used by other users and organizations to identify certificates that are no longer valid.

Isolation

System isolation is used when you have a particularly sensitive host or system that needs to be separated from the general population of users and hosts on the network. Often this is done after an incident to allow the system to run without causing further damage, particularly if malware or ransomware is involved, or if data needs to be collected for investigation.

For very sensitive systems, both physical and logical segmentation would be ideal. This might include dedicated subnets, switches, and routers. It also might mean the use of encryption for all traffic between that particular host and others. It obviously should require different authentication methods for access, including multifactor authentication, if possible. Sensitive hosts might reside on their own specific VLAN as well, and there might be intermediate network devices that use very strict access control lists to control who accesses the system, using only explicitly allowed ports and protocols. This would likely be a special use box, not intended for anyone to access for e-mail or other general purposes. The key here is to isolate the system from the general-use network and other systems and ensure highly restrictive access to it.

Containment

When an incident occurs, the containment process stops the damage from escalating further and helps preserve the evidence for any possible future action. The number-one priority is to stop the progress of any malicious activity, be it malware or a hacking action. Often, this entails a quarantine of affected systems from unaffected systems to prevent the spread of the incident, or removal of affected devices from the network. At this point, the system(s) may undergo forensic analysis or be wiped clean, depending on policy and type of incident.

Segmentation

An organization can prevent unauthorized users from accessing sensitive hosts by segmenting those hosts from the rest of the network, either logically or physically. This can be done as a result of an incident, but more often is done as a proactive measure to ensure that damage from a future incident is minimized. Only certain groups of users may be able to access those hosts. Segmentation can be done in a variety of ways, but they generally can be categorized as either physical or logical.

Physical segmentation can involve a couple of different aspects. First of all, critical assets can be segmented from other assets in a separate physical location that has stronger security controls, whether that location is simply a different part of the building or a separate building in a different geographic area. This can not only help ensure redundancy through duplicative equipment but also ensure that if an adverse physical event occurs at one location, it spares another location where other critical assets are kept and helps promote continuity of operations. Second, physical segmentation can be achieved through network devices, such as switches and routers, by physically separating hosts from being on the same physical network segment or cable. This can be especially advantageous if a piece of fiber or Ethernet cable is cut, for example, or the organization suffers a power loss to parts of its infrastructure that may not affect other parts due to the physical device segmentation.

Logical segmentation can also be employed using encryption methods. It's not uncommon to see sensitive information or even all traffic from specified hosts be encrypted and sent over unencrypted links that are shared with nonsensitive hosts. Each host that transmits or receives encrypted traffic must be specially configured to do so and can be set up to communicate only with other hosts that use the same encryption algorithms and keys. You'll also often see VLANs used to logically segment networks within an organization.

Cross-Reference

Network segmentation is also discussed in Domain 3, Objective 3.3.

Security Orchestration, Automation, and Response

As previously introduced in Domain 1, Objective 1.5 in the context of threat hunting, *security orchestration, automation, and response (SOAR)* is the name given to platforms that are dedicated to unifying the security tools, processes, and methods that are used across an enterprise. SOAR platforms are designed to integrate all the efforts an organization devotes to collecting, aggregating, and analyzing data and converting it to useful information used to make critical security decisions. Obviously, SOAR platforms are great for a variety of situations, such as threat and vulnerability management and security operations, but they are also useful in incident response. Response and post-incident activities often utilize two SOAR features, runbooks and playbooks (as described next), to ensure that the proper steps occur with a minimum of on-the-fly human intervention.

Runbooks

Runbooks are a set of rules that can be largely automated and, while they can indeed include human elements, often are used to automate features such as threat response, threat intelligence enrichment, and other activities that the SOAR platform can orchestrate. These rules are generally condition-based, so instead of following a step-by-step pattern, they are triggered by preset conditions.

Playbooks

Similar to a traditional checklist, a *playbook* lists step-by-step actions that need to occur within the SOAR process. The actions typically need to be performed by humans, so the playbook serves as the definitive guide to ensure that any documentation, required reporting, or other mandated actions that require human involvement and decision-making occur exactly when they should.

EXAM TIP You will often see the terms *playbook* and *runbook* used interchangeably by professionals, but you should understand the nuance. Playbooks are more human-based and linear in nature, while runbooks are more conditions-based and automated.

REVIEW

Objective 4.4: Given an incident, apply mitigation techniques or controls to secure an environment After an incident has occurred and the preliminary data has been collected for investigative purposes, the next common step is to quickly begin remediation to limit the damage and improve the organization based on lessons learned. Common mitigation areas include reconfiguring endpoint controls, improving configurations of security systems, segmentation, isolation, containment, and using SOAR playbooks and runbooks.

4.4 QUESTIONS

1. __________ can be largely automated and, while they can indeed include human elements, often are used to automate features such as threat response.
   A. Playbooks
   B. Incident response plans
   C. Runbooks
   D. SIEMs
2. Post-incident, Alex has identified an affected host that needs to be separated from the general population of users and hosts on the network. Which of these is her best approach?
   A. Remediation
   B. Isolation
   C. Environment
   D. Capabilities

4.4 ANSWERS

1. **C** Runbooks can be largely automated and, while they can indeed include human elements, often are used to automate features such as threat response.
2. **B** System isolation is used when you have a particularly sensitive host or system that needs to be separated from the general population of users and hosts on the network.

Explain the key aspects of digital forensics

In adjusting to the legalities of prosecuting computer crimes, most companies have trained their employees from the incident and response team in the proper collection and preservation of forensic evidence of computer crimes. Because the evidence is usually electronic in nature, it can easily be tampered with by an uneducated investigator, which would cause the evidence to be legally invalid in a court of law. Therefore, the art of computer forensics is a critical part of evidence collection necessary for prosecuting computer crimes.

Digital Forensics

Forensics is the act of acquiring and preserving evidence to use in court as part of a legal proceeding. Typical forensics of crimes such as theft and murder include gathering evidence such as fingerprints, weapons, and even DNA samples to help prosecute a suspect. In the computer world, evidence of a cybercrime can be difficult to properly obtain and preserve so that it will be allowed as evidence in a court of law. Because of its nature, most computer crime evidence is electronic, which can easily be erased, modified, and tampered with. After a computer crime—such as a server attack—is committed, an initial investigation by the network administrator can quickly ruin evidence the attacker left behind if the investigation is not conducted properly.

Documentation and Evidence

This section outlines some of the special procedures required when acquiring and preserving evidence of a computer crime, which includes preserving the incident environment, collecting evidence, determining the order of volatility, and retaining a chain of custody of the evidence. Many of these same procedures are also used within *e-discovery*, where data is being collected for legal purposes that don't require the same level of forensic detail as a formal investigation. In the case of e-discovery, the legal counsel generally receives the data without expert analysis having taken place and conducts their own investigation; however, these are completely related concepts, because often, if the court suspects that data is missing or could have been tampered with, the court will order a follow-on forensic investigation.

EXAM TIP If a system is rebooted after a security compromise, certain evidence could be destroyed in the process, such as memory contents and system logs.

Legal Hold and Admissibility

In the event that your organization's legal counsel determines that evidence should be collected for any reason, be it a pending investigation, potential litigation, or other situation where evidence would be required, a *legal hold* is formally initiated. A legal hold halts the usual backup and disposition processes and immediately puts your personnel into data preservation mode. Without these procedures being followed, your organization is at risk of losing required data to protect itself in a legal situation, including the ability to use the data within a trial or other legal setting, and it is the company's responsibility to make reasonable efforts to act as soon as possible to preserve data that might become evidence. If a court determines that data has not been preserved properly, with a clear record of how the proper processes have been followed, the court can rule that the data is *inadmissible*, meaning that it cannot be submitted as evidence in the court proceeding. Therefore, working with your organization's legal counsel to better understand legal holds and how to respond appropriately to one could save your organization from fines or sanctions.

Video

If an incident may have been captured by video surveillance, such as the theft of computer equipment, the surveillance video is potential evidence and must be preserved. If the theft took place in a secured area, it might be possible to analyze the access logs of employees who logged into the secured area at the time. If the company uses magnetic access cards for doors, a log can be created showing who went in and out at a certain time. In this case, only the video surveillance could show who was in possession of the access card, as the card might have been lost by or stolen from the original user.

Make multiple copies of the video evidence to make sure you have additional copies if the original is damaged or lost. Surveillance video on tape should be transferred to a computer as a digital video file for backup purposes and more efficient retrieval.

Chain of Custody

When collecting evidence of a computer crime, maintaining a proper chain of custody is extremely critical. A *chain of custody* requires that all evidence be properly *tagged* with information detailing who secured and validated the evidence, how they did so, and when they did so, and when and to whom that person transferred the evidence. This process must also occur for everyone who encounters the evidence. Unfortunately, electronic evidence can be volatile, and in a court of law it can be easily dismissed because of possible tampering. Computer media can be easily destroyed, erased, or modified, so handling this evidence requires strict procedures. All media must be stored in a secure room or container that has restricted access that is logged fastidiously. In addition to the chain-of-custody process, you must also consider *preservation* challenges such as humidity, temperature, electrostatic discharge, and other environmental issues that can affect electronic devices and digital storage media.

If additional copies of data need to be made, reliability and integrity must be ensured so the copies can be considered tamperproof. Obtain a hash of the data so that a checksum can be created for comparison later to prove the data was not tampered with. (See "Hashing" later in this objective.) Any devices or media containing data need to be carefully catalogued, tagged, and then sealed away to prevent tampering. Magnetic media should be write-protected to prevent the data from being overwritten.

If all evidence has been properly secured, identified, tagged, and stored, it can be considered solid and admissible in court. A clear chain-of-custody log ensures this process was completed without the possibility of data modification.

KEY TERM A **chain of custody** ensures that evidence has been handled with the utmost care and lists the persons who have had access to the evidence.

Timelines of Sequence of Events

When collecting data evidence from your systems, be aware that not all network devices or servers may have their clocks synchronized, and the timestamp that one device puts on an action that appears in the logs may be different from that of another device's timestamp. There is also the issue of time zones and how different types of devices stamp times. One device may use UTC (Coordinated Universal Time) without time zone offsets, while other systems may insert their own time zone offsets, depending on their configuration. When collecting and organizing your evidence, be aware of the issue of time offsets between different devices and time zone issues. Legally, you need to account for any time discrepancies in your evidence.

Reports

The *forensic report* is a document that describes the details of gathering, securing, transporting, and investigating evidence. Within this report, it is important to meticulously detail all the areas discussed in the previous sections, focusing on accuracy and comprehensiveness. The forensic report will likely be the basis of any legal action, and if it is inconsistent, contradictory, or missing key details regarding the phases of the forensic process, some or all of the evidence will likely be deemed inadmissible by the court.

Along with reporting on progress and findings, it is also important to track and report the resources expended on the detailed forensic analysis. While many organizations can easily quantify the amount spent on new computing equipment, other expenditures should be considered as well. For example, how much employee time (labor hours) was spent on the analysis process? This is considered an opportunity cost, or time that could have been spent on other activities that are central to completing the organizational mission. These hidden costs can easily add up to more than the price of new IT equipment.

Network, System, and Event Logs

Collecting and preserving evidence from a computer crime primarily concerns keeping and storing any event logs or audit trails that detail step by step what the attacker was doing. Log files will contain specific date and timestamps corresponding to each aspect of an intruder's activity, including login credentials, commands used, and files accessed.

When an incident occurs, avoid panicking. If you suddenly reboot a network device or server to ward off the attacker, you not only disrupt access to that server for legitimate users, but you could also destroy valuable evidence in the form of audit trails and timestamps on files that might have been changed by the intruder.

Make sure you preserve copies of your log files before letting too much time elapse after the incident. Log files, especially event logs or network logs from firewalls and routers, can roll over very quickly; older log files may be deleted to make resources available for new ones. By immediately making copies of the log files, you ensure they are not accidentally deleted or lost.

Interviews

It is possible that, depending on the nature of the incident, you may have witnesses who need to have their statements recorded as evidence. For example, in the case of a physical theft, an employee might have caught sight of an unidentified person in the building. You must take a statement of where she saw the individual and at what time, and she must provide a detailed description. It is also possible that a witness might have noticed screen activity on a server that resulted in the initial incident alarm.

What is most important is interviewing and recording the witness statements as soon as possible after the incident. Over time, the witnesses may forget specific details, and it is important to have as much information recorded as possible while the incident is fresh in their memory.

Acquisition and Preservation

Collecting evidence and then preserving it safely and appropriately are crucial aspects of incident response. Depending on the type of incident, there could be physical evidence, logs, system images, screen captures, and camera video, each of which needs to be carefully collected, preserved, and protected from tampering. This section covers some of the most important elements of acquisition and preservation that you should know.

Order of Volatility

When collecting forensic data evidence, it is important to realize that any type of digital data has a specific *volatility*, meaning that over time, the veracity or ability to recall the data declines. Some data is more persistent and less volatile; for example, a printout of a log file or a copy of the file on backup tape is less volatile than a live data log file on hard disk that is constantly being modified and overwritten. The RAM (discussed shortly) of a computer system is extremely volatile because the data is not persistent and can change at any time within a matter of seconds.

When capturing data for forensics, especially in the initial stages directly after an incident, you must consider the levels of volatility and focus your efforts on preserving the most volatile types of data before moving on to less-volatile data. Your early focus should be on system memory or crash dump files, error messages on the screen, and log files before moving on to less-volatile data.

Disk

In many cases, the entire contents of your hard drive, or an entire server with an array of hard drives, needs to be saved as evidence of your security incident. It is a best practice to create a system image, which is a snapshot of your entire data system at a specific time. The system image allows you to preserve the state of your data after the incident so that you can resume operations with your server, while the image of your hard drive is stored elsewhere.

If you do not make a system image, you could lose important log files, network traces, and crash dump files that get overwritten over time. You must also adhere to legal requirements to ensure that the digital evidence is not tampered with after the incident.

System images are typically saved to an external hard drive, after obtaining a hash to verify their integrity, and then stored in a secure place. Your disk-imaging software and image drive need to provide bit-for-bit accuracy to create an exact image of your original drive and prevent alteration after the image is created for legal reliability.

Random-Access Memory

Conducting forensics on random-access memory (RAM) is similar to doing so on disks, with one major consideration: RAM is much more volatile, meaning that if power is lost or removed from the memory, it loses its contents. This makes it incredibly important that, when systems are isolated after an event, they must not be powered down, if at all possible. RAM contains a wealth of information resident within memory that can be recovered as evidence, such as running services and processes, any network connections, and passwords that have been unencrypted and stored within the RAM. Further, some malware and other potential indicators of compromise (introduced in Domain 1, Objective 1.3) only run within active memory. Losing this means losing valuable information for an investigation. Especially with RAM capture, it is critical to document the steps that were taken to gather the information, as well as the tools used, as you'll likely change the contents of memory and will need to prove that the changes were acceptable to facilitate admissibility.

Swap/Pagefile and Cache

When a program is to be executed, the data that is required to run the program is copied from the hard disk into memory, where it is then used by the CPU. This provides greater performance than reading directly from the disk, and files in the memory can be used repeatedly. Because of this, the swap/pagefile (otherwise known as *pagefile.sys* on a Windows machine), as well as the cache, can let you know what has been executed recently on the system.

OS

Collecting forensic data from an operating system (OS) requires understanding the specific nuances of the individual OS itself. For example, Windows file systems and Linux/Unix file systems use different formats (e.g., NTFS versus ext4). Further, there are different locations within the operating system that are OS-dependent that should be prioritized. For example, on Windows systems, the registry holds a wealth of information within the registry keys.

Another important place to potentially recover files is the recycle bin, where files may have been "deleted" but not fully erased from a system. Again, these methods are OS dependent.

Device

Mobile devices can provide a wealth of information for an investigation, much of which can be used for forensic purposes, such as e-mails, SMS messages, photos, and GPS positioning. However, there are some considerations when looking to conduct forensic operations on a mobile device. First, just as with a traditional computing device, don't remove power or reboot the mobile device; first determine if you can recover any volatile memory. Acquiring evidence from mobile devices requires tools that are specialized for mobile forensic data collection, which often are tailored to the specific mobile OS. Because mobile devices can be tracked via cellular or Wi-Fi signals, be sure to store a mobile device in a Faraday bag or container to help prevent unwanted communications or even a remote wipe before you've gained access to its data.

Firmware

Firmware is essentially software code embedded in hardware that provides features such as executing the OS and encryption services, among others. If firmware is maliciously altered, it can shuttle data to unwanted sources without even scratching the surface of the OS (or alerting any antivirus protections). Consider the very real scenario where the firmware has been updated en route (potentially through an attack on the supply chain) to a government organization by a hostile nation-state threat actor to side channel data back to the actor. Potentially the only way to determine what occurred is through a review of the firmware. In this case, the firmware code itself would need to be compared with a known-good copy of the manufacturer's firmware to determine any discrepancies. Further, data would need to be collected regarding the running output, meaning how it executes and interacts with the hardware and software. To use the previous scenario, this would provide valuable *strategic intelligence* and *counterintelligence*, meaning that it could be analyzed to better understand the adversary capabilities, as well as to build better processes and technologies to protect against those capabilities.

Artifacts

The previous sections have mentioned different *artifacts*, or pieces of data that provide a clearer picture during an investigation and should be collected, including logs, metadata, the cache, registry keys, and other evidence of activities that may have been occurring. However, in certain cases, evidence of an attack may only occur as an error or diagnostic image that appears on the screen. You may even have a full transcript of the command-line instructions entered by an intruder during an attack. In this case, you will have to use a screen capture image program to take a snapshot of your current screen. This must be performed before any other action. If you clear the message, you may lose your evidence if it does not also appear in the log files. Screen capture files should be accurately labeled and time-stamped, and you should also use hashing to preserve the integrity of the file to prove that it was not altered or tampered with.

On-Premises vs. Cloud

As organizations move to the cloud, they must keep in mind, through the barrage of marketing hype, that the cloud is essentially a data center hosting its resources. Although your organization can outsource a good bit of operations to cloud service providers (CSPs), it can't outsource all of the risk, and certainly not the impact of a negative event. To that end, having a solid agreement with any CSP your organization does business with is absolutely critical if conducting digital forensics becomes necessary. There are also important legal considerations that pertain to digital evidence in the cloud.

Right to Audit Clauses

We've talked about incident response, but the ability to conduct forensics is also essential. However, it's not as simple as just asking the CSP nicely for permission to conduct forensics when something bad happens; you must plan ahead with the correct agreements in place. Remember that the CSP has the control over the resources in place and, without these agreements, you may be out of luck to conduct your investigation. One of the most important aspects that should be considered is a *right-to-audit clause*, which simply gives your organization the right to gain forensic data from the CSP if a breach or other negative event has affected your portion of the cloud environment. This clause is also great for a variety of other contexts, including auditing the CSP's compliance and service levels.

Regulatory, Jurisdiction, and Legal Considerations

Previous objectives have discussed both regulatory requirements and jurisdiction in the context of data governance; this section applies those same considerations to forensics. First, if your system processes or stores any government data, you should expect that, in the event of a breach or other negative cyber incident, you will be required to submit to that government's forensic analysis to determine the who, what, when, where, and why of the situation. Further, if the system (even without your knowledge) was used to conduct illegal activities (say, by an employee), you'll likely have law enforcement knocking on your door as well. This is where *jurisdiction* comes in. Especially in situations where a system is cloud hosted, the jurisdiction of the physical location of the data center where the system is hosted is applicable, meaning that a court order issued for forensic analysis within a different jurisdiction likely will not apply.

Cross-Reference

Additional information on breach notification is available in Domain 5, Objective 5.5, while regulations are covered in more depth in Domain 5, Objective 5.2.

Similarly, the physical location of the CSP's data center will determine the laws that guide the requirement to notify affected users in the event of a data breach. It is important to consider all of these factors well before an incident requiring forensic analysis, ideally before choosing a CSP.

Integrity

Integrity ensures that your data is consistent and has never been modified by unauthorized persons or manipulated in any intentional or accidental manner. Integrity also includes nonrepudiation methods to ensure information can be trusted from the supposed sender or user. Protecting the integrity of data is one of the most critical parts of the forensic process; as previously discussed in this objective, the ramifications of failing to protect data integrity include inadmissibility of evidence. This section discusses some different methods of ensuring integrity that you need to consider when conducting a forensic investigation.

Hashing

For legal reliability, you need to be able to prove that files haven't been altered in any way from the time of the original data capture. This supports *nonrepudiation*, which as you previously learned is the term used to describe the inability of a person to deny or repudiate an action they performed, the origin of a signature or document, or the receipt of a message or document. To help preserve data integrity, you can create a hash of the file immediately after the incident. A *message digest*, or *hash*, is used in encryption systems to create a "fingerprint" for a file. Hashing preserves message integrity by ensuring that the original data has not been tampered with. There are several complex message digest algorithms that are widely used for data integrity checking. When comparing hashes for data to verify integrity, the hashes must match for the files to be verified. If the hash does not match, the file has been altered since the original capture.

Cross-Reference

For more details on data integrity, nonrepudiation, and hashing, see Domain 2, Objective 2.8.

Provenance

The *provenance* of data is akin to metadata (discussed in Objective 4.3, earlier in this domain), in that it's data about data. In this case, provenance is the data regarding the origin and ownership of data, almost a historical log. This is valuable for a forensic investigation, as it can show where data was created and any changes that were made along the way. As data is often changed many times during its life cycle, understanding the provenance helps the investigator understand how data was created, how it has changed, and how it ended up within the investigator's purview.

Data Recovery

Data can be damaged or missing in a variety of ways. A laptop could have been accidentally dropped and damaged, and the drive no longer functions. Important files could have been accidentally erased by a user that need to be recovered. Unfortunately, other scenarios exist where data has purposefully been deleted or damaged and needs to be recovered for investigation, either on disk drives or memory cards. Data recovery tools can help recover this lost data, either for investigation or just bad luck. As an example, if data becomes corrupted on a hard drive, tools can be used on the drive to salvage files and return them back to the company on a clean drive or removable media. This is an often expensive process, but can prove invaluable in many critical situations.

REVIEW

Objective 4.5: Explain the key aspects of digital forensics When gathering documentation and evidence as part of digital forensics, always consider the requirements to ensure its admissibility. Keep a chain of custody of evidence to prevent tampering (and to prove in court that it didn't occur) and collect the timelines of sequence of events. To preserve evidence, ensure that systems are isolated but power is maintained if at all possible. Gather information based on order of volatility. Understand the different types of data to acquire. Save audit and activity logs, take screenshots, and make a system image for evidence. Understand the differences in conducting forensics in a cloud environment versus on premises. Use hashing to preserve data evidence integrity.

4.5 QUESTIONS

1. You have received a call from the legal department to halt regular operations due to pending litigation by a disgruntled former employee. What is this called?
   A. Data collection
   B. Litigation review
   C. Legal policy
   D. Legal hold
2. You are collecting forensic evidence from a recent network intrusion, including firewall logs, access logs, and screen captures of the intruder's activity. Which of the following concepts describes the procedures for preserving the legal ownership history of evidence from the security incident?
   A. Damage control
   B. Audit trail
   C. Escalation
   D. Chain of custody
3. A web server recently crashed because of a denial-of-service attack against it. Based on the order of volatility, which of the following pieces of evidence would you preserve first?
   A. Website data
   B. Screen capture of crash error message
   C. Printout of web access logs
   D. Web server configuration files

4.5 ANSWERS

1. **D** A legal hold is a formal directive from legal counsel that puts the organization into data collection and preservation mode in the event of pending litigation, investigation, audit, or other circumstance where the data may be required.
2. **D** Keeping a chain of custody requires all evidence to be properly labeled with information detailing the personnel who secured and validated the evidence. This can ensure the evidence wasn't tampered with in any way since the time it was collected.
3. **B** When collecting forensic data evidence, be aware that certain types of data are more volatile over time. In this case, the error message on the web server should be captured as a screenshot before the server is restarted. The message will disappear after restart, and unless it appears in the logs, you may have no other record of it.

About the Online Content

This book comes complete with TotalTester Online customizable practice exam software with 200 practice exam questions.

System Requirements

The current and previous major versions of the following desktop browsers are recommended and supported: Chrome, Microsoft Edge, Firefox, and Safari. These browsers update frequently, and sometimes an update may cause compatibility issues with the TotalTester Online or other content hosted on the Training Hub. If you run into a problem using one of these browsers, please try using another until the problem is resolved.

Your Total Seminars Training Hub Account

To get access to the online content you will need to create an account on the Total Seminars Training Hub. Registration is free, and you will be able to track all your online content using your account. You may also opt in if you wish to receive marketing information from McGraw Hill or Total Seminars, but this is not required for you to gain access to the online content.

Privacy Notice

McGraw Hill values your privacy. Please be sure to read the Privacy Notice available during registration to see how the information you have provided will be used. You may view our Corporate Customer Privacy Policy by visiting the McGraw Hill Privacy Center. Visit the **mheducation.com** site and click **Privacy** at the bottom of the page.

Single User License Terms and Conditions

Online access to the digital content included with this book is governed by the McGraw Hill License Agreement outlined next. By using this digital content you agree to the terms of that license.

Access To register and activate your Total Seminars Training Hub account, simply follow these easy steps.

1. Go to this URL: **hub.totalsem.com/mheclaim**
2. To register and create a new Training Hub account, enter your e-mail address, name, and password on the **Register** tab. No further personal information (such as credit card number) is required to create an account.

   If you already have a Total Seminars Training Hub account, enter your e-mail address and password on the **Log in** tab.
3. Enter your Product Key: **`7p3m-0cf3-9hc0`**
4. Click to accept the user license terms.
5. For new users, click the **Register and Claim** button to create your account. For existing users, click the **Log in and Claim** button.

   You will be taken to the Training Hub and have access to the content for this book.

Duration of License Access to your online content through the Total Seminars Training Hub will expire one year from the date the publisher declares the book out of print.

Your purchase of this McGraw Hill product, including its access code, through a retail store is subject to the refund policy of that store.

Restrictions on Transfer The user is receiving only a limited right to use the Content for the user's own internal and personal use, dependent on purchase and continued ownership of this book. The user may not reproduce, forward, modify, create derivative works based upon, transmit, distribute, disseminate, sell, publish, or sublicense the Content or in any way commingle the Content with other third-party content without McGraw Hill's consent.

Limited Warranty The McGraw Hill Content is provided on an "as is" basis. Neither McGraw Hill nor its licensors make any guarantees or warranties of any kind, either express or implied, including, but not limited to, implied warranties of merchantability or fitness for a particular purpose or use as to any McGraw Hill Content or the information therein or any warranties as to the accuracy, completeness, correctness, or results to be obtained from, accessing or using the McGraw Hill Content, or any material referenced in such Content or any information entered into licensee's product by users or other persons and/or any material available on or that can be accessed through the licensee's product (including via any hyperlink or otherwise) or as to non-infringement of third-party rights. Any warranties of any kind, whether express or implied, are disclaimed. Any material or data obtained through use of the McGraw Hill Content is at your own discretion and risk and user understands that it will be solely responsible for any resulting damage to its computer system or loss of data.

Neither McGraw Hill nor its licensors shall be liable to any subscriber or to any user or anyone else for any inaccuracy, delay, interruption in service, error or omission, regardless of cause, or for any damage resulting therefrom.

In no event will McGraw Hill or its licensors be liable for any indirect, special or consequential damages, including but not limited to, lost time, lost money, lost profits or good will, whether in contract, tort, strict liability or otherwise, and whether or not such damages are foreseen or unforeseen with respect to any use of the McGraw Hill Content.

TotalTester Online

TotalTester Online provides you with a simulation of the CompTIA Security+ exam. Exams can be taken in Practice Mode or Exam Mode. Practice Mode provides an assistance window with hints, references to the book, explanations of the correct and incorrect answers, and the option to check your answer as you take the test. Exam Mode provides a simulation of the actual exam. The number of questions, the types of questions, and the time allowed are intended to be an accurate representation of the exam environment. The option to customize your quiz allows you to create custom exams from selected domains or chapters, and you can further customize the number of questions and time allowed.

To take a test, follow the instructions provided in the previous section to register and activate your Total Seminars Training Hub account. When you register you will be taken to the Total Seminars Training Hub. From the Training Hub Home page, select **CompTIA Security+ Passport (SY0-601) TotalTester** from the Study drop-down menu at the top of the page or from the list of Your Topics on the Home page. You can then select the option to customize your quiz and begin testing yourself in Practice Mode or Exam Mode. All exams provide an overall grade and a grade broken down by domain.

Technical Support

For questions regarding the TotalTester or operation of the Training Hub, visit **www.totalsem.com** or e-mail **support@totalsem.com**.

For questions regarding book content, visit **www.mheducation.com/customerservice**.

Index

A

B

C

D

F

G

H

I

M

O

P

Q

R

S

T

U

V

W

X

Z